RIZZOLI
NEW YORK

FLORENCE

IN DETAIL

A Guide for the Expert Traveler

In Association with the

Herald INTERNATIONAL Tribune
THE WORLD'S DAILY NEWSPAPER

First published in the United States of America in 2003 by
Rizzoli International Publications, Inc.
300 Park Avenue South
New York, NY 10010

Copyright © 2003 Italy Weekly

2007 2008 2009 2010 2011 / 10 9 8 7 6 5 4 3

Library of Congress Control Number: 2002096020

ISBN-13: 978-0-8478-3117-3
ISBN: 0-8478-3117-5

Designed by Lisa Vaughn-Soraghan, Two of Cups Design Studio

Printed in China

Table of Contents

Foreword

By Fred Plotkin

he visitor to Florence brings demands and expectations to this city that are required of few other places. Yes, one might want romance in Paris, nostalgia in Vienna, excitement in New York, or sizzle in Rio. But Florence is asked to provide things that are much more elusive: a sense of proportion and the magical spell of genius.

The capital of Tuscany bestrides the Arno River, which is not a remarkable waterway. Yet along these banks have walked Dante, Boccaccio, Savanarola, Giotto, Masaccio, Botticelli, Michelangelo, da Vinci, Brunelleschi, Leon Battista Alberti, Galileo, Verdi, Puccini, and thousands of unknowns who made Florence an undisputed cradle of talent and intellect.

In this city, the art of power reached its zenith with the calculated patronage of the Medici family. Florentine arts and crafts were exported far and wide in the Renaissance, spreading the idea that this city was superior not merely for the power it could wield but for the beauty it could create.

Here, too, was born the urban census, created by Alberti to document Florence's illustrious citizenry. We can credit Alberti with coining the word "snob," which was an abbreviated reference for nouveau riche merchants who were not of noble blood. They were "s.nob," or "senza nobiltà."

And at the very end of the 16th century, a group of artists and thinkers who called themselves the Camerata Fiorentina, created a new art form that would grow to be the greatest of them all: opera lirica, which we simply call opera. It is still presented at the Teatro della Pergola as it has been for centuries, and now flourishes at the Teatro Comunale and the Teatro Goldoni as well.

This legacy of reason, proportion, and genius can weigh heavily on modern Florentines. They are at once custodians of a grand tradition, yet are also its prisoners. What can they possibly achieve that would rival Michelangelo's *David,* Botticelli's *Birth of Venus,* or Brunelleschi's dome? The most that is usually asked of a modern Florentine is directions to the nearest museum or leather shop.

There is, however, a remarkable tradition that modern Florentines maintain and build upon: the use of their hands to produce that which the mind envisions. No city in Italy can rival Florence in *artigianato,* artisanal crafts that still produce things of beauty. Whether these are made of leather, silk, paper, fabric, wood, glass, or other materials, the dexterity of the Florentine craftsman is second to none. Wander a few steps away from the most congested tourist streets and you will hear the sounds of the work of these craftsmen. It is in their workshops (or *bottegas,* as they have been known for centuries) that Florentine artistry persists.

And while appreciating these crafts, we learn another one of the many secrets that Florence jealously guards: Art requires time.

Whether one is making art or beholding it, the passage of time reveals insights that a quick look could never yield. In a place where the Uffizi,

Bargello, Accademia, Palazzo Pitti, and the Museo dell'Opera del Duomo are only the very top of the list of repositories of Florentine genius, you must quickly accept that one cannot "do" Florence. And the ambitious traveler who ventures off the well-worn paths to sites will be richly rewarded: admire the unsurpassable Pontormo painting in Santa Felicita, the Casa Buonarroti (dedicated to the life and work of Michelangelo), the church of Santo Spirito, and the gorgeous Teatro della Pergola.

Like it or not, one must adopt a policy of *"Poco, ma buono"* (loosely translated as "Do less, but do it really well") to experience what Florence has to offer. A mad dash through a gallery will leave you with only fleeting impressions. Spend ten minutes in front of one painting and you will see remarkable things that a two-minute look could not reveal; spend an hour in front of that same painting and your life will be changed. To really pause and reflect, whether in front of a sculpture or a dish of gelato, is to find the presence of art and genius in all things.

The reason, then, that we love Florence is not for the inanimate treasures that reside within its thick walls. We love Florence because it challenges and inspires us, instructing us that time well spent is knowledge and experience earned. This is not a city where time stands still. Florence is a place where time has meaning, and where we find our place in the ongoing, still-flourishing carnival of human possibility.

Fred Plotkin is a much-admired expert on all things Italian. He is the author of *Opera 101, Classical Music 101, Italy for the Gourmet Traveler,* and four Italian cookbooks.

Introduction

Florence is one of the great cities of art and architecture in the world, a cradle of the Renaissance that should not be missed on any tour of Italy. But, as Edith Wharton once remarked about Rome, a city always has a clearly visible "foreground"—in the case of Florence, the Palazzo Vecchio, the Duomo, the Uffizi Gallery—and a more concealed "background" of somewhat hidden jewels. The foreground is usually the province of the classic sightseeing tour and the conventional guidebook. The background is for the traveler interested in discovering the city known only to the real connoisseur and for the return visitor.

There are many popular guides available on Florence, but none of them is specifically geared to the "background traveler." This is why we've introduced our "In Detail" series.

We have divided Florence into five areas: its four historical neighborhoods—San Giovanni, Santa Croce, Santa Maria Novella, and Santo Spirito, also known as the Oltrarno—and the immediate surroundings outside the walls of the historical center. For each area we compiled a chapter with two major components:

Fundamentals—with descriptions of the better-known monuments and sites, accompanied by the very personal views of special observers, such as Henry James, Charles Dickens, or Lady Sidney Morgan.

Walking Tours, Focuses, and Commercial Points of Interest—with less well-known destinations, and a selection of snapshots on the best each area has to offer in terms of lodging, eating, and shopping.

We hope you enjoy your trip to Florence, and once there, remember that you can find the *International Herald Tribune* on most newsstands.

Claudio Gatti

HOW TO USE THIS GUIDE

Florence in Detail is organized by neighborhood—four in all, plus one chapter on the small towns surrounding Florence—with cultural attractions featured in several sections within each chapter:

➤**Fundamentals**: Entries on major sites.

➤**Walking Tours**: Itineraries that take you to sites within the neighborhood that feature off-the-beaten-path treasures. Within each **Walking Tour**, one site has been identified with our logo that we highly recommend. "**Our Pick**" sites are marked on the cultural maps in each chapter and on the map at the front of the book, so that you can easily make Rizzoli's favorite sites the focus of your trip.

➤**Focus**: Following each **Walking Tour**, a site from the tour is described in depth.

➤**Other Points of Interest**: Additional noteworthy cultural sites.

➤**Museums**: Museums of every type are featured, from the Uffizi Gallery to the Carriage Museum.

➤**Commercial Points of Interest** sections feature **Hotels & Inns**; **Restaurants & Cafés** (which includes bars); and **Specialty Shops**.

A note about pricing: We have included approximate ranges of prices for Hotels & Inns and Restaurants. We have not included pricing information for cafés and bars.

How to Use the Maps

Each chapter has one map marked with cultural sites and another marked with commercial points of interest. Each map has a key on the right-hand side listing all of the entries alphabetically and each is assigned a number.

Best of Florence: An extensive "Best of" chapter features listings and descriptions of Florence's exceptional offerings in the following categories:

- Best Markets
- Best Jewelry and Gift Shops
- Best Artisans' Shops on the Oltrarno
- Best Gourmet Stores
- Best Bars
- Best Bread
- Best Gelato and Pastry Shops

Each entry in this chapter lists the neighborhood where it can be found. Each "Best of" listing is marked on the commercial maps at the bottom of the key. If a listing appears in one of the neighborhood chapters as well as in the "Best of" chapter, an asterisk * will indicate that it can also be found in the "Best of" chapter.

Restaurants: All prices are for one.

€	Under 50
€€	50–75
€€€	or 75–100
€€€€	Above 100

Hotels & Inns: Prices are for double rooms. Unless noted with an *, hotels include breakfast.

€	Under 100
€€	100–200
€€€	200–300
€€€€	300 and above

At press time, the exchange rate for euros to American dollars was nearly equal.

How to Use This Guide

Santa Maria Novella
(CULTURAL)

1 Cappella Rucellai (or Cappella del Santo Sepolcro)
2 Casa-Galleria di Giovanni Michelazzi
3 Colonna della Croce al Trebbio
4 Colonna della Giustizia
5 Galleria Corsini
6 Giardino Orti Oricellari
7 Giotto's Crucifix
8 La Rimessa del Carro
9 Loggia del Porcellino (or Loggia del Mercato Nuovo)
10 Loggia di San Paolo
11 Loggia Rucellai
12 Museo della Casa Fiorentina Antica
13 Museo e Chiostri Monumentali di Santa Maria Novella
14 Museo Marino Marini
15 Officina Profumo-Farmaceutica di Santa Maria Novella
16 Ognissanti
17 Oratorio dei Barelloni
18 Oratorio di San Francesco dei Vanchetoni
19 Palazzetto Neogotico dello Scultore Ignazio Villa (Hotel Albion)
20 Palazzo Antinori
21 Palazzo Bartolini-Salimbeni
22 Palazzo Buondelmonti
23 Palazzo Calcagni-Arese
24 Palazzo Corsi Salviati
25 Palazzo Corsini
26 Palazzo Corsini al Prato
27 Palazzo Davanzati
28 Palazzo dello Strozzino
29 Palazzo dei Capitani di Parte Guelfa
30 Palazzo della Canonica
31 Palazzo di Valfonda
32 Palazzo Gianfigliazzi, Lungarno Corsini, 2
33 Palazzo Gianfigliazzi, Lungarno Corsini, 4
34 Palazzo Larderel
35 Palazzo Lenzi
36 Palazzo Ricasoli
37 Palazzo Rucellai
38 Palazzo Spini-Feroni
39 Palazzo Strozzi
40 Palazzo Torrigiani (Hotel Porta Rossa)
41 Palazzo Vecchietti
42 Piazza Santa Maria Novella
43 Piazza Santa Trìnita
44 Ponte Santa Trìnita
45 Porta al Prato
46 Porticina di Via delle Belle Donne
47 Rotonda Barbetti
48 San Gaetano
49 San Paolino
50 Santa Maria Maggiore

Santa Croce
(COMMERCIAL)

Hotels & Inns
1 Hotel Hermitage
2 Hotel Regency
3 Il Cenacolo Residence
4 J and J

Restaurants & Cafés
5 Acqua al 2
6 All'Antico Vinaio
7 Alle Murate
9 Bar Sant'Ambrogio
10 Caffè Concerto
11 Caffè Fiorenza
12 Caffè Rivoire
13 Cantinetta del Verrazzano 1
14 Cibreo
15 Cocotrippone
16 Corte Armonica
17 Dino
18 Dolci e Dolcezze*
19 Enoteca Baldovino
20 Enoteca Pinchiorri
21 Gelateria Badiani
22 Gilda Bistròt
23 I Fratellini
24 Il Francescano
25 Il Pizzaiuolo
26 L'Antico Noè
27 La Baraonda
28 La Pentola dell'oro
29 Le Mosacce
30 Osteria de' Benci
31 Osteria del Caffè' Italiano
32 Osteria delle Tre Panche
33 Pasticceria Ruggini
34 Perché No?*
35 Ruth's
36 Salamanca
37 Tavola Calda da Rocco
38 Trattoria Baldovino
39 Vini
40 Vivoli Gelateria*

Shopping
42 Gabriella Nanni*
44 JuJu
46 La Tartaruga
47 Paperback Exchange

Best of
50 Da Noi
51 Gelateria Veneta
52 Mercato delle Pulci
53 Mercato Sant'Ambrogio

TIME LINE

DATE	EVENT
59 B.C.	Florence (called Florentia) is founded by the Romans as a town for retired Roman military.
A.D. 250	Eastern merchants bring the idea of Christianity to Florence and Saint Minias is martyred in the city.
313	Emperor Constantine gives Christianity official status.
552	Florence is attacked by Totila the Goth.
c. 569	Florence is conquered by the Lombards and becomes part of their kingdom.
774	Charlemagne, King of the Franks, begins a campaign to drive the Lombards out of Tuscany; as a reward he is given Florence and other parts of Tuscany to rule.
1107	The Florentines, with the conquests of some nearby castles, begin to enlarge their territory.
1115	A fire breaks out in the borough of Santi Apostoli. It is the first of many that will affect the city over the next couple of centuries.
1125	Florence captures and destroys the neighboring hilltown of Fiesole.
1154	The Florentines defeat the Pistoiesi in the castle of Carmignano.
1216	The beginning of a conflict between the most important families in Florence—the Guelphs (supporters of the pope) and the Ghibellines (supporters of the Holy Roman Empire).
1218	All of the countryside is forced to pledge allegiance to the city of Florence.
1224	The Florentines build a fortress in Val d'Arno to protect the city and the road to Arezzo from the hostile nobility in the countryside.
1229–1235	Florence fights a war against Siena. The exile of the Guelphs from Florence is followed by reforms and new civic regulations which establish a Leader of the People and a council of twelve elders.
1251	The Guelphs return and some Ghibelline families are expelled.
1252	The first gold florin is minted.
1255	Construction is begun on the Palazzo dei Capitani del Popolo (now the Bargello).
1260	The Battle of Montaperti (September 4): The Florentines, along with their allies, Guelphs from Lucca and other cities, suffer a bloody defeat at the hands of the Sienese. Many Florentine Guelphs voluntarily go into exile. The popular government falls.
1261–1265	The Ghibellines are the majority in the city.
1265	Dante Alighieri is born.
1266	The Ghibellines go into exile and the Guelphs return.
1268	Florence wins a war against Pisa.
1269	Construction begins on the original church of Santo Spirito, later completely renovated by Filippo Brunelleschi.
1278	The Dominican church of Santa Maria Novella is begun in Florence and the Campo Santo is begun in Pisa.
1294	Work begins on Santa Maria del Fiore, the cathedral of Florence.

DATE	EVENT
1299	Work begins on the Palazzo Vecchio in Florence, designed by Arnolfo di Cambio.
1302	Dante begins writing *The Divine Comedy* (published in 1307).
1345	Work begins on the Ponte Vecchio.
1348–1393	The Black Death spreads through Florence, killing half of the Tuscan population by the time it ends.
1349–1351	Giovanni Boccaccio writes *The Decameron*.
1350	The Florentines occupy Colle, San Gimignano, and Prato.
1375	Giovanni Boccaccio dies. Work begins on the Loggia della Signoria.
1377	Filippo Brunelleschi is born.
1378	Lorenzo Ghiberti is born.
1384	The Florentines buy the city of Arezzo.
c. 1386	Donato di Niccolo di Betto Bardi, called Donatello, is born.
1402	The Florence Baptistery doors competition is held.
1406	After a long siege, Pisa falls to Florence.
1416–1420	Donatello completes his statue of Saint George for Orsanmichele (now housed in the Bargello).
1419	Work is begun on the Foundling Hospital of the Innocents by Brunelleschi.
1421	The Florentines buy the port of Livorno from the Genovese.
1424–1428	Masaccio and Masolino work on frescoes in the chapel of Santa Maria del Carmine (including Masaccio's famous *Life of Saint Peter* cycle).
1434	Cosimo the Elder returns from exile and comes to power. Brunelleschi completes the dome for the cathedral of Florence. Work begins on San Marco.
1442–1445	Fra Angelico frescoes the walls of the cells of the convent of San Marco.
1444	Michelozzo begins work on the Palazzo Medici on Via Larga.
1451	Amerigo Vespucci (who gave his name to the New World) is born in Florence.
1452	Leonardo is born in Vinci, outside Florence.
1459	Benozzo Gozzoli paints the chapel in the Palazzo Medici (now called Palazzo Medici-Riccardi).
1464	Cosimo the Elder dies.
1466	Donatello dies.
1469	Lorenzo the Magnificent comes to power.
1470	Leon Battista Alberti finishes the facade of Santa Maria Novella.
1475	Michelangelo Buonarroti is born.
1478	The Pazzi Conspiracy: The wealthy Pazzi family tries and fails to assassinate Lorenzo the Magnificent and seize control of Florence.
1480	Botticelli completes his *Primavera*.
1485	Botticelli completes his *Birth of Venus*.
1492	Lorenzo the Magnificent dies.
1494	Charles VIII of France attacks Florence, Piero de' Medici abandons the city, and Girolamo Savonarola seizes power. Leonardo's statue *Judith and*

DATE	EVENT
	Holofernes is placed in front of the Palazzo Vecchio to symbolize the end of Medici rule.
1498	Savonarola's political enemies have him executed for heresy.
1504	Michelangelo completes his *David,* which is placed in front of the Palazzo Vecchio (now housed in the Accademia Gallery).
1513	Giovanni de' Medici, the son of Lorenzo the Magnificent, is crowned Pope Leo X.
1521	Pope Leo X dies; Giulio de' Medici is crowned Pope Clement VII.
1529–1530	Between October and August there is a siege of Florence by the combined forces of Pope Clement VII and the Holy Roman Emperor, Charles V of Spain. The Republic falls after ten months of disease and starvation. Medici rule is restored in Florence.
1531	Alessandro de' Medici takes power and makes himself the Duke of Florence.
1532	Posthumous publication of Machiavelli's *The Prince.*
1533	Catherine de' Medici marries Henri III, king of France.
1534	Pope Clemente VII dies.
1537	Duke Alessandro is assassinated and succeeded by Duke Cosimo I.
1539	Cosimo I marries Eleonora of Toledo.
1540	Cosimo I changes his residence from the Palazzo Medici on Via Larga to the Palazzo Vecchio. Giorgio Vasari is responsible for redecorating most of the apartments.
1549	Duchess Eleonore de' Medici buys Palazzo Pitti.
1550	The Boboli Gardens and Garden of the Simples are begun.
1570	Cosimo I is granted the title Grand Duke of Tuscany.
1574	Cosimo I dies and is succeeded by his son, Francesco I.
1633	Galileo is excommunicated because his experiments and astronomical observations contradict the teachings of the Roman Catholic Church.
1642	Galileo dies under house arrest in Arcetri, near Florence.
1737	The end of the Medici dynasty; rule passes to the Austrian House of Lorraine.
1743	Death of Anna Maria Ludovica, the last of the Medici.
1765	Grand Duke Leopoldo I introduces many social reforms, including the abolition of the death penalty.
1784	The Academy of Fine Arts is founded by Grand Duke Leopold.
1865–1870	Florence becomes the capital of the unified Kingdom of Italy. The population is around 194,000. The area of the Mercato Vecchio is demolished to make way for Piazza Repubblica.
1896	First performance of Puccini's *La Bohème.*
1933–1935	Construction of the train station at Santa Maria Novella.
1944	The Ponte Vecchio is the only bridge left standing.
1966	Floodwater from the Arno rises to 19 1/2 feet above street level, destroying houses, monuments, and artwork (some of which is still being restored).
1993	The Uffizi Gallery and other buildings are damaged by terrorist bombings.

A Brief History of Florence

The Etruscans migrated to Italy from Asia Minor around the year 900 B.C. and settled in Etruria (now Tuscany, Lazio, and Umbria). In the 6th century they created the Dodecapolis, a confederation of 12 Etruscan centers. In 508 B.C., threatened by Rome, the Etruscans attacked it, but they failed to conquer it. In 395 B.C. they fought a second, very violent war. The Roman army captured the town of Veii, in Lazio, which signaled the beginning of the downfall of the Etruscan civilization. By 205 B.C. all of Tuscany was under Roman control. In 90 B.C. the Etruscans were given Roman citizenship.

In 59 B.C. Florence (called Florentia, meaning "flowering") was founded, and plots of land were given to loyal members of the Roman army. By the 3rd century A.D., the city had developed into an important trade center (it was near the Via Cassia, which led from Rome to the north) and had a population of 10,000.

After the fall of the Roman Empire, Florence was repeatedly attacked by the Goths and suffered heavy damage. By the 6th century, the population had dropped to less than 1,000. The Longbards ruled from 570 until Charlemagne drove them out in 774, when he made Florence part of the French country of Tuszien, initially governed from Lucca. In that period, the population grew, trade was rejuvenated, and in 854 Florence merged with Fiesole.

When Count Hugo moved his home from Lucca to Florence in A.D. 1000, the city entered an important period of cultural growth and architectural and artistic achievement. During the 11th century, Florence was a central part of the ecclesiastical reform movement and therefore a focal point in the growing conflict between papal and secular authority. Under Countess Matilda of Canossa (1046–1115), the city turned its back on the German emperor and put its allegiance with the pope. By 1172, the population had risen to 30,000 and work began on new city walls, which for the first time incorporated the area south of the Arno River.

Art and architecture were characterized by the Romanesque style at this time. Early Romanesque churches, such as Sant'Antimo (9th century), have round arches and Roman-style columns and arcades, while the church of Santi Apostoli (786) actually used columns from ancient Roman baths. In the 10th and 11th centuries, the later Romanesque churches of Santo Stefano al Ponte, Santa Margherita, San Miniato al Monte, and San Lorenzo (the first cathedral of Florence) were built, as was the Baptistery.

Trading, manufacturing, and refining of textiles brought wealth to the city, and in 1252 the first gold coin, the *fiorino d'oro* (gold florin) was minted. It became the most stable currency in Europe. Money and a new understanding of geometry led to the construction of a new cathedral (begun in 1294).

Throughout the 12th and 13th centuries, the Florentines captured much of the surrounding countryside, and by 1300 the population exploded to 100,000. That was also a period of political conflicts, when the Commune (city government) became the setting for a long-lasting feud between the Guelphs (supporters of the pope) and the Ghibellines (supporters of the Holy Roman Emperor).

In the 12th century, the skyline of Florence was defined by approximately 170 defensive towers, built on top of aristocratic families' houses to protect them during local fights. The towers were reduced to a maximum height of 132 feet in 1250. In the same period, the great churches of Santa Maria Novella (1246) and Santa Croce (c. 1295), and the Palazzo del Capitano del Popolo (begun in 1255) and the Palazzo Vecchio (c. 1300), were built.

Gothic architecture, introduced to Tuscany by the French Cistercian monks who built the abbey of San Galgano in 1218, prevailed in Florence from the mid-13th to mid-15th centuries. Pointed arches, spiked pinnacles, and soaring vertical space were typical of this style, as was the transfer of buttressing to the exterior of the building (so that the arches and piers supported the vaulting and the roof, as well as the walls).

Sculpture of this era was characterized by natural but idealized poses, where the interplay of bodies and clothing was presented in exaggerated, elongated forms. Painting was mainly executed on panels and glass (as opposed to the later technique of the fresco). Medieval art in general was intended as an aid to prayer and contemplation and was characterized by stylized figures and the use of gold, symbolizing purity. There was no detailed background or spatial depth.

Florence struggled through the entire 14th century. In 1302 Dante was exiled for his political beliefs, and in 1333 the Arno River flooded the city, which was later struck by periodic famines and fires. The Florentine army also suffered military defeats against Pisa (1315) and Lucca (1325), while the collapse of important banks in 1346 plunged the city into economic crises. From 1348 to 1393 the Black Death raged through Tuscany killing half of Florence's population.

The 14th century produced great writers, such as Dante, Boccaccio, and Petrarch, and artists, such as Giovanni and Nicola Pisano, Cimabue, Giotto, Duccio di Buoninsegna, Ambrogio Lorenzetti, and Arnolfo di Cambio.

In 1413, the Medicis assumed the role of papal bankers and became the leading family in the city. With a few interruptions, directly or indirectly, they ruled Florence for the next three centuries. The Medicis restored peace and stability to Florence, and, with other wealthy banking and merchant families, patronized the arts, setting the stage for the artistic awakening known as the Renaissance.

Inspired by ancient Roman art and classical ideas, Renaissance artists rejected the stylized art of the earlier medieval era and studied human anatomy. Their art was characterized by a use of perspective, realistic backgrounds, and the depiction of saints as real people rather than idealized figures. Their works were influenced by classical documents and scenes from mythology but also by everyday life, which then became a "legitimate" subject for art. Supported by wealthy benefactors, many artists flattered their patrons by including them in recognizable landscapes and city backgrounds as onlookers or protagonists in the scene.

Filippo Brunelleschi, the father of Renaissance architecture, was inspired by the purity and simplicity of classical Roman buildings. This style is reflected in his first true Renaissance work, the loggia of the Foundling Hospital of the Innocents (begun in 1419), with its elegant lines and simple arched bays. Classical cornices were molded in Roman style, and the plain facade is made of gray sandstone and white plaster, in striking contrast to the richly ornamented Gothic style.

The political life of the city at that time was not always stable. In 1478 the wealthy Pazzi family tried and failed to assassinate Lorenzo the Magnificent (a plot known as the Pazzi conspiracy). In 1494, the Medici family briefly lost control of the city when Charles VIII of France attacked Florence, and Piero de' Medici was forced to abandon it. Florence was subsequently declared a Republic, under the leadership of religious fundamentalist Girolamo Savonarola. He ordered the burning of profane books and art (known as the Bonfire of the Vanities). That same year, da Vinci's statue *Judith and Holofernes* was placed in front of the Palazzo Vecchio to symbolize the end of Medici rule. In 1498, Savonarola's political enemies had him executed for heresy, but the Republic lived on for another 30 years.

Between October 1529 and August 1530 Florence was kept under siege by 40,000 troops—the combined forces of Pope Clement VII (a Medici) and the Holy Roman Emperor, Charles V of Spain. The Republic fell after ten months of hardship and Medici rule was once again restored in Florence.

In the late phase of the Renaissance known as mannerism (c. 1530–1620), artists rejected the emphasis on harmony and idealized forms, proportions, and compositions that had been developed during the early Renaissance. Mannerist features include a dynamic style, elongated forms, and deliberately contorted poses. Compositions are usually complicated and crowded, with an irrational use of light and the abandonment of strict association of color with objects. Inspired by Michelangelo's *Holy Family* (1507), mannerist artists also brought new life to traditional biblical subjects.

Under Cosimo I, who took over in 1570, and his heirs, Florence experienced a long period of peace and prosperity. The population expanded from 59,000 in 1552 to about 80,000 by the end of the 17th century. The 17th century was characterized by political and economic problems, exacerbated by the Thirty Years War, but the Medici family didn't stop patronizing artists and scientists, including Galileo, who was excommunicated in 1633 and died under house arrest in 1642. Although some churches in Florence were given new baroque facades, Florence was not transformed by baroque architecture the way Rome was, and the Florentine version of this style is very classical in spirit and not as bold or as exuberant as elsewhere in Italy. The Medici dynasty ended in 1737, when the Austrian Dukes of Lorraine came into power.

In 1799, Napoleon conquered the city, and ruled it until 1815. In 1860, with the Risorgimento, Italians joined forces to overthrow their foreign rulers, and in 1865 Florence was named the capital of newly unified Italy. In 1870, the capital was moved to Rome.

Finding the Top Shops, Bars, and Markets

Best Markets

Located in the central Piazza dei Ciompi in the Santa Croce neighborhood, the Mercato delle Pulci, first set up in 1963, is Florence's trademark flea market. Thirty picturesque stalls built of metal and wood sell a wide variety of old and antique items—from 1800s furniture, to turn-of-the-century clothes and dolls, and 1950s radios.

Around the corner from Piazza del Duomo, right beside the Brancacci Chapel, is the Mercato di San Lorenzo in Piazza San Lorenzo, which, along with the Mercato del Porcellino (or Mercato Nuovo) on Via Porta Rossa, offers the widest selection of leather goods in town.

Florentines and tourists with an eye for a bargain crowd these two venues daily looking for suede and leather jackets, bags, and suitcases. The two markets also sell high-quality straw goods, such as bags and hats, and Florentine souvenirs.

On Tuesdays, a city tradition for women of all ages and fashion styles is to go to the Mercato delle Cascine in the sprawling Parco delle Cascine, the largest park in the city, to buy designer clothes at relatively cheap prices. Many stalls sell last year's top designer fashions with minor imperfections at hefty discounts.

Great for food is the Mercato di Sant'Ambrogio in Piazza Ghiberti. Most of the fruit and vegetables are brought in fresh daily from farms in the nearby Chianti and Mugello countryside. Some farmers also sell delicious homemade jams, preserves, and cakes.

The Mercato Centrale, right beside the Mercato di San Lorenzo, is Florence's main food market and offers daily the city's widest selection of meats, fruits, and vegetables. Particularly impressive is the colorful display of seasonal fruits and vegetables on the market's first floor.

Mercato Centrale
Piazza del Mercato Centrale; open: Mon.–Fri. 7 A.M.–2 P.M., Sat. 4–7 P.M.; closed: Sun. Mercato del Porcellino (or Mercato Nuovo) Piazza del Mercato Nuovo; open: daily 9 A.M.–8 P.M. (Apr.–Oct.), Tues.–Sat. 9 A.M.– 7:30 P.M. (Nov.–Mar.); closed: Sun.–Mon. (Nov.–Mar.).

Mercato delle Cascine
Parco delle Cascine; open: daily 7 A.M.–2 P.M. (summer), Tues. 8 A.M.–2 P.M. (winter); closed: Wed.–Mon. (winter).

Mercato delle Pulci
Piazza de' Ciompi; open: daily 9 A.M.–8 P.M. (Apr.–Oct.), Tues.–Sat. 9 A.M.–7:30 P.M. (Nov.–Mar.); closed: Sun.–Mon. (Nov.–Mar.).

Mercato di San Lorenzo
Piazza San Lorenzo; open: Mon.–Fri. 7 A.M.– 2 P.M., Sat. 4-7 P.M. (interior), Tues.–Sun. 9 A.M.–8 P.M. (exterior); closed: Sun. (interior), Mon. (exterior).

Mercato di Sant'Ambrogio
Piazza Ghiberti; open: daily 7 A.M.–2 P.M.

Best Jewelry and Gift Shops

Gabriella Nanni is the place to find jewelry at the right price. Near the Ponte Vecchio, the shop offers bracelets, rings, and necklaces with beautiful semiprecious stones or colorful Murano glass. They are designed by Gabriella, and it is a pleasure to discuss the pieces with her while trying to decide which to buy. You can spend just the right amount for your gifts or even more for yourself.

More than a store, Limelight is a workshop—and an experience. Highly original minimalist jewelry made with pieces of colored glass, often recycled, and silver is sold at very reasonable prices. The shop also offers quality craftsmanship with ultra-modern designs, such as aluminum clocks and picture frames that are more costly but so unique that they are worth it.

Pampaloni is a beautiful store just off Piazza Santa Trìnita that offers, aside from traditional silverware and china, its own production of designs in silver. Especially interesting and unique are the "Bicchiero-grafia," glasses glazed in silver, originally designed in the 17th century and reproduced with exceptional craftsmanship. Quite special are their candlestick holders in the shapes of letters of the alphabet.

Gabriella Nanni

(Santa Croce; see map pg. 118) Via Lambertesca, 28r; tel.: 055-214838; open: Mon.–Sat. 9:30 A.M.–1 P.M., 3:30–7 P.M.; closed: Sun.; credit cards accepted: all major.

Pampaloni

(Santa Maria Novella; see map pg. 156) Borgo Santi Apostoli, 47r; tel.: 055-289094; open: Tues.–Sat. 10 A.M.–1 P.M., 3:30–7:30 P.M.; closed: Sun.–Mon.; credit cards accepted: all major.

Best Artisans' Shops on the Oltrarno

Until the 1200s Florence was a warring city of landowners and peasants that offered little space for artistic endeavors. Starting in the 13th century, with the beginning of the Renaissance, Florence became the economic and cultural capital of Europe, but the new ruling class was made up of bankers and merchants, while artisans still remained marginalized as craftsmen in the lesser arts. Still, an elite group of artisans emerged from this period with a visibility and a civil importance they never had before: they were the painters, sculptors, and architects who would eventually give the city the fame that it carries to this day.

Lorenzo Villoresi, a perfumer who works with skills and talent that could have been passed down by an alchemist in the days of the Medici, is a modern-day heir to that tradition. As he says, he is "a craftsman who is also an artist." And although Florence is now crowded with stores selling mass-produced goods, there are many true artisans left in town. San Niccolò, Lorenzo Villoresi's neighborhood, is a good area to find them.

Villoresi's office is perched on the top floor of a 15th-century palazzo on the narrow Via de' Bardi. Upon entering the front doors below, wafts of rich mixed scents linger in the stairwell. Arriving in his office, one is struck by the walls, which are covered with shelves upon shelves of scents and essences. These small brown bottles contain the fruit of Villoresi's long, dedicated search for the best essences from around the world. He has traveled high and low for these scents, and he is capable of producing the perfect combination for any personalized perfume requested by his clients.

At the University of Florence, Mr. Villoresi studied philosophy and psychology, and he stumbled upon a few exotic scents during his visits to India and the Orient while observing those cultures. Upon his return to Florence, he began giving bits of mixed scents from his travels to friends. At a certain point one of these friends asked if he would be interested in creating scented candles for Fendi, and his career began.

What made him a success in the world of perfumes is his background, his studies, and his drive to always create a product that is unique and worthy of true artisan craft. He has never stopped traveling the world searching for new scents to add to his collection, which now holds over 1,000 different essences.

To create a personalized scent, a private seating with Mr. Villoresi is required. He will delve into a client's psyche to find out exactly what odors spark which memories. It almost becomes a therapy session out of which a scent is created that will then enhance the individual's mood.

To see and buy the work of other interesting artisans in the neighborhood, start with a visit to a shop on the opposite side of Via de' Bardi from Villoresi's offices. Il Torchio, an established fixture for about three decades, is crammed with paper goods and a bookbinding workshop that spills into the display area. A unique assortment of hand-decorated paper, photo albums, address books, and diaries are piled high. The expert and swift skill with which the paper goods are made are a pleasure to watch while sifting through the various designs and products.

It is well worth a small detour to Mannina at this point. Although this shop in Via Guicciardini, at No. 16r, is not officially in the San Niccolò neighborhood, it comes highly recommended and is really only just a few steps away. The storefront modestly displays a few elegant and conservative shoes; inside, space is tight, with just enough room to try on a pair. It is well worth squeezing in because the store offers the rare treat of custom, handmade shoes.

Turning back toward the heart of San Niccolò on the same street, another store window appears on the right side at No. 115r. The striking glint of gold and jewels beckons the visitor to enter the shop of Alessandro Dari. In the window display alone there are several pieces of work that confirm this jeweler as an artist of rare talent. Inside, the shop is filled with display cases, a studio, and living space, all fit into a churchlike room with high, arched ceilings. Like his work, Mr. Dari is eclectic. He is a pharmacist by night and a jeweler and sculptor by day. His work is already renowned in the United States. A ring made of two identical towers in gold and bronze, which he designed as part of a collection dedicated to the memory of the terrorist attacks on the World Trade Center, was displayed at Barney's in New York. In his shop he has divided the collection into various themes. There are cases titled Churches, Castles, Crowns, Alchemy and Magic, Sin, Music, Butterfly, and Fossils. Somehow the jewels separated into these cases all match their titles. Among various works and sculptures along the wall is a cast of a tabernacle Mr. Dari created for the Oblate Order of Florence. The actual tabernacle is finished in mother-of-pearl, diamonds, and rubies. Alessandro Dari is a master gold worker and restorer who has built his skill at *botteghe* in Siena and Florence, following the oldest gold-making traditions.

Following along, again on the right, at No. 95–97r is Lisa Corti Home Textiles Emporium. A bright spot of color in an otherwise dark, tortuous street, this shop offers a wide display of hand-printed fabrics, bed covers, cushions, shawls, curtains, and pottery to name but a few of the cheerful objects packed inside this little space. The designer has successfully managed to combine Indian and African themes into creative Italian productions. There is also another location on Via de' Bardi at No. 58.

Continuing on almost to the end of Via San Niccolò, at No. 2, where the tower of the same name becomes visible, is Certini, a shop specializing in wrought iron objects. For the last 30 years, Certini has occupied an old church. For the most part, the leafy and floral work is designed as lamps and candleholders, but there are also a variety of hangers, mirrors, tables, bathroom objects, and more. Although some of their crafts can already be found in some of the most exclusive American shops, it is a treat to go directly to the location where all of the items are actually made.

Alessandro Dari

(Santo Spirito; see map pg. 202)
Via San Niccolò, 115r; tel.: 055-244747; website: www.alessandrodari.com; e-mail: alessandrodari@libero.it; open: Mon.–Sat. 9 A.M.–1 P.M., 3:30–7:30 P.M.; closed: Sun.; credit cards accepted: all major.

Certini

Via San Niccolò, 2; tel.: 055-2342694; open: Mon.–Fri. 8:30 A.M.–12:30 P.M., 2:30–5:30 P.M.; closed: Sat. and Sun.; credit cards accepted: none.

Il Torchio

(Santa Spirito; see map pg. 202)
Via de' Bardi, 17; tel.: 055-2342862; open: Mon.–Fri. 9:30 A.M.–1:30 P.M., 2:30–7 P.M., Sat. 9:30 A.M.–1 P.M.; closed: Sun.; credit cards accepted: all major.

Lisa Corti Home Textiles Emporium

(Santo Spirito; see map pg. 202)
Via de' Bardi, 58; tel.: 055-2645600; website: www.lisacorti.com; e-mail: firenze@ lisacorti.com; Mon. 3:30–7:30 P.M., Tues.–Sat. 10 A.M.–1 P.M., 3:30–7:30 P.M.; closed: Sun.;

credit cards accepted: all major. Piazza Ghiberti, 33; tel.: 055-2001200; open: Mon. 3:30–7:30 P.M., Tues.–Sat. 10 A.M.– 2 P.M., 3:30–7:30 P.M.

Lorenzo Villoresi
(Santo Spirito; see map pg. 202)
Via de' Bardi, 14; tel.: 055-2341187; fax: 055-2345893; open: Mon.–Fri. 9 A.M.–1 P.M., 2–6 P.M. but only by appointment; closed: Sat.–Sun.; credit cards accepted: all major.

Mannina
(Santo Spirito, see map pg. 202)
Via Guicciardini, 16r; tel.: 055-282895; open: daily 9:30 A.M.–7:30 P.M.; credit cards accepted: all major.

Best Gourmet Stores
Pegna is the haute couture of gourmet in downtown Florence. The shop offers a wide selection of fresh, local delicacies as well as foreign packaged food (such as English muffins) that you are unlikely to find anywhere else in the city. Pegna also offers a home delivery service.

At Da Noi, Bruno Tramontana, a former chef with the city's hippest restaurant, Enoteca Pinchiorri (see entry pg. 122), prepares dishes from local 15th- and 16th-century recipes. His Swedish wife, Sabine, takes care of the sweets and numbers among her pièces de resistance cookies and chocolates. Da Noi offers a catering service as well.

Galanti makes homemade specialties such as lasagna and ravioli as well as sauces, meats, and cooked vegetables. The shop sells a wide variety of cheeses and cold cuts.

Da Noi
Via Fiesolana, 46r; tel.: 055-242917; open: Mon.–Tues., Thurs.–Fri. 9 A.M.–3 P.M., 5–7:30 P.M., Wed. 8 A.M.–3 P.M., Sat. 9 A.M.– 3 P.M.; closed: Sun.; credit cards accepted: none.

Pegna
(San Giovanni; see map pg. 68)
Via dello Studio, 8; tel.: 055-282701; website: www.pegna.it; e-mail: info@

pegna.it; open: Mon.–Sat. 9 A.M.–1 P.M., 3:30–7:30 P.M.; closed: Wed. afternoon and Sun.; credit cards accepted: all major.

Best Bars
Perched on the banks of the Arno River, Capocaccia is the trendiest bar in the city for an American-style brunch on Sundays. But it also does a great Milan-style aperitif at night, when a wide variety of delicacies, including pasta dishes, are on hand for those who decide to chill out here after work.

Giacosa on Via della Spada turned from a staple of Florentine tradition to a hip place to see and be seen after fashion designer Roberto Cavalli bought the place and refashioned it into a garment store-cum-bar, decorated with his trademark leopard prints. The renovated Giacosa offers a whole new variety of snacks along with the bar's traditional delicacies such as *torta della nonna* and *marron glacés*. A house staple is the superbly prepared local aperitif, the Negroni.

The nearby Procacci, a beautiful 19th-century store that also sells gourmet products such as Fauchon pâtés, offers the best mignon truffle sandwiches you will ever taste. Another specialty to savor with a glass of house wine is Procacci's butter and anchovy sandwich.

An 18th-century café in Piazza della Repubblica, Gilli is loved by foreigners and locals alike as a piece of Florence's history. Bartenders in liveried jackets prepare house cocktails such as the Spadolini, a Gilli creation made with spumante and kiwi in honor of the late Florentine Giovanni Spadolini, a former prime minister.

Also excellent is the bar's hot chocolate, though some Florentines would argue in favor of Rivoire's sweeter version of the beverage. The other historic café that has been serving clients since Florence was the capital of Italy, Caffè Rivoire is located directly in front of the Palazzo Vecchio. The bar offers chocolates sold in beautiful boxes that make delicious presents for special occasions.

Caffè Rivoire

(Santa Croce; see map pg. 118)
Piazza della Signoria, 5r; tel.: 055-214412;
open: Tues.–Sun. 8 A.M.–11:30 P.M.; closed:
Mon.; credit cards accepted: all major.

Capocaccia
Lungarno Corsini, 12–14r; tel.: 055-210751;
open: daily 12:30 P.M.–2 A.M.; credit cards
accepted: all major.

Giacosa—Roberto Cavalli
Via della Spada, 10r; tel.: 055-2776328;
www.caffegiacosa.com; open: Mon.–Fri.
7:30 A.M.–8:30 P.M.; Sat. 8 A.M.–8:30 P.M.;
closed: Sun.; credit cards accepted: all major.

Gilli
Piazza della Repubblica, 39r; tel.: 055-
213896; open: daily 7:30 A.M.–midnight;
closed: Tues.; credit cards accepted: all major.

Procacci
(Santa Maria Novella; see map pg. 156)
Via Tornabuoni, 64r; tel.: 055-211656; open:
Mon.–Sat. 10:30 A.M.–8 P.M.; closed: Sun.;
credit cards accepted: all major.

Best Bread
No *schiacciata*, a scrumptious bread made
with Tuscan olive oil, tastes like Pugi's, the
bakery where even Florentines pressed for
time are willing to stand in line for one of
the many *schiacciata* specialties of the house.
Also delicious is the *pan di ramerino,* a local
dessert bread traditionally made by bakeries
that is cooked with rosemary and raisins.

Another cornerstone of quality bread is
Buti, the place to go for fans of *grissini.*
Apart from the wide variety of bread
sticks, Buti bakes delicious olive and nut
loaves and *schiacciata*. The bakery makes
all sorts of cakes and sweets, including the
house's specialty, a Bavarian pudding.

The perpetually crowded Via Gioberti,
dubbed the 100-shop street, is a food
shopper's dream featuring many top-
quality bakeries. Among the best is Pan per
Focaccia. Their specialty is Florence's
traditional *pane casalingo,* an unsalted,
crusty bread baked in wood ovens that
nourished generations of Tuscan farmers.

The *grissini* and *schiacciata* are also very
good, and clients can have cakes and
pastries made to order.

Il Forno di Stefano Galli is also a
favorite venue for *schiacciata* junkies and is
well-known for its selection of *focacce* and
loaves.

Buti
Via Boccaccio, 47r; tel.: 055-571208; open:
Mon.–Sat. 7 A.M.–1:30 P.M., 4:30–7:30 P.M.;
closed: Sun.; credit cards accepted: none.

Pugi
Viale de Amicis, 49r; tel.: 055-669666; open:
Mon.–Sat. 7 A.M.–1:30 P.M., 4:45–8:20 P.M.;
credit cards accepted: none.

Best Gelato and Pastry Shops
Vivoli is synonymous with ice cream in
Florence. Its creamy gelato is widely
considered the best in town, rivaled only
by that of Gelateria Veneta and Perché No?
Vivoli also makes delicious coffee mousse
and chocolate mousse with almonds.
Perché No? serves up a record 56 flavors,
making decisions difficult and repeat visits
necessary.

Right beside Gelateria Veneta stands
Dolci e Dolcezze, a paradise for gourmets.
Giulio Corti, who imports a special butter
from the Netherlands to make his unique
pastry dough, can seduce the staunchest
dieters with the house's trademark bitter
chocolate cake, banana and *gianduia*
pastry, and a wide variety of Bavarian fruit-
cakes.

Giurovich uses the best quality ingredients for its specialties, including
Neapolitan delicacies such as *sfogliatelle.*
The kranz, filled with homemade candied
fruit, the *millefoglie,* and the bongo, a
chocolate cake filled with whipped cream,
are just three of the many delicacies of one
of Florence's most beloved pastry shops.

Robiglio was established in the 1920s
by Pietro Robiglio. Now as popular as ever,
it remains an obligatory stop for *krapfen*
fans. Another specialty is Robiglio's
country-style cake, which clients have
savored since the 1930s. The shop offers a

catering service and undisputedly has the best *budino di riso*, a typical Florentine pastry made with rice.

Finally, we suggest Latteria Frilli, one of Florence's best ice cream shops. Located just inside the gates of the old city wall, this microscopic gelaterie offers just a few select flavors made fresh in the kitchen behind the counter.

Dolci e Dolcezze
(Santa Croce, see map pg. 118)
Piazza Beccaria, 8r; tel.: 055-2345458; open: Tues.–Sat. 8:30 A.M.–8:30 P.M., Sun. 9 A.M.–1 P.M., 4:30–7:30 P.M.; closed: Mon.

Gelateria Veneta
Piazza Beccaria, 7r; tel.: 055-2343370; open: Mon.–Sat. 8 A.M.–8 P.M., Sun. 8 A.M.–1 P.M., 3 P.M.–8 P.M.

Giurovich
Viale Don Minzoni, 26r; tel.: 055-574752; open: Tues.–Sat. 7:30 A.M.–8 P.M., Sun. 7:30 A.M.–7 P.M.; closed: Mon.

Latteria Frilli
Via San Miniato, 5r; open: Thurs.–Tues. 11 A.M.–midnight (summer), Thurs.–Tues. 11 A.M.–8 P.M. (winter); closed: Wed.

Perché No?
(Santa Croce, see map pg. 118)
Via Tavolini, 19r; tel.: 055-2398969; open: daily 11–midnight (summer), noon–8 P.M. (winter); closed: Tues. in winter.

Robiglio
(Santa Maria Novella, see map pg. 156)
Via Tosinghi, 11r; tel.: 055-215013; open: daily 8 A.M.–8 P.M.; Via dei Servi, 112r; tel.: 055-212784; open: Mon.–Sat. 8 A.M.–8 P.M.; closed: Sun.

Vivoli Gelateria
(Santa Croce, see map pg. 118)
Via Isola delle Stinche, 7r; tel.: 055-292334; open: Tues.–Sat. 7:30 A.M.–midnight, Sun. 9:30 A.M.–midnight; closed: Mon.

San Giovanni

By Laura Collura Kahn

ny tour of the San Giovanni quarter must start from the **Duomo**, or the cathedral of **Santa Maria del Fiore**, Florence's main church, on which the city's most illustrious artists worked. It was started in 1296 by Arnolfo di Cambio, continued by Giotto, and finished in 1436 by Filippo Brunelleschi with his spectacular dome. On its right rises the **Campanile di Giotto**, a slender bell tower sporting the same three-hued marble that covers the cathedral. Visitors can obtain a breathtaking view of Brunelleschi's dome from the top. Facing the church is the baptistery, or **Battistero di San Giovanni**, an octagonal baptistery from the 11th century covered in white and green marble, accessible on the east side of **Piazza San Giovanni**. The nearby **Museo del Duomo** contains sculptures and decorations from the baptistery and the cathedral. This ensemble of structures rises upon the city's spiritual heart, harmonic **Piazza del Duomo**, completed in the 19th century.

Walking east, a tour of the many Medici-related sites in this area begins with a stop at the **Palazzo Medici-Riccardi**, today's Prefecture, built in 1444. It features the first example of Michelangelo's *inginocchiate,* "on the facade," windows, so-called because they rest on large windowsills, as if kneeling on them.

A detour on the left leads to **Piazza San Lorenzo**, dominated by the basilica's magnificent, unfinished facade designed by Michelangelo and enlivened by an open-air market. Also designed by Michelangelo was the annexed **Biblioteca Laurenziana**, which contains Italy's largest collection of manuscripts. The complex comprises the **Cappelle Medicee**, the burial site for the Medicis.

Proceeding north, stop at the **Mercato Centrale**, an iron-and-glass structure housing a grocery store, designed in 1874 by Giuseppe Mengoni.

Back to the Via Cavour, walk to bench-equipped **Piazza San Marco**, overlooked by the church and convent of **San Marco**, built in 1299. A section of the convent is today the **Museo di San Marco**, containing paintings by Fra Angelico. Off the square is the **Galleria dell'Accademia**, housing the magnificent *David* by Michelangelo, started in 1501, when the artist was 26.

Via Battisti leads to **Piazza della Santissima Annunziata**, considered Florence's most perfectly proportioned piazza, surrounded by three loggias and the church of **Santissima Annunziata**, a favorite site for weddings.

Farther along Via Cavour, conclude the tour at a 13th-century door to the city, **Porta San Gallo**.

Opposite, The Cupola del Duomo

Via d. Cinque G...
F. Ceruso
PIAZZA
d. Vittoria
Puccini
Via d.
della
F. Rudini
XX
Settem
Via XIV Maggio
Via
Via
F.
Crispi
Viale G.
il
Mille
Via d. Statuto
Piazza d.
Costituzione
Via
Viale
Via Leone
Via Poliziano
Lorenzo
Via Bandino
Ma

Strozzi

Fortezza
Da Basso
Viale S.
Via B.
Lavagn
Via S. Caterina d'Alessandria
Via d. Ruote
Via d. Duca d'Aosta

Via Filippo
16
Via Strozzi
Via d. Pratello
Via Barbano
Via Dolfi
Via Ridolfi
Via Poggi
Via Bartolommeo
San Zanobi
Santa Reparata
Campo reggi
Via d. Lun
Galbo
10
Via d. Fortezza
PIAZZA
della
Indipendenza
8
Via Valfonda
Pza del
Crocifisso
Via Guelfa
Via XXVII Aprile
19
11
Via Cennini
Faenza
15
Via Fiume
Via Nazionale
Via Chiara
Panicale
Via Sorsola
Via Guelfa
32
PIAZZA
S. Marco
Piazza
Adua
4
Pza della Nazione
Via Taddea
P.za d.
Mercato
Centrale
21
Via de' Ginori
Via Cavour
13
27
Via S. Antonino
Zannoni
Via d. Ariento
37
Via d. Suta
Via de' Noce
Borgo la Noce
5
Via de' Pucci
S. Maria Novella
Piazza d. Unità Italiana
Via del Melarancio
Piazza Madonna d. Aldobrandini
7
S. Lorenzo
3
P.za S. Lorenzo
Via de' Cori
31
Via de' Martelli
V. de' Billi
S. Maria de i Fiore (Duomo)
Piazza
S. Maria
Novella
Via Panzani
Via d. Giglio
Via d. Alloro
Via de' Banchi
Via de' Cerretani
Battistero
12
Piazza d.
S. Maria
Pl Fiore
(Duomo)
25
Scala
Via Moro
Pza di Paolino
Pza d. Ottaviani
V. d.Trebbio
V. d. Antinori
Via de' Rondinelli
Via de' Pecori
P.za di S. Giovanni
2
Duomo
6
Pza d. Capitolo d.Canonica
14
Via del
Via de' Belle Donne
Via de' Vecchietti
Via Roma
24
V. dell'Oche
Pza di S. Benedetto de' Bonizzi
Via d. Spada
Pza S. Pancrazio
Via de' Giacomini
Via de' Tosinghi
Pza S. Maria in Campo
V. d. Vigna Nuova
Via de' Corsi
Campidoglio
Brunelleschi
Tosinghi
Via d. Adimari
Pza d. Giglio
Vic. d. Alberghi
Borgo
Via d. Federighi
Via de' Fossi
V. d. Sole
PIAZZA
della
Repubblica
Speziali
Via del Corso
Pza d. Donati
V. d. Strozzi
Calzaiuoli
Pza de' Tre Re
Via d. Tavolini
Pza S. Maria in Campo
Vic. d. Strozzi
Pza de' Rucellai
Goldoni
Pza S. Miniato fra le Torri
V. Orsanm
V. Dante Alighieri
Via d.

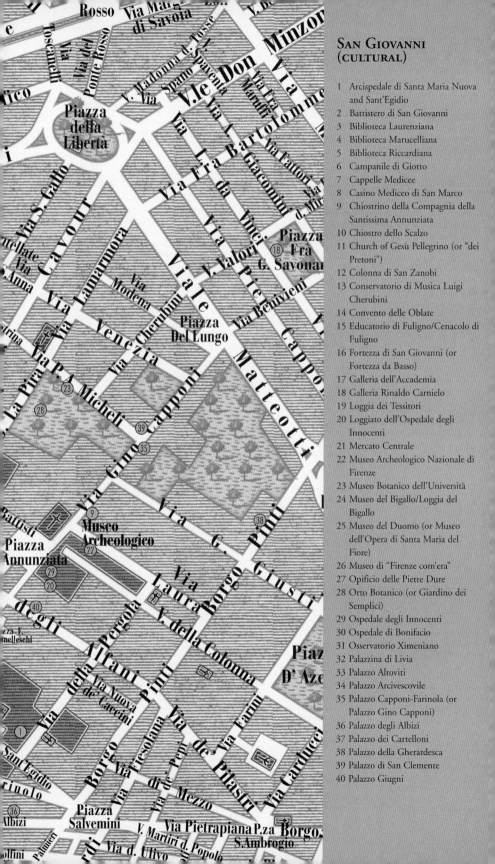

SAN GIOVANNI (CULTURAL)

1. Arcispedale di Santa Maria Nuova and Sant'Egidio
2. Battistero di San Giovanni
3. Biblioteca Laurenziana
4. Biblioteca Marucelliana
5. Biblioteca Riccardiana
6. Campanile di Giotto
7. Cappelle Medicee
8. Casino Mediceo di San Marco
9. Chiostrino della Compagnia della Santissima Annunziata
10. Chiostro dello Scalzo
11. Church of Gesù Pellegrino (or "dei Pretoni")
12. Colonna di San Zanobi
13. Conservatorio di Musica Luigi Cherubini
14. Convento delle Oblate
15. Educatorio di Fuligno/Cenacolo di Fuligno
16. Fortezza di San Giovanni (or Fortezza da Basso)
17. Galleria dell'Accademia
18. Galleria Rinaldo Carnielo
19. Loggia dei Tessitori
20. Loggiato dell'Ospedale degli Innocenti
21. Mercato Centrale
22. Museo Archeologico Nazionale di Firenze
23. Museo Botanico dell'Università
24. Museo del Bigallo/Loggia del Bigallo
25. Museo del Duomo (or Museo dell'Opera di Santa Maria del Fiore)
26. Museo di "Firenze com'era"
27. Opificio delle Pietre Dure
28. Orto Botanico (or Giardino dei Semplici)
29. Ospedale degli Innocenti
30. Ospedale di Bonifacio
31. Osservatorio Ximeniano
32. Palazzina di Livia
33. Palazzo Altoviti
34. Palazzo Arcivescovile
35. Palazzo Capponi-Farinola (or Palazzo Gino Capponi)
36. Palazzo degli Albizi
37. Palazzo dei Cartelloni
38. Palazzo della Gherardesca
39. Palazzo di San Clemente
40. Palazzo Giugni

Via d. Cinque Gio... • Via F. Cerna... • PIAZZA d. Vittoria • Puccini • Febbra...

ucci • Via XIV Maggio • Via d. • Via della • Via d. Statuto • F. Crispi • F. Ruffini • XX • Settem • Milt • Via Landino • Ma

ria • Piazza d. Costituzione • Via Viale • Via Leonel • G. • Via Poliziano

Strozzi • Via Lorenzo • il • Lavagn

Fortezza Da Basso • Viale S. • S. Caterina d'Alessandria • Via d. Ruote • V. Duca d'Aos • Via B. • Lup

Via Filippo • Via Pratello Strozzi • V.le di Barbano • Via Poggi • Via Bartolommei • San Zanobi • Reparata • Galilo • Campo reggi • 45 • 61

Via • Via Valfonda • Via d. Pratello • V. Ridolfi • Via di Fortezza • Piazza della Indipendenza • Via San • Via XXVII • Santa Reparata • 64

Pza del Crocifisso • Via Guelfa • Via Cennini • Faenza • Via XXVII Aprile • Via • 57 • Piazza S. Marco • 54

Piazza Adua • Via Fiume • Via Nazionale • 59 • Via Chiara • Panicale • Via Sorsola • Via Guelfa • Via Cavour • 64

le F.S. ovella • 75 • Via Taddea • P.za d. Mercato Centrale • Via de' Ginori

zza della azione • Via Zannonia • Via d. Ariento • 62 • Borgo • Via la Noce • Via de' Giuta • 42 • 44 • Via de' Pucci • 43

S. Maria Novella • Via S. Antonino • Via Amorino • Piazza Madonna d. Aldobrandini • Piazza d. Unità Italiana • Via del Melarancio • 53 • za S. Lorenzo • 60 • 47 • Via del

Piazza S. Maria Novella • Via d. Giglio • Via d. Alloro • S. Lorenzo • 63 • V. de' Bitti • 65 • S. Maria Bufalini

Scala • Via Panzani • Via dei Banchi • Via de' Cerretani • Battistero • Piazza d. • S. Maria Del Fiore (Duomo) • 49

za di Paolino • Via Moro • d. Sole • Fiatina • Via de' Pecori • 52 • S. Giovanni • Piazza d. • 50 • 69 • 73 • Via del

Pza d. Ottaviani • Via de' Giacomini • Via de' Vecchietti • P.za del Olio • Duomo • Pza d. Capitolo • Canonica • de' Bonizzi • 46

Pza S. Pancrazio • Via de' Corsi • Campidoglio • Brunelleschi • Via Roma • Tosinghi • V. dell'Oche • 56 • V. d. Alberighi • 67

V.d. Trebbio • d. Antinori • Via d. Agli • Via Calzaiuoli • Vic. d. Adimari • 78 • Via d. • Corso • 48

V. de' Tornabuoni • V. d. Strozzi • Pza d. Strozzi • Piazza della Repubblica • Pza del Tre Re • Via de' Speziali • Pza de' Donati • Via del • Pza S. Maria in Campo • Borgo

V.d. Vigna Nuova • Vic. d. Strozzi • V.d. Sassetti • Pellic • S. Miniato fra le torri • V. Dante Alighieri • Via de'

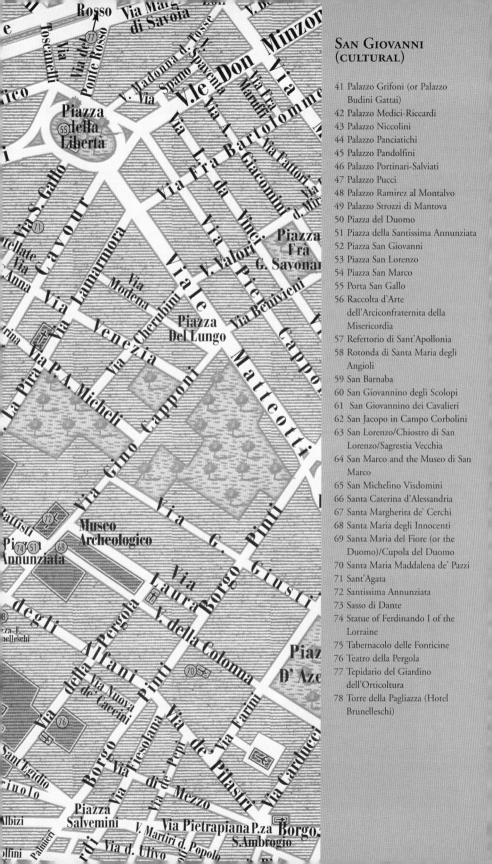

San Giovanni
(CULTURAL)

BATTISTERO DI SAN GIOVANNI (BAPTISTERY OF SAN GIOVANNI)

Piazza del Duomo; tel.: 055-2302885; open: Mon.–Sat. noon–6:30 P.M., Sun. 8:30 A.M.– 1:30 P.M.; admission: €3.

➤ Dedicated to Saint John the Baptist, patron saint of Florence, the baptistery is the oldest structure in Piazza del Duomo. During the age of Dante, who was christened here in the early 14th century, the baptistery was built over a large Roman edifice, probably a big *domus* (house). It was formally consecrated in the 11th century by Pope Nicholas II. The pilasters, capitals, and triangular pediments that decorate its marble exterior demonstrate the enduring influence of the antiquity on Florentine architecture and anticipate the arrival of the Renaissance.

The four bronze doors to the baptistery are world famous for their virtuosity. The door that serves as the public entrance (the south door) is the oldest. Begun in 1330 by Andrea Pisano, the south door's upper panels, which chronicle the life of John the Baptist, and lower panels, which depict the theological and cardinal virtues, are distinctly Gothic but exhibit a sense of

Doors of the Baptistery of San Giovanni

freedom and ease uncharacteristic of that period. The commission for the north door, built between 1403 and 1424, went to 25-year-old Lorenzo Ghiberti, who won a city-wide contest that featured stiff competition from 20-year-old Filippo Brunelleschi. (Each artist submitted a bronze sculpted plaque depicting the Sacrifice of Isaac; both plaques are now located at the Bargello Museum for side-by-side comparison. The plaque currently on the baptistery is a copy.) The north door's eight lower panels depict the evangelists and the doctors of the Church, surmounted by scenes from the Life and Passion of Christ. Together, they comprise a carefully balanced composition, so highly admired by Ghiberti's patrons, that he received a second commission for the baptistery's east end. Begun a year after the completion of the north door, the east door, called the Porta del Paradiso or "Gate of Paradise," is Ghiberti's undisputed masterpiece. The 27 years it took him to complete the work were the sculptor's artistic prime. Working with 10 large panels, instead of the 20 small ones in the tradition of Pisano, Ghiberti imbued his metalwork with an illusion of depth never before seen in relief sculpture. Moving from top to bottom, the panels depict the Creation and Fall of Adam and Eve, the history of Noah, the story of Esau and Jacob, scenes from Exodus, and the lives of Saul and David. (Four of the panels are copies. The originals are in the Museo del Duomo).

To the side of Porta del Paradiso there are two porphyry columns that were a present from the citizens of Pisa to the Florentines. (This was the only present that they ever gave to the Florentines, with whom they were constantly embroiled in wars or territorial disputes.) The columns were part of the spoils of war in one of the Pisani's many conquests in the Middle East. The people of Pisa thought they had magic power and that the marble of the column would reflect the face of people who had committed crimes but remained unpunished. When the Florentines erected the two columns in the baptistery they couldn't see any reflection (apparently the Pisani had "opacized" the columns with smoke before giving them to the Florentines) and soon concluded that they did not have any special powers. From

Giotto's Campanile

to be completed by Andrea Pisano and Francesco Talenti in 1359. The thickness of its walls was doubled in order to support the weight of its heavily decorated exterior. The present exterior is in fact a pared-down version of Giotto's design. Parts of the original exterior are now housed within the Museum of the Duomo (see pg. 33). Climb the 414 steps to the top of the tower for sweeping views of Florence's rooftops, as well as an unparalleled perspective on the cupola of the cathedral by Brunelleschi.

CAPPELLE MEDICEE (MEDICI CHAPELS)

Piazza Madonna degli Aldobrandini, 6; tel.: 055-2388602; website: www.sbas.firenze.it; open: daily 8:15 A.M.–4:50 P.M. (Apr.–Nov.), 8:15 A.M.–1:50 P.M. (rest of the year), closed 2nd and 4th Sun., 1st and 3rd Mon., holidays. (last admission 30 minutes before closing); admission: €6.

➤ This complex of apselike structures houses the Cappella dei Principi (the Chapel of the Princes) and the Sagrestia Nuova (New Sacristy) of the San Lorenzo basilica.

The Chapel of the Princes has a markedly gloomy interior. Its lofty proportions and octagonal shape, designed under the reign of Cosimo I, were intended to immortalize the Medici progeny. Under the colossal tombs, carved from oriental granite and green Corsican jasper, Cosimo I and his line are, in fact, buried. The empty niches above some of the tombs were supposed to hold statues, similar to those that decorate the tombs of

this story, Italians get their saying, *"Fiorentini ciechi e Pisani traditori,"* or "The Florentines are blind and the Pisani are traitors."

CAMPANILE DI GIOTTO (GIOTTO'S BELL TOWER)

Piazza del Duomo; tel.: 055-2302885; open: daily 8:30 A.M.–6:50 P.M.; admission: €6.

➤ The Gothic bell tower, or campanile, immediately to the right of the Duomo's facade, is 269 feet (82 meters) of pink, green, and white marble. It was originally designed by Giotto, but the master died shortly after construction began, leaving it

CAMPANILE

But perhaps the best image of the absence of stale melancholy or wasted splendour . . . in the Florentine impression and genius, is the bell-tower of Giotto, which rises beside the Cathedral. No beholder of it will have forgotten how straight and slender it stands there, how strangely rich in the common street, plated with coloured marble patterns, and yet so far from simple or severe in design that we easily wonder how its author . . . should have fashioned a building which in the way of elaborate elegance, of the true play of taste, leaves a jealous modern criticism nothing to miss.

Henry James, "The Autumn in Florence," in *Italian Hours*

Ferdinando I and Cosimo II.

Designed and executed by Michelangelo, the New Sacristy is definitely very distinct from the Sagrestia Vecchia, or Old Sacristy, of Brunelleschi (see pg. 43). Working under the commission by Pope Leo X in 1520, Michelangelo forged a new style of architecture, both inspired by and in defiance of the carefully measured compositions of his predecessor. The vertical layout of Michelangelo's arches, cornices, niches, and high-stretching pediments and windows liberates this interior space from Brunelleschi's absolutism and expresses a level of dynamism that the Old Sacristy lacks. The principal monuments, also by Michelangelo, begin with the Tomb of Lorenzo the Magnificent and His Brother Giuliano. Carved in 1521, it depicts the Virgin Mary with the Christ child. Flanking its right and left sides are Saints Damian and Cosma, respectively, designed by Michelangelo. Saint Damian was executed by Raffaello da Montelupo, while Saint Cosma was completed by Giovanni Angelo Montorsoli. The monument to Giuliano, duke of Nemours, occupies the right wall and features allegorical subjects. Night (left) and Day (right) lounge on the sarcophagus. Facing them on the opposite wall are Dusk (1531) and Dawn (1531–1532), reclining on the sarcophagus of the monument to Lorenzo, duke of Urbino (1533).

Michelangelo's Tomb of Lorenzo the Magnificent in the Cappelle Medicee of San Lorenzo

Cupola del Duomo (Cupola of the Duomo)

Piazza del Duomo, in Santa Maria del Fiore, tel.: 055-2302885; open: Mon.–Fri. 8:30 A.M.–6:50 P.M., Sat. 8:30 A.M.–5 P.M.; closed: Sun.; admission: €6.

➢ Among the architectural contributors to Santa Maria del Fiore, no one, perhaps, is more significant than Filippo Brunelleschi, who Vasari characterized as "an architectural genius sent down by heaven to bring new form to an architecture that had gone astray." The new form that Brunelleschi conceived in 1429 still reigns as the quintessential cupola, or dome, of Christian architecture.

Undoubtedly the greatest architectural feat of the 15th century, Brunelleschi's ambitious design fully expressed his faith in the integration of art and science, an essential postulate in Renaissance theory. More conventional modes of construction, which relied on scaffolding, were useless to Brunelleschi, who needed to cover the immense space left by the cathedral's preexistent octagonal drum. The drum, in fact, was so expansive that its diameter (139 feet, or 42 meters) far outstretched the length of the tree trunks that would have traditionally covered the void and formed the base of the scaffolding. The guiding principle of Brunelleschi's design, meanwhile, relied upon a system of forces, converging at the cupola's apex, where the lantern and its weight could absorb the inward thrust and evenly redistribute it outward. This self-sustaining force, according to a memorandum sent by Brunelleschi to the cupola's commissioners before work began in 1420, was a mere theoretical assumption. The architect's mathematical guesswork was inevitably confirmed in practice, as his cupola surged into the air, without a scaffolding, supported by the integrity of its own design.

On January 17, 1600, as a violent thunderstorm hit Florence, lightning struck the gilded copper ball by Andrea Verrocchio that had been put on top of Brunelleschi's cupola in 1472. The ball rolled down to the pavement of the piazza; a marble circle marks the exact place where it fell.

FORTEZZA DI SAN GIOVANNI (OR FORTEZZA DA BASSO)

Viale Filippo Strozzi 1; tel: 055-49721; open: for exhibits only.

➤ Designed by Antonio di San Gallo and erected in 1534 by Alessandro de' Medici to strengthen his position in the city as first duke of Florence, this massive fortress is considered a landmark in the history of military architecture. Alessandro, who thought of the building as a safe haven in times of trouble, was killed here by his cousin in 1537. Over the centuries, the structure was used as a prison, an arsenal, and military barracks. In 1967, it was heavily renovated and turned into an exhibition center. Each year, the famed Pitti fashion shows are held inside the fortress. In 1978, a large prefabricated steel structure was erected inside the walls surrounding the fortress. A similar round one was built in 1987, and a third pavilion is in the works. The Fortezza houses a restoration center for works of art, complete with a science lab.

GALLERIA DELL'ACCADEMIA (ACCADEMIA GALLERY)

Via Ricasoli, 60; tel.: 055-2388609; website: www.sbas.firenze.it/accademia; open: Tues.–Sun. 8:15 A.M.–6:50 P.M.; closed: Mon., Jan. 1, May 1, Dec. 25; admission: €6.50.

➤ Founded in 1784 by Grand Duke Pietro Leopoldo, the gallery's aim was to amass a collection of Florentine masterpieces that would inspire students at the adjoining Accademia di Belle Arti (Academy of Fine Arts), providing them with examples against which they should measure themselves. (It is for this reason that the duke chose only Florentine works, since they were unquestionable masterpieces.) It is now home to some of Michelangelo's greatest sculptures, as well as paintings by many of his contemporaries.

Lining the main corridor of the Michelangelo Gallery are four of the artist's famous slaves (c.1521–1530). These unfinished marble works were originally intended to adorn the tomb of Pope Julius II, and the figures, who seem to be struggling to free themselves from the marble they are trapped in, are among Michelangelo's most dramatic pieces.

Between two ...Matthew, also... Commissione... oversaw the ... Duomo, the st... cathedral's mai... years until it wa... the end of this c... contrast to the ra... and the *Four Pris...* ...ost highly refined of Michelangelo's masterpieces, the *David* (1501–1504). In carving the statue from one enormous block of marble, Michelangelo achieved a technical feat without precedence, while also breaking figurative ground in his unorthodox representation of the widely known biblical hero. Unlike Donatello's *David,* for example, which portrays an effeminate youth, sword in hand, beside the decapitated head of Goliath (currently in the Bargello Museum), Michelangelo presents a young man, striking a defiant posture, with a provocative gaze directed at his giant adversary. In its original location, in front of the Palazzo Vecchio in Piazza della Signoria (it has been replaced by a copy), the statue was intended to both deter foreign attackers and to provoke a sense of civic pride in Florence's ability to stand its

Michelangelo's Dying Slave *at the Galleria dell'Accademia*

...such an attack take place. [...]ee wings that stem from the [...]rridor contain a number of works [...]Michelangelo's contemporaries. In the right wing is *Venus and Cupid* (c. 1532) by Jacopo Pontormo. On the right side of the gallery is an intricately painted wooden chest, the *Cassone Adimari,* which was done by Scheggia, Masaccio's stepbrother, around 1440. The chest was part of a bride's trousseau and depicts details of Florentine daily life and a picture of the bridal party in front of the baptistery. There are also two paintings by Sandro Botticelli, the *Madonna of the Sea* (attributed by some to young Filippino Lippi) and the *Madonna and Child with the Young Saint John and Angels* (c. 1470). *The Visitation* (c. 1470) is among the first of a cycle of paintings that Perugino completed while in Florence. To the left is the entrance to the Gipsoteca Bartolini, a sculpture gallery with plaster casts that were used for creating marble sculptures— there are 285 busts. On the left side of the wing are the Sale Bizantine (Byzantine Hall) with *Mary Magdalene and Stories from Her Life,* by the Maestro della Maddalena, *Virgin Mary Enthroned with the Christ Child and Four Saints,* by the Maestro di San Gaggio, and the *Tree of Life,* by Pacino di Bonaguida. The small hall on the right has 22 panels by Taddeo Gaddi (c. 1330) and a crucifix (after 1340) by Bernardo Daddi. The Salone della Toscana (Tuscany Room) is full of 19th-century sculptures and paintings by members of the Accademia.

LOGGIATO DELL'OSPEDALE DEGLI INNOCENTI

Piazza della Santissima Annunziata

➣ With this elegant portico, which extends across the building's entire front of the Ospedale degli Innocenti, Brunelleschi, in 1419, updated the traditional Florentine architectural style. The new design, experts say, created a continuity between the void of the square and the fullness of the palazzo. In addition, Brunelleschi used geometry to enhance the portico's harmony, making the arches as wide as the columns are tall, so that the loggia appears to be a series of cubes. The building, financed by the Silk-Workers Guild, or *Arte della Seta,* was built by Francesco della Luna to allude to the function of the building, a foundling hospital or orphanage. In 1487 Andrea della Robbia produced the terra-cotta works placed in the arches, each representing a newborn baby. Frescoes by Bernardino Poccetti decorate the area under the portico. The door on the left side features a 1459 fresco by Giovanni di Francesco, while the one on the left bears a much later work (1843) by Gasparo Martellini.

MERCATO CENTRALE

Piazza del Mercato Centrale; open: see p. 16 for hours; closed: Sun.

➣ Located in the piazza of the same name and completed in 1874, the Mercato Centrale offers locals and tourists alike the chance to sample a wide variety of Florentine foods under one roof. Its construction called for the demolition of several free-standing historical buildings to create ample indoor space for the food

SPEDALE DEGLI INNOCENTI

. . . another image, classically, tenderly Florentine: of the Spedale degli Innocenti, the first architectural work of the Renaissance, that exquisite asylum designed by Brunelleschi for the city's foundlings, with ten glazed terracotta roundels, by Andrea della Robbia, of babies, swaddled, each in a different position, aligned, as if in a nursery, over the graceful pale-yellow portico.

Mary McCarthy, *The Stones of Florence*

Mercato Centrale

shops. Made of cast iron with high windows, the interior is divided into two levels with several walkways to allow easy browsing for shoppers.

Museo del Duomo (or Museo dell'Opera di Santa Maria del Fiore) (Museum of the Duomo)

Piazza del Duomo, 9; tel.: 055-2302885; open: Mon.–Sat. 9 A.M.–6:50 P.M., Sun. and public holidays 9 A.M.–1 P.M.; admission: €6.

➤ The Museum of the Duomo has stored artwork since the 15th century. In 1891 the rooms were converted into a museum that exhibits fragments of sculptures from Piazza del Duomo, the baptistery, and the facade and interior of Santa Maria del Fiore. One of the most important of these is Ghiberti's *Gates of Paradise* panels from the baptistery doors, which were removed after the flood of 1966. Four of the original reliefs from the east door, which depict the Creation, Cain and Abel, the Life of Joseph, and David and Goliath, are on display. Once the restoration is completely finished, these pieces will be joined by the rest of the door.

The first room of the museum is devoted to Brunelleschi and includes a small bust of him, as well as tools used by 15th-century masons. There are also models for the construction of the cathedral dome. Also on the ground floor are wooden models for the facade of the Duomo, including a facsimile of the plans by Arnolfo di Cambio, and some statues he carved for its niches, such as the *Madonna of the Glass Eyes*. There are also four statues carved between 1408 and 1415 for the four niches on the bottom and to the side of the main door of the Duomo. In order from left to right, they are: Nanni di Banco's *Saint Luke*, Donatello's *Saint John*, Bernardo Ciuffagni's *Saint Matthew*, and Niccolo Lamberti's *Saint Mark*. Make sure to look at the two famous *cantorie* (1431–1438) by Luca della Robbia and Donatello, probably executed by organ-lofts for the Duomo, and Donatello's *Mary Magdalene* (1455), expressively carved in wood. The latter depicts a repentant Magdalene, ravaged by old age and shrouded in tufts of her own overgrown hair. Also by Donatello are a number of Old Testament figures including the prophet Habbakuk (1423–1425), often referred to as *"lo zuccone"* ("pumpkin head") because of its oval head.

On the staircase is one of Michelangelo's final sculptures, the *Pietà*. He worked on it until the age of 80, and it was intended to decorate his tomb, but upon his death it was still unfinished. The Virgin Mary, Christ, and Nicodemus are the authentic work of the master (the face of Nicodemus is thought to be a self-portrait). The figure of Mary Magdalene, however, is the awkward contribution of Michelangelo's pupil.

On the second floor are choir stalls by Donatello and Luca della Robbia from the 1430s. Carved in marble and decorated with colored glass and mosaic, both of them depict children playing musical instruments and dancing. There are also lunettes by Andrea della Robbia, a statue of Boniface VIII by Arnolfo di Cambio, and bas-reliefs by Nanni di Banco, Andrea Pisano, and Tino di Camaino.

PALAZZO MEDICI-RICCARDI

Via Cavour, 1; tel.: 055-2760340; website: www.palazzo-medici.it; open: daily 9 A.M.– 7 P.M.; closed: Wed., May 1, Dec. 25; admission: €5.

➢ When Michelozzo received the commission from Cosimo the Elder to build the Medici a place of residence in 1444, the architect was confronted by the challenge of creating a mansion worthy of his proprietor's great name, a mansion that would later play host to Lorenzo the

Palazzo Medici-Riccardi

Magnificent's princely court, as well as Charles VII of France. On the other hand, the palazzo's design had to be somber, or else it would stir suspicions that the Medici, who already considered themselves the unofficial rulers of Florence, were moving toward outright sovereignty. Michelozzo's final design would strike a successful balance that quickly became the prototype for Florentine mansions to follow. The building combines elements of medieval fortification with the grace and elegance of classical architecture. Composed of three stories, the structure rises from street level in heavily rusticated stonework that gradually softens over a succession of cornices. The top level is virtually smooth, crowned by a powerful, overhanging cornice that takes direct inspiration from antiquity. The barred windows at street level, topped by triangular pediments, were added in 1517, long after the palazzo's completion in 1462.

In his design of the interior courtyard and chapel, however, Michelozzo definitively breaks from medieval appearances to forge fine examples of Renaissance architecture. The courtyard is surrounded by a tall portico and twin windows. The decorative medallions, carved in Donatello's workshop, bear the Medici coat of arms as well as classical themes. The first staircase to the right, in the courtyard, leads into the chapel. Here, Michelozzo's richly coffered ceilings and patterned flooring are complemented by a glorious cycle of frescoes (1459) by Benozzo Gozzoli depicting the Procession of the Magi. These highly imaginative compositions depict an assortment of lively animals, hunting scenes, delightful landscapes, and famous figures from Florentine high society.

The Medici family made the palace their primary home until 1540; in 1659 the Riccardi family purchased it and made several changes, including the addition of a new wing that now houses the headquarters of the local representative of the Interior Ministry, or Prefecture. The first stairway on the right leads to the Cappella dei Magi, or Chapel of the Magi (Three Wisemen), a square chapel with a small apse. There are inlaid-wood choir stalls along the walls, the ceiling is made of carved and painted wood, and the floor is decorated with inlaid marble. A wonderful

Piazza della Santissima Annunziata

fresco cycle from the early Renaissance, the *Procession of the Magi* by Benozzo Gozzoli (1459–1460), adorns the walls. The depiction of the landscape and the figures (many of whom represent members of the Medici family) simultaneously celebrate the Medici family and the birth of Christ.

The Palazzo Medici-Riccardi also houses the Galleria, one of the most valuable examples of Florentine baroque art. Its vault is painted with the *Allegoria of the Medicis* by Luca Giordano (1682–1685), depicting various scenes representing the history of this illustrious family.

PALAZZO NICCOLINI

Via de' Servi, 15; closed to the public.

➢ Palazzo Niccolini was designed by Domenico Baccio d'Agnolo in 1548–1550. Its beautiful facade is typical of Florentine palaces of this period, but the graffiti decorations were added in the 19th century. The small courtyard also has graffiti decoration, and in the garden beyond is an elaborate double loggia, probably by Giovanni Antonio Dosio. The interior is adorned with frescoes by Volterrano, Gimignani, Colonna, and Meucci.

PALAZZO PANCIATICHI

Via Cavour, 2; closed to the public.

➢ Designed by Carlo Fontana, the Palazzo Panciatichi currently houses Tuscany's regional council.

PIAZZA DEL DUOMO

➢ A casual survey of Piazza del Duomo's layout would suggest that its monumental buildings were configured to fit within the piazza like a key within its keyhole. To the contrary, the space around the Duomo and the baptistery has undergone numerous transformations over a period of almost 700 years before assuming its present state of conformity. The most recent addition to the piazza, the cast iron gate that fences in the Duomo, stands in heavy contrast to the breathing room Florence's religious center used to enjoy. Until the addition of this gate, the two doors that flank the cathedral's left and right sides were often kept open, affording many Florentines the luxury of passing under Brunelleschi's cupola while crossing the piazza. The palazzi that currently seal off the south end of the Duomo, meanwhile, were only built in the 19th century. Prior to their construction between 1826 and 1830, the piazza expanded well beyond the rear of the Duomo and could hold crowds of up to 30,000 people.

PIAZZA DELLA SANTISSIMA ANNUNZIATA

➢ One of the city's most enjoyable piazzas, this square's origins date to the latter half of the 13th century. However, much of its present character is due to Filippo Brunelleschi's Loggiato dell'Ospedale degli Innocenti (1419–1451), and the

SAN MARCO

*I went the other day to the secularised Convent of San Marco . . .
passed along the bright, still cloister and paid my respects to Fra
Angelico's Crucifixion, in that dusky chamber in the basement. I
looked long; one can hardly do otherwise. The fresco deals with
the pathetic on the grand scale, and after taking in its beauty you
feel as little at liberty to go away abruptly as you would to leave
church during the sermon.*

Henry James, "Florentine Notes," in *Italian Hours*

portico, whose rounded arches helped create a harmonious urban space. In the center of the piazza stands a bronze statue of Grand Duke Ferdinando I on horseback, the last work of Giambologna, finished by his pupil Pietro Tacca in 1608. Tacca also designed the square's two fountains, completed in 1629, which are adorned with figures depicting sea monsters.

PIAZZA SAN GIOVANNI

➢ Along with the adjacent Piazza del Duomo, Piazza San Giovanni once formed the nucleus of Florence's religious life and has since become the unofficial intersection of the city's tourist activity. Centered around the baptistery bearing the same name, the piazza came to resemble its current appearance in 1289, when it was paved over and elevated to accommodate the height of Piazza del Duomo. While the piazza's size was significantly increased with the removal of the baptistery's sarcophagi a few years later, its perimeter remained relatively confined until 1885, when the facade of the Palazzo Arcivescoville was demolished.

PIAZZA SAN LORENZO

➢ During business hours, a throng of market stalls occupies this piazza and its adjoining streets, where merchants hawk everything from fine leather goods to soccer jerseys. Immersed in the tumult of the marketplace is the *Monument to Giovanni dalle Bande Nere* (1540), carved by Baccio Bandinelli in tribute to Cosimo I de' Medici's father, a ruthless mercenary

commander. Behind it rises the facade of the basilica of San Lorenzo.

PIAZZA SAN MARCO

➢ Dominated by the baroque facade of the church of San Marco, this piazza consists of a shady island of park benches and leafy trees, encircled by a roundabout of steady car traffic. At the center of the island surges an equestrian monument of General Manfredo Fanti (1873) by Pio Fedi.

PORTA SAN GALLO

➢ Built in 1284–1285 Porta San Gallo remained one of the principal doors in the circle of medieval walls that once surrounded Florence and divided its historical center from the rest of the modern city until 1865. That year, the walls were torn down so that Giuseppe Poggi could build his *circonvalazione,* a chain of avenues that still encircles the city's historical center. Poggi's project salvaged Porta San Gallo along with Porta al Prato and Porta alla Croce, building piazzas around them and, thus, giving them the monumental status they now enjoy.

San Marco and the Museo di San Marco

Piazza San Marco; tel.: 055-287628 (church); open: daily 7 A.M.–noon, 4–8 P.M. (church); 055-2388608 (museum); Mon.–Fri. 8:15 A.M.–1:50 P.M., Sat. 8:15 A.M.– 6:50 P.M., Sun. 8:15 A.M.–6:50 P.M. (last admission 30 minutes before closing) (museum); closed: first, third, and fifth Sun. and second and fourth Mon. of each month, holidays; admission: €4.

➢ The church of San Marco was first built in the 14th century and then rebuilt by Michelozzo in the 15th century. While home to a number of notable works, including the *Virgin Mary and Saints* (1509) by Fra Bartolomeo and a crucifix (1425–1428) by Fra Angelico, the church has long played second fiddle to its famous convent. Among the convent's inhabitants were Saint Antoninus, bishop of Florence, and the two artists mentioned above: Fra Giovanni da Fiesole, known as Fra Angelico, and Fra Bartolomeo. Its most

Detail of a statue on the facade of San Marco

notorious inhabitant, however, was the prior Girolamo Savonarola, the antagonistic reformer who figured heavily in the founding of Florence's Republic. After the Republic fell, Savonarola was arrested, and the church bell pealed throughout the city. Know as the "Piagnona," the bell is now located in the Sala del Capitolo of the convent's museum.

The convent's library (1441), among Michelozzo's finest works, is located just before the cells. It has a well-balanced, spacious interior, composed of three aisles and supported by elegant arches. A plaque near the entrance of the library marks the spot where Savonarola was detained the night of April 8, 1498. Two months later he and two of his monks were executed in Piazza della Signoria.

Most of the Museum of San Marco is devoted to Fra Angelico, the convent's most prolific painter. Some of the artist's best-known works are located in the Sala dell'Ospizio. *The Last Judgment* (1431) applies conventions inherited from Gothic art, such as gold leaf and high detail, to those of the Renaissance: perspective, balance, and realism. The Linaioli's *Madonna* (1433) was the artist's first public commission and contains some of the finest figures he ever painted. As in *The Last Judgment,* the *Annalena Madonna* (c. 1434) exhibits the same use of color and attention to detail belied by a geometric organization of space.

Fra Angelico's presence is most strongly felt on the first floor, beginning in the monk's cells, where the artist executed a cycle of frescoes (1442–1445) intended to inspire meditation. They depict the Life of Christ, the Life of the Virgin Mary, and the mysteries of the Christian religion. While Fra Angelico probably sketched all of the preliminary drawings, he completed the frescoes with the help of assistants, producing mixed results. One of the artist's masterpieces, the *Annunciation* (c. 1442), faces the stairway. A familiar theme in Fra Angelico's repertoire, here the artist's rendering of Gabriel and the Madonna exhibits a degree of monumentality disproportionate to that of their austere architectural setting. Such disproportion would become one of the central postulates of Renaissance painting, which sought to emphasize human forms over their inanimate backgrounds.

The convent's cloister, the Cloister of Sant'Antonino, was built by Michelozzo before 1440. Frescoes decorate the walls depicting scenes from the Life of Domenican Saint Antonino Pierozzi. Other paintings were done by Fra Giovanni, including the four lunettes above the door and the ones at the corner of the cloister. The Great Refectory contains 16th- and 17th-century works by Giovanni Antonio Sogliani, Fra Paolino, Jacopo Vignali, Lorenzo Lippi, Jacopo Ligozzi, and others. On the back wall is a fresco, *Saint Dominic and His Brethren Fed by Angels*, by Sogliani. The refectory is dominated by the great fresco by Sogliani that occupies the interior wall. The Crucifixion is depicted in the upper half of the fresco, and the Dominicans' Providence is in the lower half. Also visit the Refettorio Piccolo, or small refectory, where Domenico Ghirlandaio frescoed his intricately decorated *Last Supper* (1480).

The Museo di Firenze Antica is situated in the cells of the Foresteria, the former guest quarters of the convent. The museum houses the material salvaged from the demolition of the Mercato Vecchio and part of the ghetto at the end of the 19th century (these were replaced by what is now Piazza della Repubblica). The museum includes numerous architectural fragments dating from the medieval and early Renaissance periods. At the end of the corridor are the rooms that were occupied by Savonarola from 1482–1487 and 1490–1498. His cell contains two portraits of him by his supporter and fellow friar, Fra Bartolomeo.

SANTA MARIA DEGLI INNOCENTI

Piazza della Santissima Annunziata, 12; tel.: 055-243670; open: early morning only.

➤ Brunelleschi's Loggiato dell' Ospedale degli Innocenti leads into the church of Santa Maria degli Innocenti, renovated in neoclassical style by Bernardo Fallani in 1786. The vault bears a fresco, *Moses Saved from the Waters,* by Sante Pacini, who also painted the canvas *The Dream of Saint Joseph,* which is hanging above the

accordion on the right side of the altar. The opulent 17th-century altar comes from the church of San Pier Maggiore, now destroyed. The baptismal font, an imitation of the one in Parma's baptistery, dates back to the end of the 14th century.

SANTA MARIA DEL FIORE (OR THE DUOMO)

Piazza del Duomo; tel.: 055-2302885; website: www.operaduomo.firenze.it; open: Mon., Tues., Wed., Fri. 10 A.M.–5 P.M., Thurs. 10 A.M.–3:30 P.M., Sat. 10 A.M.–4:45 P.M., Sun. 1:30–4:45 P.M. (first Sat. of every month 10 A.M.–3:30 P.M.; crypt open: same as church); admission: €3.

➤ Upon the Duomo's inception in 1296, Florence's fathers envisioned a structure that would serve as an emblem of the city it crowned, setting a precedent for its own age and those to come. Such high ambitions would lead to over 150 years of ongoing construction and innovation, from the foundations laid by Arnolfo di Cambio to the punctuation expressed by Brunelleschi's cupola. In between these monumental brackets, Giotto, Andrea Pisano, and Francesco Talenti each made their own significant contributions to the Duomo's grandeur. The pink, green, and white facade that currently dons the cathedral's exterior, however, is a 19th-century imitation of the Gothic style. On the north side, couched between the nave and the transept, is the Porta della Mandorla, or Almond Door, cast in bronze, surmounted by the 15th-century carving of the Virgin Mary of the Assumption by Nanni di Banco. The mosaic that fills the tympanum, directly above, depicts the Annunciation by Florentine painter and sculptor Domenico Ghirlandaio.

Despite the sumptuous embellishments to the cathedral's exterior, its interior is distinguished by a relative lack of adornment. Upon entering through the main doors, one is immediately taken aback by the hollow space that comprises the church's nave. On Easter Sunday, April 26, 1478, this solemn interior hosted one of the most dramatic scenes in Florence's history. The Pazzi family, great rivals of the Medici, conspired with the pope to assassinate Lorenzo the Magnificent during

Duomo and Campanile as seen from the Palazzo Vecchio

Easter mass. The two assassins, disguised as monks, infiltrated the Duomo, intending to stab the patriarch once the service reached its climax: the ringing of the bell. Instead, Lorenzo's younger brother Giuliano bore the brunt of the Pazzi treachery. He was stabbed to death while Lorenzo took refuge in the New Sacristy. The bronze doors of the New Sacristy, behind which the older brother locked himself, are still there, at the east end of the church, to the left of the sanc-tuary. The sanctuary itself offers an awe-inspiring view of the underbelly of Filippo Brunelleschi's massive cupola. Decorating its surface is Giorgio Vasari's *The Last Judgment* (1572–1579), completed five years after his death by Federico Zuccari. Also notable is the first bay of the south aisle of the nave, where a portrait of Brunelleschi was carved by one of his pupils. In 1972, Brunelleschi's tomb was discovered in the crypt, directly below the site of the portrait.

On the left side of Santa Maria del Fiore, on a stone shelf on top of one of the pillars, is the head of an ox. It was put there to honor all of the animals that helped build the Duomo. Oxen were often given the heaviest and most dangerous materials to move and carry.

SANTISSIMA ANNUNZIATA

Piazza della Santissima Annunziata; tel.: 055-266181; open: daily 7 A.M.–12:30 P.M., 4–6:30 P.M.

➢ Founded as an oratory in 1250 for the fraternity of the Servants of Maria, the basilica of Santissima Annunziata was first expanded by Leon Battista Alberti in 1477 according to designs from 1444 by Michelozzo. It was not consecrated until 1516.

An elegant portico, facing Piazza della Santissima Annunziata, dominates the church facade. Its central arch features a mosaic of the Annunciation by Domenico Ghirlandaio. Through this arch is the Chiostrino dei Voti, which contains one of the most important cycles in the history of Renaissance art, executed by an eclectic group of masters. Compare the nuance of mannerist works like the *Visitation* by Jacopo Pontormo (1514–1516) and the *Assumption*

(1517) by Rosso Fiorentino to watermark works of the High Renaissance like the *Wedding of the Virgin Mary* (1513) by Franciabigio and the *Birth of the Virgin Mary* (1514), Andrea del Sarto's masterpiece.

At the far end of the cloister is an entrance leading into the richly decorated baroque interior of the basilica. Painted just above this entrance is another masterpiece by del Sarto known as the *Madonna del Sacco* (1526). The Cappella della Compagnia di San Luca at the opposite end of the nave contains Pontormo's fresco, *Virgin Mary, Christ Child and Saints*.

Cloister of Santissima Annunziata

Walking Tour 1:

Discovering the Art Behind the Leather Market Carts: Renaissance Jewels in San Lorenzo

By Rosanna Cirigliano

The best time to catch a true glimpse of San Lorenzo's nature is between 7 and 8 P.M., when the steel shutters of neighborhood shops come crashing down, accompanied by the rumble of wheels on the cobblestone pavement. The open-air market stalls filled with tourist trinkets and leather jackets are packed up. Dozens of work-worn street vendors pass by, bent double like Indian rickshaw carriers, pulling their loaded carts to nearby warehouses. It is only then that the many beautiful buildings of medieval and Renaissance origin come into view, providing entrance for the visitor to a little-known world of artistic and scientific treasures.

Liberated from nearby wall displays of shoes and T-shirts, the doorway to the **Osservatorio Ximeniano** at No. 6 Piazza San Lorenzo, Italy's oldest meteorological and historic astronomical observatory, is distinctly visible. The observatory takes its name from Leonardo Ximenes, who, aside from founding the observatory in 1756, was also a hydraulic engineer, a mathematician, and a geographer to Grand Duke Pietro Leopoldo. Since its inception, the observatory has continued to publish a daily bulletin on meteorological and seismic activity. It has also conserved a number of scientific instruments, dating from antiquity to present day, in the observatory library.

Atop the observatory's medieval tower, and with the endless stretch of canopy covering the market stands gone, the delicate dome of the Sagrestia Vecchia, part of the San Lorenzo church complex, comes clearly into sight. It was here, thanks to Brunelleschi's design and Donatello's embellishments, that the Renaissance movement took form in the 1420s.

Walk around the church down the now-nearly empty Via dell'Ariento to the end of Via Sant'Antonino to find an unusual Renaissance building at No. 11, the **Palazzo dei Cartelloni**, now adapted for use as an art school. The palazzo is decorated with stone scrolls praising the achievements of Galileo, a native son of Florence who had fallen into disrepute because he refused to bend the laws of science to accommodate theology.

When Vincenzo Viviani, Galileo's favorite disciple, purchased the Palazzo dei Cartelloni in the 17th century, he commissioned Francesco Nelli to

Brunelleschi's Sagrestia Vecchia at San Lorenzo

redesign the facade as a memorial to the scientist. Nelli inserted a bust of
Galileo into the wall and two large marble scrolls on either side of the main
entrance. There are also images of the moons of Jupiter, which Galileo discovered, in addition to his family coat of arms.

The elaborate decoration was in defiance of the Inquisition, which had
called Galileo to Rome and forced him to publicly renounce his discovery
that the earth moves around the sun and not vice versa. He was forced to live
in exile, his teachings prohibited, and the Church forbade any monuments to
be built in his honor. Viviani was never reprimanded for his tribute to
Galileo, and the palace has remained essentially intact.

In contrast to the Palazzo dei Cartelloni, a building in the neighborhood
that has been renovated and changed several times in its 1,700-year history is
the church of **San Lorenzo** itself. Its present look is the work of Brunelleschi,
who was hired by the first Medicis to give their parish church a complete face-
lift. The rugged exterior of the basilica belies the elegance of its interior. In
fact, the simple surface of *pietra grezza,* or rough-hewn stone, was supposed to
be substituted by a grand facade designed by Michelangelo, but the change was
never executed. Brunelleschi's interior, on the other hand, is a highly polished
masterpiece crafted in *pietra serena.* Begun in 1420, it features a nave
supported by rounded arches and flanked by barrel-vaulted aisles. These
elements, which favor harmony and balance over the surging grandiosity of
Gothic architecture, influenced Florentine architecture for years to come.

Among the artistic masterpieces located in the church is the *Marriage of
the Virgin Mary* (1523) by noted mannerist painter Rosso Fiorentino. It is
located in the second chapel on the right. The church's pulpits feature panels
by Donatello, begun in bronze, during the artist's later years, and finished in
bronzelike wood after his death. The pulpit on the right depicts the

Martyrdom of Saint Lawrence and the Resurrection of Saint Lucas, the Derision of Christ, Mary at the Tomb, the Descent into Purgatory, the Ascension, and the Pentecost. The pulpit on the left depicts the Deposition, Flagellation, Saint John the Evangelist, Oration in the Garden, Christ before Caifa and Pilate, and the Crucifixion. The large fresco at the head of the left aisle is the *Martyrdom of Saint Lawrence* (1565–1569) by Agnolo Bronzino.

Brunelleschi's revival of the ideals of Greek and Roman design, and an emphasis on expressing mathematics in architecture, is evident in the **Sagrestia Vecchia** (Old Sacristy, 1421–1429), off the north transept of the church. There, rounded arches, Corinthian columns, a segmented dome, and the cool gray stone and warm golden plaster produce a balanced symmetry. Donatello's bold decorations—including terra-cotta and stucco reliefs of episodes from the lives of Saint John (to whom the sacristry is dedicated), the evangelists, Saint Stephen, and Saint Lawrence, as well as the reliefs of saints and martyrs on the bronze doors—have been held by some art historians as somewhat intrusive. The bust of Saint Lawrence, while attributed to Donatello, is widely believed to be the highly refined work of Desiderio da Settignano.

Like Michelangelo's better-known Sagrestia Nuova (New Sacristy), off the south transept, home to the tomb of Giuliano de' Medici, the Sagrestia Vecchia contains several other sarcophagi, including one by Andrea del Verrocchio (1472) made of gaudy porphyry and bronze and framed by white marble. It contains the remains of Lorenzo the Magnificent's father, Piero "the Gouty," and his uncle Giovanni. The marble tomb at the center of the room, studded with angel heads, laden with vegetable festoons, and enriched by the Medici coat of arms, belongs to Giovanni di Bicci de' Medici and his wife Piccarda Bueri (1434). This immodest monument was crafted by Andrea Cavalcanti, known as "Il Buggiano."

The Sagrestia Vecchia's finishing touch is the deep blue of the azurite dome above the main altar by Giuliano d'Arrigo, "Il Pasello." It is the background for a precise star chart of the night sky on July 4 or 5, 1442, when the sacristry was finally finished.

Back on Via Faenza behind the church, at No. 42, is the **Cenacolo di Fuligno**, a refectory frescoed with a depiction of the Last Supper once thought to be by Raphael. Its design was later attributed to Perugino, and its execution mainly to the artistic circle of this High Renaissance master. A little farther on, at No. 48, is the neoclassical facade of the **Educatorio di Fuligno**, a former convent and girls' school to which the refectory once belonged. It is filled with little-seen masterpieces of different periods.

The Educatorio started as a hermitage dedicated to Saint Onofrio at an unspecified date around the year 1000. It was transformed into a convent and completed in 1429. This was the former convent of Augustinian monks before it passed into the hands of the Franciscan Tertiaries, an order founded by Ginevra Bardi, widow of Albertaccio degli Alberti, who purchased it to provide a home for fellow noblewomen from Umbria who arrived in Florence as laysisters and followers of the Blessed Angela of Foligno.

Before the order became enclosed in 1616, the nuns at Fuligno, as they were known in Florence, gave commissions to well-known artists. Several had

R
OUR PICK

their workshops in the neighborhood, including Bicci di Lorenzo (1373–1452), son of Lorenzo di Bicci (1353–1427). Despite a new use of perspective as a visual language by Brunelleschi and Masaccio, Bicci di Lorenzo remained uninfluenced by his illustrious contemporaries. In the manner of his father, Bicci continued creating frescoes in the international Gothic style, which was by that time beginning to wane in favor of Renaissance art.

His works at Fuligno are full of late medieval grace, the figures so deli-cately depicted as to seem almost insubstantial, yet so brilliantly colored with vermilions, russets, delicate greens, and rose as to thrust them into the phys-ical world. To accentuate his palette, Bicci used a lapis-lazuli background instead of the traditional gold.

The frescoes—including a Nativity and Crucifixion on the ground floor and a serenely beautiful Annunciation and Saint Margaret on the floor above—were detached after the 1966 flood and have only just now been put back. Some, like the Crucifixion, were not replaced over their underdrawings (sinopie), allowing for a rare exposition of normally concealed sketches. Looking at the frescoes, their magical sensation is augmented by the fact that the figures are drawn in a descending scale of importance, with the main characters the largest, and saints, nuns, patrons, and bystanders ever smaller.

At the Cenacolo di Fuligno, Bicci di Lorenzo's son, Neri di Bicci, painted a Last Supper (1462) in the same late-Gothic style. The sisters apparently thought its appearance outdated so they commissioned a new one to be painted on top of it by Perugino some years later. He retained the unusual subject of Christ and the apostles in the garden of Gethsemane in the upper part.

Standing at a distance, the incredible painted spatial depth—so pronounced that the fresco almost seems to be receding into a niche—is apparent. Judas, according to tradition, is across from Christ and looking at the viewer. The harmonious composition and soft colors emanate a sense of peace. When the sisters moved to the convent of Sant'Ambrogio in 1800, the refectory became a workshop where carts and wagons were painted; this stopped when someone discov-ered what they thought was a hidden Raphael.

Until the nuns abandoned Fuligno, they dedicated them-selves to caring for and some-times educating such paying (or charitable) female boarders

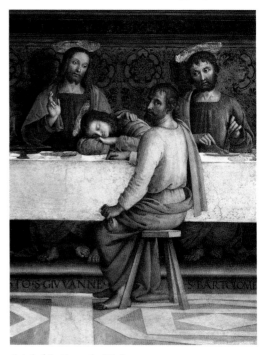

Detail of the Cenacolo di Fuligno

as widows, orphans, servants, and even a young Turkish slave at the Medici court. One woman who involuntarily stayed at Fuligno was Ginevra degli Albizi, former lover of Cosimo I and mother of his illegitimate son, Giovanni. She was forced to live there by her husband, Carlo Panciatichi. Cosimo had arranged the marriage of Ginevra and Carlo after bringing Panciatichi back from exile and pardoning him for murder and a dissipated life in exchange for a hefty sum of money. Ginevra's consolation lay in writing letters to her son and contemplating an oil painting, *Crucifixion, Mary, and Saint John* (1558) by Alessandro Allori, disciple of Bronzino. It is still at Fuligno, above the main altar in the church.

Also note the tabernacle on the left side of the facade decorated with a fresco by Giovanni da San Giovanni, *Madonna and Child Among Saints.*

In 1829, following the suppression of religious orders under the Napoleonic laws, Fuligno became a religious school for girls (hence the "Educatorio") where they learned arithmetic, weaving, knitting, and cooking. It remained open until 1973. The complex has recently been restored, and some of the rooms have been adapted as a senior citizens' center as well as a playroom for children.

FURTHER INFORMATION

Cenacolo di Fuligno
Via Faenza, 42; tel.: 055-286982; website: www.polomuseale.firenze.it; open: Tues., Thurs., Sat. 9 A.M.– noon; admission: donation is suggested.

Educatorio di Fuligno
Via Faenza, 48; tel: 055-210232; open: by appointment only.

Osservatorio Ximeniano (Ximenian Observatory)
Piazza San Lorenzo, 6; tel.: 055-210420; open: by appointment only.

Palazzo dei Cartelloni
Via Sant'Antonino, 11; closed to the public.

San Lorenzo
Piazza San Lorenzo, 9; tel./fax: 055-216634; open: Mon.–Fri. 10 A.M.–5 P.M.; admission: €2.50

FOCUS: San Barnaba

Via Panicale, 9, corner of Via Guelfa;
tel.: 055-216634; open: Sun. mass
5–7 P.M.

By Stacy Meichtry

San Barnaba

An eye window, pierced through the humble facade at the corner of Via Guelfa and Via Panicale, marks the church of San Barnaba, erected by the Republic of Florence in 1322 as a gesture of gratitude toward the Guelf party. The Guelfs, who led Florence to victory over the Ghibellines in the battle of Campaldino on June 11, 1289, are commemorated by one of the two coats of arms located above the church's ogival entrance. The coat of arms depicting an eagle thrashing an undersized dragon is that of the Guelf party, while the red cross of the other coat of arms symbolizes the Florentine people.

Standing in heavy contrast to this 13th-century arrangement is the glazed terra-cotta lunette of the Madonna and Child. It was added by the shop of Giovanni della Robbia in the years after 1520 when the Carmelites inherited San Barnaba from the Augustinians, the church's original tenants.

While the exterior of the San Barnaba has remained relatively intact since its founding, its interior was significantly altered during the 18th-century renovations, which added the heavy coffered ceiling above the nave. Poorly preserved on the left-hand wall are the remains of a 13th-century fresco, painted in the style of Spinello Aretino but attributed to Lorenzo di Bicci. The altarpiece, depicting the Assumption, is not the celebrated work of Botticelli, but an inferior piece by an unknown 15th-century painter. Botticelli's famous altarpiece executed for San Barnaba currently rests in the Uffizi.

Walking Tour 2:

The Frescoes and Friezes around Piazza San Marco: Sketches from the Cloisters

By Stacy Meichtry

The environs of Piazza San Marco have a consistency uncommon to most Florentine neighborhoods. The streets conform to a rigid, gridlike pattern, the architecture is austere, and pedestrians are rare. In the late 1400s San Marco was a bastion of fervent reformism. From here, Domenican prior Girolamo Savonarola orchestrated a spiritual revolution that saw its climax in the expulsion of the Medicis and the notorious Bonfire of the Vanities, held in Piazza della Signoria. Roughly a year later, the mobs would reconvene at the same spot to burn Savonarola himself. Ever since the smoke cleared, however, the neighborhood has proven itself a worthy host to important works of art, many of which actually owe their preservation to the religious establishment.

Just off of Piazza San Marco, at Via XXVII Aprile, is the entrance to the **Refettorio di Sant'Apollonia,** the refectory, or dining hall, where Andrea del Castagno frescoed his ground-breaking *Last Supper.* Proceed through a vestibule, decorated with an assortment of 13th- and 14th-century altarpieces, to the lofty room where the Benedictine monks came to break their daily bread. Lining the lateral walls of the hall are other works by Andrea, including a tablet of the *Pietà,* its preparatory cartoon, and *Christ Crucified with Mourners Saint Benedict and Saint Romualdo.* The monumental fresco at the end of the room is the *Last Supper,* surmounted by scenes from the Passion of Christ: the Crucifixion, Deposition, and Resurrection.

Completed in 1450, Andrea's composition was unlike any before it. Christ's revelation unfolds under a loggia, drafted in strict geometrical terms. The ceiling and pavement follow rigorous checker and diamond patterns. Each of the three walls is lined by square panels, different in color but even in measurement, spacing, and number. These linear parameters give the design an unprecedented sense of depth and perspective, which heavily contrasted with the flatness of his predecessors.

This contrast is evident in the blistering white rectangle posing as a highly artificial dinner table at the foreground of the composition. It bisects the carefully engineered perspective study in the form of a flat, dimensionless slab, cutting Christ and the apostles in half at the waist while formally isolating Judas, the only apostle seated in front of the table. He is depicted in an archaic profile pose, minus a halo, his head bowed in shame.

Orto Botanico

Returning to San Marco, make a left on Via Cavour and follow it out of the piazza. At No. 69 is the entrance to the **Chiostro dello Scalzo**, home of the confraternity of San Giovanni, known for walking barefoot, or *scalzo,* during the procession of the cross. This apparent eccentricity was interpreted as not only a demonstration of poverty but a reflection of it. When, in 1509, the confraternity commissioned Andrea del Sarto to fresco the walls of their court-yard in monochrome, rather than full color, the public consensus was that the decision had been made out of economic, rather than aesthetic, necessity.

Completed in 1526, the *Life of Saint John the Baptist* was painstakingly extended over a 17-year period by detours in del Sarto's personal and profes-sional life. These detours included a trip to France, which established his reputation as a master, as well as a streak of infidelities that his wife, Lucrezia del Fede, committed in his absence.

The cycle is of particular interest to followers of Andrea del Sarto because it traces his artistic development both figuratively and literally. Compare the *Baptism of Christ* (1519), at the extreme right of the far wall, to the *Birth of Saint John* (1526), second from the right on the right wall. In the former, del Sarto mimics Leonardo da Vinci with delicately drawn figures set in an ethe-real landscape of heavy boulders and botanical minutia. In the latter, the artist exhibits a fully digested application of Michelangelo, with bold figure studies in highly contorted positions.

Flanking the doorways at each end of the cloister are four virtues—Faith, Hope, Charity, and Justice—also by del Sarto. *The Benediction of Zachary* and *The Meeting of Baby Jesus and Baby Saint John* are inferior works by his assis-tant Franciabigio.

Across the street from the Chiostro dello Scalzo is Via della Dogana, which branches off from Via Cavour to blossom in a bright cluster of vegeta-tion at its opposite end. Cropped by the faceless facades that line Via della

Dogana, this burst of plant life is only one patch in an expansive quilt of well-manicured grounds that belong to the **Orto Botanico**, also known as the Giardino dei Semplici (Garden of the Simples).

Named for the raw ingredients, or "simples," used by medieval apothecaries in preparing medicines, the garden was established by Dominican nuns for the purpose of growing medicinal herbs, and was acquired by Cosimo I in 1545. The Medici coat of arms that hangs over the historic entrance on Via la Pira commemorates this takeover. The epitaph SENARUM DUX (Duke of the Sienese) was added to the arms 12 years later, when Florence became a grand duchy of France.

Located within the Museo di Storia Naturale (Museum of Natural History), the garden is one of the oldest of its type, and its grounds cover 400 acres and feature 6,000 different plants from all over the world. It includes a 16th-century vegetable garden and greenhouse and open gardens with a magnificent palm tree collection, irises, and swamp vegetation. The ancient trees such as sequoia, oak, and cedars date from two centuries ago and the oldest specimen, a yew tree, was planted in 1720. One garden was restructured in the 19th century to include tropical plants and flowers native to Tuscany. Around the garden are small museums on various topics such as geology and mineralogy.

The entrance on Via Micheli opens up onto a large expanse of flower beds, interspersed with gravel pathways and lined with large trees. While the trees date back through the centuries to when the garden was run by botanist Luca Ghini, most of the flower beds were restructured at the end of World War II. During the war, the city had found itself cut off from its cemeteries, making the flower beds a popular place to bury the dead.

Via Gino Capponi lies at the other end of Via Micheli. Make a right on this street and proceed to No. 4. The glazed terra-cotta lunette marks the age-worn entrance to the **Chiostrino della Compagnia della Santissima Annunziata**. The *Annunciation between Members of the Confraternity* by Santi Buglione is partially visible underneath layers of soot. The white-robed figures flanking each side of the lunette are the hooded members of the Compagnia, a lay association devoted to the Virgin that founded the cloister in 1572.

Today, the cloister is inhabited by the Società Dante Alighieri, an association offering language courses and other services to foreigners in Italy. During business hours, the doors remain open to a steady influx of students flowing under the lunette and into the cloister's picturesque courtyard.

The placement of potted palms at the center of the courtyard seems somewhat out of place, if not wholly conspicuous. While the struggling palms receive plenty of sun from this spot, they also interfere with the structural harmony of the courtyard's elegant Corinthian columns and barrel-arched wings. In doing so, they also provide a convenient subterfuge to mask the unbridled gore decorating the courtyard's perimeter.

The *Martyrdom of the Apostles* (1585–1590), which, in graphic detail, depicts the apostles being crucified, decapitated, bull whipped, burned, and cooked alive, is the work of painters Andrea Boscoli, Bernardino Monaldi, Giovanni Balducci, Cosimo Gheri, and Bernardino Poccetti. Presiding over each of these scenes are architectonic renderings of the virtues. Art, Prudence,

Temperance, Fortitude, Faith, Hope, Charity, and Justice are a hung jury, as each reacts to the brutal events in a range of expressions varying from shock and grief to curiosity and indifference.

Just beyond the courtyard is a vestibule that now functions as a busy reception room to the Società Dante Alighieri. Vaulted high above the administrative clamor is another cycle of frescoes by the same group that decorated the courtyard. This composition, however, provides a sober depiction of scenes from the Passion of Christ.

Exiting the cloister, proceed down Via Gino Capponi until it terminates at Piazza della Santissima Annunziata. Bordered by elegant loggias on three sides and pointed toward Brunelleschi's massive cupola on it fourth, this piazza ranks among Florence's most harmonious public spaces.

While the piazza owes its design to Brunelleschi, the only structure that bears his official signature as artist and builder is the **Ospedale or Spedale degli Innocenti**. *Spedale* translates to hospital, but this building was actually an orphanage, named for Herod's Massacre of the Innocents following the birth of Jesus. Built in 1419, it embodies the humanitarian spirit of civic art during the Florentine Rennaissance. When it opened in 1444 it was the first orphanage in Europe, and part of the building is still used for that purpose.

Brunelleschi gave the orphanage one of his most innovative creations in the graceful loggia (1419–1426) that forms the building's expansive facade and is a masterpiece of simple Renaissance design. It is decorated with glazed terra-cotta roundels added by Andrea della Robbia around 1498, depicting babies wrapped in swaddling clothing, an image that became the enduring symbol of this first-of-its-kind institution.

At the left side of the portico there is a special door with a rotating circular stone, or *ruota,* upon which mothers used to anonymously place their

Chiostro delle Donne at the Ospedale degli Innocenti

unwanted newborns. They would then ring the bell that clamored through the hallways inside the *spedale,* and a nun would come, rotate the wheel, and take the child.

Within the building there are two elegant cloisters built from Brunelleschi's designs. The Chiostro degli Uomini, or Men's Cloister, the larger of the two, was built between 1422 and 1445. It is decorated with designs of cherubs and roosters, which were scratched into the wet plaster. The Chiostro delle Donne, Women's Cloister (1438), leads to a gallery housing some paintings from former children at the orphanage, including an *Adoration of the Magi* (1488) by Domenico Ghirlandaio. The contradictions facing charitable institutions of such size and scope find representation in this masterpiece. In the foreground, the kings gather around the baby Jesus, offering their support and devotion to the infant and his mother. The highly detailed portraits that pepper this illustrious crowd were drawn from members of Florence's leading families, many of whom were among the hospital's best patrons. Meanwhile, in an isolated scene off in the not-too-distant background, a miniaturized version of the Massacre of the Innocents can be seen. Soldiers, wielding instruments of war against unarmed mothers, litter the landscape with infant corpses still wrapped in their rags.

Within the *spedale,* one can also find paintings by Piero di Cosimo and Botticelli, and sculptures by Luca della Robbia. Francesca della Luna engineered the complex web of open courtyards, triple-decker porticoes, and intersecting corridors that circulates through the hospital's interior.

FURTHER INFORMATION

Chiostrino della Compagnia della Santissima Annunziata (Cloister of the Compagnia of Santissima Annunziata)
Via Gino Capponi, 4; tel.: 055-2478981; open: by appointment; admission: free.

Chiostro dello Scalzo
Via Cavour, 69; tel.: 055-2388604; open: Mon.–Sat. 8:30 A.M.–2 P.M.; closed: Sun.; admission: free.

Orto Botanico (or Giardino dei Semplici) (Garden of the Simples)
Via P. A. Micheli, 3; tel.: 055-2757402/2757406; open: Mon., Wed., Fri.–Sat. 9 A.M.–noon.; closed: Tues., Thurs., Sun.; admission: free.

Ospedale degli Innocenti (Foundling Hospital of the Innocents)
Piazza della Santissima Annunziata, 12; tel.: 055-203711; open: Thurs.–Tues. 8:30 A.M.–2 P.M.; closed: Wed.; admission: €4.

Refettorio di Sant'Apollonia (Refectory of Sant'Apollonia)
Via XXVII Aprile, 1; tel.: 055-2388607; fax: 055-2388699; open: daily 8:15 A.M.–1:50 P.M.; admission: free.

FOCUS: Santa Maria Maddalena de' Pazzi

Borgo Pinti, 58; tel.: 055-2478420; open: daily 9 A.M.–noon, 5–7 P.M.

By Stacy Meichtry

In 1492, the Pucci family commissioned Pietro Perugino to fresco a cumbersome wall in the chapter house of Santa Maria Maddalena de' Pazzi. The challenge lay in the structure of the wall, which was definitively divided into three parts by its arched ceiling.

Rather than fight these structural limitations, Perugino fully embraced them, extending the arches to the base of his composition with architectonic columns and painting his scenes in between. The finished composition assumes the appearance of a triptych with divided scenes depicting (from right to left) Saint John the Evangelist and Saint Benedict, Christ on the cross adored by Mary Magdalene, and the Virgin and Saint Bernard.

A study of the landscape, however, reveals that the separate scenes are in fact unified in perspective. Delicately brushed hillsides, trees, and waterways roll and wind their way through each of the segments. The dividing arches, therefore, do not function as borders of a triptych, but rather as an elaborate framework designed to intensify the monumental figures they confine.

Mary Magdalene is chosen to share space with Christ, due to the inspirational role she played in the foundation of the church in

Courtyard of Santa Maria Maddalena de' Pazzi

Door of Santa Maria Maddalena de' Pazzi

1240. Built by the order of the "Convertite," or converts, the church and its convent served a group of penitent women who, like the Magdalene, had repented for their licentiousness and were thus "converted" into respectable wives of God.

In 1442, Pope Eugenius IV ordered the removal of the Convertite and demolished their church, thus paving the way for the structure that stands today. Designed by prolific renaissance architect and sculptor Giuliano da Sangallo, the complex is a highly unorthodox tandem with a courtyard, which wraps elegantly porticoed Ionian columns around an expansive quadrangle of grass, anchored by a simple facade rising in the background.

The interior of the church, also by Sangallo, consists of a single nave flanked by deep chapels on the right and left. These chapels once contained works by such masters as Botticelli, Domenico Ghirlandaio, and Perugino. In 1810, however, a Napoleonic decree dissolved the monastery of Santa Maria Maddalena de' Pazzi, along with every other monastery in Florence. These works were therefore relocated and are now at the Louvre, in Paris, and the Uffizi.

From the sacristy of the church you can access the former chapter house of the monastery, which holds a Crucifixion by Perugino (1493–1496). The fresco was painted as if it was being seen through the arches that divide up the walls.

Walking Tour 3:

Medieval Footnotes to the Renaissance

By Stacy Meichtry

The impact of the Renaissance on medieval Florence is usually measured by the diameter of Brunelleschi's cupola. The iconic monument marks a peak in Renaissance ingenuity, but the nature of the climb itself is best understood from the foot of the **Torre della Pagliazza**.

Located steps from Piazza del Duomo, the round brick tower barely clears the shadowy confines that presently form Piazza Santa Elisabetta. During the Greco-Gothic wars of the 6th century, however, the Pagliazza was one of two lookout points along the walls that protected the former Roman colony of Florentia, making it one of the city's highest and outermost points. It is the only part of the Byzantine walls to have survived these wars. Although it is believed to have been built upon a complex of Roman baths, the tower's name derives from medieval times, when it was used as a prison and its inmates slept on mats made of *paglia,* or straw. The *"stinche,"* as Florence's first municipal prisons were called, were notoriously inhospitable facilities that demanded the outrageous payment of one florin a day from their inmates. Those who paid received their fair share of the rations; those who didn't received harsh treatment in return.

Roughly 1,000 years later, the tower finds itself imprisoned by the Hotel Brunelleschi, the four-star tourist stronghold that incorporated the Pagliazza in 1988. Just as the architect's massive cupola reduces the Pagliazza tower to a stump on the Florentine skyline, his namesake hotel engulfs the cylindrical tower, leaving only half of it visible to the public. And though the hotel museum, kept under lock and key in the tower's excavated foundations, pays tribute to the Pagliazza in the form of chipped ceramics and other precious artifacts, its warlike days are long gone. Like so

Torre della Pagliazza

Loggia del Bigallo

many of Florence's other respected medieval monuments, the Pagliazza has entered into a state of limbo, wherein ancient towers, columns, and chapels are seldom recognized, and then only as a footnote to the Renaissance.

The arched wings and bifora windows of the **Loggia del Bigallo** form a corner that points right at the facade of the Duomo, through the most heavily trafficked intersection the city has ever known. For this very reason the Compagnia della Misericordia, a medieval charity institution dedicated to the care of orphans, commissioned the construction of the loggia in 1351 as a sort of high-visibility lost-and-found. For days upon end, abandoned and injured children were put on display to await reunion with their parents. When such reunions failed to materialize, the children went into the permanent care of the Misericorderia, which often placed the orphans in homes of noble families. In 1425, the Compagnia del Bigallo replaced the Misericorderia in its charitable vocation and still functions to this day.

But while the charity survives, the loggia it once operated no longer commands attention. The orphans have been replaced by horse-and-buggy carriages, which dock along the loggia's gated perimeter to feed on hay while their jockeys solicit potential passengers from the throngs of tourists gravitating toward the Duomo.

Housed in the oratory formerly operated by the Misericordia, the **Museo del Bigallo** exhibits frescoes that once decorated the loggia, such as Niccolò di Pietro Gerini's sober work, *The Captains of the Misericordia Entrusting Injured and Abandoned Children to their 'Mothers'.*

The collection also includes an altarstep by Ridolfo del Ghirlandaio, paintings by Domenico di Michelino and Jacopo del Sellaio, and sculptures by 14th- and 15th-century Tuscan artists, but the true masterpiece of the museum is the fresco of the Madonna of the Misericordia (1342). Executed by the circle of Bernardo Daddi, the fresco depicts a bullet-shaped Mother Mary, rising like a mountain from behind Florence's undersized medieval skyline. Enrobed in a mantle that lists each of the seven charities in neatly inscribed tondi, the mammoth Madonna is flanked by groups representing the Florentine nobility, their hands piously folded and knees obediently bent.

Despite its disproportion, the miniature skyline offers a faithful rendering of what the city might have looked like in the Middle Ages. Dominant among the dwellings and encircled by ramparts is the octagonal dome of the Baptistery of San Giovanni. The humble church, across the piazza from the baptistery, meanwhile, is none other than the Duomo, rendered somewhat impotent by its missing cupola, still 87 years away.

Also missing from the picture is the **Colonna di San Zanobi**, which sprouted up beside the baptistery 22 years later, in 1384. The marble column, crowned with a simple cross, rises on the spot where, on January 26, 409 A.D., a dead elm tree miraculously bloomed as the remains of San Zanobi were passing by en route to the ancient church of Santa Reparata. That church was eventually demolished in order to lay the Duomo's grand foundations.

Today, the legacy of Santa Reparata is remembered by the church of **San Michelino Visdomini**. The site for this church was chosen by the Visdomini family in the 11th century for its proximity to Santa Reparata— it stands just off the northern end of Piazza del Duomo on Via de' Servi. And yet the simple facade does not reflect that which the Visdomini knew.

Like the ancient church that came before it, San Michelino was also demolished in the name of the new cathedral, which needed space for its high courts. These courts were later relocated, allowing San Michelino to be rebuilt in the 14th century in the exact same spot. The church was further renewed in 1660 when its monks commissioned a makeover in the baroque style.

Housed within San Michelino's sober interior are works that date back to its humble reconstruction. The colored patches along the transept walls are the remains of 14th-century frescoes. According to Vasari, *The Sacred Conversation* is Pontormo's definitive masterpiece. Completed in 1518, the painting is contemporary with many of Raphael's oil-on-panels and, like many of these, Pontormo here uses the *sfumato* technique, developed by da Vinci, to shroud his figures in darkness. However, Pontormo used shadow to fracture perspective rather than establish it. The Holy Family emerges from darkness in segments: a pyramid of floating heads and dismembered limbs. Only the Christ Child remains intact. Exercising a preternatural sense of agility, he escapes from his mother's arms, rebounds off Joseph's lap, and pirouettes toward an audience of saints.

FURTHER INFORMATION

Colonna di San Zanobi
Piazza San Giovanni, next to the Baptistery

Loggia del Bigallo
Piazza San Giovanni, 1

Museo del Bigallo
Piazza San Giovanni, 1; tel.: 055-2302885; open: Tues.–Sun. 10 A.M.–1:30 P.M., 3–6:30 P.M. (call ahead); closed: Mon.; admission: €3.

San Michelino Visdomini
Piazzetta di San Michele, corner of Via de' Servi and Via Bufalini; tel.: 055-292448; open: Mon.–Sat. 8 A.M.–noon, 4–5:30 P.M., Sun. 10 A.M.–noon (mass 11:30 A.M.).

Torre della Pagliazza (Hotel Brunelleschi)
Via Santa Elisabetta, 3; tel.: 055-27370; fax: 055-219653; by appointment.

Opificio delle Pietre Dure

Via degli Alfani, 78; tel.: 055-2651357; website: www.opificio.arti.beniculturali.it; open: Mon.–Wed., Fri.–Sat. 8:15 A.M.–1:30 P.M., Thurs. 8:15 A.M.–6:30 P.M.; closed: Sun. and public holidays; admission: €2.

By Stacy Meichtry

Focus

57

In 1558, Grand Duke Francesco I de' Medici sectioned off a part of the Uffizi to house a workshop for semiprecious stones, the Opificio delle Pietre Dure. To be exact, the Opificio was expected to generate new decor for San Lorenzo's Cappella dei Principi, where Francesco I's illustrious ancestors are memorialized, from stones like lapis lazuli and malachite. The artisans of the Opificio were so successful in their endeavors that demand for their unique brand of mosaic tabletops on heraldic crests quickly spread throughout Europe.

This success lives on in the worldwide reputation that the Opificio has garnered as a leading restorer of stonework, semiprecious or not. It has operated out of the ex-monastery of San Niccolò di Cafaggio at No. 78 Via degli Alfani since 1796, when the workshop finally moved out of its space in the Uffizi. Unlike many historically prominent institutions, which currently count on the financial support of Italy's ministry of culture, the self-sufficient Opificio proudly maintains its autonomy as an economically viable enterprise.

Dedicated to the history of the workshop and the techniques of the trade itself, the adjacent Museo dell'Opificio delle Pietre Dure exhibits a large sampling of sculpture, furniture, models, and other rare art objects crafted from semiprecious stones. The collection highlights include an 18th-century model of the Cappella dei Principi, a mosaic Medici coat of arms flanked by putti, and a red marble bust of Cosimo I de' Medici by Bernardo Buontalenti. Also noteworthy are the mosaic "portraits" of Cosimo III, pieced together from polychrome stone to give the composition the depth and richness of an oil painting.

The upper level of the museum focuses on the labor behind the artwork. Dominated by a line of original Opificio workbenches, the room displays a massive collection of tools, ranging from heavy machinery to more delicate, finely tuned instruments.

Other Points of Interest

ARCISPEDALE DI SANTA MARIA NUOVA (HOSPITAL OF SANTA MARIA NUOVA) AND SANT'EGIDIO

Piazza di Santa Maria Nuova; open: by appointment only via written request (contact the Direzione Generale Azienda Sanitaria di Firenze at Piazza Santa Maria Nuova, 1, 50122 Firenze, tel. 055-27581, fax 055-2758378.

➢ Founded in 1288 by Folco Portinari, father to Dante's beloved Beatrice, the Hospital of Santa Maria Nuova is the oldest hospital in Florence. During the great plague (c. 1348), it expanded to serve over 200 patients, creating separate wards for male and female patients adjacent to its in-house church, Sant' Egidio (built at the turn of the 15th century). In 1420, the complex was further embellished with the addition of cloisters by Bicci di Lorenzo and the expansion of Sant'Egidio. Two years later, Lorenzo Monaco finished his monumental *Coronation of the Virgin* for the church's altar. This was later substituted in 1483 by Hugo Van der Goes's masterpiece, known as the *Trittico Portinari*. Both of these works now rest in the Uffizi. Between 1430 and 1461, Domenico Veneziano, Piero della Francesca, Andrea del Castagno, and Alessio Baldovinetti took turns at frescoing the new chorus of Sant'Egidio. The finished product yielded one of the most impressive cycles of the Florentine Renaissance. The interior of the church also includes a large marble tabernacle by Bernardo Rossellino from 1450 with a door designed by Ghiberti. On the right side of the church is the cloister, the Chiostro delle Medicherie, which includes the glazed terra-cotta *Pietà* by Giovanni della Robbia, as well as the *Madonna and Child with Two Angels*, which dates from the 14th century.

The hospital owes most of its current appearance, however, to artists of the 16th century; Giambologna, Alessandro Allori, and Bernardo Buontalenti. Giambologna added a series of stucco decorations to the men's ward, Allori frescoed the chapel at the head of the men's ward and the walls and ceiling of the women's ward, and Buontalenti designed the loggia that forms the hospital's monumental facade.

CASINO MEDICEO DI SAN MARCO

Via Cavour, 57; closed to the public.

➢ Currently home to the Court of Appeals, the Casino Mediceo was built by mannerist architect Bernardo Buontalenti as a laboratory for scientific study. Under the direction of Grand Duke Francesco I, these studies became primarily sculptural. In 1588, the duke founded the Opificio delle Pietre Dure here, the "Factory of Stone," where Florence's leading artists were invited to experiment. The casino's main entrance consists of a portale-terrazza. Also by Buontalenti, this handsome architectural arrangement crowns the main door with a refined balcony which accesses a second-story window. The entire composition is framed in *pietra serena* to heavily contrast with the harsh *intonaco* of the expansive facade. In the courtyard is a fountain with a statue of Diana attributed to the school of Giambologna.

CHIOSTRO DI SAN LORENZO (CLOISTERS OF SAN LORENZO)

Piazza San Lorenzo, in San Lorenzo; tel.: 055-216634; open: daily 9 A.M.–noon, 3:30–6:30 P.M.; admission: free.

➢ At the end of the left aisle of the basilica of San Lorenzo, a brief flight of stairs leads into the cloisters of the church. Preceded by a well-manicured hedge garden, the first cloister was remodeled by 15th-century architect Michelozzo in the style of Brunelleschi. The second cloister bears the marks of the 14th-century style, predating the influence of the prolific architect.

CHURCH OF GESÙ PELLEGRINO (OR "DEI PRETONI")

Via degli Arazzieri, 8; open: inconsistently.

➢ Located on the right at the intersection of Via degli Arazzieri and Via San Gallo, this building is now home to the Association of Italian Catholic Schoolteachers. It was built from 1584–1588 by Giovanni Antonio Dosio for Cardinal

Alessandro de' Medici (who, in 1605 became Pope Leo XI). The interior has a rectangular layout with roof trusses and is decorated with a series of frescoes (stories of the Life of Jesus and of the apostles) and altarpieces by Giovanni Balducci, known as Il Cosci, from 1590. Arlotto Mainardi (1396–1484), known as Piovano Arlotto, was a member of the Congregation of the Pretoni, which was based here. The congregation assisted and hosted those secular priests that passed through Florence on their pilgrimages. Arlotto became famous for his works and asked to be buried in the church; he prepared the text of his own epitaph: "Piovano Arlotto had this tomb made for himself and any who would enter."

In the past, Via degli Arazzieri was a simple lane known as Via del Faggio di San Marco, which cut through the fields that surrounded the ancient convent of San Marco. In 1545, Grand Duke Cosimo I gave it to a company of tapestry makers (*grazzieri*) from Flanders to start up the famous Medici tapestry workshop, giving the street its name.

Trompe l'oeil by Giuseppe del Moro at the Palazzina di Livia

CONVENTO DELLE OBLATE

Via dell'Oriuolo, 24; tel.: 055-2616545; open: Mon.–Wed. 9 A.M.–2 P.M., Sat. 9 A.M.–7 P.M., closed Thurs., Fri., Sun., holidays; admission: €2.70.

➤ Adjacent to the Arcispedale of Santa Maria Nuova is the simple structure that once served as the women's ward prior to the hospital's expansion in 1348. Thereafter, the former ward became a permanent home to the sisters of the Convento delle Oblate. Dedicated to providing care for the crippled, the sisters continued to operate at this site up until 1936, when the convent was transferred to the town of Careggi. Today, the convent hosts the Museo di Firenze Com'era (see pg. 67).

LOGGIA DEI TESSITORI

Via San Gallo

➤ The five arcades that comprise this early-16th-century loggia were originally the trading grounds of the Weavers Guild.

OSPEDALE DI BONIFACIO (HOSPITAL OF BONIFACE)

Via Duca d'Aosta; tel.: 055-49771; fax: 055-4977616; open: by appointment only via faxed request.

➤ Founded as early as 1377 by Bonifacio Lupi, the hospital was transformed in 1787 by Giuseppe Salvetti, who added an elegant arcade to its exterior. The 17th-century *Last Supper*, frescoed in the hospital's refectory, is by Fabrizio Boschi. Today, the Hospital of Boniface houses the offices of the Questura, the national police headquarters.

PALAZZINA DI LIVIA

Piazza San Marco, corner of Via degli Arazzieri; closed to the public.

➤ In the late 18th century, Bernardo Fallani built this small palace for the dancer Livia Malfatti Raimondi, the mistress of Grand Duke Pietro Leopoldo of Lorena. The most interesting room to note is the large central salon with recently restored frescoes by Giuseppe del Moro.

Palazzo Altoviti
(or Palazzo dei Visacci)

Borgo degli Albizi, 18; closed to the public.

➤ This mansion first came into being when its owner, Baccio Valori, commissioned architect G. B. Caccini to unify three preexistent structures with a single facade. Executed in 1600, the facade was enriched in the years that followed with 15 marble statues, depicting portraits of Florentines (1600–1604). The unmistakable bust above the main door is that of Cosimo I. Valori, considered one of Florence's most learned noblemen, was also the chief librarian at the Biblioteca Laurenziana and thus stood in good favor with the Medici.

Palazzo Arcivescovile

Via dei Cerretani, corner of Piazza San Giovanni; closed to the public.

➤ Just behind the Baptistery of San Giovanni is the Palazzo Arcivescovile, the mansion of the archbishop. Founded as early as the 14th century, the palace burned down in 1533 and was rebuilt by Giovanni Dosio between 1573 and 1584. When the piazza underwent expansion at the turn of the 17th century, the Palazzo Arcivescovile's facade was demolished and rebuilt in an abbreviated form. Its courtyard, meanwhile, is a well-preserved 16th-century composition with loggias on three sides, supported by Doric columns.

Palazzo Capponi-Farinola
(or Palazzo Gino Capponi)

Via Gino Capponi, 26; closed to the public.

➤ This street honors Gino Capponi (1792–1876), the statesman-historian whose grandiose home, the Palazzo Capponi-Farinola, was designed by Carlo Fontana and built in 1698–1713 by Alessandro Cecchini. The huge palace has a fine garden. The poet Giuseppe Giusti died here suddenly in 1850. The rooms on the ground floor are frescoed by such 18th-century Florentine painters as Giandomenico Ferretti, while the staircase is frescoed by Matteo Bonechi.

Palazzo degli Albizi

Borgo degli Albizi, 12–14; closed to the public.

➤ The Albizi were a powerful family in Florence in the 1200s. This structure includes both a palazzo and their private home. The former, considered the family's major residence, was renovated in the early 16th century, when the plasterwork visible today replaced the previous rough wall. The latter, instead, retains its medieval characteristics, including the coat of arms on the facade.

Palazzo della Gherardesca

Borgo Pinti, 99; closed to the public.

➤ Between 1713 and 1720 Antonio Ferri expanded what was once a Renaissance *palazzetto* into a full-scale baroque mansion replete with a rare-plant garden, richly decorated salons, and fully frescoed apartments. The elegant courtyard at the center of these enlargements, however, dates back to the original structure. Built according to designs by Giuliano da Sangallo in the late 15th century, the porticoed courtyard takes its inspiration from Roman triumphal arches. The 12 bronze-colored bas-reliefs, depicting allegorical themes, are by Bertoldo, a pupil of Donatello.

Palazzo di San Clemente

Via Micheli, 2; closed to the public.

➤ Attributed to architect Gherardo Silvani, this 16th-century structure now hosts the University of Florence's School of Architecture. The frescoes decorating the ground floor, by Volterrano, depict Saint Martin and the Poor.

Palazzo Giugni

Via Alfani, 48; open: closed to the public.

➤ Designed by the prolific mannerist architect and sculptor Bartolomeo Ammannati, the Palazzo Giugni was built as part of the architect's urban plan for the area. The Giugni family coat of arms hangs in the elegant courtyard, just beyond the main entrance. Past the courtyard lies a well-manicured garden, dominated by Lorenzo Migliorini's monumental grotto. The mansion's richly furnished salons and apartments are occupied by the International Lyceum Club for Ladies, which has used this space since 1953 for concerts, exhibitions, and lectures. In 1910, Italy's first Impressionism exhibition was held here. The 17th-century gallery contains works by Alessandro Gherardini (c. 1691).

PALAZZO GRIFONI (OR PALAZZO BUDINI GATTAI)
Via dei Servi, 51; closed to the public.

➤ The Palazzo Grifoni is the exposed-brick structure at the mouth of Piazza della Santissima Annunziata. Built between 1563 and 1574 according to designs by Bartolomeo Ammannati, it is currently the headquarters of the government for the province of Florence and of the president of the region of Tuscany.

PALAZZO PANDOLFINI
Via San Gallo, 74; closed to the public.

➤ The Palazzo Pandolfini was designed by Raphael and executed by his students Giovan Francesco and Aristotile da Sangallo. The massive portal that dominates the facade formally divides the exterior into two separate sides. The right side consists of only a single floor, surmounted by a terrace. The left side rises in two elegant stories of gabled windows, crowned by a heavy cornice.

PALAZZO PORTINARI-SALVIATI
Via del Corso, 6; closed to the public.

➤ Currently home to the Banca Toscana, the Palazzo Portinari-Salviati dates back to 1470, when the Portinari family built their mansion over medieval apartments where Beatrice Portinari, their ancestor of Dantean fame, once lived. What remains of the Portinari mansion lies at the center of the current building in the form of faint structural traces. The rest of the palazzo reflects the expansion that took place under the ownership of the Salviati family who purchased the mansion in 1546. The interior features a courtyard-turned-salon, lined with Tuscan columns and decorated with a fresco, *Enthroned Madonna and Child with Saints John the Baptist and*

Zanobi, dating from the 14th century. Preceding this space is the imperial courtyard, frescoed by Alessandro Allori. The cycle, depicting stories from the life of Ulysses, was intended to complement the stories of Hercules in Santa Croce's famous Pazzi Chapel.

PALAZZO PUCCI
Via de' Pucci, 6; tel.: 055-298061; closed to the public.

➤ In 1560 the Pucci family, who had been allied with the Medicis, became their bitter enemies when Pandolfo de' Pucci was expelled from the Medici court after being accused of immorality. Pandolfo was furious and decided to get revenge by hiring hit men to assassinate Cosimo I. The plan was that the men would position themselves on the ground floor of the Palazzo Pucci, on the corner of Via de' Servi. They would wait there for Cosimo I to pass, as he always did on his walk to Santissima Annunziata. An accomplice hidden behind a window in the upper floors was to give them a signal that Cosimo was approaching the building. The plot was discovered before it could be carried out and Pandolfo de' Pucci was tried, convicted, and sentenced to be hung. Cosimo I continued to walk to Santissima Annunziata but, to play it safe, he decided to have that window boarded up. The window is still there, the same as it was over 400 years ago.

PALAZZO RAMIREZ DI MONTALVO
Borgo degli Albizi, 26; closed to the public.

➤ Bartolomeo Ammannati built this palazzo for the Castilian nobleman Ramirez di Montalvo in 1568. The facade is dominated by an elegantly carved niche that holds the Medici coat of arms. This choice of decoration was made in honor of Eleonora of Toledo and Cosimo I, both of whom Ramirez served. The somewhat deteriorated graffito etchings are attributed to Vasari or Bernardino Poccetti. They depict the virtues of consonance: imperatives for those in the service of a sovereign.

PALAZZO STROZZI DI MANTOVA

Piazza del Duomo; closed to the public.

➤ Located next to the Museum of the Duomo, the Palazzo Strozzi di Mantova is an oversized mansion with two facades, each consisting of three levels. On the ground floor are heavy stone portals. Embedded in the upper registers are gabled and architrave windows.

ROTONDA DI SANTA MARIA DEGLI ANGIOLI

Via del Castellaccio, corner of Piazza Brunelleschi and Via degli Alfani; closed to the public.

➤ This octagonal structure was originally the oratory of the Camaldolesi Monastery. In form it is reminiscent of classical rotundas, especially the Temple of Minerva Medica in Rome. Brunelleschi began work on it in 1433, but his funding dried up after his patron shifted resources to pay for the war against Lucca. It was restored in 1936, and is currently used by the University of Florence. It now hosts the Linguistic Center of the University of Florence.

San Giovannino degli Scolopi

SAN GIOVANNINO DEGLI SCOLOPI

Via de' Martelli, corner of Via de' Gori; open: inconsistently.

➤ Begun in 1579 by architect Bartolomeo Ammannati, this church presents a classically inspired facade fancifully highlighted with mannerist elements. The twin columns that support the facade's two registers evoke the spirit of Michelangelo's design for the vestibule of the Laurentian Library. The lofty interior features lateral chapels, divided by Ionic pilasters, containing a number of 17th-century works.

SAN GIOVANNINO DEI CAVALIERI

Via San Gallo, 60; open: inconsistently.

➤ San Giovanni dei Cavalieri derives its name from the order of monks, devoted to Saint John of Jerusalem, who occupied the adjacent monastery in the 16th century. The order apparently had ties with the confraternity of the Knights of Malta.

The interior is divided into a nave and two aisles by pilasters that support a ceiling of heavy rafters. On the high altar is the *Nativity* (1435) by Bicci di Lorenzo. His son, Neri di Bicci, painted the adjacent *Coronation of the Virgin,* a work of limited innovation that draws heavily on the *Crucifixion,* a highly refined 15th-century work by Lorenzo Monaco located in the choir.

SAN JACOPO IN CAMPO CORBOLINI

Via Faenza, 43; closed to the public.

➤ Currently part of an art school, the church of San Jacopo was founded in 1206 by the bishops of Florence and Fiesole. The numerous coats of arms that stud the main door, the portico, and the capitals supporting the portico, belong to the Templars and the Knights of Malta, who were associated with San Jacopo. Inside the church are several well-conserved inscriptions, etched by various members of the order in memory of their commandants and priors. Of particular note for its delicacy and dynamism is the sepulcher of Prior Luigi Tornabuoni

Detail of San Giovannino dei Cavalieri

(1515), which Vasari attributes to Cicilia, a Fiesolian sculptor. The rest of the interior is bare, aside from the 16th-century crucifix in polychrome wood.

SANT'AGATA

Via San Gallo, 112; open: contact the adjacent Military Hospital at tel. 055-472021 or 055-582615.

➢ Adjacent to the Ospedale di Bonifacio, the church of Sant'Agata was consecrated in 1569. Before then, it was a secular structure known as the Casa delle Donne di Bibbiena. Inside are two notable frescoes by Giovanni Bizzelli depicting the martyrdom and burial of Saint Agatha. These flank the high altar, which holds the highly imaginative *Wedding at Cana*, painted by Alessandro Allori.

SANTA CATERINA D'ALESSANDRIA

Via Santa Caterina d'Alessandria, in front of Via E. Poggi; tel.: 055-470027; open: for mass 9 A.M., 11 A.M., 5 P.M.

➢ Built in the 19th century, this church was restored beginning in 1937 according to designs by the architect Achille Cetica. The baptismal chapel has a neo-

Renaissance statue of *Saint John the Baptist* by Mario Moschi (1941) and a painting of the Annunciation by Edoardo Gelli (an artist from Lucca who studied under Antonio Ciseri at the Fine Arts Academy in Florence). With the images of the Pietà and the Adoration in the chapel to the right of the entrance, the Annunciation formed a triptych painted from 1911–1916, originally located in the apse of the church.

SANTA MARIA DE' RICCI

Il Corso, in front of No. 31; tel.: 051-215044; hours: every day 10:30 A.M.–6 P.M., Mon. and Thurs. afternoons closed; admission: free.

➢ Santa Maria de' Ricci was built in 1508, but the facade and entrance were renovated in 1610 by Gherardo Silvani. The interior was reconstructed in 1769 by Zanobi del Rosso, and he created one of the most sober naves of the baroque period. There is a fresco of the Assumption of the Virgin Mary by Lorenzo del Moro and *The Virgin Mary Presenting Saint Camillo de Lellis to the Glorious Trinity* by Agostino Rosi (18th century). On the walls of all of the chapels are eight paintings by Giovanni Camillo Sagrestani, depicting scenes from the Life of the Virgin. In the first chapel on the right is *Saint Margaret of Antioch,* from the second half of the 14th century and attributed to the Master of the Annunciation of Legnaiuoli and *A Cripple Asking Saint Margaret for Her Blessing,* by Cosimo Gamberucci. An interesting painting in the second chapel is *Saint Augustine Distributing Church Goods to the Poor,* by Francesco Mati. On the walls of the presbytery are two frescoes from the 18th century, done by Stefano Amigoli. In the sacristy is *God the Father Sending the Archangel Gabriel to Mary,* by Francesco Mati.

SASSO DI DANTE (DANTE'S STONE)

Piazza delle Pallottole, at Via dello Studio

➢ When Dante was living in Florence there was a specific spot where he loved to sit and write, think, or simply be inspired by his surroundings. He could stay for hours watching the early stages of construction of the Duomo. At the intersection of Via dello Studio and Piazza delle Pallottole there is a house overlooking Piazza del Duomo where a stone proudly marks the spot with the inscription SASSO DI DANTE, or Dante's stone.

STATUE OF FERDINANDO I OF LORRAINE

Piazza della Santissima Annunziata

➤ In the center of Piazza della Santissima Annunziata there is a bronze statue of Ferdinando I, of the Lorraine family, sitting on a horse. The mold for the work was done by Giambologna and it was then finished by Pietro Tacca. On the back of the pedestal Ferdinando insisted on having a queen bee surrounded by a swarm of bees, with the inscription MAJESTATE TANTUM ("Only Majesty"). The queen bee obviously represents the grand duke.

Biblioteca Laurenziana

TABERNACOLO DELLE FONTICINE (TABERNACLE OF THE LITTLE WATER FOUNTAINS)

Via Nazionale, in front of Via dell'Ariento

➤ This large tabernacle is decorated with a beautiful and monumental terra-cotta completed by Giovanni della Robbia in 1522. It represents the Madonna and child, Saint John the Lesser, and four other saints.

TEATRO DELLA PERGOLA (PERGOLA THEATER)

Via della Pergola, 18-32; tel.: 055-22641 (theater), 055-2264337 (museum); fax: 055-2264350; website: www.pergola.firenze.it; open: by appointment only; admission: €2.50.

➤ Built in wood by Ferdinando Tacca in 1656, the Pergola Theater is now the best-known theater in Florence. It was rebuilt in brick a century later, and it acquired its present style after undergoing restructuring in 1828. Theater accessories—such as lighting fixtures and the wheel that was used to raise the stalls to the stage's level—are now exhibited under the stage. There are also various pieces of memorabilia on exhibit, such as the footstool Giuseppe Verdi used while directing *Macbeth*.

TEPIDARIO DEL GIARDINO DELL'ORTICOLTURA (GREENHOUSE OF THE HORTICULTURAL GARDEN)

Via Vittorio Emanuele II, corner with Via XX Settembre (entrance also at Via Bolognese, 17); open: sunrise to sundown; admission: free.

➤ Just off Via Bolognese, this horticultural garden is celebrated for its grandiose greenhouse. Constructed in 1879 by Giacomo Roster for the Horticultural Society of Tuscany, the greenhouse offers a splendid example of Victorian wrought iron.

Museums

BIBLIOTECA LAURENZIANA (LAURENTIAN LIBRARY)

Piazza San Lorenzo, 9; tel. 055-210760; website: www.bml.firenze.sbn.it; open: Library: Mon., Fri., Sat. 8 A.M.–1:50 P.M.; Tues.–Thurs. 8 A.M.–5 P.M.; Museum: open only during exhibits; admission: free (€3 when there is an exhibit).

➤ Pope Clement VII commissioned Michelangelo to create this wonderful 16th-century library in order to house Cosimo the Elder's manuscripts. Off the corridor that connects the church of San Lorenzo to its first cloister is the vestibule to the Laurentian Library. The staircase leading up to the library entrance is among the most innovative of Michelangelo's architectural designs. Two flights of *pietra serena* cascade toward a bottom flight, made of steps that spread out like pools underneath a waterfall. The staircase was actually completed in 1559 by noted mannerist sculptor Bartolomeo Ammannati, who worked from drawings and other instructions from his correspondence with Michelangelo. The rest of the room follows suit with the staircase, mixing white marble with gray *pietra serena*. The wide columns, heavy cornices, and windowless window frames serve the vestibule's lofty interior more as architectural ornaments than as structural supports, anticipating the arrival of the baroque period.

Just beyond the staircase is the *sala di lettura*, or reading room. Also by Michelangelo, this space is organized according to a strict gridlike progression of carved wooden reading desks. The ceiling is coffered to complement the desks and the depth of perspective they create. The library itself houses a collection of over 10,000 original manuscripts, making it

Biblioteca Marucelliana

the largest library in Florence. Among these are texts by Virgil, Leonardo da Vinci, Petrarch, Machiavelli, and, of course, Michelangelo.

BIBLIOTECA MARUCELLIANA (MARUCELLIAN LIBRARY)

Via Cavour, 43–47; tel.: 055-27221; website: www.maru.firenze.sbn.it; open: Mon.–Fri. 8:30 A.M.–7 P.M., Sat. 8:30 A.M.–1:45 P.M., closed: Sun.

➢ Founded at the turn of the 18th century, this library was opened to the public in 1752. Its collection consists of over half a million volumes, texts, and manuscripts dating back to the Middle Ages. Among these are letters by 19th-century writer Silvio Pellico and manuscripts by poet Ugo Foscolo.

BIBLIOTECA RICCARDIANA (RICCARDIAN LIBRARY)

Via de' Ginori, 10, in the Palazzo Medici-Riccardi; tel.: 055-212586; open: Mon.–Wed., Fri.–Sat. 9 A.M.–5 P.M., Thurs. 9 A.M.–3 P.M.; closed: Sun.; admission: free.

➢ This library was founded by Riccardo Romoli Riccardi at the end of the 1600s and was opened to the public in 1715. It has a series of reading rooms frescoed by Luca Giordano (1632–1705) and decorated with 18th-century furniture. It also houses a collection of rare editions and precious manuscripts, including Dante's *Divine Comedy*. In 1945 the library was enlarged with the addition of the collection of volumes on the history of Florence belonging to the Biblioteca Moreniana.

CONSERVATORIO DI MUSICA LUIGI CHERUBINI (LUIGI CHERUBINI CONSERVATORY OF MUSIC)

Piazza Belle Arti, 2; tel.: 055-292180; closed to the public.

➢ The Conservatory of Music, responsible for training some of Italy's finest musicians, is named after the Florentine composer Luigi Cherubini (1760–1842). It features an important musical library containing many original manuscripts by composers like Monteverdi and Rossini.

The Museum of Musical Instruments has a collection of instruments begun by the Medici and the Lorraine grand dukes, including Antonio Stradivari's Viola Medicea (1690); a harpsichord by Bartolomeo Cristofori, who invented the piano in the early 18th century; and violins and cellos by Amato, Guarneri, Ruggeri, and Stradivari that is now on permanent display at the Accademia di Belle Arti (see pg. 31).

GALLERIA RINALDO CARNIELO (RINALDO CARNIELO GALLERY)

Piazza Fra G. Savonarola, 3; tel.: 055-2616539; temporarily closed.

➤ The home and studio of Rinaldo Carnielo (1853–1910), in Piazza Savonarola, is now a small gallery dedicated to the sculptor's works. Born in Bosco (Treviso) in 1853, Carnielo eventually moved to Florence and attended the Accademia di Belle Arti (Academy of Fine Arts). He was instructed by the master sculptor Aristodemo Costoli, who influenced his style. In 1878 his frustration at his poverty and the death of his father resulted in the dramatic *Dying Mozart*. Presented at the Paris Exposition in 1878, the sculpture was hugely successful and catapulted Carnielo to fame.

MUSEO ARCHEOLOGICO NAZIONALE DI FIRENZE (NATIONAL ARCHAEOLOGICAL MUSEUM OF FLORENCE)

Via della Colonna, 36; tel.: 055-23575; fax: 055-242213; website: www.firenzemusei.it/archeologico; open: Mon. 2–7 P.M., Tues., Thurs. 8:30 A.M.–7 P.M., Wed., Fri.–Sun. 8:30 A.M.–2 P.M.; admission: €4.

➤ The National Archaeological Museum of Florence houses a superb collection of Greek, Etruscan, Roman, and Egyptian artifacts, most of which came from the private collections of the Medici and Lorraine families. Of particular importance are the Greek vases, such as the *François Vase*, found in an Etruscan tomb at Fonte Rotella near Chiusi. Painted and signed in 570 B.C., it is decorated with six rows of black and red figures depicting scenes from Greek mythology. The Etruscan statues were badly damaged in

the flood of 1966, and only a fraction of the collection is currently on display. One of these bronze statues, the *Chimera* (4th century B.C.), is a mythical lion, with a goat's head and a serpent as a tail, shown cowering in terror. It was discovered in 1553 and given to Cosimo I by Giorgio Vasari. *L'Arringatore* (The Orator) was found in 1566 near Lake Trasimeno in central Italy. The sculpture, which is inscribed with the name of an Etruscan aristocrat, dates from the 1st century B.C. and depicts a figure in a Roman toga who seems to be addressing an audience. Also of particular interest is the rare collection of Egyptian artifacts, such as textiles, ropes, hats, and baskets that normally do not survive over time. They were preserved in a desert tomb, along with a bone-and-wood chariot that is also on display.

MUSEO BOTANICO DELL'UNIVERSITÀ (BOTANICAL MUSEUM OF THE UNIVERSITY OF FLORENCE)

Via Micheli, 3; tel.: 055-2757402; fax: 055-289006; open: Mon., Tues., Thurs., Fri., Sun. 9 A.M.–1 P.M., Sat. 9 A.M.–5 P.M., closed Wed.; admission: €4.

➤ The museum, the largest botanical museum in Italy, was founded in 1842 by

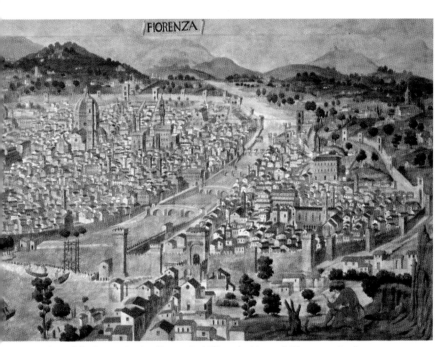

Pianta della Catena *showing Florence in 1470, at the Museo di "Firenze com'era"*

Leopoldo II. It has vegetation samples and models of plants, including some famous wax models from the early 1800s. There are also manuscripts on botany and antique herbaria (particularly interesting is a 15th-century engraved herbarium), as well as a fine wood collection. The Tropical Herbs Garden has one of the world's best collections of samples from Ethiopia and Somalia.

Museo di "Firenze com'era"

Via dell'Oriuolo, 24; tel.: 055-2616545; open: Mon., Tues., Wed. 9 A.M.–2 P.M., Sat. 9 A.M.–7 P.M. (last admission 30 minutes before closing); closed: Thurs. and Fri., Jan. 1, Easter, May 1, Aug. 15, Dec. 25; admission: €2.70.

➤ The museum, whose name translates to "The Museum of Florence How It Was," is dedicated to the history of Florence and the development of the city. Located in the former Oblate convent, it has drawings, plans, and paintings from the 15th through the 20th centuries. The *Pianta della Catena* is a 19th century copy of a woodcut from the 15th century and shows Florence at the height of the Renaissance. Some buildings depicted,

such as the Palazzo Pitti, can still be seen today. The Palazzo Pitti reappears in a sequence of lunettes made by the Flemish artist Giusto Utens in 1599. These show the Medici villas and gardens, as well as interesting vignettes of rural life. There is also a map of the city of Catena. Another room is devoted to a plan devised by Giuseppe Poggi, once the city architect, for destroying many buildings and remodeling the center of Florence when it was briefly the Italian capital from 1865 to 1871. He managed to clear some buildings for the new Piazza della Repubblica and its triumphal arch before an international outcry stopped the plans.

Raccolta d'Arte dell'Arciconfraternita della Misericordia (Art Collection of the Arciconfraternita della Misericordia)

Piazza del Duomo, 20; tel.: 055-239393; open: by appointment.

➤ This museum exhibits paintings, sculpture, and furniture from the 15th to 17th centuries.

Via d. Cinque Giornate

Via d. Statuto

Via della

Via F. Crispi

Via Cernaia

PIAZZA d. Vittoria

Via F. Ruffini

Via Puccinotti

XX Settembre

Viale G. Milton

Via Poliziano

Piazza d. Costituzione

Via Leone X

Viale Lorenzo

Via Landino

il Magnifico

Via Lavagnini

S.

Viale

S. Caterina d'Alessandria

Via d. Ruote

Via d. Mantellate

Via S. Anna

Via Salvestrina

Strozzi

V. Pratello

V. Barbano

Via Dolfi

Via Poggi

Via Bartolommeo

Via d. Ridolfi

Piazza della Indipendenza

Via Zanobi

Santa Reparata

Campo-reggi

V. Duca d'Aosta

Lupi

Via d. Fortezza

Via San

Via XXVII Aprile

Via S. Gallo

Via d. Dogana

Via G. La Pira

ilippo

Via

Via d. Forteza

Via Guelfa

Piazza S.Marco

za del cifisso

Via Cennini

Via Faenza

Via Nazionale

Via Panicale

Via Chiara

Via S. Orsola

Via Taddea

Via Guelfa

Via Cavour

Via C. Battisti

Piazza S.S.Annunz

Via Fiume

Via d'Ariento

Via S. Antonino

P.za d. Mercato Centrale

Via Ginori

Via de' Servi

Piazza d. Unità Italiana

Via Panzani

Via d. Melarancio

Piazza Madonna d. Aldobrandini

Borgo La Noce

Via de' Ginori

Via Ricasoli

deg

Piazza F. Brunelleschi

Piazza del Castellaccio

Via del

S.Lorenzo

Via Cori

Via de' Martelli

Via de' Pucci

Via Bufalini

S. Maria Del Fiore (Duomo)

P.za di S.Maria Nuova

Via Santa

Via de' Cerretani

Battistero di S. Giovanni

Piazza d.

Via de' Pecori

Via Roma

Duomo

P.za d. Capitolo

Canonica dell'Oche

Via d. Proc

Via dell' Oriuolo

aria ella

Moro

V.d.Trebbio

Via d. Antinori

Via degli Agli

Via de' Vecchietti

Vic. d. Adimari

Tosinghi

de Bonizzi

Borgo degli Albizi

Via de' Giacomini

Via de' Corsi

Campidoglio

Piazza della Repubblica

Calzaiuoli

Via d. Alberghi

P.za S. Maria in Campo

V. d. Strozzi

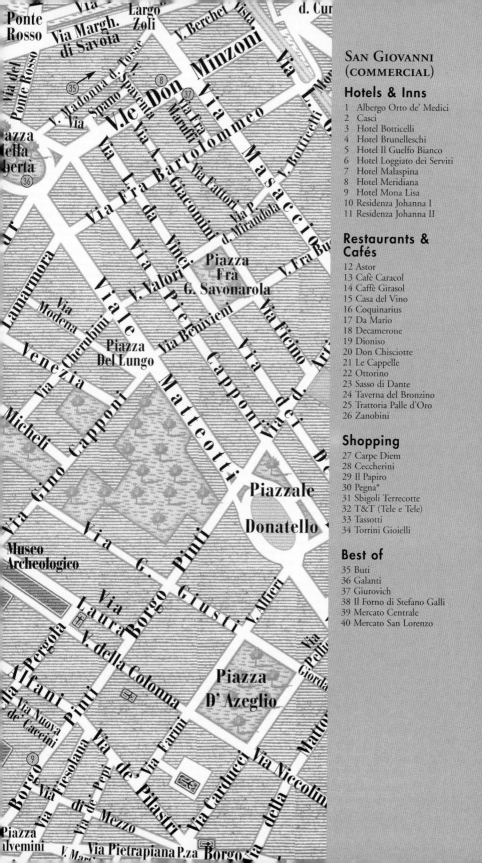

SAN GIOVANNI
(COMMERCIAL)

Hotels & Inns

1 Albergo Orto de' Medici
2 Casci
3 Hotel Botticelli
4 Hotel Brunelleschi
5 Hotel Il Guelfo Bianco
6 Hotel Loggiato dei Serviti
7 Hotel Malaspina
8 Hotel Meridiana
9 Hotel Mona Lisa
10 Residenza Johanna I
11 Residenza Johanna II

Restaurants & Cafés

12 Astor
13 Café Caracol
14 Caffè Girasol
15 Casa del Vino
16 Coquinarius
17 Da Mario
18 Decamerone
19 Dioniso
20 Don Chisciotte
21 Le Cappelle
22 Ottorino
23 Sasso di Dante
24 Taverna del Bronzino
25 Trattoria Palle d'Oro
26 Zanobini

Shopping

27 Carpe Diem
28 Ceccherini
29 Il Papiro
30 Pegna*
31 Sbigoli Terrecotte
32 T&T (Tele e Tele)
33 Tassotti
34 Torrini Gioielli

Best of

35 Buti
36 Galanti
37 Giurovich
38 Il Forno di Stefano Galli
39 Mercato Centrale
40 Mercato San Lorenzo

HOTELS & INNS

Albergo Orto dei Medici

Via San Gallo, 30; tel.: 055-483427; fax: 055-461276; website: www.ortodeimedici.it; e-mail: hotel@ortodeimedici.it; category:★★★; number of rooms: 31, including 4 with balconies and views of San Marco or of roofs downtown; credit cards accepted: all major; access to internet: none; €€.

☛This hotel is in an old patrician palace in the heart of the city.

Casci

Via Cavour, 13; tel.: 055-211686; website: www.hotelcasci.com; category:★★; number of rooms: 24; credit cards accepted: all major; access to internet: from common area; €–€€.

☛Ideal for families, the Casci offers baby-sitting, a parking garage, and more in an elegant 15th-century palazzo.

Hotel Botticelli

Via Taddea, 8; tel.: 055-290905; fax: 055-294322; website: www.hotelbotticelli.it; e-mail: info@hotelbotticelli.it; category:★★★; number of rooms: 34; credit cards accepted: all major; access to internet: from common area; €€–€€€.

☛Located in a 16th-century palazzo just behind the Mercato di San Lorenzo, this hotel has a central location with rooms that are spacious and simply furnished.

Hotel Brunelleschi

Piazza Santa Elisabetta, 3, in the Torre della Pagliazza; tel.: 055-27370; fax: 055-219653; website: www.hotelbrunelleschi.it/; e-mail: info@hotelbrunelleschi.it; category:★★★★; number of rooms: 96, including 2 suites on the top floor with a view of the Duomo and the Campanile; credit cards accepted: all major; access to internet: from common area; €€€€.

☛While the 5th-century Byzantine tower that punctuates the facade of the Hotel Brunelleschi once served as a prison, it now houses two penthouse suites offering 360-degree views of Florence. Though not as picturesque, the hotel's other 94 rooms are rich in accommodations, with rates to match. There is also a renowned restaurant.

Hotel Il Guelfo Bianco

Via Cavour, 29; tel.: 055-288330; fax: 055-295203; website: www.ilguelfobianco.it; e-mail: info@ilguelfobianco.it; category:★★★; number of rooms: 42 and 1 apartment; credit cards accepted: all major; access to internet: yes; €€–€€€.

☛In a building that dates back to the 17th century, the Guelfo Bianco is situated on one of the busiest streets in the city center, but the soundproofed, air-conditioned rooms are quiet and comfortable. Lodging includes a continental breakfast.

Hotel Loggiato dei Serviti

Piazza della Santissima Annunziata, 3; tel.: 055-289592/289593; fax: 055-289595; website: www.loggiatodeiservitihotel.it; e-mail: info@loggiatodeiservitihotel.it; category: ★★★; number of rooms: 29 (room 30 has a view of the Duomo); credit cards accepted: all major; access to internet: no; €€€.

☛The Hotel Loggiato dei Serviti is a unique hotel located in one of the most beautiful piazzas in Florence, under the portico of the Loggiato dell'Ospedale degli Innocenti by Filippo Brunelleschi. It was constructed by Antonio da Sangallo in 1527 for the Servite priests, hence the name.

Hotel Malaspina

Piazza Indipendenza, 24; tel.: 055-489869; fax: 055-474809; website: www.malaspinahotel.it; e-mail: info @ malaspinahotel.it; category:★★★ deluxe; number of rooms: 31, including 4 that lead into Piazza Indipendenza; credit cards accepted: all major; access to internet: yes; €€.

☛This hotel is located in one of the oldest remaining piazzas in Florence. It is shaded by many large trees even though it is just a few steps from the historical center of the city. It is a comfortable and pleasant place with antique furniture.

Hotel Meridiana

Viale Don Minzoni, 25; tel.: 055-576552; website: www.meridiana-hotel.it; category:★★★; number of rooms: 67; credit cards accepted: all major; facilities: air-conditioning, sauna; access to internet: from common area; €€–€€€.

☛Built at the beginning of the 20th century, the Meridiana was recently renovated and is just ten minutes from the historic city center. Ideal for individual travelers or those with families, the hotel offers all the modern amenities. Only breakfast is available downstairs in the dining room, but a string of cafés and restaurants are steps away. All rooms are equipped with air-conditioning.

Hotel Mona Lisa

Via Borgo Pinti, 27; tel.: 055-2479751; fax: 055-2479755; website: www.monnalisa.it; category: ☆☆☆☆; number of rooms: 30; credit cards accepted: all major; access to internet: yes; €€–€€€.

☛Pleasant and elegant, the hotel Mona Lisa has a quiet garden and a nice collection of antique furniture filling the rooms.

Residenza Johanna I

Via Bonifacio Lupi, 14; tel.: 055-481896; fax: 055-482721; website: www.johanna.it; e-mail: lupi@johanna.it; category: ☆☆; number of rooms: 10; credit cards accepted: all major; access to internet: none; €.

☛This residence offers comfortable, utilitarian rooms at a very reasonable price.

Residenza Johanna II

Via delle Cinque Giornate, 12; tel.: 055-473377; fax: 055-4634197; e-mail: cinque giornate@johanna.it; category: ☆☆; number of rooms: 6; credit cards accepted: all major; access to internet: none; €.

☛After the success of the Residenza Johanna I, this second location was opened not far away from the first and with the same arrangements: comfortable rooms with minimal services at very reasonable prices.

RESTAURANTS & CAFÉS

Astor

Piazza del Duomo, 20r; tel.: 055-2399000; open: Mon.–Sun. noon–3 A.M.; credit cards accepted: all major.

☛This recently redone cocktail bar and disco pub is of minimalist, modern design. Snacks are served with drinks, dinner, and occasionally live music later on in the evening.

Cafè Caracol

Via de' Ginori, 10r; tel.: 055-211427; website: www.cafecaracol.com; open: Tues.–Sun. 5:30–7 P.M. (happy hour), 7:30–11:30 P.M. (dinner), 11:30 P.M.–2 A.M. (drinks), Sun. brunch 12–2:30 P.M.; closed: Mon.; credit cards accepted: all major; €.

☛Cafè Caracol has a warm, colorful atmosphere and the most authentic Mexican food in Florence. Foreigners are attracted by happy hour, when margaritas, piña coladas, daiquiris, and beer are half-price, and are accompanied by salsa and chips. Quesadillas and enchiladas reign at dinner.

Caffè Girasol

Via del Romito, 1r; tel.: 055-474948; e-mail: girasol@inwind.it; open: Tues.–Sun. 8 A.M.–2 A.M.; closed: Mon; credit cards accepted: all major.

☛This Caribbean-themed bar offers strong exotic drinks.

Casa del Vino

Via dell'Ariento, 16r; tel.: 055-215609; open: Mon.–Fri. 9:30 A.M.–5:30 P.M., Sat. 10 A.M.–3:30 P.M.; closed: Sun.; credit cards accepted: all major.

☛This small enoteca behind Florence's Mercato Centrale has one of the city's best wine lists. Owner Gianni Migliorini will proudly pour his collection, and patrons always enjoy his *crostini* and cold snacks.

Coquinarius

Via delle Oche, 15r; tel.: 055-2302153; open: Mon.–Sat. noon–10:30 P.M.; closed: Sun.; credit cards accepted: Visa, MasterCard.

☛This wine bar/café offers light meals from breakfast until evening. There is a wide selection of wines offered by the glass.

Da Mario

Via Rosina, 2r; tel.: 055-218550; website: www.trattoriamario.com; open: Mon.–Sat. noon–3:30 P.M.; closed: Sun.; credit cards accepted: none; €.

☛Located at the periphery of San Lorenzo's busy market place, this family-run establishment packs it in during the lunch hour. The menu offers authentic Florentine fare such as *pappa al pomodoro,* and hearty soups and stews.

Decamerone

Viale Spartaco Lavagnini, 40a/b; tel.: 055-496450; open: daily 11:30 A.M.–3:30 P.M., 6 P.M.–2 A.M.; credit cards accepted: all major.

☛A nice spot for an aperitif. Drinks are served with a variety of appetizers.

Dioniso

Via San Gallo, 16r; tel.: 055-217882; open: Mon.–Sat. noon–midnight, Sun. 7 P.M.–midnight; credit cards accepted: all major; €.

☛This Cuban restaurant of minimalist design emphasizes its kitchen rather than its image. It offers dishes such as chili.

Don Chisciotte

Via C. Ridolfi, 4-6r; tel.: 055-475430; fax: 055-485305; open: Mon. 7–10:30 P.M., Tues.–Sat. noon–2:30 P.M., 7–10:30 P.M.; closed: Sun., Mon. at lunch, and month of Aug.; credit cards accepted: all major; €.

☛Elegant, creative cuisine, and a good wine selection make Don Chisciotte an excellent choice. Specialties include *zuppa di pesce alla toscana* (Tuscan fish soup), *pasta fresca ai porcini e tartufi* (fresh pasta with porcini mushrooms and truffles), *and ravioli di branzino con salsa di scampi* (sea bass ravioli with shrimp scampi).

Le Cappelle

Piazza Madonna, 11r; tel.: 055-217700; open: Tues.–Sun. 11:30 A.M.–10:30 P.M. (summer), 11:30 A.M.–2:30 P.M., 6:30–10:30 P.M. (winter); closed: Mon.; credit cards accepted: all major; €.

☛Located in the historic frescoed Palazzo Benci, this is the place for traditional Tuscan fare. This includes *penne strascicate,* short pasta that finishes cooking in a skillet of meat and tomato sauce lightened with cream. *Ossobuco* and veal chops are among the main courses, and a fresh, seemingly made-to-order fruit salad (*macedonia*) brings any meal to a nice ending.

Ottorino

Via delle Oche, 20r; tel.: 055-215151; open: Mon.–Sat. 12:15–2:15 P.M., 7:15–10:15 P.M.; closed: Sun. and month of Aug.; credit cards accepted: all major; €.

☛Ottorino stands right by the Duomo, and is thus patronized by tourists and Florentines alike. There are ample choices, but their specialties are *taglierini con calamari e rucola* (taglierini with calamari and arugula) and *scaloppina di vitella ripiena di parmigiano* (calf scallopini filled with Parmesan).

Sasso di Dante

Piazza delle Pallottole, 6r; tel.: 055-282113; open: daily noon–2:30 P.M., 7–10:30 P.M.; credit cards accepted: all major; €.

☛Located in a small piazza just adjacent to the Duomo, the limited outdoor seating area at Sasso di Dante offers a splendid view of part of the cathedral. Good lighter fare is also served.

Taverna del Bronzino

Via delle Ruote, 25r; tel.: 055-495220; fax: 055-4620076; open: Mon.–Sat. 12:30–2:30 P.M., 7:30–10:30 P.M.; closed: Sun. and month of Aug.; credit cards accepted: all major; €€.

☛This restaurant is housed in a 15th-century palazzo that has connections with the Florentine painter Bronzino, hence the name. The atmosphere is reserved; the surroundings are airy and beautifully furnished. The antipasti and wide choice of pastas are characteristically Tuscan, while the *secondi piatti* (main courses) are more Florentine. There is a good wine selection.

Trattoria Palle d'Oro

Via Sant'Antonino, 43r; tel.: 055-288383; open: Mon.–Sat. noon–2:30 P.M., 6:30–10 P.M.; closed: Sun.; credit cards accepted: all major; €.

RESTAURANTS & CAFÉS

☞If you arrive after one in the afternoon or after eight at night the restaurant will be packed full of Italians who go for a quick counter lunch or leisurely sit-down meal. Made-to-order sandwiches, pastas, and main courses are available. On Fridays the specialty is *caciucco,* a spicy fish stew. The menu changes daily and according to the season.

Zanobini

Via Sant'Antonino, 47r; tel.: 055-2396850; open: Mon.–Sat. 8:30 A.M.–2 P.M., 3:30–8 P.M.; closed: Sun.; credit cards accepted: all major.
☞Not far away from the train station on a street that leads to Florence's Mercato Centrale, Zanobini has a vast selection of wines by the glass or the bottle.

SPECIALTY SHOPS

Carpe Diem

Via Ricasoli, 52r; tel.: 055-292281; open: Tues.–Sat. 10 A.M.–7 P.M.; closed: Mon.; credit cards accepted: all major.
☞Near the Accademia Gallery, this shop is tasteful and elegant. There is a collection of clothing and accessories by Moschino.

Ceccherini

Via de' Ginori, 31–33–35r; tel.: 055-217584; open: Mon.–Fri. 9 A.M.–1 P.M., 3:30–7:30 P.M., Sat. 9 A.M.–1 P.M.; closed: Sun.; credit cards accepted: all major.
☞Designed by Baccio d'Agnolo, the 16th-century Palazzo Taddei is now home to Italy's oldest and most prestigious music store.

Il Papiro

Piazza del Duomo, 24r; tel.: 055-281628; website: www.ilpapirofirenze.it; open: Mon.–Sat. 9:30 A.M.–7:30 P.M., Sun. 10 A.M.–6 P.M.; credit cards accepted: all major.
☞This lovely shop sells handmade paper goods. Most of the products are done in a typical Florentine marbled design.

*Pegna

Via dello Studio, 8; tel.: 055-282701; website: www.pegna.it; e-mail: info@pegna.it; open: Mon.–Sat. 9 A.M.–1 P.M., 3:30–7:30 P.M.; closed: Wed. afternoon and Sun.; credit cards accepted: all major.
☞This gourmet grocery shop has been patronized by both Florentines and foreigners alike since it first opened in 1860.

Sbigoli Terrecotte

Via Sant'Egidio, 4r; tel.: 055-2479713; website: www.sbigoliterrecotte.it; open: Mon.–Sat. 9 A.M.–1 P.M., 3–7:30 P.M.; closed: Sun.; credit cards accepted: all major.
☞An array of pottery—from unglazed garden pots to hand-decorated tableware—can be found at Sbigoli Terrecotte.

T&T (Tele e Tele)

Via de' Ginori, 2r; tel.: 055-280123; fax: 055-290563; open: Mon. 3–7:30 P.M., Tues.–Sat. 10 A.M.–1:30 P.M., 3–7:30 P.M.; closed: Sun.; credit cards accepted: all major.
☞In addition to a beautiful collection of fabrics, T&T sells an array of carpets, pillows, ethnic furniture, and candles.

Tassotti

Via dei Servi, 9; tel.: 055-2645477; open: daily 10 A.M.–1 P.M., 2–7 P.M.; credit cards accepted: all major.
☞This beautiful stationery store specializes in handmade paper goods and boxes covered with intricately patterned paper with flowers, butterflies, or other motifs.

Torrini Gioielli

Piazza Duomo, 10r; tel.: 055-2302401; website: www.torrinishop.it; e-mail: shop@torrini.it; open: daily 10 A.M.–7 P.M., Sat. 10 A.M.–1 P.M. (summer), daily 10 A.M.–7 P.M., Mon. 3–7 P.M. (winter); closed: Sun.; credit cards accepted: all major.
☞In business since 1369, this jewelry store is the oldest in the world. The high quality is still apparent in the creative gold and silver jewelry and in the elegant watches.

Santa Croce

By Laura Collura Kahn

Centered around the geometrically shaped square of Santa Croce and the Franciscan establishment by the same name, this quarter was once known as the working-class neighborhood of Florence, complete with wool-dyeing mills, justice courts, and a prison. In keeping with the Franciscan friars' bent for mingling with the populace, the medieval **Piazza Santa Croce** was the city's gathering place and is still a favorite spot for improvised soccer matches.

The church of **Santa Croce**, a Pantheon-like burial site for many illustrious Florentines, including Michelangelo and Niccolò Machiavelli, was started in 1294, consecrated in 1443, and completed with a neo-Gothic facade in the 18th century. Annexed at the back are the **Museo dell'Opera di Santa Croce**, containing Cimabue's famous crucifix, damaged in the 1966 flood and later restored, and the 15th-century **Cappella de' Pazzi**, named after a Renaissance family whose name meant "crazy" and who set up an ill-fated conspiracy to oust the Medicis.

To enter the museum, visitors must walk through the church's cloisters, or the **Chiostri di Santa Croce**, designed by Filippo Brunelleschi. Walking west, you can stop at the **Museo Nazionale del Bargello**. Now a museum housing the world's top collection of Renaissance painting and Donatello's statue of David, the building was once much feared—it was the site of public executions. A few blocks away is the **Casa di Dante**, with its parsimonious collection of Dante Alighieri memorabilia.

Farther west is **Orsanmichele**, a church that was originally built by Arnolfo di Cambio in 1290 as a grain market. Nearby is the medieval **Palazzo dell'Arte della Lana**, the palace of the powerful guild of the wool drapers.

South, at the center of town, stand Florence's most renowned sights, starting with the austere **Piazza della Signoria**, the city's political headquarters from the Renaissance onward. Over the square looms the **Palazzo Vecchio**, built in 1298 to house the Republican government and then taken over in 1540 by Grand Duke Cosimo I, the patriarch of the Medici dynasty. In its courtyard is the **Fontana del Puttino**. In front of the palazzo, visitors can admire a copy of Michelangelo's statue of David and peruse the much-maligned **Fontana del Nettuno** by Bartolomeo Ammannati and the unwieldy *Hercules and Cacus* by Baccio Bandinelli—two rare examples of lower-quality art in Florence.

Off the square is the **Galleria degli Uffizi**, Giorgio Vasari's first architectural work. Today it is Italy's leading museum. Inside is also the **Corridoio Vasariano**, a walkway linking the gallery to the Palazzo Pitti and containing 700 paintings.

Opposite, Detail of the facade of Santa Croce

Via Indipendenza

Via XXVII Aprile

Via G. La Pira

Via P. A. Micheli

Via d. Dogana

Via C. Battisti

PIAZZA S.Marco

Via Gino C.

Museo Archeologico

Via S. Giovanni

Via Nazionale

Via Chiara Panicale

Via d. Ariento

Via Guelfa

Via Taddea

Via Sorsola

Via de' Ginori

Via Cavour

Via de' Servi

Via dei

PIAZZA S.S.Annunziata

Piazza E. Brunelleschi

Via della Pergola

Via degli Alfani

P.za d. Mercato Centrale

Borgo La Noce

Via di Sta.

P.za S. Lorenzo

Via de' Martelli

Via de' Billi

Via Pucci

Via Ricasoli

Via dei Castellaccio

Via Nuova de' Caccini

S.Lorenzo

Piazza Madonna Aldobrandini

Bgo. S. Lorenzo

Via Panzani

Via de' Cerretani

Battistero P.za di S. Giovanni

Piazza d. Duomo

Via de' Pecori

S. Maria Del Fiore (Duomo)

Via Bufalini

P.za di S. Maria Nuova

Via Sant'Egidio

Via della

Via Fiesolana

Boreo

P.za dei Cavallari

P.za di S. Olio

Duomo

Campanile

V. d. Canonica

P.za d. Capitolo

P.za di S. Benedetto de' Bonizzi

Via Portinari

Via dell' Oriuolo

Piazza Salvemini

Campidoglio

Via de' Vecchietti

Via de' Tosinghi

V. dell'Oche

V. dei Giglio

V. dei Alberighi

P.za S. Maria in Campo

42

Via dei

Via G. Verdi

PIAZZA della Repubblica

Via de' Sassetti

S. Anselmi

S.Miniato Fra le Torri

Cavaliceri

V. de'

Via de' Speziali

Calimala

V. de' Medici

Via dei Calzaiuoli

Via del Corso

P.za dei Tre Re

P.za dei Donati

Via de' Tavolini

V. Dante Alighieri

58

43

Borgo degli Albizi

Via de' Giraldi

Pandolfini

66

49

Via de' Pepi

Via G. Verdi

V. M.

P.za di S. Orsanm.

53

67

Via del Cimatori

Bargello

63

Ghibellina

Via de'

Vigna Vecchia

45

V. M.

Porta Rossa

38

V. d. Lamberti Arte d. Lana

Via d. Magazzini

V. d. Condotta

Piazza Firenze

Via d. Acqua

Burella

Isola d. S. Simone

59

Via de' Lavatoi

Vic. d. Panico

V. d. Terme

Calimaruzza

Piazza d. S.ta Cecilia

Piazza d. Signoria

Palazzo Vecchio

36

39

Burella

Via dell'

Anguillara

Via da Verrazzano

V. Pinzochere

40

48

47

V. de' Gondi

Borgo de'

Greci

44

Piazza di S. Croce

50

Via Por S. Maria

Via Lambertesca

Galleria D. Uffizi

V. de' Castellani

P.le d. Uffizi

35

Via del Corno

Via Vinegia

Via Borgognona

de' Peruzzi

37

57

51

Ponte Vecchio

Girolami

Lung. d. Archibusieri

Lung. A. M. de' Medici

V. d. Saponai

P.za di Giudici

Piazza S. Remigio

55

Via Neri

V. d. Vagellai

Malenchini

Piazza Mentana

65

41

Piazza S. Croce

46

Biblioteca Nazionale

V. de' Bardi

P.za de' Rossi

Stracciatella

Pza di S. Maria Sopr'Arno

Fiume Arno

Lungarno Gen. Diaz

Lungarno d. Grazie P.za dei Cavalleggeri

Costa di San Gi

Via de' Bardi

Lungarno Torrigiani

Ponte alle Grazie

Lungarno Serristori

Costa de Magnoli

Corso dei Tintori

V. dei Renai

P.za Demidoff

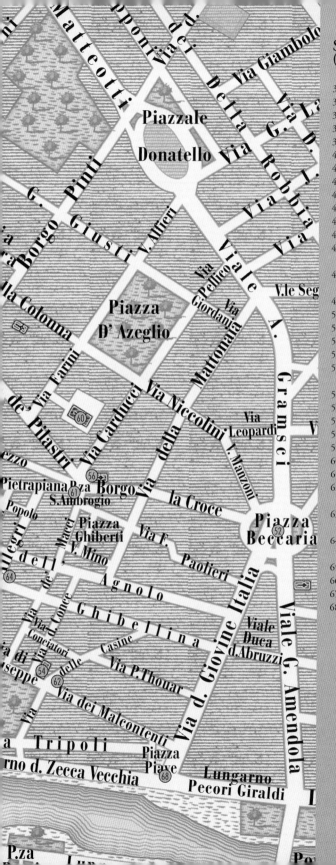

CAPPELLA DE' PAZZI (PAZZI CHAPEL)

Piazza Santa Croce; tel.: 055-290832/ 244619; open: Mon.–Sat. 9:30 A.M.–5:30 P.M., Sun. 1–5:30 P.M.; closed: Jan.1, Dec. 25–26; admission: €5

➤ Situated at the far end of the first cloister of Santa Croce is the idyllic Pazzi Chapel, designed by Filippo Brunelleschi. Begun by the artist in 1429, this fine example of Renaissance architecture was built over a period of almost 50 years. The elegant portico that frames the main door is supported on each side by three Corinthian columns. These are then surmounted by an attic that evokes the spirit of a triumphal arch. The barrel vault underneath the arch features a small cupola adorned with glazed terra-cottas by Luca della Robbia.

The interior of the chapel follows in step with that of the Old Sacristy of San Lorenzo. It consists of two rooms, each defined by strict geometry: square spaces topped by a cupola. Of the 12 tondi that decorate the walls, the one of the apostles is one of della Robbia's masterpieces. The four spandrels inside the cupola depict the evangelists, and were executed by Brunelleschi.

CASA DI DANTE (DANTE'S HOUSE)

Via Santa Margherita, 1; website: www.museocasadidante.it; open: daily 10 A.M.–5 P.M., Sun. 10 A.M.–1 P.M.; closed Mon. and last Sunday of each month, Jan. 1, Dec. 25; admission: €4

➤ Restored in the early 1900s, this building houses a small museum dedicated to the famous poet's life and work. This is not the real house where Italy's greatest poet lived, but a reconstruction that dates back to the beginning of the 20th century. The ground floor has temporary exhibits of modern art and sculpture, while the collection linked to Dante is located on the upper floors. The collection is divided into periods and themes of the poet's life—his youth, his time in exile, his time in the military, and his love for literature, paintings, and maps of Florence. On the top floor there is a collection of antique copies of *The Divine Comedy* in different languages. The rooms of the ground floor are adapted for temporary exhibits.

Cappella de' Pazzi

Corridoio Vasariano

Vasari designed this corridor in 1565 to allow his leading patron, Cosimo I, to pass from the Palazzo Vecchio to the Uffizi to the Palazzo Pitti unimpeded by the public and unexposed to the sun. The corridor is now open to the public and can be accessed from inside the Uffizi Gallery. The section that stretches over the Ponte Vecchio holds a famous collection of self-portraits, including those by Vasari and Bernini. There are also works by other Italian artists such as Annibale Carracci, Guido Reni, and Artemisia Gentileschi, and by foreign ones such as Rubens, Rembrandt, Van Dyck, and Velázquez.

CHIOSTRI DI SANTA CROCE (CLOISTERS OF SANTA CROCE)

Piazza Santa Croce; tel.: 055-244619; open: Mon.–Sat. 9:30 A.M.–5:30 P.M., Sun. 1–5:30 P.M.; closed: Jan.1, Dec. 25–26; admission: €5

➤ These charming 14th-century cloisters, together with the Pazzi Chapel and the works of art located in the convent of the church, comprise the Museo dell'Opera di Santa Croce (see pg. 117). Access the first cloister through an entrance flanking the basilica's right side. At the center of the cloister is a bronze warrior by Henry Moore and *God the Father, Seated,* by Baccio Bandinelli. The adjacent refectory contains a masterpiece by Gothic artist Cimabue—a crucifix that was heavily damaged by the flood of 1966.

CORRIDOIO VASARIANO (VASARI CORRIDOR)

In the Uffizi; tel.: 055-294883; open: by appointment only.

➤ The most visible section of this "secret" passageway stretches across the Ponte Vecchio, atop the shops that line the eastern (upstream) side of the bridge.

FONTANA DEL NETTUNO (NEPTUNE FOUNTAIN)

Piazza della Signoria

➤ Between 1563 and 1575, Bartolomeo Ammannati and his assistants, including Giambologna, created a monumental fountain to match the greatness of the ruler it celebrated: Cosimo I de' Medici. Made possible by the construction of Florence's first aqueduct, the fountain features an oversized Neptune, god of the sea, carved in marble. The awkward statue, nicknamed "Biancone" ("Big White One"), oversees a court of graceful satyrs and sea goddesses, cast in bronze. At the foot of the fountain's basin, a bronze epigraph marks the exact spot where hellfire-and-brimstone preacher Girolamo Savonarola and two of his followers were executed on May 23, 1498. They were first hung and then burned at the stake. Their ashes were poured into the Arno River.

FONTANA DEL PUTTINO (PUTTINO FOUNTAIN)

Piazza della Signoria, in the courtyard of the Palazzo Vecchio; tel.: 055-2768325.

➤ Upon entering the interior of the Palazzo Vecchio, one happens upon an antique courtyard. Designed by Arnolfo di Cambio as a nucleus to the original medieval building, in 1453 this space underwent renovations by Michelozzo in the style of the High Renaissance. Upon the wedding of Francesco de' Medici to Jane of Austria in 1565, the court was refashioned yet again. The grotesques that adorn the courtyard's walls and columns and the cycle of frescoes, *Views of the Hapsburg Empire,* were all added by Vasari and his assistants. The fountain at the center of the courtyard is the Puttino Fountain. Erected for the same occasion, the fountain replaced a humble medieval well with elegant work by Francesco del Tadda and Raffaello di Domenico, under Vasari's direction. Surmounting the fountain is a copy of the bronze statuette *Putto with Dolphin* by early Renaissance master Andrea del Verrocchio. The original, which was taken from the gardens of the Villa Medicea di Careggi and placed atop the fountain for Francesco's wedding, is now located in the Terrace of Juno, inside the palazzo.

GALLERIA DEGLI UFFIZI (UFFIZI GALLERY)

Piazzale delgi Uffizi, 6; tel.: 055-2388551 (reservations: 055-294883); website: www.uffizi.firenze.it; open: Tues.–Sun. 8:15 A.M.–6:50 P.M. (last admission 45 minutes before closing); closed Mon., Jan. 1, May 1, Dec. 25; admission: €6.50

Detail of the Fontana del Puttino

➤ Built by Vasari at the request of Cosimo I, the Uffizi provided the offices of the city magistrates with a single, central location. Whereas these offices had previously been scattered throughout Florence, they now rested safely between the Palazzo Vecchio, Cosimo I's then-place of residence, and the Palazzo Pitti, his future place of residence. Thus, the duke architecturally unified the government that he had already unified politically.

The Uffizi Gallery came into being after Francesco I, Cosimo I's son, commissioned Buontalenti in 1581 to enclose the loggia that once ran along the third floor of the east wing. In 1584, an octagonal gallery was constructed within the enclosure to house the most prized possessions of the Medici art collection (now Room 18). This initial addition would expand throughout the years as Vasari began adding works from those artists of the 16th century whom he chronicled in his famous book, *Lives of the Artists.* In the centuries that followed, works from the classical and Gothic periods would be acquired, along with acquisitions from Flanders, making the Uffizi not only the first art museum of modern Europe but perhaps one of the most complete art collections in the Western world.

Lining the Uffizi's wood-paneled corridor is the collection of Greek and Roman sculpture, which played a fundamental role in the development of the museum. The corridor wraps around each of the Uffizi's wings—east, south, and west—ending back where it began: at the east hall. Here, in chronological order, the painting gallery begins with works dating from the 13th through the 15th century.

Room 2 is dominated by three large Madonnas displayed side by side. To the right is the *Maestà di Santa Trìnita* (c. 1280) by Cimabue. To the left is the *Madonna Rucellai* (1285) by Duccio da Buoninsegna, from the Sienese school. In the center is Giotto's *Madonna di Ognissanti* (1310). While the earlier works display a strict sense of symmetry characteristic of Gothic and Byzantine styles, the realism in the facial expression of Giotto's Madonna, combined with the artist's attention to perspective, distinguishes the *Madonna di Ognissanti* as a precursor to the Renaissance.

Of the numerous masterpieces present in Room 7, three in particular played key roles in the development of Renaissance painting. Paolo Uccello dominates the room with his *Battle of San Romano* (late 1430s), one of the panels that comprises a monumental triptych (the other panels are housed in the National Gallery in London and the Louvre in Paris). Here, Uccello's deftly foreshortened figures seem superimposed upon one another, horse upon rider, imbuing the chaotic battle scene with an unprecedented sense of volume. The two portraits of the Duke and Duchess of Urbino, meanwhile, are widely considered the first examples of portraiture in Renaissance painting. Executed by Piero della Francesca around 1465, these works are distinguished by the artist's use of detail to characterize each figure: the duchess's opulent necklace and the duke's wrinkled skin. The delicately lit background offsets each figure with distant perspectival landscapes, another cornerstone of Renaissance portraiture. The other notable works in this room include the *Virgin Mary with Christ Child and Saint Anne,* painted by Masaccio around 1424 in tandem with his master Masolino, and Domenico Veneziano's *Virgin Mary, Christ Child and Saints* (c. 1445).

Room 8 and part of Room 9 are devoted to paintings by Filippo Lippi. The elegance and refinement of works such as the *Coronation of the Virgin Mary* (1441–1447) and the *Virgin Mary with Christ Child* show a distinctive use of line and contour that would greatly influence Sandro Botticelli, his student. Insofar as the works of the master were precursors to the masterpieces of the pupil, these Lippi paintings function as a preface to those of Botticelli in Rooms 10 through 14. Two pillars of the Uffizi collection, the *Birth of Venus* and the *Primavera,* were painted by the artist at the height of his talent as both a painter and poet. In each, Botticelli expresses humanist ideals though lyrical compositions that "revive" the themes of classical art. In the *Birth of Venus,* the love goddess emerges from her shell to strike one of the most indelible poses in Western culture; in the *Primavera,* she presides over the arrival of spring. Between these allegorical masterpieces hang *Pallas and the Centaur, Madonna of the Pomegranate,* and *Calumny.* Botticelli executed the last of these near the end of his career, when the artist found himself disillusioned with the ideals of humanism and heavily influenced by the preachings of Savonarola. Opposite the *Birth of Venus* is the *Portinari Triptych,* a masterpiece by

Botticelli's Allegory of Spring, *at the Galleria degli Uffizi*

Flemish painter Hugo van der Goes. Completed around 1478, the painting shows the influence of Italian art in the size and stature of its monumental figures. The meticulous detail and realism with which van der Goes rendered his figures, on the other hand, would have an equivalent effect on Italian painters to come.

The next room holds two early masterpieces by Leonardo da Vinci. They are the *Annunciation* and the unfinished *Adoration of the Magi*. Painted by da Vinci at the age of 20, the *Annunciation* already exhibits the artist's typical *sfumato* technique, which creates a hazy background landscape. The figures in the foreground, however, are devoutly traditional, both in terms of their positioning and the painter's use of line. In the *Adoration of the Magi*, da Vinci breaks with convention, positioning the sacred family—Mary, Joseph, and the Christ child—in a triangular arrangement that dominates the composition. The shed and the procession of the Magi, meanwhile, comprise an indistinct background of shadowy forms. Sharing space with da Vinci works is the *Baptism of Christ* (1475) by Verrocchio. Da Vinci, a one-time apprentice in Verrocchio's workshop, painted the angel to the right of Christ.

The triangular composition of the sacred family is revisited in Room 25, not by da Vinci, but by one of the few artists who could rival his genius. Upon its completion in 1504, the *Tondo Doni* by Michelangelo was considered highly unconventional, even by Renaissance standards. The Madonna assumes an extremely contorted posture as she reaches over her shoulder to balance a lively Christ child. Joseph forms the last point of the triangle, offering support to the child as he moves toward his mother's embrace. The gaze that the figures concentrate on one another interlocks the family in a highly intimate exchange, separate from John the Baptist, who looks on to the right, and the promiscuous crowd of nudes, who fraternize in the background.

The next room contains several portraits by Raphael. Of these, the portrait of Pope Leo X is the artist's most mature work. Painted during Raphael's Roman period, it testifies to his reputation as a supreme colorist. As in the *Veiled Lady*

(at the Palazzo Pitti), Raphael provides rich texture to the pope's habit through a harmonious variation of reds. The *Madonna of the Goldfinch* (1505–1506), dates back to Raphael's formative years, showing a variety of influences, from Leonardo to Fra Bartolomeo.

Room 28 is devoted to Titian. Among the works present is a true masterpiece: the *Venus of Urbino*. While many of Titian's contemporaries in Tuscany might have spoiled the goddess's graceful figure with the use of hard lines, the Venetian painter relied solely on the effects of alternating hues to achieve his objectives. The result is a titillating nude whose sensual contours created a scandal upon its unveiling in 1538. The other works in the room include the tranquil *Flora*, painted around 1520, and *Venus and Cupid* (c. 1550).

The *Madonna of the Long Neck*, located in Room 29, is a fine example of mannerist painting. Aside from stretching the Madonna to unnatural proportions, Parmigianino also burdens her with a cadaverous Christ child so as to simultaneously evoke the imagery of a Pietà.

Early works by Caravaggio (1573–1610) are contained in Hall 43. They are the *Bacchus*, painted when the artist was only 20 years old; *Medusa*, an oil on canvas designed as a cover for a shield; and the *Sacrifice of Isaac*, which features a cameo appearance by the model who posed for *Medusa*. Works by Rembrandt are on view in Room 44. Rubens and Van Dyck are featured in Room 41.

Loggia dei Lanzi (or Loggia della Signoria)
Piazza della Signoria

➤ The loggia was constructed in the late 14th century to serve the Signoria, the Commune magistrates, during public ceremonies. It later became the unofficial campgrounds of the German guards, or the *lanzi*, who protected the Palazzo Vecchio under the reign of Alessandro I de' Medici. In the 16th century Cosimo I made the loggia into a kind of "laboratory" for sculptors. Now, it is one of the few places where world-class sculpture can be enjoyed free of charge. Among these are a number of restored Roman sculptures (at the rear of the loggia) and works by Giambologna. In the foreground is the *Rape of the Sabine Women* (1583), a dramatic marble group that twists and writhes. The piece's contortion is renowned for the constant shift in perspective it precipitates on the viewer. Also present is Giambologna's *Hercules with the Centaur Nessus* (1599), which attempts a similar sense of contortion, but with less success. Missing from the front left of the loggia is Benvenuto Cellini's monumental *Perseus,* holding the freshly decapitated head of Medusa, which is currently undergoing restoration at the Uffizi Gallery. Begun in 1545, the statue presented a number of technical casting challenges because of its size. The *Perseus* did not assume its place in the loggia until 1554, where it stood in direct competition with Michelangelo's *David,* in Piazza della Signoria.

Michelangelo, including his famous *Bacchus* (1497). This depiction of the Roman god of wine, with a small satyr crouched next to him, was Michelangelo's first major work. While bearing heavy influences from antique sculpture, the statue's classical *contrapposto* stance seems a result of the effects of heavy drinking. Michelangelo captures his subject in mid-stumble, imbuing *Bacchus* with a sense of potential, if not wholly realized, motion. For this unique effect, it is widely considered the first work of Michelangelo's maturity.

The *Tondo Pitti* (1504–1506) also shows signs of early innovation. In this unfinished relief, Michelangelo attempts to apply da Vinci's *sfumato* painting technique to sculpture. Also featured are *David-Apollo* (1530–1532) and *Brutus* (1539), the only bust in Michelangelo's repertoire, which, Vasari writes, was modeled after the "brutal" Lorenzino de'

MUSEO NAZIONALE DEL BARGELLO (NATIONAL MUSEUM OF BARGELLO)

Via del Proconsolo, 4; tel.: 055-2388606 website: www.polomuseale.firenze.it; open: daily 8:15 A.M.–1:50 P.M.; closed second and fourth Mon. and first and third Sun. of each month, Jan. 1, May 1, Dec. 25; admission: €4

➤ Built between 1255 and 1261, incorporating an existing tower, the Bargello is located on the corner of Via Ghibellina and Via del Proconsolo. Originally named the Palazzo del Capitano del Popolo (Palace of the Leader of the People), it is the oldest surviving seat of government in Florence. In 1574 it became a prison and the home of the chief of police and changed its name to Palazzo Bargello, which is slang for "cop." This was the beginning of the building's decay, which ended in 1865 when it was entirely renovated and became Italy's first national museum. Today, along with its large arms collection, it is home to one of the world's most important collections of Renaissance sculpture and mannerist bronzes, and boasts works by Donatello, Verrocchio, della Robbia, and Michelangelo.

The museum is on three floors. To the right of the entrance is the Sala del Cinquecento, which has many works by

Donatello's David, *at the Museo Nazionale del Bargello*

Medici (who murdered Duke Alessandro). Competing with Michelangelo for space are several works by one of his contemporaries, sculptor Benvenuto Cellini. The statue at the center of the collection is *Narcissus,* carved in marble. The bronze statuettes *Minerva* and *Jupiter* originally decorated the base of his masterpiece *Perseus,* once located in the Loggia della Signoria. The bronze plaque that hangs on the wall is called *Perseus Delivering Andromeda.* It too once decorated the base of *Perseus* and represents relief work characteristic of the mannerist period. The *Winged Mercury* by Giambologna, another master of mannerism, rounds off the room with its agility and grace.

In the courtyard, once used for public hangings and torture, is a staircase built by Neri di Fioravante (1345–1367). There are also six allegorical statues by Ammannati and another statue, *Ocean,* by Giambologna. The second-floor balcony is filled with statues of animals by Giambologna, including one of a turkey.

To the right is the Salone del Consiglio General, which features mostly works by Donatello. The largest piece is *Saint George* (1416), which was removed from its niche at Orsanmichele. Carved in marble, it exemplifies the influence of classical art on

the master. Of the two Davids present in the room, the one cast in bronze circa 1440 is the world-famous one—the first nude statue by a Western artist since ancient times. It shows David without any appearance of triumph or pride. The other, carved from marble between 1408 and 1409, is from Donatello's youth. Other important works are Donatello's *Marzocco* (1418–1420), the symbolic lion that used to reside in Piazza della Signoria; the bust of Niccolò da Uzzano; and the *l'Atys-Amor,* also by Donatello. Before exiting the second floor, take note of the famous panels by Lorenzo Ghiberti and Filippo Brunelleschi depicting the Sacrifice of Isaac. While Ghiberti's version beat Brunelleschi's in the competition for the north door of the baptistery of Florence's cathedral, the latter artist's panel is widely considered the first example of Renaissance sculpture. Also noteworthy is the Islamic Room and the Chapel of Mary Magdalene, frescoed in about 1340 by the school of Giotto.

The third floor of the Bargello features halls devoted to the works of Giovanni and Andrea della Robbia, including three glazed terra-cottas: *Bust of a Youth, Madonna degli Architetti,* and *Madonna del Cuscino.* Verrocchio emphasized realism in his work, which is evident in his delicate

Orsanmichele

bronze *David* (1470), in the middle of the Verrocchio Room. Also noteworthy is his *Dama col Mazzolino,,* (c. 1480). The Arms and Armor Collection is also on the third floor and features interesting objects.

ORSANMICHELE

Via dell'Arte della Lana; tel.: 055-284944; open: Tues.–Sun. 10 A.M.–5 P.M.; closed Mon., Jan. 1, May 1, Dec. 25; admission: free

➤ Orsanmichele derives its name from the 8th-century church, dedicated to Saint Michael, which once stood beside several vegetable gardens *(orti)*. Arnolfo di Cambio built one of the first public loggias in Florence over this site, which became home to the city's grain market. After the citywide fire of 1304 and a succession of enlargements in 1337, the loggia underwent a major remodeling in 1367. Soon afterward the presence of a sacred image that was believed to be miraculous made it a destination for pilgrimages, and the space was converted into a church and named Orsanmichele, a variation on Orto San Michele. Above the arcade, two stories were added where storage of food and grain could continue in case of famine. After the government of the Signoria moved their offices into this space toward the end of the 15th century, they ordered each of the major guilds in Florence to decorate the exterior of Orsanmichele. Each guild, therefore, commissioned a sculpture of its patron saint to fill the niches that line the chapel's four walls.

The wall that faces Via Calzaiuoli features (from left to right) a bronze Saint John the Baptist (1416) cast by Ghiberti for the Drapers Guild; a hyper-realistic bronze group of the Doubting Thomas (1484) by Verrocchio for the merchants' court; and a bronze Saint Luke (1562) by Giovanni da Bologna, known as Giambologna, for the Guild of Judges and Notaries. Facing Via Orsanmichele are three marble works by Donatello: *Saint Peter* (1413), made for the Butchers Guild; *Saint Philip* (1410), made for the shoemakers, attributed to Nanni di Banco, and a copy of the famous Saint George (1416), carved for the armor merchants and sword cutlers. The original is preserved in the Bargello Museum, along

with the bas-relief of Saint George and the Dragon that originally accompanied it. The latter is considered Donatello's most sophisticated work in relief. The only marble group on this wall is Nanni di Banco's *Four Crowned Saints* (1408), created for the master stonecutters and carpenters. This group is complemented with a bas-relief that depicts the craftsmen at work. Facing Via dell'Arte della Lana are more contributions by Ghiberti. He cast *Saint Matthew* in 1422 for the money changers and *Saint Stephen*, four years later, for the wool merchants. *Saint Eligius* (1416), the patron saint of the blacksmiths, is by Nanni di Banco. The wall along Via dei Lamberti is lined by *Saint Mark* (1411–1413) by Donatello, *Saint James,* attributed to Niccolò di Piero Lamberti, the *Madonna of the Rose* (1400), attributed to Pietro di Giovanni Tedesco, and, finally, *Saint John the Evangelist* (1515) by Baccio da Montelupo. They were carved for the Textile, Furriers, Doctors and Apothecaries, and Silk Merchants and Goldsmiths Guilds, respectively.

PALAZZO DELL'ARTE DELLA LANA

Via dell'Arte della Lana, 1, at Via Orsanmichele; closed to the public.

➤ Currently home to the Società Dantesca, this 16th-century structure is the former headquarters of the weavers' guild, considered the city's most powerful corporation during the Middle Ages and Renaissance. The plaque on the west wing of the structure commemorates 1308, the year in which the palazzo became the headquarters of all guilds and thus the seat of Florence's oligarchic power. The arched skyway connecting the mansion to Orsanmichele was constructed by Buontalenti in 1569. The rest of its current appearance, however, reflects restructuring done in 1905. Enter the palazzo and cross this pathway to access the museum at the top of Orsanmichele, which currently holds many of the sculptural works that once filled the church's exterior niches.

PALAZZO VECCHIO

It is vast, it is strong, it is stern; it is splendid, proud-looking and majestic. Nor are minor details wanting to assist its historic eloquence . . . It is strangely irregular in form, being, in fact, most comically crooked; but enquire why it is so, and you will find that it is because the building of it straight, would have obliged the thin-skinned citizens to permit a portion of it to rest upon ground once occupied by the dwellings of the Uberti, a Ghibelline faction whom they had routed and banished, after knocking their houses about their ears.

Frances Trollope, *Italy and the Italians*

Palazzo Vecchio (or Palazzo della Signoria)

Piazza della Signoria; tel.: 055-2768325;
website: www.comune.firenze.it;
open: Mon.–Sun. 9 A.M.–7 P.M.,
Thurs. 9 A.M.–2 P.M.
(last admission 1 hour before closing);
closed Mon., Jan. 1, Easter,
May 1, Aug. 15, Dec. 25;
admission: €6

➤ Surmounted by its Gothic bell tower, the austere, almost windowless, facade of the asymmetrical Palazzo Vecchio forms the architectural centerpiece of Piazza della Signoria. Originally designed by Arnolfo di Cambio as a civic counterpart to his Duomo, and completed in 1322, this building was first home to the heads of the Florentine Commune, the *Priori*, in the 14th century, and therefore the palazzo was known as the Palazzo dei Priori. A huge bell, used to call citizens to meetings or to warn them of danger, was put on top of the tower in 1310.

The building earned the title of Palazzo della Signoria in the 15th century, when the Republic located its government, the *Signoria*, within the palace walls. Not until the mid-16th century did the Palazzo Vecchio receive its current name. With the fall of the Republic and the return of the Medici reign, a new residence (the Palazzo Pitti) was erected on the other side of the Arno, making the Palazzo della Signoria the "old palace," or Palazzo Vecchio.

While the Gothic facade of the Palazzo Vecchio remains faithful to the building's medieval beginnings, one can discern the nature of its structural evolution by walking along the palazzo's left side. Porta di Tramontana leads into the Sala d'Arme, or Arm's Room, the only interior space left from the medieval period. The rest of the structure along Via de' Gondi reflects a succession of enlargements, beginning in 1495 with the addition that now houses the Salone dei Cinquecento and ending in the 16th century with the addition that stretches all the way to Via dei Leoni.

The Palazzo della Signoria is the only building in the whole city that has both Guelph and Ghibelline battlements, or *merli*. The Guelph ones are square fortifications on top of the gallery, while the ones done by the Ghibellines are shaped like a swallow's tail and are on top of the Torre di Arnolfo, the tower surmounting the building. The coats of arms that were painted in 1353 underneath the arches of the gallery of the palazzo were used as the symbol of the Florentine Republic. The red cross on a white background is the insignia of the Florentine people; the red lily on a white background is the symbol of the city; the red and white coat represents the union of Fiesole and Florence; the gold keys on a red background are the emblem of the papacy. They symbolize the recognition and trust that the Republic was supposed to have toward the pope (who is represented by the keys of Saint Peter); *Libertas* (liberty), written in gold with a dark blue background, is the coat of arms of the *Priori* and represents the people who are in charge of the guilds; the red eagle gripping a green dragon on a white background is the coat of arms of the *Parte Guelfa* (Party of the Guelphs); the white lily on a red background is the old coat of arms of the city; the gold lilies (the symbol of France) on a dark blue background are the coat of arms of Carlo d'Angiò, who brokered the historic peace between the Guelphs and the Ghibellines; the gold lilies with a black and gold band set in an azure background represent the coat of arms of Roberto d'Angiò.

The two coats of arms of Florence represent two very different points in the history of the city. The older ones, from the time when the Ghibellines were in power, depict a white lily on a red background. This was used until the middle of the 13th century, when the Guelphs defeated the Ghibellines and marked this radical change by inverting the colors in the city's coat of arms.

To the right of the entrance of the Palazzo Vecchio is Francesco I's study. The small, windowless room designed by Vasari contains paintings and frescoes dealing with the natural sciences, including one depicting Nature and Prometheus surrounded by the four elements. On the third floor, the Quartiere degli Elementi (Quarter of the Elements) is a series of

Palazzo Vecchio

rooms with allegories of Earth, Fire, Air, and Water by Vasari and his assistants (1555–1558). Eleonora of Toledo, the wife of Cosimo I, had a suite of rooms decorated for her with scenes of virtuous and faithful women. In one of these rooms there is a fresco of Penelope waiting faithfully for her husband, Odysseus, to return from the Trojan War. The Cappella di Eleonora (Eleonora's Chapel) has biblical frescoes by Bronzino (1540–1545), including some wonderful frescoes of Egyptian soldiers pursuing Moses and the Jews as they cross the Red Sea. The Sala dei Gigli (Hall of Lilies) has a fresco on the wall by Ghirlandaio with various Roman characters and a restored bronze group, *Judith and Holofernes,* by Donatello. As you exit this room you will enter the three halls that comprise the Donazione Loeser, a collection of 14th- to 16th-century sculptures donated to the city council by the American art critic Charles Loeser in 1928.

The Sala dei Dugento, usually closed to the public, is part of the Palazzo Vecchio's original medieval structure. It currently serves as a chamber to the *consiglio comunale,* or "town council." The ceiling's ornate coffers and elaborate friezes, featuring the coat of arms of the Republic of Florence, were executed by Benedetto and Giuliano da Maiano and assistants in 1472.

The Salone dei Cinquecento was built between 1495 and 1496 by Antonio da Sangallo, Simone del Pollaiuolo, and Francesco di Domenico. This large hall, or *salone,* was commissioned by Savonarola to house the 500, or *cinquecento,* members of the Republic he founded after the expulsion of the Medici. After Cosimo I brought the Medici back to the palazzo in 1540, the despot remodeled the hall in a manner that would exude absolute power. At the left end of the room stands the Tribuna d'Udienza (1542–1543) by Baccio Bandinelli, a raised platform, originally intended to hold the ducal throne. The rest of the area would have served as an audience chamber and occasional reception hall for such celebrations as the wedding of Francesco de' Medici to Jane of Austria. The walls and ceilings are sumptuously coffered with allegories and battle scenes by Vasari. The central coffer features a godlike Cosimo I. Before these pieces were executed, Michelangelo and da Vinci had been commissioned to work side by side on a cycle of frescoes that would have depicted the Battle of Cascina and the Battle of Anghiari by each artist respectively. Amidst much anticipation and hype, the masters never progressed beyond their preliminary cartoons, drafted along the *salone* walls. Nevertheless, the cartoons were heavily studied by Florentine artists up until their replacement by Vasari.

Among the sculptures currently present in the *salone* are *Florence Triumphing Over Pisa*, by Giambologna, and Michelangelo's *Genius of Victory*. This marble group of Genius slaying Might was intended for the tomb of Pope Julius II. It ended up being given to Cosimo I by Michelangelo's nephew.

Piazza della Signoria

➣ Whereas the space around Piazza del Duomo has diminished over time, the area that surrounds Piazza della Signoria has grown significantly. These patterns of growth reflect a fundamental shift in thought, separating the spiritual role of the Church from the civic and economic affairs of the state. During the Middle Ages, the piazza was comprised of a small square that stretched along the facade of the Palazzo Vecchio, known then as the Palazzo dei Priori, the seat of Florentine political power. Between 1560 and 1580, at the peak of the High Renaissance, the piazza extended its reach to the Arno River's edge when Giorgio Vasari included an adjacent *piazzale* in the design of the Uffizi. It was around this period that many

of the monumental statues that now give the piazza its dramatic appearance were installed. Among these are the *Equestrian Monument to Cosimo I de' Medici* (1594–1598) by Giambologna, and *Neptune Fountain* (1563–1575) by Bartolomeo Ammannati and assistants. The heavily ridiculed *Hercules and Cacus* was commissioned in 1534 by Duke Alessandro de' Medici as a symbol of dynastic power. Installed beside the statue of David, *Hercules and Cacus* was intended to counterbalance the Republican reputation of Michelangelo's dominant masterpiece. The original *David* (1501–1504), as opposed to the marble copy that currently resides in the piazza, was initially intended for the top of the Duomo. But after the fall of Medici rule and the rise of the Republic, the graceful statue of the triumphant David found a home in Florence's political center. Upon returning to power, the Medicis appropriated the *David* as a symbol of the diplomatic successes they achieved in fending off the brute force of larger, foreign militaries. The copies of Donatello's *Marzocco* and *Judith and Holofernes* are the piazza's oldest symbols of civic pride. The original *Marzocco,* now in the National Museum of Bargello, features a lion that symbolizes Florence. The gore of *Judith and Holofernes* (1482–1485) acted as a warning to foreign invaders and is now housed within the Palazzo Vecchio.

A curiosity is the profile of a man carved into one of the stones to the right of the entrance of the Palazzo Vecchio. It is believed to be Michelangelo.

PIAZZA DELLA SIGNORIA

It belongs only to Italy, and more particularly to Florence, to open Galleries in the streets for the study of the artist and the admiration of amateurs; and to expose in her public places and highways those treasures of sculpture, which would make the value of royal cabinets, or be enshrined in the imperial collections of other nations. Of this the Piazza del Gran Duca at Florence (once the Piazza Pubblica) [now Piazza della Signoria] is the most striking illustration.

Lady Sydney Morgan, *Italy*

Replica of Michelangelo's David, in Piazza della Signoria

Piazza Santa Croce

➤ During the Middle Ages and early Renaissance, this piazza was a leading venue for public events. These included sermons by Saint Bernardine of Siena, considered one of the greatest preachers of the Franciscan order.

Piazza Santa Croce was where games of *calcio fiorentino,* a form of soccer dating back as early as the 16th century, were usually held. On the left side of the piazza, opposite the facade of the church of Santa Croce, there is a roundel on the wall that is divided into four red and white squares. On the other side of the piazza, on the ground floor of the frescoed Palazzo dell'Antella, there is a marble disk dated February 10, 1565. These two objects were once used to mark the midpoint of the playing field.

Today, annual matches of *calcio fiorentino* are still held in the piazza, with players dressed in traditional period costume. In preparation for the event, a heavy layer of dirt is poured over the piazza's expansive center to form the field, while bleachers crowd against the antique palazzi, creating a makeshift stadium.

The Palazzo Serristori is the oldest of these, dating back to the 15th century. The 17th-century Palazzo dell'Antella displays an elegantly frescoed exterior. Decorative traits of this kind complement the colorful facade of the basilica of Santa

Croce, which stands at the piazza's east end. The basilica and its adjoining cloisters were probably the landmarks worst affected by the flood of 1966. After the water receded, mud deposits remained, measuring as high as nine feet (three meters) inside the basilica and 16 feet (five meters) in the adjoining cloisters.

Ponte Vecchio

➤ In 996, this bridge was already known as the Ponte Vecchio or "Old Bridge." It repeatedly collapsed, in 1117 and then again in 1333, and it was rebuilt for the last time in 1345 by Neri di Fioravante. Aside from the structural merits of Fioravante's three-arch design, a combination of location (it crosses the Arno at the river's most narrow point) and good fortune (in 1944, it was the only bridge along Florence's stretch of the Arno that the retreating German army didn't demolish) has allowed it to endure throughout time. After the bridge's reconstruction in 1345, shops began to line its edges. These consisted mostly of butchers and herbalists until Ferdinando I, grand duke of Florence, made it a hub for gold- and silversmiths.

At that time, the Ponte Vecchio had four imposing towers placed at its four corners and was the only fortified bridge in the city. In 1565 Giorgio Vasari began planning a passageway to allow Cosimo I to reach the Palazzo Pitti from the Palazzo Vecchio without stepping into the street. He decided that the most direct route involved breaking through the towers on the Ponte Vecchio, but he faced the objections of the Mannelli family, who owned the last remaining original tower on the bridge. Cosimo I therefore made the architect change his plans and that section of the Vasari Corridor was built around the tower instead of through it. Because of this, the tower remains intact today.

SANTA CROCE

Piazza Santa Croce; tel.: 055-244619/ 2466105; open: Mon.–Sat. 9:30 A.M.–5 P.M., Sun. and public holidays 1–5 P.M.; closed: Jan.1, Dec. 25–26; admission: €5 (includes entry to Museo dell' Opera di Santa Croce)

➤ This Gothic church was begun in 1295 under the direction of Arnolfo di Cambio and was finally finished almost a century later. The facade and bell tower are 19th-century neo-Gothic additions, flanked by a monument to Dante from the same period.

Home to the Franciscan order, the basilica's lofty interior was designed to accommodate the great number of fervent followers who regularly gathered here for mass. Up until 1566, a large partition bisected the nave, separating the monks from the laypeople. The partition was removed in accordance with measures implemented by Cosimo I and directed at the Franciscans during the Counter-Reformation. Lining the aisles of the basilica, between the altars, are tombs belonging to many of Florence's greatest minds. For this reason, Santa Croce is often referred to as the "Florentine Pantheon." Starting from the door and proceeding down the right aisle are the tomb of Michelangelo, a memorial to Dante Alighieri (1829), a memorial to 18th-century author Vittorio Alfieri, and the tomb of Niccolò Machiavelli (1787), featuring the famous epitaph: TANTO NOMINI NULLUM PER ELOGIUM ("No praise can be high enough for so great a name"). A *pietra serena* group of the Annunciation by Donatello follows directly after. Illuminating the altars that rest in between each of these monuments are beautiful stained-glass windows from the 14th and 15th centuries.

Located across the right transept, adjacent to the main chapel, are the Bardi Chapel and the Peruzzi Chapel, respectively. Each of these contains frescoes executed by Giotto between 1320 and 1325. While now considerably diminished by inadequate preservation techniques, the series once demonstrated the virtuosity of a master working at the height of his artistic powers. The frescoes in the Bardi Chapel depict the Stories of Saint Francis; those in the Peruzzi

Ponte Vecchio and the Arno

Santa Croce

Chapel depict the Stories of Saint John the Evangelist (right wall) and the Stories of Saint John the Baptist (left wall).

Proceeding back up the left aisle, at the foot of the *Pietà* by Angiolo Bronzino, is the tombstone of sculptor and architect Lorenzo Ghiberti and his son Vittorio. Between the second and third altars is the 18th-century tomb of Galileo and his pupil Vincenzo Viviani.

SANTA CROCE

At the end of this very ancient square, stands the Church of la Santa Croce, the Westminster Abbey of Tuscany; or as the natives proudly call it—*"Il Pantheon di Firenze"* . . . The Santa Croce is contemporary with the Duomo. What ages of gigantic design were the thirteenth, fourteenth, and fifteenth centuries in Italy. What vigour and freshness in the conceptions of that national genius, which sprang forth, at the call of freedom, from the torpidity engendered by a barbarous despotism, like light from chaos.

Lady Sidney Morgan, *Italy*

Walking Tour 1:

Temples and Tabernacles: Sant'Ambrogio, a Traditional Neighborhood with "Foreign" Roots

By Carla Rossi

Stumbling upon Florence's church of Sant'Ambrogio and the neighborhood surrounding it is a pleasant surprise after battling the crowds around the Duomo and the Uffizi. Although it is actually only a 15-minute walk from the central Duomo, Sant'Ambrogio could just as easily be in another world. In fact, it is one of just a handful of areas that can still be called truly Florentine, even though it is named after a holy foreigner: the Milanese bishop, Saint Ambrose.

A morning is enough to explore this small neighborhood tucked inside the larger area of Santa Croce. Taking a detour on foot from Piazza del Duomo, it is a pleasant walk down narrow streets closed to traffic. Borgo degli Albizi, a small street behind the Duomo off Via del Proconsolo, can be followed west to Piazza Salvemini. There the street turns into Via Pietrapiana and the neighborhood begins. After all the cars and scooters, it is a relief to find that the only vehicles allowed to pass here are small electric buses, which can also be used to get to Sant'Ambrogio. The A bus, which heads directly into the middle of Sant'Ambrogio, can be taken at Santa Maria Novella Station.

Almost immediately, on the right side of the street, is Piazza dei Ciompi, named after a dyers' and wool-workers' revolt (the *ciompi* were "wool-workers") in 1378. The **Loggia del Pesce** dominates this side of the piazza. Originally located in Piazza della Repubblica, it was designed by Giorgio Vasari and was erected in 1567. Vendors of fish (*pesce,* in Italian) once crowded under its arches. The structure was moved to its present location in the early 1900s after the old central market was torn down. It is made up of 18 Doric columns and terra-cotta representations of colorful fish.

Behind the loggia is the antique market, which looks more like a flea market. There are various stands that sell all kinds of things, from cheap to pricey, and it is worth a quick look around. On the last Sunday of every month, when the market is open all day, it expands into the streets, almost doubling in size. (On weekdays the market closes for lunch from 1–4 P.M., and on Saturdays it closes for good at 1 P.M.)

Moving on along Via Pietrapiana, the next stop is the church and piazza of Sant'Ambrogio—the heart of the neighborhood. The piazza, though not the most spectacular in Florence, has its gems. An upward glance at the corner of Via dei Macci reveals the **Tabernacolo di Sant'Ambrogio**. It consists of a beautiful glazed terra-cotta by Giovanni della Robbia (1525). Opposite the church is the Oratorio dell'Agnolo, a narrow and unusual structure from the 15th century wedged between Via di Mezzo and Via dei Pilastri.

The church of **Sant'Ambrogio**, which dates from sometime between the 5th and 9th centuries, is one of the oldest in Florence. The facade, renovated most recently in 1880, is unimpressive, but inside there are several works well worth seeing.

OUR PICK

Legend has it that the church was built in honor of a visit by then-Bishop Ambrose of Milan. Historians have varying theories on when the church was constructed. The most probable says it was built in 400 by Bishop Zanobi of Florence, a close friend of Ambrose. He apparently decided to erect it where Ambrose resided during his visit. In this period, Zanobi began a campaign called "rapid Christianization," pushing for several church construction projects in order to convert the still-numerous pagans. A second hypothesis is that the church was built by Benedictine monks in the 800s. Whatever its origins, the structure underwent drastic renovations in the 1200s and to this day maintains a Gothic style, best characterized by the windows in the nave.

Upon entering the church, to the right is the fresco of the enthroned Madonna with Saints Bartholomew and John, attributed to Andrea Orcagna. The curious arches along the wall were added by a Renaissance architect who, in the process, did not hesitate to destroy several works that would have been of great historical value today. At the time the church also housed the

Loggia del Pesce

The Synagogue of Florence

Sant'Anna 'Metterza' by Masaccio and Masolino, *The Crowning of the Virgin Mary* by Filippino Lippi, and Botticelli's *Pala della Convertite*, all works now in the Galleria degli Uffizi.

In 1700 Sant'Ambrogio underwent further renovations and the architect Foggini added a quite intriguing baroque apse that houses an altar inlaid with semiprecious stones. To the left of the main altar is the Cappella del Miracolo (Chapel of the Miracle). This was built in 1481–1483 to host a vial holding blood found in 1230 in the bottom of a goblet that an elderly priest had forgotten to clean the night before. This miracle turned the church into a destination for religious pilgrims for centuries afterward. The tabernacle is by Mino da Fiesole, whose remains are also kept in the church. The candelabras are by one of the della Robbias, and the frescoes commemorating the miraculous event are the work of Cosimo Rosselli. In the course of the most recent restorations of the church, the rough drafts of these frescoes were mounted on the wall just in front of the chapel. They are of interest because in these sketches Rosselli drew all of the figures nude, possibly to help himself remember the forms that the clothes would cover.

Outside of the church to the left is one of the best stands in the city for tripe, a Florentine specialty, while just a block down Via dei Macci is a cluster of some of the best restaurants in Florence as well as the Mercato Sant'Ambrogio, the meat and produce market, where even the pickiest palates will find something delightful to taste (open: Mon.–Sat. 7 A.M.–2 P.M.).

In the opposite direction from the market on Via Farini, behind huge, gray iron gates, is the **Synagogue** of Florence. Built following the design of three architects, Treves, Falcini, and Micheli, its Moorish design and exotic gardens are a stark contrast to the generally severe Florentine style. The temple was inspired by Constantinople's Byzantine church Hagia Sophia, and the walls and ceilings are completely covered in arabesques. The mosaics and frescoes inside are by Giovanni Panti, and the arabesque decorations in the apse are by Giacomo del Medico. Just before the exit of the temple, a staircase to the right leads up to the museum. Built to tell the history of the Jewish community in Florence, it offers a collection of objects from daily and religious life, including marriage contracts, instruments used for circumcision, and, of particular value and importance, a 17th-century *paròkhet,* used to cover the ark holding the Torah.

On the right after leaving the synagogue is Piazza d'Azeglio, the last piazza in the neighborhood. Huge plane trees offer the only green space in the area. A small carousel attracts local children, and a number of houses lining the piazza name characters of varying fame who once sojourned there. It is the perfect place to catch one's breath before leaving Sant'Ambrogio and returning to the crowded center around the Duomo.

FURTHER INFORMATION

Loggia del Pesce
Piazza dei Ciompi

Sant'Ambrogio
Piazza Sant'Ambrogio, corner of Borgo la Croce; tel.: 055-240104; open: daily 7:30 A.M.–noon, 4–7:30 P.M.

Synagogue
Via Luigi Carlo Farini, 4; tel.: 055-245252; open: Sun.–Thurs. 10 A.M.–3 P.M., Fri. 10 A.M.–2 P.M. (Nov.–Feb.), Sun.–Thurs. 10 A.M.–5 P.M., Fri 10 A.M.–2 P.M. (Mar.–May, Sept.–Oct.), Sun.–Thurs. 10 A.M.–6 P.M., Fri. 10 A.M.–2 P.M. (Jun.–Aug.); closed: Sat.; admission: €4.

Tabernacolo di Sant'Ambrogio
(Tabernacle of Saint Ambrose)
Piazza Sant'Ambrogio, corner of Via dei Macci

FOCUS: Cimitero degli Inglesi

Piazzale Donatello; tel.: 055-582608; open: Mon. 9 A.M.–noon, Tues.–Fri. 4–6 P.M. (summer), 2–5 P.M. (winter); closed: Sat.–Sun.

By Sara Carobbi

The Cimitero degli Inglesi, or English Cemetery, also known as the Protestant Cemetery, was opened in 1828 as a burial ground for protestants, mostly from Great Britain. It stood next to the destroyed Porta Pinti on a piece of land granted by the Grand Duke Leopold the year before. However, as the property was bought by the Swiss, the English community decided to build a new graveyard, which led to the opening of the Cimitero degli Allori in 1878 and the closure of the original burial site.

The cemetery walls were demolished in 1865 with the implementation of the Poggi project, a plan meant to create larger avenues as Florence had become the capital of the newly reunified Italy. The cemetery was encircled with new avenues and therefore isolated from the surrounding traffic. Thus it became a romantic isle where many artists found inspiration. As a consequence, the neighborhood around it, including the aptly named Via degli Artisti, or Artists Street, became home to many ateliers.

A number of famous people were buried in the Cimitero degli Inglesi between 1840 and 1865. Amongst them, the poet Elizabeth Barrett Browning, whose grave, raised on six columns and situated on the left-hand side of the central path, was designed by Robert Browning, sculpted by Lord Leighton, and finished by Luigi Giovannozzi. The Pre-Raphaelite tomb located behind Browning's grave is that of Holman Hunt's wife Fanny, who was 23 when she died in

Fiesole. Other well-known people buried here include Isa Blagden, Arthur Hugh Clough, Walter Savage Landor, Frances Trollope, Giovanni Pietro Vieusseux, founder of the literary cabinet Gabinetto Scientifico Letterario, the preacher Theodore Parker, and the young daughter of Andrew Boeklin, whose fantastic vision of the famous painting *L'Isola dei morti* was, in fact, inspired by the cemetery.

Cimitero degli Inglesi

Walking Tour 2:

Galileo Meets Michelangelo in a Renaissance Neighborhood

By Sarah Rose Leiwant

The neighborhood of Santa Croce has always been a sacred meeting place. Long before the piazza of the same name was laid out in stone, crowds gathered in the square to hear Franciscan preachers deliver oratories dedicated to the Holy Cross. In the 16th century, residents would assemble to play a medieval form of soccer there, known as *calcio fiorentino*.

But these days, Piazza Santa Croce is best known for the church dominating the square, the cafés and restaurants around its perimeter, and the charming Renaissance homes in the quieter alleyways.

A tour of its palaces and museums will also illuminate Florence's role as a center of science, and will turn up evidence of some of the wealthiest families, including Michelangelo's, who made their homes here.

In 1657, Florence founded the world's first scientific institution, the Accademia del Cimento (Academy for Experimentation), in memory of Galileo. It has taken on a new life as a large part of the **Museo di Storia della Scienza**, located in Piazza de' Giudici on the bank of the Arno River.

The building, Palazzo Castellani, houses a small but interesting collection of scientific instruments that reflect Florence's contributions to the field during the Medici rule. A large portion of the collection was owned by the Medici grand dukes, although the museum, originally called the Museo delle Scienze Fisiche e Naturali (Museum of Physics and Natural Sciences), was opened in 1775 by Grand Duke Pietro Leopoldo of Lorraine, the dynasty that succeeded the Medicis.

Parts of the museum pay tribute to the Pisa-born scientist Galileo Galilei (1564–1642). The exhibits include his telescopes and the lens he used to discover the four largest moons of Jupiter in 1610. Large-scale reconstructions of his experiments with motion, velocity, weight, and acceleration are sometimes demonstrated by the attendants.

In 1632, after teaching at universities in Pisa and Padua, Galileo published a defense of the Copernican theory of astronomy. He was condemned to death by the Inquisition in 1633 for believing that the Earth was not the center of the universe. His life was spared, however, with the help of Grand Duke Ferdinando, and he lived as a virtual prisoner in his home in Florence until his death nine years later. (The condemnation of 1633 was canceled by Pope John Paul II in 1992.)

Some of the Accademia del Cimento's inventions, including early thermometers, barometers, and hygrometers, are on display. The ground floor houses the library of the Istituto di Storia della Scienza. It holds 80,000 volumes, many of which belonged to the Medici and Lorraine grand dukes.

On the second floor are mathematical instruments from 16th- and 17th-century Florence, including huge globes used to illustrate the motion of the planets and stars. There are also astrolabes, sundials, compasses, 18th- and 19th-century microscopes, and the nautical instruments invented by Sir Robert Dudley, an Elizabethan marine engineer employed by the Medici dukes to build a harbor at Livorno. Finally, there is Lopo Homem's map of the world,

Sfera armillare (armillary sphere) at the Museo di Storia della Scienza

dating from the mid-16th century. Also, be sure to peek in at the interesting array of clocks on the second floor.

Continue west along the Arno, to Piazza Mentana, and from there take a left on Via della Mosca, which eventually will lead to Piazza San Remigio. As early as the 9th century, this piazza became a pit stop for French pilgrims en route to Rome. The church of **San Remigio** was built on this site in the 11th century, but the present church dates from the 13th century. The exterior is made of *pietra forte,* and the interior is a restored Gothic hall. The cross vaulting is decorated with worn 14th-century roundels of saints.

A follower of Giotto's master, Cimabue, known as the Master of San Remigio, painted the beautiful 13th-century panel of the Madonna and child in the chapel to the right of the sanctuary. The opposite chapel, to the left of the sanctuary, has a 1591 painting of the Immaculate Conception by the Florentine artist Jacopo Chimenti, known as Empoli. Adjacent to this chapel is a neo-Renaissance cornice by Luigi Camrai-Digny that holds a wood panel called *San Remigio Baptizes Clodeveo.* Executed in 1821, the panel is among the finer examples of works by the master Tuscan Romantic painter Giuseppe Bezzuoli.

In a room below the bell tower, or campanile (admission upon request), there are monochromatic frescoes depicting hunting scenes.

Walk back to the beginning of the piazza and take a left on Via dei Neri. At the end of this street, turn right onto Via de' Benci, which will lead you to the **Museo della Fondazione H. P. Horne.**

OUR PICK

The Palazzo Alberti-Corsi, which houses the museum, is a wonderful example of a Renaissance *palazzetto* (small town house) and was constructed in the late 15th century. Built for the Alberti family in 1489, the town house was rebuilt upon its acquisition by the Corsi clan. They, in turn, commissioned Simone del Pollaiuolo, better known as Cronaca, to carry out the renovations. In collaboration with Andrea Sansovino and the shop of Giuliano da Sangallo, Cronaca completed the project, which contributed the small, harmonious courtyard as its finishing touch.

In 1917, the building was left to the state by the English architect and art historian Herbert Percy Horne (1864–1916), who also donated his small but charming collection of paintings, sculptures, and decorative arts, mostly dating from the 14th to 16th centuries.

Horne first visited Florence in 1904 and bought the Palazzo Corsi seven years later. He carefully restored every detail (down to the doors and shutters) so that it would look the same as it had when it was first built; he lived on the top floor for the last few months of his life.

The arrangement of the rooms is typical of Renaissance residences, with the work and storage areas at the ground level and the apartments above. The Alberti family had made their money from the flourishing cloth trade in Florence at that time and put their wool-dyeing vats in the basement and their drying racks in the courtyard. The kitchen was built on the top floor to prevent fumes from spreading through the whole house; it now contains Horne's collection of Renaissance cooking utensils.

Many of the charmingly displayed contents of the house had to be restored after the flood of the Arno in 1966 and several of the museum's 17th- and 18th-century drawings have been transferred to the Uffizi Gallery,

Fondazione Horne

but there are still a few gems in the house: Giotto's 13th-century polyptych of Saint Stephen; a Madonna by Bernardo Daddi (c. 1312–1348); a Madonna and child attributed to Simone Martini (1283–1344); an altarpiece depicting the stories of Saint Julian by Masaccio; a triptych of Saints Margaret, John Gualberto, and Catherine of Alexandria; a Holy Family by Domenico Beccafumi; and a relief of the Madonna and child by Jacopo Sansovino. There are also wonderful pieces of 15th-century furniture and majolica (brightly painted pottery).

Across Via de' Benci from the museum is the **Palazzo Busini-Bardi**. Attributed to Brunelleschi by Vasari, the palazzo was erected sometime around the year 1430.

Since 1576, the palazzo has housed the Camerata de' Bardi. Founded in part through the patronage of humanist, mathematician, poet, composer, and Greek scholar Count Giovanni Bardi of Venice, this academy of music and poetry redefined the foundations of vocal music, giving birth to such operatic conventions as the bel canto and the melodrama. Vincenzo Galilei, father of Galileo and a composer of madrigals, also took part in the Camerata de' Bardi, as did poet Ottavio Rinuccini and the composer and singer Giulio Caccini.

Continuing northwest on Via de' Benci, you will pass the **Torre degli Alberti**, on the corner of Via de' Benci and Borgo Santa Croce. This stone tower, built in 1200, now houses a pizzeria. In warm weather you can sit outside and have a coffee and brioche on the small 15th-century loggia.

Across Via Verdi from Piazza Santa Croce (which Via de' Benci turns into at the piazza) extends Via Torta, "crooked street." This canyonlike passage winds along a path that still conforms to the perimeter of what was once a Roman amphitheater, known as Il Parlascio. Built between A.D. 124 and 130 with a seating capacity of 20,000, the amphitheater has since been replaced by a procession of mansions. Their rounded facades line the left side of Via Torta, continuing down Via Bentaccordi and terminating in Piazza Peruzzi. The last mansion in line, at No. 3, is the 13th-century **Palazzo Peruzzi**, a collection of buildings that extends as far as the Borgo de' Greci. Aside from being the primary residence of one of Florence's most powerful banking families from its construction in the 13th century up until its sale to the Bourbon del Monte in 1772, this complex is distinguished by the unique way it conforms to the curvature of Via Bentaccordi as it flows into Piazza de' Peruzzi. This is due to the fact that the foundations of these buildings, like the buildings of Via Torta, are sitting over the perimeter of the ancient Roman amphitheater. On the left, at No. 12, is the Palazzo di Ubaldino Peruzzi, reconstructed in the mid-17th century and attributed to Gherardo Silvani. The most important structure is known as the Bourbon del Monte and was built at the end of the 13th century. The main entrance is at No. 3 Borgo de' Greci. The inner courtyard survives as a shadow of its former self; its original structure can be discerned in the quadrangular pilasters in *pietra forte* and the grand arcade on the second level. Note the numerous sightings of the family's coat of arms, with six pears (Peruzzi means "little pears"). The enduring presence of the Peruzzi coat of arms on nearly every mansion in the piazza testifies to the extent to which the family nearly monopolized the area, using the public square as their own courtyard.

Follow Via Verdi to Via Ghibellina and turn right; after a few minutes you will reach **Casa Buonarroti**, which is both the former house of Michelangelo (whose last name was Buonarroti) and a museum dedicated to his works. Michelangelo bought this group of three houses as an investment in 1508 but lived here only briefly. His nephew Leonardo united the houses into one building and later descendants added what they could to the sizable collection of works there. In 1858, the last member of this branch of the Buonarrotis turned the house into a museum and a tribute to the family.

As you wander around the second floor you will see small rooms beautifully decorated by Michelangelo the Younger, the master's grand-nephew.

They constitute one of the most esteemed examples of 17th-century Florentine style. His tiny wooden study, nestled into the Stanza della Notte e del Dì (Room of Night and Day), demonstrates an ingenious use of space. There are also portraits of Michelangelo and some of his works, including his earliest known sculpture, the *Madonna della Scala*; a marble rectangular relief carved in 1490–1492; a dramatic relief, the *Battle of the Centaurs*; and a wooden model of his never-used design for San Lorenzo.

Downstairs there is a collection of Etruscan and Roman works assembled by Michelangelo the Younger, beautiful pottery and dishes, as well as other paintings by Michelangelo.

FURTHER INFORMATION

Casa Buonarroti (Buonarroti's House)

Via Ghibellina, 70; tel.: 055-241752; website: www.casabuonarroti.it; open: Mon.–Sun. 9:30 A.M.–2 P.M.; closed: Tues, Jan.1, Easter, Apr. 25, Aug. 15, Dec. 25; admission: €5

Museo di Storia della Scienza (Museum of the History of Science)

Piazza de' Giudici, 1; tel.: 055-265311; website: www.imss.fi.it; open: Mon., Wed., Thurs., Fri. 9:30 A.M.–5 P.M., Tues. and Sat. 9:30 A.M.–1 P.M. (June 1–Sept. 30), Mon., Wed., Thurs., Fri., Sat. 9:30 A.M.–5 P.M., Tues. 9:30 A.M.–1 P.M. (Oct. 1–May 31); closed: Sun. and public holidays; admission: €6.50

Museo della Fondazione H. P. Horne

Via de' Benci, 6; tel.: 055-244661; open: Mon.–Sat. 9 A.M.–1 P.M.; closed: Sun. and public holidays; admission: €5.

Palazzo Busini-Bardi

Via de' Benci, 5; closed to the public.

Palazzo Peruzzi

Borgo de' Greci, 3; closed to the public.

San Remigio

Piazza San Remigio; tel.: 055-284789; open: daily 9–11 A.M., 3:30 P.M.–6:30 P.M.

Torre degli Alberti

Via de' Benci, 1r, corner of Via de' Benci and Borgo Santa Croce

FOCUS: Museo dei Ragazzi

Piazza della Signoria, in the Palazzo Vecchio; tel.: 055-2768224; open: tours daily 9:30 A.M.–noon, call ahead for reservations; admission: cost of tour will vary depending on the itinerary.

By Elisa Cecchi

The Palazzo Vecchio hosts the Museo dei Ragazzi, the first children's museum ever created inside one of Italy's historic landmarks. It consists of five separate areas, each with a different theme.

Each thematic area is a small world within itself, with a different atmosphere and special furnishings. Children are always accompanied by entertainers, all recent graduates trained for their task, who tailor activities to each particular age group.

From the celebrated Geographical Map Room, children take a secret passage to an area where they can learn about the architecture of the palace by testing their own building skills on models of the Palazzo Vecchio and other historic Italian buildings.

They can then clamber along a steep and narrow stairway within another secret passage to reach the "Costumes and Body" area, where they can put on historic costumes in a replica of a theater. Professional actors playing the role of Cosimo and his wife Eleonora of Toledo answer questions about etiquette, fashion, and other matters of importance to children who wish to be heard as well as seen.

On the ground floor, two laboratories—one dedicated to Galileo's experiments, called "The Spell of Lenses," and the other, "Horror Vacui?," based on the findings of the physicist Toricelli on air pressure—are geared toward little scientists in the making.

Bia and Garcia's Playroom, named for two of Cosimo de' Medici's children, is a room especially conceived for preschoolers, who can amuse themselves with the same games their Renaissance counterparts played.

Children in period costumes

Visitors are also allowed to access the roof of the hall, the Salone de Cinquecento, where they can behold the complicated system Vasari devised to prevent the heavy structure from caving in.

The discovery of the two small and precious rooms where Cosimo and his son Francesco kept the palace's treasures is a treasure in itself, while the private quarters of the grand duke offer a view of what lay behind the public facade of the Medicis. Finally, the "Stairs of the Duke of Athens" is a secret passageway built in 1342 so that the duke would be able to secretly leave the palace if need be.

Walking Tour 3:
Up and Down Via Proconsolo

By Stacy Meichtry

At the close of the 16th century, mannerist architect Bernardo Buontalenti started work on what might have been one of his most fantastic creations had he been given the chance to realize it. But before the good architect could go for it, his patron Alessandro Strozzi went broke.

The final result is Florence's **Palazzo Nonfinito**, or Unfinished Palace, a bizarre mix of different architectural periods and styles. The lower half of the facade is Buontalenti's own, distinguished by the artist's use of zoomorphic motifs to mold the facade's doors and windows. Pediments spread wings and cornices fishtail inside a cagelike wall of monotonous brick and mortar. The upper half was executed after the intervention of Alessandro's older brother, who replaced the untamed Buontalenti with a more polite, better behaved architect. In 1597 G. B. Caccini took over and imposed his rarefied neoclassicism on the palazzo facade. By this time, the mansion was already being referred to as the Palazzo Nonfinito, and after Caccini finished making his stately reforms, the nickname stuck.

Located at No. 12 Via del Proconsolo, the mansion currently houses the Museo Nazionale di Antropologia ed Etnologia (see pg. 117). The museum took its seat in the Palazzo Nonfinito in 1869, three years into Italy's nationhood, and has since exhibited a collection of wares and clothes drawn from indigenous cultures around the world.

At No. 10 Via del Proconsolo is the **Palazzo Pazzi**. Noted for its remarkable facade, where the heavily rusticated stones on the ground floor contrast with the smooth white plaster and the elegant mullioned windows of the upper floors, this palazzo is considered a masterpiece of early Renaissance architecture. Its highly refined courtyard features the same mullioned windows, which look down upon a delicate arcade of columns with capitals bearing the Pazzi heraldic crest: a dolphin. Built by Giuliano da Maiano between 1458 and 1469, the mansion was the home and headquarters of the wealthy Pazzi family, whose influence around Florence was second only to that of the Medici. In fact, the mansion is also known as "La Congiura," "The Conspiracy," for the infamous plot that the clan organized against the Medici on Easter Sunday of 1478, in an attempt to usurp their dominant rivals. The scheme ultimately failed, leaving Jacopo Pazzi, the family patriarch, to the mercy of the mob, who promptly stormed the mansion and lynched its owner.

Down the street toward the Arno River is the trapezoidal Piazza San Firenze, home of the baroque church of the same name. Across from the church, the demure facade of the **Palazzo Gondi** rises in rows of rough,

Palazzo Gondi

interlocking stones, which gradually soften to achieve a polished look toward the top. For this characteristic, in particular, the Palazzo Gondi has held a place among the city's most distinguished homes since its conception by Giuliano da Sangallo in 1490. And yet, for nearly the first 400 years of the palazzo's existence, it too was left unfinished. Not until 1874 did the Gondi family find a suitable replacement for Giuliano. Giuseppe Poggi, Florence's prolific, post-Unification builder, was given the commission and, to his credit, did a faithful job of filling in the blanks left by Giuliano da Sangallo. These amendments include the addition of a seventh vertical row of windows to widen the mansion's profile and the creation of a third door to balance the addition.

Cautious homeowners that they were, the Gondi family have managed to retain possession of their namesake mansion to the present day. For this very reason, the Palazzo Gondi is not open to the public. But a flower shop, which rents space in the facade's central door, offers a generous view of the palazzo's refined courtyard, which it currently uses as a showroom. Thus, da Sangallo's carefully proportioned *cortile* now overflows with vegetation. Greenery sprouts in bushels around the gray *pietra serena* fountain; cactus plants stand guard under the white, *intonaco* portico; and flamboyant palms brush against Corinthian columns.

In between the Palazzo Gondi and the Palazzo Nonfinito, just past the point where Via Dante Alighieri runs into Via del Proconsolo, rests one of Florence's first churches, the **Badia Fiorentina**. Founded in the year 978 by Countess Willa, mother of Marquis Ugo of Tuscany, the Badia records many of the city's most fundamental changes over the course of its own 500-year metamorphosis. Dedicated to the Benedictine order of monks upon its founding, the church later was incorporated into the city's medieval walls for use as a military fort. Its distinct cone-shaped bell tower, meanwhile, was once

OUR PICK

the official town clock, tolling on the hour, every hour. Still among the highest landmarks on the Florentine skyline, the noble campanile has recently begun to tilt precariously close to total collapse. To correct its geriatric posture, the tower must temporarily rely upon steel scaffolding for support while its foundations undergo reinforcement.

The complex is best experienced from the inside out. Start with Filippino Lippi's oil-on-panel masterpiece, *The Apparition of the Madonna to Saint Bernard,* to the immediate left upon entering the nave; then proceed directly to Vasari's *Assumption* on the main altar. The elaborate marble tomb, beneath the main altar, was sculpted by Mino da Fiesole between 1461 and 1481 for the remains of Marquis Ugo of Tuscany. The legendary marquis, who died in 1001 after helping to found the *comune* of Florence, was given a hero's remembrance by Mino's magnificent monument, which provides a startling depiction of the dearly departed carved into the sarcophagus lid. Renovations by Arnolfo di Cambio in the 13th century and Matteo Segaloni during the baroque period radically altered the proportions, layout, and style of the church, yet the march toward modernity has not trampled the memory of the marquis. His legacy is inexhaustibly preserved in the red and white heraldic crests that inhabit nearly every corner of the Badia's lofty interior.

The Badia's cloister, located behind the presbytery, is perhaps the city's most picturesque. Known as the **Chiostro degli Aranci**, or Cloister of the Oranges, for the fruit tree idyllically planted at its center, the courtyard is bordered by a double-decker arcade on all four sides. The frescoed lunettes on the upper tier were probably executed between 1436 and 1439 by the anonymous Master of the Cloister of the Oranges. They appropriately depict stories of the animated life and times of Saint Benedict. The scene in which the saint

Chiostro degli Aranci

unequivocally throws himself into a ravine so as not to give into the temptation to sin, however, is the work of a young Agnolo Bronzino. Before leaving the Badia, duck into the Cappella Pandolfini. This simple cubical, crowned by a hemispherical dome, was once a church dedicated to Saint Stephen, where Giovanni Boccaccio, author of the *The Decameron,* gave his first public reading of Dante's *The Divine Comedy.*

Walking west on Via Dante is the tiny Piazza San Martino, dominated by the medieval building known as the **Torre della Castagna**, or "Chestnut Tower." The Priori delle Arti, or Council of the Guilds, began gathering in this elegant edifice as early as 1282 to deliberate some of the most controversial cases. With their influence quickly expanding past *comune* borders, the *Priori* would eventually move their conferences to the more prominent Palazzo Vecchio. The Torre della Castagna, therefore, provides a portrait of the Florentine oligarchy in its nascent period. Locking themselves within the tower for days on end so as not to have their decisions influenced by outsiders, the members used to vote by casting chestnuts into a small bag, hence the name of the tower.

Further Information

Badia Fiorentina
Via del Proconsolo, at Via Dante Alighiri; tel. 055-264402; open: daily 7 A.M.–7 P.M.; closed: Mon.

Chiostro degli Aranci (Cloister of the Oranges)
Via del Proconsolo, at Via Dante Alighieri, in the Badia Fiorentina; open: Mon. 3 P.M.–6 P.M.

Palazzo Pazzi
Via del Proconsolo, 10, at the corner of Borgo degli Albizi

Torre della Castagna
Piazza San Martino, 1, at the corner of Via Dante Alighieri

Palazzo Gondi
Piazza San Firenze, 2; closed to the public.

Palazzo Nonfinito
Via del Proconsolo, 12; tel. 055-2396449 (National Museum of Anthropology and Ethnology); open: daily 9 A.M.–1 P.M.; admission: €4

Piazza San Martino, off Via Dante Alghieri; tel.: 055-281259; open: Mon.–Sat. 10 A.M.–noon, 3–5 P.M.; closed: Sun.

By Stacy Meichtry

The Oratorio di San Martino Buonomini, a *chiesetta,* or "little church," that inhabits the first floor of an otherwise nondescript medieval dwelling along Via Dante, is identifiable by the lunette above its doorway.

It depicts Saint Martin (San Martino del Vescovo), the patron saint of the 15th-century congregation, whose anonymous members, or "good men," famously offered assistance to impoverished citizens victimized by the ongoing factional wars that plagued Florence. Founded in 1441 by Antonio Pierozzi, prior of the Dominican order at San Marco, future archbishop of Florence, and current saint, the congregation's mission was to raise alms for the needy while maintaining absolute secrecy. More than 500 years later, the group still operates out of this humble setting, providing charitable care to Florence's "poor and ashamed."

The frescoes that circumscribe the oratory's closet-size interior are attributed to Domenico Ghirlandaio and his assistants Filippino Lippi, Pietro di Cosimo, and Lorenzo di Credi. The cycle on the right wall depicts the good men practicing their charitable works—administering alms and assisting birth. The cycle on the left wall depicts the works of the Misericordia, another charitable institution.

The frescoes over the altar depict the life of Saint Martin. In the most prominent of these, the warlike saint, sword in hand, slashes a slice from his disproportionately long cloak to clothe a naked beggar.

The polychrome wooden bust on the altar provides an emaciated, thin-lipped portrait of founder Antonio Pierozzi. It is carved by the early Renaissance master Andrea Verrocchio, whose penchant for frighteningly realistic portraits earned him a place among the pantheon of great Florentine sculptors.

Other Points of Interest

Biblioteca Nazionale Centrale (National Central Library)

Piazza dei Cavalleggeri, 1; tel.: 055-249191; website: www.bncf.firenze.sbn.it; open: Mon.– Fri. 8:15 A.M.–7 P.M., Sat. 8:15 A.M.–1.30 P.M.; closed: Sun; admission: free

➤ Prominently situated in Piazza dei Cavalleggeri is the National Central Library of Florence with its prominent facade highlighted by twin bell towers. Though built between 1911 and 1935, the origins of the library date back to 1714 when Antonio Magliabechi, a prominent Florentine, donated in his will over 30,000 books in order to create the city's first public library. As the collection grew, the library moved to various locations, including the Uffizi, before a modern structure was selected over a site that once housed army barracks. After 1885, it became the official central depository where one could find a copy of any book published in Italy. The present site suffered damages during the great flood in November 1966, but thanks to the efforts of hundreds of volunteers most of its contents were rescued intact.

The library contains many rare and unique works of historical and artistic value including an early edition of Dante's *The Divine Comedy* with engravings attributed to Botticelli and several signed works by Galileo and Machiavelli, among others.

Complesso di San Firenze

Piazza di San Firenze

➤ Widely considered the finest example of baroque architecture in Florence, the facade of the San Firenze complex unifies the church of San Filippo Neri (through the left portal), an oratory (through the right portal), and a corridor leading into a splendid courtyard (center portal). It is a single, sweeping composition of angelic statues, heavy pediments, and monumental portals, all carved in sun-baked *pietra forte*. The complex inherits its name from the diminutive church of San Fiorenzo that, since 1645, had been destined for demolition in order to make room for a grandiose project designed by Pietro da Cortona under the commission of Giuliano de' Serragli. But the church of San Fiorenzo remained. The grandiosity of Pietro's design exceeded the budget of the commission, thus leaving the project unfinished. In 1668, Pier Francesco Silvani finished what Pietro began with the church of San Filippo Neri: a smaller building located to the immediate right of San Fiorenzo. In 1715, Ferdinando Ruggieri gave the newer church

Tribunal of the Complesso di San Firenze

a stylish baroque facade that not only widened the disparity between the two "twin" churches, but also anticipated the complex's present facade. In 1772, San Fiorenzo was finally demolished and an oratory of symmetrical size and proportion was built in its place, complete with a facade that matched that of San Filippo Neri. Soon after, the two churches were adjoined by monastic cells and corridors, thus giving it the final appearance of a unified "palazzo-convento."

Convento di Santa Maria di Candeli (Convent of Santa Maria di Candeli)
Via dei Pilastri, 54; closed to the public.

➤ Currently occupied by the offices of the carabinieri, the Italian police force, this fortified convent also houses in its refectory a cycle of frescoes attributed to High Renaissance painter Franciabigio. This cycle consists of an uncharacteristically serene *Last Supper* (1511–1516) surmounted by a lunette depicting the *Annunciation* (1514). The influence of Leonardo da Vinci is especially felt in the lunette, where the archangel Gabriel addresses the Virgin with the same imperial gesture seen in Leonardo's oil-panel version (now in the Uffizi). The monochromatic tablet on the adjacent wall was discovered underneath the *Annunciation* fresco. Representing the Nativity, the work is attributed to Franciabigio even though the only certain contribution of his is the monumental figure of Saint Joseph.

Lapide del Giubileo 1300 (Memorial Stone of the Jubilee of 1300)
Via Giovanni da Verrazzano, between Via Ghibellina and Piazza Santa Croce

➤ The year 1300 was a Jubilee year, and many pilgrims made a trip to Rome to receive the plenary indulgence that would absolve them of their sins. In the middle of Via Giovanni da Verrazzano there is a stone tablet that marks that year. It is written almost entirely in Latin except for the last words, which are in Italian. They say "*E andovvi Ugolino cho la moglie*" ("And Ugolino and his wife went there"). Ugolino, whoever he was, wrote this on the walls of this house upon his return from Rome to keep an everlasting memory of the trip that he had made for the Jubilee with his wife.

Lapidi delle Alluvioni (Memorial Stones of the Two Floods of November 4)
Via San Remigio, corner of Via de' Neri

➤ The two stone tablets here record two of the most disastrous floods that Florence ever experienced: the one in 1333 and the one in 1966. Although they happened hundreds of years apart, by a strange coincidence they took place on the same day, November 4. The first stone is engraved with the phrase "*Il 4 novembre 1966 l'acqua d'Arno arrivò a questa altezza*" ("On the 4th of November, 1966, the water of the Arno arrived to this height"). On the other stone there is a cross above the image of waves, with a finger pointing to the level that the water reached that day. The inscription reads "*. . . fu alta l'acqua d'Arno fino qui.*" (". . . the water from the Arno came up to here").

Loggia del Grano
Via Castellani

➤ Situated at the end of Via dei Neri, this structure was the last in a series of loggias commissioned by Cosimo II in order to give each of the guilds its own marketplace. Other structures erected during the project include the Loggia del Pesce and the Loggia del Mercato Nuovo. The Loggia del Grano was devoted to the granaries. Cereals were sold on its ground floor, under the arcade, and stored in the attic space above. The loggia was turned into a theater at the turn of the century, when actor Tommaso Salvini purchased the structure. It was later converted into a movie theater, which has since gone out of business.

Oratorio di San Niccolò del Ceppo (Oratory of San Niccolò del Ceppo)
Via Pandolfini, 5; closed to the public.

➤ Built in 1516 when the confraternity of San Niccolò del Ceppo settled in Florence, this oratory has since accumulated a number of late-16th- and early-17th-century works to decorate its stylish interior. The loggia that once preceded the oratory's entrance has been walled in to form a vestibule. The rest of the oratory's interior is covered in frescoes by Giandomenico Ferretti (1734).

Palazzo Antinori-Corsini

Borgo Santa Croce, 6; closed to the public.

➤ Constructed at the end of the 14th century, the Palazzo Antinori-Corsini has a remarkable courtyard. Bordered by porticoes at three of its four wings and accented with frescoed lunettes, the extravagant courtyard stands in heavy contrast to the sober architecture that characterizes the rest of the palazzo. The building takes its name from the Corsini family, who took over the property in 1587 and passed it on to the Antinori family in the 19th century.

Palazzo Borghese

Via Ghibellina, 100; tel.: 055-2396293; closed to the public.

➤ The Palazzo Borghese was built in record time—just six months—according to plans by Gaetano Baccani. The mansion's massive structure, a rare example of neoclassicism in Florence,

absorbed the preexistent Salviati house. Richly furnished salons and finely frescoed apartments were added to the original building. These include the Red Room and the Salon of Mirrors, begun by Baccani and finished by Gasparo Martellini.

Palazzo Cocchi-Serristori

Piazza Santa Croce, 1; closed to the public.

➤ The oldest mansion in Piazza Santa Croce, the Palazzo Cocchi-Serristori stands across the square, opposite the church. It was built after the Cocchi family came into possession of the property, which, at that time, was occupied by smaller, apartment-style houses. In 1469, the Cocchis hired Giuliano da Sangallo to build a mansion over these humble structures. The result is the present palazzo, which the architect prefaced with a highly unconventional facade of rounded arches framed by pilasters. In front of the palazzo stands a 19th-century copy of a 17th-century fountain, which marks the site of an ancient lavatory.

Palazzo degli Stiattesi

Via del Corno, 3; closed to the public.

➤ On Via del Corno sits the Palazzo degli Stiattesi, built around the 6th century with a base that dates from around the 3rd century. Its most interesting architectural feature is a very small gated window underneath one of the main windows. It was built to allow the children of the Stiattesi family to look out on the street, and had window guards to protect the youngsters from falling out.

Palazzo del Tribunale di Mercatanzia

Piazza della Signoria, entrance at Via de' Gondi, 10; closed to the public.

➤ Located at the corner of Via de' Gondi, the Palazzo del Tribunale di Mercatanzia was the place where the magistrates settled disputes between Florentine merchants. Recent archaeological excavations have shown that the site was formerly occupied by a Roman theater that housed upward of 3,000 spectators.

Palazzo Cocchi-Serristori

Porta alla Croce

PALAZZO DELL'ANTELLA
Piazza Santa Croce, 20–22; closed to the public.

➤ The decorative frescoes that adorn the expansive facade of the Palazzo dell'Antella make it one of the only structures bold enough to compete with its neighboring church. Painted between 1619 and 1620, over a brief period of 20 days, the facade marked the unification of the adjoining houses into one mansion. Designed by Giulio Parigi and painted by a team of artists working under the direction of Giovanni da San Giovanni, the frescoes' iconography depicts Virtue and Divinity. The marble tondo, under the third window from the left, is dated 1565 and marks the place were the center field line is drawn for games of *calcio fiorentino,* the Renaissance soccer matches that are still played in the piazza during the summer.

PALAZZO LAVISAN
Piazza della Signoria, in front of the Palazzo Vecchio; closed to the public.

➤ Built in 1871, the Palazzo Lavisan was a radical alteration to Piazza della Signoria. Sitting opposite the Palazzo Vecchio. This bulky structure imitates a 15th-century style and is located on the site once occupied by the church of Santa Cecilia. Both the church and a lodge were demolished to make space for the new addition, which was overseen by engineer Giuseppe Landi.

PALAZZO MORELLI
Borgo Santa Croce, 19; closed to the public.

➤ This early Renaissance mansion is noted for the refined *intonaco* graffiti designs that decorate its facade. These graffiti, or "scratched," designs were achieved by etching through the surface coat of freshly applied *intonaco* to the different-colored layers beneath, creating a bold contrast.

PALAZZO SALVIATI-QUARATESI
Via Ghibellina; closed to the public.

➤ Well known for the monumental arches that line the base of its facade, the Palazzo Salviati-Quaratesi dates back to the first half of the 13th century, when these arches served as storefronts. The rest of the structure was once a prison (1301), later a horseback-riding school (1838), and, finally, a theater. Now called Teatro Verdi, it is the second largest theater in Florence.

PALAZZO SPINELLI
Borgo Santa Croce, 10; closed to the public.

➤ Built between 1460 and 1470, the Palazzo Spinelli offers fine examples of *intonaco* graffiti on both its facade and in its tiny courtyard. The courtyard is porticoed on two sides and contains a framed water well at its center.

PIAZZA SAN PIER MAGGIORE

➤ This piazza is noted for the 11th-century church that once dominated it. Restructured in 1638 by Matteo Nigetti, the church was demolished in 1783 because it was deemed structurally unsafe. Today, all that remains of the San Pier Maggiore is the three-columned portico that sprouts in the piazza.

PORTA ALLA CROCE
Piazza Beccaria

➤ Situated at the center of Piazza Cesare Beccaria, this city gate, built in 1284–1285, is the hub from which a number of Florence's major avenues extend like spokes. Frescoed on the interior of Porta alla Croce is a lunette of the Madonna and child with saints by Michele di Ridolfo di Ghirlandaio.

SAN CARLO DEI LOMBARDI

Via dei Calzaiuoli; open: inconsistently.

➤ Adjacent to Orsanmichele, the church of San Carlo dei Lombardi strikes a distinctly Gothic pose in a neighborhood dominated by the architecture of the Renaissance. While architects Neri di Fioravante and Benci di Cione began construction as late as 1349, the church's sandstone facade and pointed-arch portal exhibits faith in the architecture of the 1200s. The interior features a cycle of frescoed lunettes depicting scenes of the Life of Saint Carlo Borromeo. They were painted in the early 17th century, when the order of Lombardi acquired the church and named it after their patron saint.

SAN GIUSEPPE AND SANTA MARIA DELLA CROCE AL TEMPIO

Via delle Casine, 9; tel.: 055-247089; open: Mon.–Sat. 5–6:30 P.M., Sun. 9:30 A.M.–noon (San Giuseppe).

➤ The heavy triangular pediment that crowns the facade of San Giuseppe is an 18th-century addition, as are the pilaster strips extending to the base of the facade and the monumental main door. The structure dates back to plans drafted in 1519 by Baccio d'Agnolo, who envisioned a nave laterally lined by three chapels. The second of these on the right contains frescoes by Attanasio Bimbacci (1705), a triptych of the Virgin and child with saints attributed to Gothic master Taddeo Gaddi, and a wooden crucifix that once accompanied the *condannati a morte,* "those sentenced to die," at their executions. These were conducted down the street at Porta alla Giustizia. The street that is now called Via San Giuseppe was then known as Via de' Malcontenti, "Road of the Unhappy," because the prisoners would follow it from the 13th-century *chiesetta,* now known as the Santa Maria della Croce al Tempio, where their sins were absolved, to the gate, where they were then executed. Located 90 feet up the street, Santa Maria della Croce al Tempio has since been deconsecrated but is closed to the public.

SANTA MARGHERITA DE' CERCHI (OR CHIESA DI DANTE, DANTE'S CHURCH)

Via Santa Margherita, 2 ; tel.: 055-215044/333-3074339; hours: daily 10:30 A.M.–6 P.M.

➤ The little church of Santa Margherita de' Cerchi, one of the oldest churches in the town, still stands as a testimony to the love that Dante had for Beatrice Portinari. Every morning Beatrice would leave her parents' house and walk to nearby Santa Margherita to pray. Dante would position himself on the corner of the other end of the street and watch her. They did this for nine years. In remembrance of this love from afar and Beatrice's devotion to the church, upon her death, her remains were placed in the church. It is also believed that Dante wedded Gemma Donati here. The Donati family was one of Santa Margherita's leading patrons; their coat of arms, in fact, decorates the 14th-century portal. The interior is a rectangular room, lit by iron-framed windows and frescoed by G. B. Perini. The fresco depicts the Glorification of Saint Margaret. The *Enthroned Madonna with Child and Saints* is the work of Lorenzo di Bicci. The tomb on the left wall is that of Monna Tessa (1327), who allegedly inspired Folco Portinari, father of Beatrice, in his medicinal discoveries.

SANTI SIMONE E GIUDA

Piazza San Simone at Via Lavatoi; tel.: 055-284789; open: Tues. 5–7 P.M.

➤ Dedicated to Saints Simon Cananeus and Judah Taddeus, the church's beginnings date back as early as the 12th century. At that time, it was a humble chapel sprouting amidst vineyards owned by the monks of the Badia. Its current appearance reflects a series of enlargements that began in 1209, when the chapel was converted into a full-size church. The memorial plaque on the facade commemorates an enlargement that took place several years later in 1243. The church's baroque interior, meanwhile, reflects changes made by Gherardo Silvani in 1630. Note the remarkable coffered ceiling. Its green and gold depressions contain the crests of the Knights of Malta. Bartolomeo Galilei, who commissioned Silvani's renovations, was in fact a knight of Malta as well as a high dignitary to the Medici court. Having exhausted his resources on the interior, however, Galilei took a more conservative approach to the exterior. The main door was refashioned with a fresco in its lunette by Nicodemo Ferrucci, and a baroque window and cornice, above, was improvised to replace the traditional rosette.

Santo Stefano al Ponte

Piazza Santo Stefano al Ponte; tel.: 055-2710732; open: Fri. 4–7 P.M.

➤ Right before crossing onto the Ponte Vecchio from Via Por Santa Maria, note the narrow alleyway on the left. At its opposite end is the eclectic facade of Santo Stefano al Ponte. The bottom half of the facade is Romanesque and reflects the early beginnings of the church, first documented in 1116. The upper half is signature Gothic architecture, as is the green and white marble arch that frames the central portal. The interior, renovated during the baroque era, currently serves as the home venue of the Orchestra Regionale Toscana. The stairwell to the presbytery is the innovative work of mannerist sculptor and architect Bernardo Buontalenti, who originally carved this spirited flight in 1574 for the church of Santa Trìnita.

Tabernacolo di Via de' Malcontenti (Tabernacle of Via de' Malcontenti)

Via de' Malcontenti, corner of Via delle Casine

➤ The construction of the church of San Giuseppe in 1519 was made possible by this humble tabernacle. In the early 15th century, the *Madonna and Child,* which dominates the tabernacle, drew considerable attention from local peasants, convinced that the painting was a miracle maker. The devotional offerings made to the tabernacle at this time were so generous that they allowed the confraternity of the Battuti Neri to finance the construction of San Giuseppe.

Tabernacolo sul Palazzo del Bargello (Tabernacle on the back of the Bargello)

On the corner between Via Ghibellina and Via dell'Acqua

➤ The painting on this tabernacle, by Fabrizio Boschi, represents Saint Bonaventure visiting plague victims (c. 1588). The frame was added in the 19th century.

Tabernacolo tra Borgo Allegri e Via Ghibellina (Tabernacle between Borgo Allegri and Via Ghibellina)

➤ This tabernacle is adorned with a 17th-century fresco representing the Holy Family. It is attributed by some scholars to Giovanni da San Giovanni.

Torre dei Donati

Borgo degli Albizi

➤ At the site of these ruins once stood the Torre dei Donati, a medieval tower. The plaque at No. 31, adjacent to the fallen tower, displays verses by Dante that commemorate the brutal assassination of Corso Donati, patriarch of the powerful Donati family, killed by his adversaries in the Cerchi family.

Torre della Zecca Vecchia (Old Mint Tower)

Piazza Piave

➤ A standing remnant of the ancient city wall, this tower stands in the center of Piazza Piave. At one time, the tower was surrounded by a cluster of other structures, including mills containing the Florence Mint (hence its name), homes, public baths known as "The Red Bricks," and the Bastion of Mongibello (designed by Antonio da Sangallo in the 16th century), which was concealed inside the ancient church of Santa Maria della Croce al Tempio.

Museums

ACCADEMIA DEI GEORGOFILI (GEORGOFILI ACADEMY)

Via dei Georgofili, 4; tel.: 055-212114; website: www.georgofili.it; open: Mon.–Fri. 3–6 P.M.; closed: Sat.–Sun; admission: free

➤ The Georgofili Academy, which is often overlooked, was founded in 1753 to study the progress of science and its applications to agriculture, management of the environment, agricultural economy, and crop sustainability. Although it has suffered various setbacks, it has managed to survive throughout the centuries. In 1993 a bomb planted behind the Uffizi, just under the Georgofili Academy, almost destroyed the entire building. Mass restoration efforts were organized and works were put back together piece by piece. Today it houses a library on Tuscan agriculture.

DONAZIONE CONTINI-BONACOSSI

Piazzale degli Uffizi, Via Lambertesca, 6; tel.: 055-23885; open: by appointment only; admission: free

➤ The heirs of Alessandro Contini-Bonacossi donated to the state this collection of 15th- and 16th-century Tuscan and Venetian paintings and sculptures. Of particular interest are *Madonna and Saints* by Cimabue, *Madonna della Neve* by Sassetta, *San Girolamo* by Giovanni Bellini, and a *Madonna and Saints* by Bramantino. Also on view are the *Portrait of Count Giuseppe da Porto with Sons* by Paolo Veronese; the *Martyr of San Lorenzo*, a marble sculpture by Gian Lorenzo Bernini (c. 1616); the *Torero* by Goya (c. 1800); and the *Madonna Pazzi* by Andrea del Castagno (c. 1445).

GABINETTO DISEGNI E STAMPE DEGLI UFFIZI (DRAWINGS AND PRINTS OF THE UFFIZI)

Piazzale degli Uffizi; tel.: 055-23885; open: for study Mon., Wed., Fri. 8:30 A.M.–1:30 P.M.; Tues., Thurs. 8:30 A.M.–5 P.M., (open to public when there is an exhibition); closed: Sat.,Sun;

➤ This collection is housed in the Uffizi and exhibits the most important pieces of the museum's large print and graphic collec-

tion. The most important part of the exhibit is the Medici collection, especially the pieces collected by Cardinal Leopold (1617–1655). The 12,000 prints were transferred from the Palazzo Pitti to the Uffizi in the early 1700s and Grand Duke Ferdinando's prints were moved a few years after.

MUSEO DELL'ACCADEMIA DELLE ARTI DEL DISEGNO (MUSEUM OF THE ACADEMY OF THE ARTS AND DESIGN)

Via Orsanmichele, 4; tel.: 055-219642; fax 055-288164; open: by appointment

➤ The academy was founded by Cosimo I in 1563 and was transferred to the 14th-century Arte dei Beccai palace in 1975. Particularly interesting are the *Crucifixion* by Giovanni Battista, *Giuliano e Agostino* by Pontormo, two organ doors from Orsanmichele by Francesco d'Antonio, and a fresco of the Madonna with angels and saints by Mariotto di Nardo.

MUSEO DELL'OPERA DI SANTA CROCE (MUSEUM OF THE WORKS OF SANTA CROCE)

Piazza Santa Croce; tel.: 055-244619/2466105; open: Mon.–Sat. 9:30 A.M.–5 P.M, Sun. and public holidays 1–5 P.M.; Tues., Thurs. 8:30 A.M.–5 P.M., admission: €5 (includes entry to the basilica of Santa Croce)

➤ The Museum of the Works of Santa Croce, displaying architectural fragments from the construction of the Franciscan church, is located in the convent to the right of Santa Croce. Inside is a crucifix by Cimabue (damaged by the 1966 flood) and a gilt-bronze statue of Saint Louis of Toulouse by Donatello. There are also frescoes by Taddeo Gaddi, such as the *Tree of the True Cross* and a *Last Supper* that was used as the model for later refectory decorations; a fresco by Domenico Veneziano with Saint John the Baptist and Saint Francis; and fragments of the large fresco, *Triumph of Death, the Last Judgment and the Inferno*, by Andrea Orcagna. The cloister has a bronze sculpture called *Warrior* by Henry Moore and *God the Father, Seated* by Baccio Bandinelli. The domed Pazzi Chapel (see pg. 80) was built by Brunelleschi between 1429 and 1470.

Museo di Arte e Storia Ebraica (Museum of Jewish Art and History)

Via L. C. Farini, 4; tel.: 055-2346654; fax: 055-244145; open: Sun.–Thurs. 10 A.M.–3 P.M. (Apr.–Sept. open until 5 P.M.), Fri. 10 A.M.– 2 P.M.; closed Sat.; admission: €4

A.M.–1:30 P.M.; closed: Sat.; admission: €4.

➢ This museum, located in the modern, Moorish-style synagogue of Florence (see pg. 96), illustrates the life of the Jewish community within the city of Florence through a photographic exhibit and a model reproducing the location and architecture of the Jewish ghetto, which was demolished at the end of the 1800s. It also contains one of the greatest collections of Jewish ritual artifacts in Europe. The objects, largely donated by local families, date back to the 16th century, and thereby document the history of the Florentine Jewish community.

Museo Diocesano di Santo Stefano al Ponte (Diocesan Museum of Santo Stefano al Ponte)

Piazza Santo Stefano, 5; tel.: 055-2710732; open: Fri. 3:30–6:30 P.M. (other times for groups, by appointment only); admission: free.

➢ The church of Santo Stefano al Ponte, so-called because it is next to the Ponte Vecchio, has a small museum with works that come from the former Museum of the Archvicary. Among the paintings are the *Madonna in Trono* by Giotto, *San Giuliano* by Masolino, and the *Nativity* by Paolo Uccello. There are also fabrics and liturgical objects on exhibit.

Museo Nazionale di Antropologia ed Etnologia (National Museum of Anthropology and Ethnology)

Via del Proconsolo, 12, in the Palazzo Nonfinito; tel.: 055-2396449; fax: 055-219438; open: Mon., Tues., Thurs., Fri., Sun. 9 A.M.–1 P.M., Sat. 9 A.M.– 5 P.M.; closed Wed.; admission: €4

➢ The National Museum of Anthropology and Ethnology is housed on the ground and second floors of the Palazzo Nonfinito. The museum was founded in 1869 by Paolo Mantegazza and was the first museum of its kind in Italy, with objects from different areas around the world. The first 12 halls (with the exception of Hall IV, VII, and VIII) contain objects from Africa, including wood and straw containers, lucky charms, necklaces, and wooden statues. Halls XIV through XIX have artifacts from the Americas, including a rare feathered mantle by people native to eastern Brazil (Hall XV) and, from Mexico, a statue made from trachyte, a form of volcanic rock, that depicts the god of the sea (Hall XVIII). Among the objects in the following rooms, many devoted to Asia, there are idols, ceramics, and musical instruments. There are also objects that Captain Cook brought back from his 1779 voyage through the Pacific, including human heads from the Solomon Islands, sterns and prows of Maori canoes, and a "Heva"—a costume worn by Tahitian priests to funerals (Hall XXV). Articles of clothing, weapons, and boats from China, New Guinea, and India are also on display.

Via XXVII Aprile
Via Dogana
Via S. Gallo
Via G. La Pira
Michelli
Via Cappo
d.

Via Guelfa
Via Cavour
Via S.Orsola
Via S. Reparata

Piazza S.Marco
Via C. Battisti
Via Gino

Museo Archeologico
Via

P.za d. Mercato Centrale
Via Taddea
Borgo la Noce
Via d. Stufa
Via de' Ginori
Via Ricasoli
Via dei Servi
Piazza S.S.Annunziata
Via Laura
V. della

Piazza degli Alfani
Via della Pergola
V. Pinti

S.Lorenzo
P.za d. Olio
Via de' Gori
P.za S. Lorenzo
Bgo S. Lorenzo
Via de' Martelli
V. de' Bilfi
Via de'
Via Pucci
Piazza F. Brunelleschi
Via del Castellaccio
Via de' Pucci
Via Nuova de' Caccini
47

retani
Pecori
P.za dei cavallari
Battistero P.za di S. Giovanni
Piazza d.
S. Maria Del Fiore (Duomo)
Via Bufalini
P.za di S. Maria Nuova
Borgo Pinti
28

Via Roma
Vic. d. Adimari
Fosinghi
Duomo
Campanile
P.za del Capitolo d.Canonica
V. dell'Oche
Pza di S.Benedetto de'Bonizzi
Via dei Pucci
Via Sant'Egidio
50
Via Fiesolana
Via de' Pepi
Mez

Piazza della Repubblica
Via dei Calzaiuoli
P.za d. Speziali
P.za dei Giglio
Vic. di S. Albrighi
Via de' Medici
Via del Corso
Via dell' Oriuolo
Pza S. Maria in Campo
Piazza Salvemini
26
V. Pi
Via Martiri d. Po
44

S. Miniato fra le Torri
V. de' Cavalieri
Pellicceria
Borgo degli Albizi
46
Via de' Giraldi
V. Seggiole
Pandolfini
43
Via d. Ulivo
41

Rossa
Via Calimala
Via Orsanm.
Tavolini
V. Dante Alighieri
13 34
P.za dei Tre Re
Via de' Donati
29
Borgo degli Albizi
V. d. Palmieri
Via Ghibellina
V. d. Pepi
36
Via d. Fico
7

Via Por S. Maria
Lamberti Arte d. Lana
48 23 39
Cimatori
45
Barg
V. d. Isola
V. d. Pinzochere
27

V. d. Terme
11
Via delle Farine
Palazzo Vecchio
P.za d. Condotta
Piazza S.Firenze
Via d.
V. d. Vigna Vecchia
49 31
Via G. Verdi
Via de' Macci
20
Kristofano
Borgo Allegri
Via Giusti

P.za di Parte Guelfa
Vacchereccia
P.za d. Signoria
P.le d. Uffizi
Borgo dei Greci
Burella
5
40
S.Simone
P. Lavatoi
Torta
Via Verrazzano
38
19
24

42
Via Lambertesca
Galleria D. Uffizi
V. de' Gondi
Via d. Corno
Via Vinegia
Piazza Mentana
33
6
8
Via de' Neri
Piazza di S. Croce
Piazza de' Peruzzi
Via de' Bentacordi
30
Borgo S. Croce
Via Magliabechi
Biblioteca Nazionale
S. Croce

Ponte Vecchio
1
Girolami
Lung. d. Archibusieri
Lung. A.M.I. de' Medici
P.za de' Giudici
V. d. Saponai
Piazza Mentana
Malenchini
V. d. Vagellai
Borgo S. Croce
Via a
Lungar

P.za di S. Maria Sopr'Arno
Fiume Arno
Lungarno Gen. Diaz
Lungarno d. Grazie
P.za dei Cavalleggeri

Costa di San Giorgio
Via de' Magnoli
Lungarno Torrigiani
Lungarno de' Bardi
Ponte alle Grazie

Via di San Giorgio
V. dei Bardi
P.za Demidoff
Lungarno Serristori
Renai
Via di San Niccolò

Via dei Bastioni

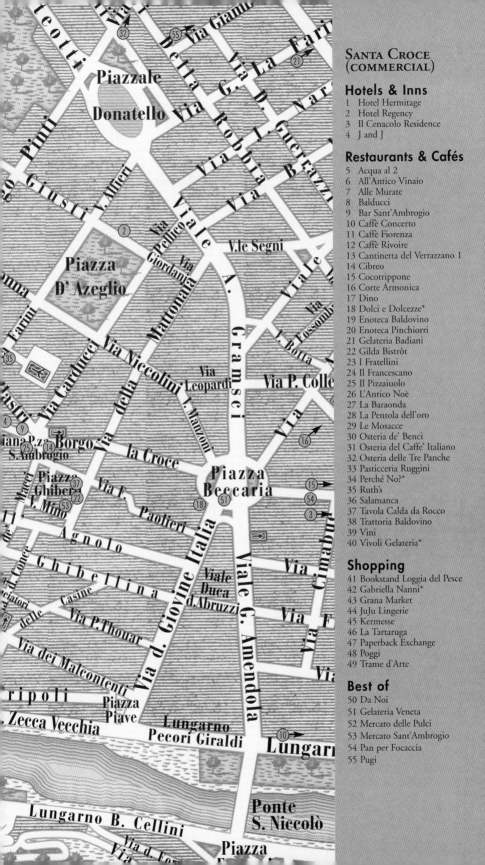

Santa Croce
(COMMERCIAL)

Hotels & Inns
1 Hotel Hermitage
2 Hotel Regency
3 Il Cenacolo Residence
4 J and J

Restaurants & Cafés
5 Acqua al 2
6 All'Antico Vinaio
7 Alle Murate
8 Balducci
9 Bar Sant'Ambrogio
10 Caffè Concerto
11 Caffè Fiorenza
12 Caffè Rivoire
13 Cantinetta del Verrazzano 1
14 Cibreo
15 Cocotrippone
16 Corte Armonica
17 Dino
18 Dolci e Dolcezze*
19 Enoteca Baldovino
20 Enoteca Pinchiorri
21 Gelateria Badiani
22 Gilda Bistrôt
23 I Fratellini
24 Il Francescano
25 Il Pizzaiuolo
26 L'Antico Noè
27 La Baraonda
28 La Pentola dell'oro
29 Le Mosacce
30 Osteria de' Benci
31 Osteria del Caffè' Italiano
32 Osteria delle Tre Panche
33 Pasticceria Ruggini
34 Perché No?*
35 Ruth's
36 Salamanca
37 Tavola Calda da Rocco
38 Trattoria Baldovino
39 Vini
40 Vivoli Gelateria*

Shopping
41 Bookstand Loggia del Pesce
42 Gabriella Nanni*
43 Grana Market
44 JuJu Lingerie
45 Kermesse
46 La Tartaruga
47 Paperback Exchange
48 Poggi
49 Trame d'Arte

Best of
50 Da Noi
51 Gelateria Veneta
52 Mercato delle Pulci
53 Mercato Sant'Ambrogio
54 Pan per Focaccia
55 Pugi

HOTELS & INNS

Hotel Hermitage

Piazza del Pesce, Vicolo Marzio, 1; tel.: 055-287216; fax: 055-212208; website: www.hermitagehotel.com; e-mail: florence@hermitagehotel.com; category:★★★; number of rooms: 28, including 8 with a view of the Arno River; credit cards accepted: all major; access to internet: none; €€€.

☛The Hotel Hermitage is a small, pleasant, old-style hotel right off the bustling Ponte Vecchio.

Hotel Regency

Piazza Massimo d'Azeglio, 3; tel.: 055-245247; fax: 055-2346735; website: www.regency-hotel.com; e-mail: info@regency-hotel.com; category: ★★★★★; number of rooms: 35, including 2 suites with a view of the park; credit cards accepted: all major; access to internet: yes; €€€–€€€€.

☛The Hotel Regency is a very elegant hotel where all of the modern comforts are combined with traditional decor and service. It is located in one of the quieter piazzas of the city.

Il Cenacolo Residence

Via San Salvi, 47; tel.: 055-677608; fax: 055-661375; website: www.residenceilcenacolo.it; category: ★★★; number of rooms: 8, plus 14 apartments; credit cards accepted: all major; access to internet: yes; € (monthly rates available).

☛Il Cenacolo Residence is a nice place in a more residential neighborhood of Florence that is still close to the historical center. Rooms can be rented for a long period of time or a minimum of three days.

J and J

Via di Mezzo, 20; tel.: 055-26312; fax: 055-240282; website: www.cavalierehotels.com; category: ★★★★; number of rooms: 19 suites; credit cards accepted: all major; access to internet: yes; €€€.

☛The ground floor of this converted 16th-century convent has two drawing rooms decorated with Persian rugs, old furniture, and a collection of art books. A stone staircase leads up to the 19 suites, which feature coffered or frescoed ceilings.

RESTAURANTS & CAFÉS

Acqua al 2

Via della Vigna Vecchia, 40r; tel.: 055-284170; website: www.acquaal2.it; e-mail: stefanoin@inwind.it; open: daily 7:30 P.M.–1 A.M.; credit cards accepted: all major; €.

☛A well-established restaurant in the center of the city, the kitchen of Acqua al 2 offers international cuisine to a young crowd and theatergoers. It stays open late.

All'Antico Vinaio

Via dei Neri, 65r; tel.: 055-2382723; open: Tues.–Sat. 8 A.M.–3 P.M., 5–9 P.M., Sun. 8 A.M.–3 P.M.; closed Mon.; credit cards accepted: all major

☛This place takes tradition seriously. Tuscan reds are abundant and the drinking decor consists of dark wooden furniture and whitewashed walls. There is also a good selection of cured meats and cheeses.

Alle Murate

Via Ghibellina, 52r; tel.: 055-240618; website: www.caffeitalino.it; open: Tues.–Sun. 7:30–11 P.M.; closed Mon.; credit cards accepted: all major; €€.

☛Alle Murate is a very warm restaurant offering traditional yet creative southern Italian cuisine. It is popular among tourists. Specialties include *minestra di fave a purea e cicoriell* (fava bean soup with chickory), *tortelli di branzino al sugo di peperoni gialli* (sea bass tortellini with yellow pepper sauce), *tortelli con crema di piselli e cozze* (tortellini with cream of peas and mussels), and *stufatino di seppie con carciofi* (cuttlefish stew with artichokes). There is also a good wine selection.

Bar Sant'Ambrogio

Piazza Sant'Ambrogio, 7r; tel.: 055-241035; open: daily 9–3 A.M.; closed: Sun. morning; credit cards accepted: none.

☛This is a relaxed bar with outdoor seating in the summer and an interesting mix of music. Good, strong aperitifs, which cost €4 during happy hour (6–10 P.M.).

Caffè Concerto

Lungarno Colombo, 7; tel.: 055-677377/ 674496; website: www.caffeconcerto.net/; open: Mon.–Sat. 12:30–2:30 P.M., 7:30– 11 P.M.; closed: Sun.; credit cards accepted: all major; €.

☛A very charming restaurant along the Arno River, the Caffè Concerto features a wood-panelled dining room inside and, in the summer, garden seating outside on a terrace perched over the Arno. Specialties include *baccalà fritto* (fried cod), *tartare di manzo Chianino* (Chianina beef tartare), *tortiglioni con moscardini* (shrimp tortiglioni), and *gnocchi allo zafferano con crema di cicoria* (saffron gnocchi with chicory cream).

Caffè Fiorenza

Via dei Calzaiuoli, 9r; tel.: 055-216651; open: daily 8–1 A.M.; credit cards accepted: all major.

☛Some of the best ice cream in Florence can be found here, with more than 24 homemade flavors to choose from.

*Caffè Rivoire

Piazza della Signoria, 5r; tel.: 055-214412; open: Tues.–Sun. 8 A.M.–midnight; closed: Mon.; credit cards accepted: yes.

☛One of the best-known cafés in Florence, Caffè Rivoire is located in Piazza della Signoria. Patrons can enjoy a splendid view of the Palazzo Vecchio while sipping delicious hot chocolate.

Caffelatte–La Latteria

Via degli Alfani, 39r; tel.: 055-2478878; open: Mon.–Sun. 8–midnight; credit cards accepted: none.

☛This small café/tea room/health-food bar sells a variety of organic products. It is a pleasant place to enjoy freshly squeezed fruit juice or a homemade dessert.

Cantinetta del Verrazzano

Via dei Tavolini, 18-20r; tel.: 055-268590; website: www.verazano.com; open: Mon.–Sat. 8 A.M.–9 P.M.; closed: Sun. and public holidays; credit cards accepted: all major.

☛Near Piazza della Signoria, this is a more recent addition to the Florence wine trail. Matching the estate's fine wines to high-quality cheeses, salamis, and vegetables from the Chianti area, all of which are served with freshly baked breads, has proved a huge success.

Cibrèo

Via de' Macci, 122r; tel.: 055-2341100; website: www.cibreo.com; e-mail: cibreo.fi@tin.it; open: Tues.–Sat. 12:50–2:30 P.M., 7:30–11:15 P.M.; closed: Sun.–Mon., Aug.; credit cards accepted: all major; €€.

☛A long-time favorite among food connoisseurs, this is one of the most successful places in Florence. Next door, Il Cibreino offers the same cuisine for somewhat lower prices. The menu changes according to the season with specialties like *pappa al pomodoro, sformato di patate e ricotta* (potato and ricotta soufflé), *calamari in zimin,* and *torta di formaggio e arancia amara* (cheese and orange cake).

Cocotrippone

Via Gioberti, 140r; tel.: 055-2347527; open: Mon.–Sat. 12:30–2:30 P.M., 7:30–11 P.M.; closed: Sun.; credit cards accepted: none; €.

☛Cocotrippone is a traditional trattoria in one of the best shopping districts. Specialties include *ribollita, panzanella,* and *zucchine ripiene di carne* (zucchini stuffed with meat).

Corte Armonica

Viale M. Fanti, 53b; tel. and fax: 055-5532392; open: Mon.–Sat. 11 A.M.–11:30 P.M.; closed: Sun.; credit cards accepted: all major; €.

☛Overlooking the courtyard of the 14th-century Villa Martelli, this restaurant is in a beautiful setting and offers exclusively organic vegetarian dishes.

Dino

Via Ghibellina, 49r; tel.: 055-241452; open: Tues.–Sat. 12:30–2:30 P.M., 7:30–10:30 P.M., Sun. 12:30–2:30 P.M.; closed: Mon. for lunch; credit cards accepted: all major; €.

☛Dino offers traditional Tuscan cuisine and a good wine selection. Specialties are *tortelli con fegatini di pollo* (chicken liver tortellini) and *mousse di ricotta con amaretti* (ricotta mousse with amaretti biscuits).

*Dolci e Dolcezze

Piazza Beccaria, 8r; tel.: 055-2345458; open: Tues.–Sat. 8:30 A.M.–8:30 P.M., Sun. 9 A.M.–1 P.M., 4:30–7:30 P.M.; closed: Mon.; credit cards accepted: all major.

☛The delicious desserts at Dolci e Dolcezze come in individual servings to eat on the spot, or as entire cakes that can be ordered for just the number of people eating. A small sign boasts that the chocolate cake is the best in the world, and it's probably true.

Enoteca Baldovino

Via San Giuseppe, 18r; tel.: 055-2347220; open: Mon.–Sat. noon–4 P.M., 6 P.M.–midnight, Sun. noon–midnight; credit cards accepted: MasterCard, Visa.

☛Near the delicious Trattoria Baldovino (see pg. 124), this wine bar serves top-notch food and wine. The decor is casual, with menu items listed on a blackboard and strings of onions and dried tomatoes hanging from the ceiling.

Enoteca Pinchiorri

Via Ghibellina, 87; tel.: 055-242777; website: www.enotecapinchiorri.com; e-mail: enotecca@relaischateaux.com; open: Tues., Wed. 7:30–10:30 P.M., Thurs.–Sat. 12:30–2 P.M., 7:30–10 P.M.; closed: Sun.–Mon.; credit cards accepted: all major; €€€€.

☛Located in a 16th-century palazzo near Santa Croce, with its own courtyard, this is the only two-star Michelin restaurant in Florence. There is an excellent, if pricey, wine list and cheese selection. It is impossible to get in without a reservation. The specialties of the house are *zuppetta di porcini con ragù d'agnello e uova di quaglia* (porcini mushroom soup with lamb and quail eggs), *frittelle di baccalà con pappa al pomodoro* (fried cod with pappa al pomodoro), and *tortelli con ragù di salsiccia d'agnello* (tortellini with lamb sausage sauce).

Gelateria Badiani

Viale dei Mille, 20; tel.: 055-578682; open: Wed.–Mon. 7–1 A.M.; closed: Tues.

☛Favored by locals, Badiani is the original Florentine source for fabulous Buontalenti ice cream, the egg-yolk-rich flavor named for Francesco de' Medici's personal architect and gelato maker. There is an extensive selection of fruit flavors, along with standouts such as coffee, melon, and *riso* (rice pudding flavor).

Gilda Bistrôt

Piazza Ghiberti, 40–41r; tel.: 055-2343885; open: Mon.–Sat. noon–2:30 P.M., 7–10:30 P.M.; closed: Sun.; credit cards accepted: all major, €.

☛On the edge of the produce market, this is a nice place to try light first courses. For the second course, the *peposa* is an interesting take on a classic Florentine dish. Fish dishes from southern Italy are also a regular item on the menu.

I Fratellini

Via dei Cimatori, 38r; tel.: 055-2396096; open: daily 8 A.M.–8 P.M. (Sept.–Oct.), Mon.–Sat. 8 A.M.–8 P.M. (Nov.–July); closed: Aug.; credit cards accepted: none.

☛This wine bar is literally a hole in the wall where a glass of wine can be ordered and consumed while standing in the narrow street, which is open only to foot traffic. A variety of *panini* are also offered.

Il Francescano

Largo Bargellini, 16r; tel.: 055-241605; open: Wed.–Sun. noon–2:30 P.M., 7–11 P.M.; closed: Tues., Aug.; credit cards accepted: all major; €.

☛This restaurant, which serves typical Tuscan cuisine, was recently bought by David Gardner, owner of the nearby Enoteca Baldovino and Tattoria Baldovino.

*Il Pizzaiuolo

Via de' Macci, 113r; tel.: 055-241171; open: daily 12:30–3 P.M., 7:30–11:30 P.M.; closed: Sun.; credit cards accepted: none; €.

☛Many consider this the best pizza place in Florence, so expect to wait before sitting down. Their specialty is Neapolitan-style pizza with buffalo mozzarella.

L'Antico Noè

Volta di San Piero, 6r; tel.: 055-2340838; open: Mon.–Sat. noon–3 P.M., 7–11 P.M.; closed: Sun.; credit cards accepted: all major.

☛Crouched under a seedy passageway that leads into Piazza San Pier Maggiore, this rustic sandwich shop serves up custom-made *panini* at bargain prices. A little gem of a wine bar, it is a wonderful hideaway where patrons stand at the bar and snack on cocktail foods. In the evening, the merrymaking spills into the street in front.

La Baraonda

Via Ghibellina, 67r; tel. and fax: 055-2341171; website: www.labaraonda.net; e-mail: info@labaraonda.net; open: daily 11 A.M.–1 A.M.; credit cards accepted: all major; €

☛This inviting trattoria offers the best in Tuscan cuisine with dishes like *pappa al pomodoro, schiacciata calda al patè di olive* (hot sandwich with olive pâté), and *risotto con lattuga* (lettuce risotto). The desserts are extraordinary.

La Pentola dell'Oro

Via di Mezzo, 24r; tel.: 055-241821; open: Mon.–Sat. 12:30–3 P.M., 7:30 P.M.–midnight; closed: Sun.; credit cards accepted: all major; €.

☛This is a place to discover true Tuscan dishes. It doesn't have a sign, but the front door is almost always open and one immediately gets a glimpse of the kitchen. Specialties are *crostini, panzanella, pappardelle al cinghiale* (pappardelle with wild boar sauce), *zuppetta di mare in bianco e ortaggi* (seafood soup with vegetables), and *peposo*.

Le Mosacce

Via del Proconsolo, 55r; tel.: 055-294361; open: Mon.–Fri. noon–2:30 P.M., 7–9:30 P.M.; closed: Sat. and Sun.; credit cards accepted: all major; €.

☛This family-run restaurant serves up typical Tuscan cuisine like *ribollita* in winter and *panzanella* in the summer. Its location, just across from the Bargello and behind the Duomo, makes it a nice place to stop in for a quick meal at lunchtime.

Osteria de' Benci

Via de' Benci, 13r; tel.: 055-2344923; open: Mon.–Sat. 1–2:45 P.M., 7:30–10:45 P.M.; closed: Sun.; credit cards accepted: all major; €.

☛Right off Piazza Santa Croce, Osteria de' Benci has outdoor tables when the weather permits. Tuscan cuisine is mixed with some Roman or Milanese specialties. Spring menus include *crostone di piccione*, or toast with pigeon pâté, and thinly sliced zucchini carpaccio topped with parmesan cheese. *Pappa al pomodoro* is a specialty. Leave room for the homemade cheesecake.

Osteria del Caffè Italiano

Via Isola delle Stinche, 11/13r; tel.: 055-289368; website: www.caffeitaliano.it; open: Tues.–Sat. 12:30–3 P.M., 7:30–11 P.M.; credit cards accepted: all major; €

☛Situated inside the Palazzo da Cintoia, this is one of the most charming restaurants in town, serving genuine and very good Tuscan cuisine, such as *Tagliatelle con funghi porcini* (tagliatelle with porcini mushrooms). There is also a pizzeria connected to the restaurant that serves Neapolitan-style pizza.

Osteria delle Tre Panche

Via A. Pacinotti, 32r; tel.: 055-583724 (reservations required); open: Mon.–Sat. 12:30–3 P.M., 7:30 P.M.–midnight; closed: Sun.; credit cards accepted: all major; €.

☛The specialties at Osteria delle Tre Panche are the *tortelloni di melanzane* and the salads. It is a very small place with only three tables and a very limited wine selection.

Pasticceria Ruggini

Via dei Neri, 76r; tel.: 055-214521;
open: Tues.–Sun. 7:30 A.M.–8 P.M.; closed Mon.;
credit cards accepted: all major.

☛Crammed with sweet culinary delights of every shape, size, and color, this much-loved pastry shop with warm wood paneling is filled with glass display cases, which make it look like a jewelry shop—the merchandise is just as priceless.

*Perché No?

Via Tavolini, 19r;
tel.: 055-2398969; open: daily 11–midnight (summer), noon–8 P.M. (winter);
closed Tues. in winter.

☛In business since 1939, many locals consider this one of the best gelateria in town. There are a record 56 flavors available, 30 of which change according to the day and season. Try green pistachio.

Ruth's

Via Farini, 2a; tel.: 055-2480888;
open: daily 12:30–3 P.M., 7:30–11:30 P.M., Fri. 12:30–3 P.M.; credit cards accepted: all major; €.

☛Next door to Florence's synagogue, Ruth's offers kosher cuisine with a Middle Eastern influence. Specialties are fish couscous and vegetarian dishes.

Salamanca

Via Ghibellina, 80r; tel.: 055-2345452;
open: daily 7 P.M.–2 A.M. (Fri.–Sat. until 3 A.M.);
credit cards accepted: all major; €.

☛In this lively Spanish restaurant/bar, Florentines along with tourists, and Spanish and South American transplants, eat and drink. The paella is especially good.

Skipper

Via degli Alfani, 78r; tel.: 055-284019;
open: Mon.–Fri. noon–2:30 P.M., 8–midnight, Sat. 8–10 P.M.); closed: Sun.; credit cards accepted: all major; €.

☛In this little-known restaurant the menu changes monthly. Specialties are *gnocchetti con pancetta e pomodoro* (gnocchi with bacon and tomato) and *cotognata con salsa alla liquerizia* (quince jam tart with licorice sauce).

Tavola Calda da Rocco

Piazza Ghiberti, in the Mercato di Sant' Ambrogio; open: Tues.–Sat. noon–2 P.M.; closed Sun.;
credit cards accepted: none; €.

☛Located inside the market, right next to the meat stands, this is a good place to try local fare at cheap prices. Specialties include a variety of Florentine dishes like *panzanella* in the summer season, *ribollita* in winter, and the usual grilled meats.

Trattoria Baldovino

Via San Giuseppe, 22r; tel.: 055-241773;
open: Tues.–Sun. 12–2:30 P.M., 7–11:30 P.M.;
closed Mon.; credit cards accepted: all major; €.

☛This trendy restaurant is a good example of the type of eatery becoming increasingly popular in Florence. Forget wine flasks and prosciutto hams hanging from the ceiling, Baldovino is painted in bright, warm colors highlighted by off-beat artwork. Owner David Gardner, an avid wine lover and one of the few foreigners to make a mark in Florence's restaurant industry, blends traditional and modern recipes. Try the *orecchiette* with red cabbage pesto and fish kebabs.

Vini

Via dei Cimatori, 38r; open: Mon.–Sat. 8 A.M.–8 P.M.; closed: Sun.; credit cards accepted: none.

☛Founded more than 100 years ago, this wine bar is truly one of a kind. Clients with glasses and porchetta sandwiches in their hands linger for an entire afternoon, and elderly residents stop by to fill empty flasks with cheap red wines.

*Vivoli Gelateria

Via Isola delle Stinche, 7r;
tel.: 055-292334;
open: Tues.–Sat. 7:30 A.M.–midnight, Sun. 9:30 A.M.–midnight;
closed: Mon.

☛Also considered one of the best ice cream spots in town, the small shop is always packed with visitors.

La Bancarella

Piazza dei Ciompi; tel.: 055-4220746; e-mail: morenoceccarellli@inwind.it; open: Mon.–Sat. 9:30 A.M.–7 P.M.; closed: Sun.; credit cards accepted: none.

☛This small bookstand under the Loggia del Pesce has some great bargains on slightly outdated books.

*Gabriella Nanni

Via Lambertesca, 28r; tel.: 055-214838; open: Mon.–Fri. 9:30 A.M.–1 P.M., 3:30–7 P.M., Sat. 9:30 A.M.–1 P.M. (summer), Mon. 3:30–7 P.M., Tues.–Sat. 9:30 A.M.–1 P.M., 3:30–7 P.M. (winter); closed: Sun; credit cards accepted: all major.

☛Gabriella sells all kinds of Venetian glass as well as handmade jewelry. The shop has a very 1960s feel.

JuJu

Via Pietrapiana, 51r; open: Mon.–Sat. 9:30 A.M.–1 P.M., 3:30–7:30 P.M.; closed: Sun.; credit cards accepted: all major.

☛Although quite small, JuJu Lingerie offers an interesting selection of intimate apparel—for both men and women—by Italian designers.

La Tartaruga

Via Borgo Albizi, 60r; tel.: 055-2340845; open: Sat. 9:30 A.M.–3 P.M., Tues.–Sun. 9:30 A.M.–7:30 P.M; closed: Mon.; credit cards accepted: all major; €.

☛An "ecological" paper shop offering a unique array of cards, notebooks, photo albums, toys, and other miscellaneous items, all by local artists.

Paperback Exchange

Viadelle Oche, 4r; tel.: 055-293460; website: www.papex.it; e-mail: papex@papex.it; open: Mon.–Fri. 9 A.M.–7:30 P.M., Sat. 10 A.M.–7:30 P.M; closed: Sun.; credit cards accepted: all major.

☛This used bookstore is handy for those looking for literature in English. It has an expansive collection of new and used books of every genre.

Poggi

Via dei Calzaiuoli, 103-116; tel.: 055-216528; open: Mon.–Fri. 10 A.M.–7:30 P.M., Sat. 10 A.M.–2 P.M., Sun. 11 A.M.–7 P.M. (summer), Mon.–Fri. 10 A.M.–7:30 P.M., Sat. 10 A.M.–1 P.M., Sun. 11 A.M.–7 P.M. (winter); closed: Sun.; credit cards accepted: all major.

☛Famous for ceramics and objets d'art, this store sells a wide range of beautifully crafted porcelain and silver, as well as other decorative items to fill a house. They also carry the famous Tuscan-made figurines of Giuseppe Armani. The prices range from €40–€1,500.

Santa Maria Novella

By Laura Collura Kahn

The site of the train station, the Santa Maria Novella neighborhood, in the western section of Florence, was once aptly nicknamed "The Mecca of Foreigners." A network of small streets and wide shopping avenues, the quarter converges on the basilica of **Santa Maria Novella**, built in the late 13th century for the dogmatic, intellectual Dominican order, in a bid to counterbalance the more down-to-earth Franciscans' settlement at Santa Croce, on the eastern side of town. Inside the church, a must-see is **Giotto's Crucifix**, painted before 1312.

The church rises at the northern end of the vast **Piazza Santa Maria Novella**, the one square in the city with grass, originally created to provide the Dominicans with preaching space.

Annexed to the basilica is the **Museo e Chiostri Monumentali di Santa Maria Novella**, which includes a series of cloisters and the Cappellone degli Spagnoli, or Chapel of the Spaniards.

At the back of the basilica is the elegant train station, the **Stazione Santa Maria Novella**, built by Giovanni Michelucci in Functionalist style in 1933–1935. The much-maligned platform in front was built in 1990, the year that Michelucci died.

On the southern end of Piazza Santa Maria Novella rises the **Loggia di San Paolo**, which once fronted a 13th-century *ospedale,* or hospital, of the same name. The loggia is decorated with medallions by Luca and Andrea della Robbia.

Leaving the square behind and the loggia on the right, you will reach the **Palazzo and Loggia Rucellai**, on Via della Vigna Nuova. Built according to plans by Alberti in the mid-14th century, the three-story palazzo features the first Renaissance example of the classical stacking of orders. The loggia across the street was built in 1460–1466.

Along the Arno River is the massive **Palazzo Corsini**, a quasi-baroque structure built in the 17th century. It houses the largest private art collection in Florence, the **Galleria Corsini**. Via di Parione and Via di Porta Rossa lead to Piazza Davanzati, featuring some of the city's most ancient buildings, notably the 13th-century Torre dei Foresi and Torre dei Monaldi. These imposing structures are peppered with square holes used to insert wooden structures known as *passerelle*—passageways that allowed movement from one tower to the other during riots.

A few blocks away is the **Palazzo Strozzi**, considered the most grandiose Renaissance palazzo in town.

Opposite, Santa Maria Novella

Via d. Porta Nuova

Via P... da Pal...

Viale Bel...

Via Cittadella

Via G. Monaco

Via Perla...

Via Chiaccia e...

V.le F.lli Rosselli

Via J. da Diacceto

Via Alamanni

Staz. F.S.
Porta Al Prato

Piazzale
Porta al Prato

45

26

Via della Scala

Staz. Cen
S.ta Mari

F.lli Rosselli

57

il Prato

8

Via B. Rucellai

Via d. Orti Oricellari

55

Via Magenta

Via Montebello

Via M. Solferino

Garibaldi

47

6

Via

Corso

Italia

Via Palestro

19

56

Via S. Lucia

Via

Via d. Albero

Via del

15

Via A. Vespucci

23

58

Via Curtatone

Via Montebello

Via Melegnano

Borgo Ognissanti

Via Palazzuolo

Via Finiguerra

18

Via d. Por...

onderia

Via d. Anconella

Lungarno
di S. Rosa

Lung.

16

35

2

49

54

Piazza
d'Ognissanti

Ponte
A. Vespucci

Vespucci

Via Pisana

Via Zanella

Lungarno Le Mura di S.ta Rosa

P.za di
Verzaia

Via
Bartolini

Via d'Onofrio

Via Tiratoio

V. Piag-
gione

Lungarno Soderini

Piazza di
Cestello

al

Lun

Via F. Berni

Viale L. Ariosto

Via S. Giovanni

Borgo

Via dell'Orto

Cardatori
P.za
de' Nerli

Drago d'oro

Tessitori

San Frediano

Aleardi

Via Pucci

Via D. Burchi

Via di Camaldoli

Via del Leone

Piazza
Piattellina

Piazza d.
Carmine

B.go d.Stella

Via S. Monaca

Via del Leone

Via Maffia

S. S

Piazza

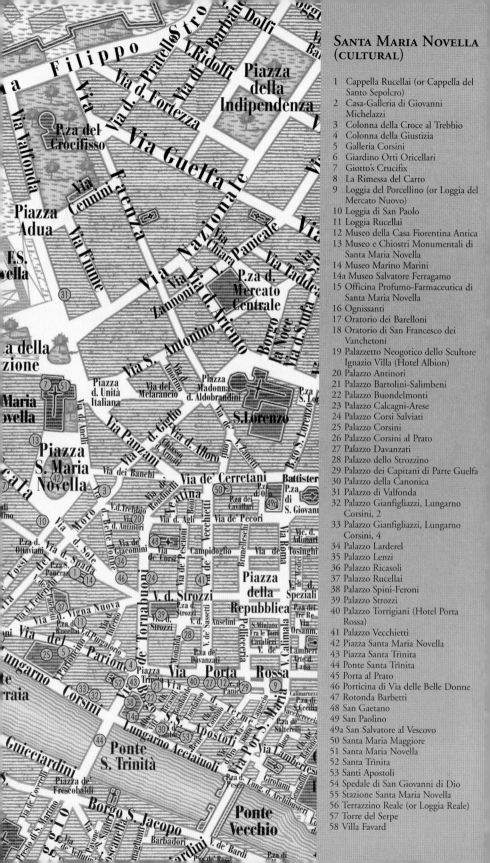

Santa Maria Novella (cultural)

Loggia del Porcellino (or Loggia del Mercato Nuovo)

Mercato Nuovo, Via Porta Rossa

➤ In the center of this loggia, built by Buontalenti between 1547 and 1551, there is a white and green marble disk that is a reproduction of a large wheel of a carriage. This wheel was once a symbol of the Republic because the Florentine troops used to gather here before a battle, assembling at the sound of the *martinella* (the traditional bell). This was also where one of the most humiliating Florentine punishments was inflicted: People found guilty of fraud were ushered into the square, led to the stone wheel, stripped, made to bend over, and then hit on their naked bottoms.

Loggia di San Paolo

Piazza Santa Maria Novella

➤ Once part of the Ospedale di San Paolo, the loggia is now all that remains of that 13th-century orphanage. In between its arches are glazed terra-cotta medallions by Andrea della Robbia. They portray Saint Dominic and Saint Francis embracing.

Palazzo Rucellai

Loggia Rucellai

Via della Vigna Nuova

➤ Across the street from the Palazzo Rucellai is the family's loggia (1463–1466). Such structures were standard accompaniments for any residence that housed families as noble as the Rucellai. The frieze that decorates the first floor of the loggia features the Rucellai coat of arms, emblazoned with a wind-filled sail. The three porticoes and fluted cornices that make up the loggia's elegant design are, like the Palazzo Rucellai, attributed to Leon Battista Alberti.

Palazzo Corsini al Prato

Via del Prato, 58; closed to the public.

➤ Begun by architect Bernardo Buontalenti in 1591 for the Acciaioli family and finished by Gherardo Silvani for their successors, the Palazzo Corsini al Prato is known for its charming garden, just beyond the antique gates at No. 115 Via della Scala. The garden is strictly divided into geometrical flower beds by a network of carefully groomed pathways. These are dotted by a collection of terra-cotta statues and furnishings.

Palazzo Rucellai

Via della Vigna Nuova, 16; closed to the public.

➤ The gridlike pattern of pilasters, cornices, and rusticated stonework that comprises the facade of the Palazzo Rucellai (1446–1451) is the first of its kind in Renaissance architecture. Designed by Leon Battista Alberti, the facade's strict uniformity was intended to reflect the solidarity of its inhabitants. The Rucellai were one of Florence's most powerful families, with close ties to the Medicis and Strozzis. They chiefly traded in wool and silk. Their success in business was due to a curious discovery by an ancestor of theirs, the merchant Alamanno del Giunta. During a trip to the Orient he noticed, when he went to relieve himself, that a certain wild herb would become a beautiful violet color when it came in contact with urine. He brought the herb to Florence, named it "oricella" and began to use it to dye cloth. The herb was cultivated in a part of the

Courtyard of Palazzo Strozzi

city that came to be known as the Orti Oricellari (Oricellari Gardens). The family took the name of the gardens, Oricellari, which later became Rucellai.

PALAZZO STROZZI

Piazza degli Strozzi, 1; tel.: 055-2776461; website: www.palazzostrozzi.org; open: daily 9 A.M.–6 P.M.; admission: free.

➢ The defining feature of the Palazzo Strozzi, the last of the great Florentine mansions, is the immense cornice that juts out from the top of its facade. At the time of its execution, the cornice was considered a highly ambitious undertaking. Cronaca was responsible for its design and might have completed the heavy cornice if not for the death of Filippo Strozzi the Younger in 1538, the palazzo's proprietor. His passing halted the project, which had been under construction since 1489. As a result, the southern side of the palazzo is still missing its share of the cornice. The

PONTE SANTA TRÌNITA

Ammannati's bridge, the most beautiful in Florence, the most
beautiful perhaps in the world, was destroyed by the Germans
during the last war and has been rebuilt, as it was. The rebuilders,
working from photographs and from Ammannati's plans, became
conscious of a mystery attaching to the full, swelling, looping
curve of the three arches—the slender bridge's most exquisite
feature—which conforms to no line or figure in geometry and
seems to have been drawn, free hand, by a linear genius,
which Ammannati was not.

Mary McCarthy, *The Stones of Florence*

rest of the exterior's design was heavily influenced by the Palazzo Medici-Riccardi, which had already been in existence 30 years prior to the Palazzo Strozzi's beginnings. The rustic stonework, the curved pediments that frame the windows of the upper stories, and the arches that form the palazzo's immense doorways, all testify to the influence of the Palazzo Medici-Riccardi. The lamps at the corners of the palazzo are rare examples of wrought iron work from the period.

The palazzo's courtyard is accessed through the main door at Piazza degli Strozzi. Also by Cronaca, the courtyard features a highly refined portico at its perimeter, surmounted by an open loggia.

Piazza Santa Maria Novella

➢ After settling in Florence, the Dominican order devoted the years between 1287 and 1325 to clearing a space, amidst the densely packed homes that surrounded their church, where large crowds could gather for public preaching. Upon its completion, Piazza Santa Maria Novella would stand in direct competition with its rival, Piazza Santa Croce, the Franciscan hub across town. During the Renaissance, Piazza Santa Maria Novella was also a popular venue for secular events. Standing at each end of the piazza, the marble obelisks by Giambologna once served as markers for the Palio dei Cocchi, an annual horse and chariot race, established in 1563. A rope tied between the two obelisks formed the

center barrier for the track while the loggia, at the southern end of the piazza, provided shade to such spectators as Cosimo I, who regularly presided over the event.

Ponte Santa Trìnita

➢ Stretching across the Arno River from Via de' Tornabuoni to Piazza dei Frescobaldi, graceful Ponte Santa Trìnita follows the seamless design of mannerist architect Bartolomeo Ammannati. Destroyed in 1944 during the German occupation of Florence, the bridge was faithfully rebuilt in its original form, using the stones that had fallen into the river bed. Originally built as a replacement to a bridge of primitive design that collapsed in 1557, the Ponte Santa Trìnita spans the width of the Arno in three harmonious arches, flanked by free-standing statues of the Four Seasons at each of its corner's ends.

Santa Maria Novella

Piazza Santa Maria Novella; tel.: 055-282187; open: daily 9 A.M.–4:30 P.M., Fri., Sun. 1–4:30 P.M.; admission: €2.50

➢ One of the most picturesque churches in all of Florence, Santa Maria Novella owes its beauty to Renaissance architect Leon Battista Alberti. While the church and bell tower were begun in 1278 and completed nearly 70 years later, the facade was still unfinished by the time Alberti inherited the project in 1458. In accordance with the rest of the church, the construction of the lower half of the facade had already been styled in the tradition of Gothic architecture. This included the intricate marquetry in green and white marble and the arched recesses, complete with marble sarcophagi. Rather than demolish what progress had already been made, Alberti built around it, blending the facade's Gothic foundations with his tastes for classical elements. He divided the line of pointed arches, which frame each of the recesses, with a barrel-vaulted arch that surmounts the central doorway. From here on up, the facade is dominated by simple, geometric designs: a rectangular partition, crowned by a triangular pediment. The original Gothic rosette, meanwhile, is complemented by radial designs for the recesses that flank the partition. Extending from the right side of the facade is a series of arched recesses, behind which lies a small cemetery whose walls are decorated with the emblems and badges of wealthy Florentines (closed to the public). Early Renaissance painter Domenico Ghirlandaio is buried here.

Garden in the Old Cemetery at Santa Maria Novella

Designed for preaching sermons, Santa Maria Novella has a vast interior, illuminated by ample sunlight. While the nave stretches for over 300 feet, its length is even further exaggerated by the manner of its construction. The arches that line the nave's edges narrow as they approach the chancel, creating the optical illusion of added depth for anyone entering the church through the main door. The interior's architectural grandiosity is further embellished by the richness of its artwork. The most significant element is the cycle of frescoes by Domenico Ghirlandaio in the Tornabuoni Chapel, the church's main chapel. Executed between the years 1485 and 1490, the frescoes depict the evangelists (vault), scenes from the Life of the Virgin (left wall), stories of the Life of Saint John the Baptist (right wall), the Coronation of the Virgin, and other stories of saints (far wall). The fact that Ghirlandaio painted with tireless attention to detail not only establishes his place among the pantheon of Florentine artists, but also lends considerable importance to his works as forms of historical documentation. He often populated his biblical scenes with portraits of members from Florentine high society. The first fresco on the left-hand wall, *Joachim Chased from the Temple,* features a self-portrait of the artist with his hand on his hip, among the group to the right.

The Chapel of Filippo Strozzi has dramatic frescoes by Filippino Lippi, including *Saint John Raising Drusiana from the Dead* and *Saint Philip Slaying a Dragon.* Italian writer Boccaccio set the beginning of his famous work, *The Decameron*, in this chapel.

The third alter of the left aisle features Masaccio's *Holy Trinity* (1427), one of the pioneering frescoes of the Renaissance because of its use of perspective and the creation of a three-dimensional effect through the use of the architecture. The figures in the picture form a triangle, symbolizing the Holy Trinity, and the viewer's eye is drawn up to Christ and God the Father at the apex of the triangle. Also note the depiction of the Virgin Mary and Saint John the Baptist as regular people instead of idealized figures, and Lorenzo Lenzi, Masaccio's patron (in red), kneeling opposite his wife. In the Gondi Chapel, to the left of the main chapel, note the wooden crucifix by Filippo Brunelleschi.

• GIOTTO'S CRUCIFIX

In Santa Maria Novella

➢ In 2001 the crucifix by Giotto in Florence's great Dominican church, Santa Maria Novella, was returned to the public after many years of restoration. The imposing 700-pound, 17-foot-tall crucifix was moved to the restoration laboratory, the Opificio delle Pietre Dure, in the late 1980s. Giotto had probably just turned 30 when he created the crucifix, which represents a watershed in Western art. Until then, Italian artists working in the International Gothic style had depicted the Crucifixion in two ways. The most common was the *Christus triumphans,* where a wide-eyed Christ is shown gazing serenely from the cross, certain of his triumph over death. This was superseded by the *Christus patiens,* a cross with a depiction of a suffering Christ. Both types were highly stylized and flat, and the central figure was accompanied by miniature non-divine figures, following the Byzantine icon canon that the composition served as a medium between God and man. Giotto, on the other hand, painted a realistic, dead, red-haired Christ with head bowed, who is firmly nailed to the cross. The dangling, outstretched arms of this humanized Christ form the top of an inverted triangle, the sides of which converge underneath a representation of Golgotha, "the place of the skull," the hill where Christ was crucified. To further emphasize his humanity, Christ's feet are placed in the midst of a small cross firmly planted on the dry earth of Golgotha. This symbolism was especially significant as the Dominicans of Santa Maria Novella were combating the spread of Catharism, a heretical faith that upheld dualism—the belief that the spiritual world was good and the visible world evil—and therefore denied the human nature of Christ. After having been displayed in different places in the church throughout its history, Giotto's crucifix is now suspended 15 feet

Giotto's crucifix in Santa Maria Novella

from the floor in its original striking position in the middle of the church, where it once served as a partition between the area where the monks prayed and people worshiped.

STAZIONE SANTA MARIA NOVELLA (SANTA MARIA NOVELLA STATION)

Piazza Stazione; tel.: 055-2352061; ticket office open: daily 6 A.M.–10 P.M.

➢ With its geometric contours, shaped by sharp angles and gridlike lines, the Santa Maria Novella Station testifies to the enduring influence of Renaissance principles in Florentine architecture. Built between 1933 and 1935, the station is technically classified as a rationalist structure for its complementary blend of form and function. Conveniently located behind the church from which its name derives, the station's 300-foot plate-glass corridor forms a veritable trunk from which platforms stem on one side while ticket offices, vendors, and waiting rooms extend from the other.

Walking Tour 1:

In the Shadow of
the Duomo: Della Robbia
and da Rovezzano

By Carla Rossi

Towering over the city of Florence, the church of Santa Maria del Fiore (the Duomo), with its famous cupola by Filippo Brunelleschi, dominates the skyline. Getting off the train, the average visitor usually heads straight for that fabled dome, hardly glancing at the many smaller churches in the central neighborhood of Santa Maria Novella. But these buildings are treasures in and of themselves, and generally devoid of the surging masses.

Moving back toward the Galleria degli Uffizi and through its piazza, the arched beginning of Via Lambertesca, which turns into Borgo Santissimi Apostoli, appears to the right. It is a narrow stone street lined with dark, imposing palazzi and intersected by even narrower side streets—one of the most intact medieval neighborhoods remaining in Florence. Tucked into the small Piazza del Limbo (so named because it was originally the cemetery for non-baptized children) is **Santi Apostoli**. The church officially dates back to the 11th century, but a Latin inscription on its facade, to the left of the main door, claims that it was actually founded by Charlemagne and consecrated by Monsignor Turpino, the archbishop of Reims. In this case, it would have been built much earlier, in the 8th century. It has been redone several times in the following centuries, with the most recent restoration project in the 1930s. During this restoration, following the common practice of the period, the church's architecture was returned to its Romanesque origins. The main entrance is from the 1500s, and possibly done by Benedetto da Rovezzano.

Inside, the church is designed in the traditional basilican form. It is divided into a nave and two aisles, emphasized by columns constructed in green marble from Prato and crowned by Corinthian capitals taken from nearby Roman baths dating from around 1 B.C. Various works by Benedetto da Rovezzano are scattered throughout the church; for example, there is the marble holy water container and the sepulchral monument to the Archbishop Oddo Altoviti (1507–1510). At the head of the left aisle is a terra-cotta tabernacle by Giovanni della Robbia.

The 15th-century **Palazzo della Canonica** that flanks Santi Apostoli houses a noteworthy copper, silver, and iron receptacle in which the legendary *pietre focaie* are stored. These "flint stones" were supposedly carried from the site of the Crucifixion by progenitor Pazzino de' Pazzi, who apparently donated the precious bounty to the leader of the First Crusade, Goffredo di Buglione, in gratitude for the latter's acts of heroism. Every Easter, the receptacle and its stones make a trip to the Duomo to assist in the Scoppio del Carro fireworks spectacle.

Next to the church and attached to the facade of the 14th-century Palazzo della Canonica is the Altoviti coat of arms, also by Benedetto da Rovezzano. Continuing along Borgo Santissimi Apostoli to Via Tornabuoni, the steep facade of the church of **Santa Trìnita** appears ahead. It is located almost at the end of Via Tornabuoni, close to the Arno River and the bridge that also adopted the name of Santa Trìnita. The basilica was constructed in the 11th century by the Vallombrosan order and was included within the city walls in 1172–1175. In the 1300s it was enlarged, and the interior was transformed into its present Gothic style. The marble facade was redone by Bernardo Buontalenti around 1593.

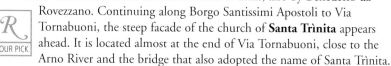

The interior of Santa Trìnita was restored to its Gothic designs after the Arno River flood in 1966 damaged the church and instigated a large restoration of all of the ancient frescoes inside. Built in the form of an Egyptian cross, the church is divided into a nave and two aisles, with five chapels on both the left and right sides. Behind the iron gates of the fourth chapel, the Cappella Bartolini-Salimbeni, and to the right is the *Story of the Virgin* by Lorenzo Monaco (1420–1425), the only early-15th-century fresco in the church that has remained completely intact.

The Cappella Ficozzi, to the left of the main altar, contains the legendary crucifix of Saint John Gualberto. Gualberto, a member of one of Florence's most powerful families, decided to pardon the murderer of his brother Ugo

Central portal of Santa Trìnita

after receiving a sign from the crucifix. He went on to become a monk, founding the Vallombrosan order in 1036. The cross was later moved from its original place at San Miniato al Monte, where Gualberto saw the sign, to the Cappella Ficozzi. Pier de' Medici ordered the move and commissioned Michelozzo to build it a proper home.

Perhaps the most important frescoes ever painted by the painstakingly detailed brush of Domenico Ghirlandaio are located in the Cappella Sassetti. Francesco Sassetti was the highly influential humanist and banker who oversaw the Medici financial empire from its earliest stages, under Cosimo the Elder, through the reign of Peter the Gout. Ghirlandaio's *Scenes from the Life of Saint Francis* (1483–1486) features a remarkably faithful portrait of Sassetti

Facade of Santa Trinita

beside renderings of his boss, Lorenzo the Magnificent, as well as poet Angelo Poliziano, Luigi Pulci, Matteo Franco, and Sassetti's children, Giuliano, Piero, and Giovanni.

Ghirlandaio's frescoes are remarkable for, among other reasons, the detailed and realistic representation of 15th-century life, including a depiction of the church's facade as it was before Buontalenti rebuilt it. On the altar of the chapel, still by Ghirlandaio, is *The Adoration of the Shepherds* (1485).

Other noteworthy works in the church include the wooden-carved Mary Magdalene, in chapel five, which Vasari attributes to Benedetto da Majano (c. 1455), and the marble tomb of Benozzo Federighi, bishop of Fiesole, whose sarcophagus stretches along the left transept beside a glazed terra-cotta by Luca della Robbia (1454) depicting Christ between the Virgin and Saint John. The adjacent sacristy, built by Lorenzo Ghiberti between 1418 and 1423, exhibits the same finesse used to build the Cappella Strozzi. Da Fabriano's *Adoration of the Magi* (1423), now held in the Uffizi, was originally executed for this sacristy.

Moving back along Via Tornabuoni and then right on Via de' Cerretani, the church of **Santa Maria Maggiore**, one of the most overlooked of the central churches, appears on the busy corner of Via de' Vecchietti. The origins of the church date back to the 11th century, making it one of the most ancient in Florence. It made up part of the original 12 priories and was the first to be dedicated to the Virgin Mary. The Romanesque bell tower was shortened in the early 17th century but, apart from this modification, has remained untouched. On the left side, facing Via de' Cerretani, is a small marble head of a woman. The head represents Berta, a well-liked woman who lived in this neighborhood around the 13th century. She never married or had children, so she decided to leave all of the money that she had saved to Santa Maria Maggiore; the money was to be used to buy a bell for the bell tower.

As a mark of gratitude, the people of the neighborhood commissioned this ancient Roman marble head so that they would always remember the generosity of Berta.

In the 13th century, the church itself was completely redone in the Gothic style for the Vallombrosan order. The work was executed by Gherardo Silvani, who clearly followed the designs of Bernardo Buontalenti. Another restoration project in the early 20th century cleared the interior of the church of its baroque additions, returning it to its Gothic design. The interior is divided into three aisles with pointed arches and square chapels. Inside one of the chapels is a series of frescoes attributed to Mariotto di Nardo (1390–1395). Currently, the left

Santa Maria Maggiore

wall of the church is being restored. Also noteworthy is the 13th-century painted wooden relief attributed to Coppo di Marcovaldo representing the Virgin and Child on the Throne.

Further Information

Palazzo della Canonica
Piazza del Limbo, 1; closed to the public.

Santa Maria Maggiore
Piazza Santa Maria Maggiore; tel. 055-215914; open: daily 7:30 A.M.– noon, 4–7 P.M.

Santa Trìnita
Piazza Santa Trìnita; tel.: 055-216912; open: daily 7:30 A.M.–noon, 4–7 P.M.

Santi Apostoli
Piazza del Limbo, 1; tel.: 055-290642; open: daily 9 A.M.–noon, 4–7 P.M.

Piazza di Parte Guelfa; open: inconsistently.

By Sarah Rose Leiwant

The Palazzo dei Capitani di Parte Guelfa is a lively complex located in Piazza di Parte Guelfa, adjacent to Piazza della Repubblica. The original structure was built around 1265 as the political seat for the victorious Guelph faction leaders, and it is actually made up of three separate buildings.

To the left, upon entering the piazza, is the former church of San Biagio. Long deconsecrated, the building has served many functions, including offices for the Guelphs, a firehouse, and, presently, a public library. On the opposite side of the piazza is the 13th-century Palazzo dell'Arte della Seta. The building that is officially called the Palazzo dei Capitani is a two-story structure with a 15th-century Gothic facade dominated by a mullioned window and a rare external staircase that leads up to the main entrance on the second floor.

The first room seen upon entering the palazzo is the Sala del Camino. It has a large fireplace above which is a depiction of the coat of arms of the Guelphs. A door to the left leads through the Sala dei Drappeggi to the Salone Brunelleschi, which the great architect added near the turn of the 15th century. The entrance to the *salone* is decorated by a marble work depicting the Virgin and child with angels, attributed to Luca della Robbia (1420–1430). The large hall was later modified by Giorgio Vasari, who added the wooden ceiling and a loggetta, which is opposite the entrance. The loggetta can be seen from Via di Capaccio.

Today, the palazzo is used for cultural events and is also the official seat of the Calcio Storico Fiorentino, a traditional soccer tournament between the four neighborhoods of Florence. The match follows ancient rules: players, dressed in traditional garb, run around in what seems more like a large brawl than a soccer game.

Although this, and all of the buildings in Piazza di Parte Guelfa, have been splendidly restored, modern history has been rather unkind to the palazzo. After centuries of modifications and daily wear, the run-down Palazzo dei Capitani was completely restored in the 1920s, only to have its roof destroyed by German bombing in 1944. It was repaired again but then flooded by the Arno in 1966. On May 23, 1993 a painstakingly long restoration project was finally finished. Four days later, a bomb planted at the nearby Galleria degli Uffizi destroyed, among other things, all of the windows in the Palazzo dei Capitani, resulting in another restoration project that was only recently finished.

Walking Tour 2:

Around Santa Maria Novella: An Ancient Pharmacy and Elegant Chapels

By Stacy Meichtry

OUR PICK

The building at No. 16 Via della Scala is somewhat difficult to locate. The street runs along the southernmost corner of Piazza Santa Maria Novella. No. 16 can be spotted by its stylish doorway squatting amidst a monotony of nondescript medieval dwellings. A fine example of mid-19th-century Liberty architecture, this doorway is one of the more recent additions to the **Officina Profumo-Farmaceutica di Santa Maria Novella**— Florence's first pharmacy.

During business hours, the door is open to a clientele of regular customers and accidental tourists. A barrel-vaulted corridor is filled with curious chamber music. At the other end is a brief flight of steps, marked by red velvet ropes. Follow the ropes under the lofty ceilings of a 14th-century Gothic vestibule until the sounds of classical music yield to the fragrances of a shimmering salesroom.

A carefully arranged jewel box of art nouveau statuettes, neo-Gothic furnishings, and diamond-cut marble pavement, the salesroom is an embodiment of the pharmacy's enduring prosperity. Crystalline urns, filled with antique perfumes, radiate from within monumental cabinets.

Painted in between the arched ribs supporting the room's ceiling is a cycle of frescoes by Paolino Sarti. Commissioned upon the creation of the salesroom in 1848, they depict the four corners of the world and were intended to glorify the pharmacy's growing fame, which at that point had already spread as far as China. Each of the allegorical figures, representing Africa, Asia, America, and Europe, is allotted its own quarter of ceiling space and thus watches over a quarter of the pharmacy's sales. These purchases still include products such as "Skin Whitening Powder" and "Vinegar of Seven Thieves," prescribed for fainting fits.

The salesroom inherits its vast interior from what was once the Cappella di San Niccolò. Before it was converted into a place of business in the 19th century, the chapel had been a place of prayer dating back to 1332. It was built adjacent to the infirmary of the monastery of Santa Maria Novella by a team of Dominican friars and was intended to offer spiritual assistance to monks suffering from physical ailments. The chapel's sacristy, in fact, still contains a cycle of 14th-century frescoes between its peaked arches. Attributed to Mariotto di Nardo, they depict scenes from the Passion of Christ. Popular among these was the exaggerated depiction of the Flagellation, a practice that the Dominican order proudly appropriated for use as an act of contrition.

Shortly after the construction of the chapel, the friars began concocting "medications" from the herbs grown in their garden. The most popular of these was rose water, which they touted as an effective antiseptic against the plague.

To see the plot of grass that marks the site of this garden, a tour must be arranged with the pharmacy's administration. In addition to the garden, however, the tour also visits the old pharmacy, where a collection of glass beakers, brass scales, and ceramic jugs still line the shelves of their original 17th-century cabinets.

In 1612, Fra Angiolo Marchisi founded the old pharmacy, thus turning the order's penchant for scientific inquiry into a money-making enterprise. Among his most prominent clients were members of the Medici family. After becoming a grand duke, Cosimo I made the pharmacy a "Foundry of His Royal Highness." The friars, in turn, devised "Water of the Queen," for Catherine de' Medici, daughter of Cosimo and wife to Henry II of France. Its creator, Giovanni Paolo Feminis, would later move to Cologne in 1725, where he changed the name of his popular formula to eau de cologne.

Portraits of Marchisi and his successors hang in the salon adjoining the antique pharmacy and the salesroom. Among the more recent portraits are those of Fra Tomas Valori, who had himself defrocked in order to save the pharmacy from a Napoleonic decree abolishing religious orders and institutions, and Fra Damiano Beni, who fully secularized the pharmacy in passing

Colonna della Croce al Trebbio

it down to his nephew, a layman. Keeping them company is Peter the Martyr, whose crest hangs on the adjacent wall.

Celebrated as the pharmacy's patron saint, Peter made a name for himself in the 13th century for persecuting Patarin heretics. The knife that decoratively hovers over Peter's head commemorates the axe that he categorically wielded in the name of God. The heretics later returned the favor, bestowing a similar axe on Peter's head, thus giving his followers their martyr and the pharmacy its saint.

To visit the site where Peter carried out God's will, cross Piazza Santa Maria Novella from Via della Scala to Via delle Belle Donne. Proceed down this narrow street to a three-way intersection where Via delle Belle Donne, Via del Moro, and Via del Trebbio converge at the **Colonna della Croce al Trebbio**. Erected in 1338, this column commemorates Peter's exploits with a Gothic capital, dominated by a heavy wooden tabernacle. The granite Crucifixion inside was carved by the school of Pisano. The four evangelists are depicted in the bas-relief beside their respective symbols.

Continue down Via delle Belle Donne until it merges with two other streets, coming from the right. One of these is Via della Spada. Follow this street along its left-hand side as glossy storefronts give way to the rustic exterior of the **Cappella Rucellai** (or Cappella del Santo Sepolcro). The entrance to this chapel is a few paces ahead, marked by the steps extending onto the sidewalk.

Tondi at the Palazzo Corsini

The chapel's solemn interior is the work of prolific early Renaissance architect Leon Battista Alberti. White *intonaco* walls conform to an austere rectangular floor plan, surmounted by a lofty, barrel-vaulted ceiling. The marble monument planted in the middle of this rectangle is the Tempietto del Santo Sepolcro. Also by Battista (1467), it is a scaled-down version of the Holy Sepulcher in Jerusalem, reproduced in the Renaissance style. Ornamental marble panels, divided by Corinthian pilasters in *pietra serena,* decorate the exterior of the temple. The interior, visible through a miniature doorway at the temple's facade, contains the sarcophagus of Giovanni Rucellai.

The chapel was originally constructed as an appendage to the church of San Pancrazio, a 9th-century church that Alberti rebuilt for the Rucellai between the 14th and 15th centuries. In the 19th century, San Pancrazio was deconsecrated and used first as a police station and then as a storehouse for tobacco. It was during this period that an iron gallery was installed along the inner walls of the nave, vertically dividing it in half.

Today, the **Museo Marino Marini** occupies this space, taking full advantage of the basilican plan it inherited from San Pancrazio to thematically display the works of Marino Marini (1901–1980), one of Italy's best-known modern sculptors. Marini is noted for his jagged bronzes, many of which are in an elemental style and are on the theme of a horse and rider. Using that subject, he was able to express a variety of emotions, from sad to exhausted, exhilarated, or erotic. The most important of these are *Gentleman on Horseback* (1937) and *Simmer* (1932). A procession of equestrian monuments lines the lower half of the nave and continues under the cupola and into the transepts.

The upper half of the nave offers an assortment of dancers, jugglers, and portraits cast in plaster of paris and naturally lit by a neoclassical lunette at the far end of the room. This semicircular window looks out onto Piazza San Pancrazio. Across the piazza is Via dei Federighi. Exit the museum and follow this street until it converges in a three-way intersection with Via della Vigna Nuova and Via del Parione.

At No. 11 Via Parione is the visitor's entrance to the **Palazzo Corsini**. Due to its imposing size and structure, however, the Palazzo Corsini is perhaps best navigated by crossing the Arno River at Ponte alla Carraia. From here, the palazzo is easily identified. Beached alongside the opposite riverbank, it is the baroque behemoth whose rooftops are audaciously studded with freestanding statues and Grecian urns.

Even more immodest, however, is Pier Francesco Silvani's design of the facade, which is defined by an expansive terrace that stretches between the mansion's lateral wings and the barrel-arched windows that run along the rear wing of the courtyard, serving as keyholes into the interior life of the mansion.

The corridor directly across from the terrace is the palazzo's main artery. Also known as the Galleria Aurora for the rich baroque frescoes that cover its interior, this hallway leads directly into the heart of the Palazzo Corsini: the Sala del Trono, or Throne Room.

The Sala del Trono combines the space of two stories in one vast interior. On the ceiling is an expansive fresco, *The Glorification of the Corsini Family* (1696), by Anton Domenico Gabbiani. Hanging from opposite ends of this work are two massive chandeliers carved in wood by Anton Francesco Gonelli. To visit this or any other interior space of the palazzo, a private tour must be arranged through the offices of Countess Livia Sanminiatelli Branca. The tour includes a tranquil 17th-century grotto, the magnificient staircase by Antonio Ferri, and the Galleria Corsini, home to one of Florence's most important private art collections.

Further Information

Cappella Rucellai (or Cappella del Santo Sepolcro)
Via della Spada, corner of Piazza San Pancrazio; tel.: 055-216912; open: call ahead.

Colonna della Croce al Trebbio
Via delle Belle Donne, at the intersection of Via del Moro and Via del Trebbio

Museo Marino Marini
Piazza di San Pancrazio, 1; tel.: 055-219432; open: Mon, Wed.–Sat. 10 A.M.–5 P.M.; closed: Tues., Sun.; admission: €4.

Officina Profumo-Farmaceutica di Santa Maria Novella
Via della Scala, 16; tel.: 055-216276; open: Mon.–Sun. 9:30 A.M.– 7:30 P.M.

Palazzo Corsini
Via Parione, 11; tel.: 055-212880; open: by appointment only.

FOCUS: Ognissanti

Borgo Ognissanti, 42; tel.: 055-2398700/284727 (church); open: Mon.–Sat. 8 A.M.–noon, 4–7 P.M., Sun. 9 A.M.–noon, 4–6 P.M. (church), Mon., Tues., Sat. 9 A.M.–noon (refectory); admission: free.

By Stacy Meichtry

Facing the Arno River with its brilliant marble facade, the church of Ognissanti (All Saints) was the hub of this neighborhood throughout the Middle Ages and Renaissance. Founded in 1251 by the order of the Umiliati, or "the humble ones," it provided a spiritual and social nucleus for an otherwise disjointed community of weavers. The baroque facade by Matteo Nigetti was added in 1637, punctuating the church's rise to prominence during the Renaissance. The glazed terra-cotta lunette above the portal depicts the Coronation of the Virgin and is by Giovanni della Robbia.

Among the church's leading patrons was the Vespucci family, whose most famous member, Amerigo, gave his name to the New World. He is depicted as a young boy in the *Madonna della Misericordia,* a late 15th-century fresco, located inside the church in the second chapel on the right. Painted by Domenico Ghirlandaio, the composition places Amerigo between the Virgin and a nobleman in a red habit. A marble plaque, set within the pavement adjacent to the fresco, marks the spot where Amerigo is buried.

Keeping him company in the crypt are the remains of Sandro Botticelli, located under a modest marble disk tucked away in the right transept. Botticelli is perhaps better celebrated by the stroke of his own brush: the frescoed tablet depicting Saint Augustine in His Studio (1480), above the confessional in the nave.

Across the nave, above an identical confessional, is a frescoed tablet of equal size and proportion, by Ghirlandaio. Executed alongside Botticelli's work, this fresco depicts a contemplative Saint Jerome.

Ghirlandaio maintains this sense of tranquility in his monumental

Last Supper, painted in the cloister refectory. Framed underneath the room's arched ceiling, the fresco incorporates the web of these arches into its composition. This creates the impression that the fresco is actually an extension of the refectory, proceeded by an exterior landscape where ducks and pheasants glide amidst fruit trees. The museum in the cloister exhibits furniture, silver objects, and fabrics.

Giovanni della Robbia's Coronation of the Virgin lunette, above the portal of the church of Ognissanti

Exterior of the Casa-Galleria di Giovanni Michelazzi

Other Points of Interest

Casa-Galleria di Giovanni Michelazzi

Borgo Ognissanti, 26; closed to the public.

➤ Just steps away from the baroque facade of Ognissanti is the Casa-Galleria di Giovanni Michelazzi, a rare example of Florentine Liberty architecture. An exuberant architectural style that took root at the turn of the twentieth century, Liberty architects sought to embellish their forms with ostentatious decoration that would enhance functionality rather than follow it. Built for Argia Marinari Vichi in 1912, Michelazzi's Casa-Galleria follows these principles to the letter, with florid art nouveau windows that immodestly span the length of the facade, showcasing the galleria's interior.

Colonna della Giustizia (Column of Justice)

Piazza Santa Trìnita

➤ An imposing monolith of oriental granite, the Column of Justice made its way from the orient to the Baths of Caracalla in Rome. It arrived in Florence in 1565, after Pope Pius IV donated it to Cosimo I to commemorate Florence's victory over Siena

on August 2, 1554. Its location, at the crossroads of Piazza Santa Trìnita, marks the place where Cosimo I received news of the important victory. In 1581 a porphyry statue of Justice, sculpted by Francesco del Tadda, was placed on top of the column; the bronze cloak was added later.

Giardino Orti Oricellari (Orti Oricellari Gardens)

Via della Scala, 85; closed to the public (to obtain special authorization to visit, call the Banca Popolare d'Etruria e del Lazio, the bank that occupies the palazzo, at tel. 055-219356).

➤ Running north on Via degli Orti Oricellari, on the left side next to the private grounds of the Palazzo Venturi-Ginori, is a large botanical garden known as the Orti Oricellari. It was famous for being the seat of the Platonic Academy founded under Cosimo de' Medici. The grounds were redesigned in the 17th century for Cardinal Giovanni de' Medici and a massive statue by Antonio Novelli, depicting the one-eyed cyclops Polyphemus from Homer's *Odyssey,* was added in 1650. The garden was finally transformed into a Romantic garden by Luigi Cambrai-Digny for the Stiozzi Ridolfi family.

LA RIMESSA DEL CARRO

Via Il Prato, 42

➤ This is where the *carro*, or cart, used on Easter morning for the traditional ceremony of the Scoppio del Carro, is kept. Every year in Florence, Easter Sunday starts off with a bang—literally. Dating back to the 12th century, the Scoppio del Carro, or "Explosion of the Cart," is one of the city's most eccentric and anticipated events. When successfully executed, it is said to ensure a good harvest. At 10 A.M. on Easter Sunday, a chariot made in 1680, called *Il Brindellone,* is pulled by four white oxen with gilded horns and wreathed in flowers. It is led through the streets from Piazzale Porta al Prato to Piazza del Duomo. A long parade of trumpeters, drummers, and flag throwers in medieval costume accompany the enormous wooden cart. Another procession starts from Santissimi Apostoli in Piazza del Limbo. During the 10 A.M. mass, the priest strikes flints together to make a spark that ignites the holy fire—which, according to tradition, was left to die as a symbol of mourning for Christ after his Crucifixion on Good Friday and was ignited again on the day of the resurrection. The flints are said to have come from the Holy Sepulcher having been brought to Florence 900 years ago, in 1101, by Pazzino de' Pazzi, who was awarded them for being the first to scale the walls of Jerusalem during the First Crusade. Smoldering charcoal is placed in a 14th-century metal container and once it has been blessed, it is carried to the Duomo. There, professional pyrotechnicians nervously check fireworks attached to *Il Brindellone.* The ceremony is entirely in their hands—and their reputations are at stake. As recently as 1909, firework masters were jailed because the Easter "explosion" went wrong. When the word "gloria" is pronounced at the end of the 11 A.M. mass at the Duomo, a mechanical dove with a rocket is ignited with the holy fire. It bursts out from the cathedral door and flies along a wire stretched from the high altar to the chariot and back, leaving a trail of smoke. If all goes well—boom!—the dove sets off a spectacular display of fireworks and makes it safely back to the altar.

ORATORIO DEI BARELLONI

Via della Scala, 9; open: inconsistently.

➤ This oratorio, also known as the Oratorio dei Santi Filippo e Giacomo, used to belong to the 14th-century hospital, the Ospedale dei Barelloni, that occupied the entire block between Via della Scala and Via Palazzuolo. This small structure, which was restored by Matteo Nigetti in 1626, has a ten-part cycle of the *Opere di carità* (Charity Works) by Cosimo Ulivelli.

ORATORIO DI SAN FRANCESCO DEI VANCHETONI

Via Palazzuolo, 17; open: usually closed but used for concerts.

➤ Built in 1602 by Giovanni and Matteo Nigetti, the Oratorio di San Francesco dei Vanchetoni is marked by a rather unremarkable sun-baked facade, crowded between competing storefronts on Via Palazzuolo. Beyond this grizzled exterior, however, is the charming rectangular oratory where the Congregation of the Christian Doctrine once met. On the ceiling are fine examples of 17th-century painting including a grandiose Medici coat of arms by Pietro Liberi, and works by Giovanni Martinelli, Domenico Pugliani, Volterrano, Cecco Bravo, and Lorenzo Lippi. While this interior is rarely left open to the public, the intercom beside the entrance is worth a try. If admitted, visit the chapel behind the altar, which holds a large 16th-century crucifix, and a charming sacristy with inlaid cupboards.

PALAZZETTO NEOGOTICO DELLO SCULTORE IGNAZIO VILLA (HOTEL ALBION)

Via Il Prato, 22r; tel.: 055-214171; closed to the public.

➤ This mid-19th-century building, with ribbed arches, offers an unusual example of the neo-Gothic style. The Milanese sculptor Ignazio Villa (1813–1895) built it for himself, although today the restoration has removed much of its decorative elements. The palazzetto currently houses a hotel.

Palazzo Antinori

Piazza Antinori, 3; closed to the public.

➢ Located catty-corner to the church of San Gaetano, this 15th-century structure is a fine example of a typical early Renaissance mansion. The palazzo was completed by Giuliano da Maiano in 1469 for Giovanni Boni before coming into the hands of the Antinori family in 1506. The facade in the courtyard, with its elegant porticoes looking onto the garden, was designed by Baccio d'Agnolo, the architect of the High Renaissance Palazzo Bartolini-Salimbeni. It consists of three registers in semirusticated stone and a central portal. The mansion also features a quaint courtyard at its center with porticoes on three sides.

Palazzo Bartolini-Salimbeni

Piazza Santa Trinita; closed to the public.

➢ A rare example of High Renaissance architecture in Florence, this palazzo is the inspired work of Baccio d'Agnolo. Completed in 1520, the structure draws heavily upon Roman architecture with a facade that combines a heavy cornice with triangular pediments and classic columns. Upon completion, the architect was widely criticized for breaking with Florentine tradition. He responded with an inscription on the architrave above the main door that said "Carpere promptius quam imitari" (It takes more courage to break from tradition than to imitate).

Palazzo Buondelmonti

Piazza Santa Trinita, 2; closed to the public.

➢ Situated behind the Column of Justice, this 13th-century mansion was the site of bitter factional disputes through most of the 14th century following the murder of Buondelmonte de' Buondelmonti on the Ponte Vecchio. In the early 16th century, Baccio d'Agnolo rebuilt the Palazzo Buondelmonti in the style of the High Renaissance. The memorial plaques on the facade commemorate the mansion's most notable residents, including humanist thinker and poet Ludovico Ariosto.

Palazzo Calcagni-Arese (now United States Consulate)

Lungarno Amerigo Vespucci, 38

➢ Located on the corner between Lungarno Vespucci and Corso Italia, this building was designed by Giuseppe Poggi in 1877. It is surrounded by the garden of Villa Favard, which was laid out in 1847.

Palazzo Corsi Salviati

Via Tornabuoni, 16; closed to the public.

➢ The beautiful Palazzo Corsi Salviati on Via Tornabuoni, now seat of the Intesa Bank, has an interesting history. The palace formed the foundation of three preexisting medieval buildings that belonged to the Tornabuoni and Tornaquinci families. Lucrezia Tornabuoni, the mother of Lorenzo the Magnificent, was born in one of these buildings. The biggest house was designed by the architect Michelozzo on the orders of Giovanni Tornabuoni. He incorporated the small piazza in the middle of the buildings into the actual palace, making the splendid courtyard that can still be seen today. Ludovico Cardi, called "Il Cigoli," built a loggia at the corner of the palazzo (at Via Strozzi and Via Tornabuoni). The Loggia del Cigoli, also known as Loggetta dei Tornaquinci, was later extended and, when the palace was moved back several yards, it ended up in the middle of the crosswalk of Via Tornabuoni. The loggia was then completely dismantled and painstakingly reassembled at another corner of the palazzo (next to Via Tornabuoni and Via dei Corsi), where it remains today.

Palazzo Davanzati

Via Porta Rossa, 13; tel.: 055-2388610; website: www.polomuseale.firenze.it; open: daily 8:15 A.M.–1:50 P.M.; closed: 1st, 3rd, 5th Mon., 2nd, 4th Sun., holidays

➢ One of the best surviving examples of 14th-century secular architecture, the Palazzo Davanzati is an amalgam of medieval and Renaissance thinking. The inviting loggia, placed at the top of the mansion, is a graceful 16th-century addition, typical of a *casa-signorile* of the Renaissance. Meanwhile, the very fact that this loggia is perched above five full stories

Room in the Museo della Casa Fiorentina Antica in the Palazzo Davanzati

when it doubled as a tower. Note the four *piombatoi di difesa* protruding from Davanzati's austere facade of rusticated stone work: they are archaic spouts, intended to deliver molten metal onto attackers beneath.

The interior houses the Museo della Casa Fiorentina Antica (see pg. 154).

PALAZZO DELLO STROZZINO

Piazza degli Strozzi, 2; open to the public.

➤ This palazzo, which houses a movie theater and an English-language school, was built in the mid-15th century for the Strozzi family. It took up the space of various apartment buildings and an entire square, Piazza della Marmora, which was turned into the palazzo's courtyard. Historians believe that Michelozzo designed the ground floor, featuring rough masonry, in or around 1458, while Giuliano da Maiano designed the first floor with smooth masonry between 1462 and 1465. The upper floor was built in the 1800s. In the 1920s, the architect Marcello Piacentini turned the palazzo into a theater, using the courtyard, complete with its ancient columns, as the main hall.

PALAZZO DI VALFONDA

Via Valfonda, 9; closed to the public.

➤ At the time of its construction in 1520, the Palazzo di Valfonda was best known for the size of its estate, which was the largest within the city walls. Built by Baccio d'Agnolo for Giovanni Bartolini-Salimbeni, the modest-sized mansion was passed onto the Riccardi, also owners of the Palazzo Medici, in 1589. Under the Riccardis, the Palazzo di Valfonda grew into its spacious location. This expansion not only involved the architectural additions of Gherardo Silvani, but also the growth of Valfonda's esteemed art collection and splendid gardens. The Sala degli Stucchi, on the ground floor, is covered in frescoes depicting the parties at the Riccardi villas and scenes of Florence by Jacopo Chiavistelli (1672).

PALAZZO GIANFIGLIAZZI

Lungarno Corsini, 4; closed to the public.

➤ This heavily modified medieval mansion was once the home of Luigi Bonaparte and Alessandro Manzoni, author of *Betrothed*.

Palazzo Gianfigliazzi (or Palazzo Masetti)

Lungarno Corsini, 2; closed to the public.

➤ The Palazzo Gianfigliazzi, later called Palazzo Masetti, was built in the 14th century, and was restored in the 17th (by Gherardo Silvani) and again in the 19th century. Among the many illustrious people who resided here are poet Ugo Foscolo, painter Francois Xavier Fabre, and writer Vittorio Alfieri.

Palazzo Larderel

Via dei Tornabuoni, 19; closed to the public.

➤ Designed by Giovanni Antonio Dosio in 1580, this signature High Renaissance mansion is considered the architect's masterpiece. The coat of arms at the corner dates back to the mansion's original owners, the Giacomini.

Palazzo Lenzi

Piazza Ognissanti, 2; closed to the public.

➤ With its graffitied stucco and overhanging facade, the Palazzo Lenzi is one of the most provocatively dressed mansions in the Santa Maria Novella quarter, let alone in Piazza Ognissanti. Built near the end of the 15th century, the mansion is currently home to the French Institute, which holds over 70,000 titles in the palazzo's library.

Palazzo Ricasoli

Piazza Goldoni; closed to the public.

➤ The design of this palazzo is attributed to Michelozzo, but construction was begun in 1480, after his death; it was completed in 1500. In 1580 a passageway was built under the road; it led to a vast garden and a loggia overlooking the river.

Palazzo Spini-Feroni

Via dei Tornabuoni, 2; closed to the public.

➤ Built at the turn of the 13th century, the Palazzo Spini-Feroni has been subject to numerous alterations over the centuries due to its prime location along the Arno River. In 1824, the mansion's tower and arch were demolished to make room for traffic along the widening lungarno. While the appearance of the mansion's current facade intimates that the building has been well-preserved since its inception, the medieval trimmings on its exterior were, in fact, added in 1875, after the brief period

Palazzo Spini-Feroni

Piazza Santa Trinita and the Colonna della Giustizia

in which the Palazzo Spini-Feroni served as city hall. This occurred in 1865, when Florence became the temporary capital of the newly united Kingdom of Italy. Prior to that, however, the palazzo had been fully decorated in the baroque style.

Palazzo Torrigiani (Hotel Porta Rossa)

Via Porta Rossa, 19; closed to the public.

➢ Originally owned by the Bartolini family, this mansion is noted among Florentine palazzi for the design of its facade, which is divided horizontally into two parts by a truss, yielding a necklike bottom half surmounted by a head of overhanging upper floors. This design was particularly useful during the Middle Ages for fending off attacks, should the enemy attempt to scale the facade. The ribbon corbels that form this truss are decorated with poppies, the heraldic symbol of the Bartolini. Rising from the center of the mansion is the ancient tower, the Torre dei Monaldi, also known as the *Rognosa* ("the scabbed one"). The palazzo was passed onto the Torrigiani family in 1559. Transformed into a *locanda,* or guesthouse, in the middle of the 19th century, it now houses the Hotel Porta Rossa.

Palazzo Vecchietti
Via degli Strozzi, 4; closed to the public.

➤ Designed by Giambologna in 1578, the Palazzo Vecchietti went unfinished until the mid-18th century when its facade was finally completed. At the corner, known as the Canto dei Diavoli, or "Devils' Chant," is the Vecchietti coat of arms, also by Giambologna, along with a copy of his bronze *Diavolino.* The original is kept in the Palazzo Vecchio. Just beyond the entrance on Via degli Strozzi is the palazzo's quaint 15th-century courtyard, lined by a graffitied loggia and a noteworthy staircase by Giambologna.

Piazza Santa Trìnita

➤ Years ago, this piazza was an important meeting place for influential figures in Florence's history; they would convene at the Column of Justice (see pg. 145) to talk about the politics of the day.

On the three sides of Piazza Santa Trìnita you can see four buildings that represent different architectural periods and styles: the Palazzo Spini-Ferroni, made of stone, which is a wonderful example of 14th-century buildings (see pg. 149); the Palazzo Buondelmonti, from the 15th-century, which is painted in a pale yellow—a classic Tuscan color—and has an elegant loggia (see pg. 147); the Palazzo Bartolini-Salimbeni, built by Baccio d'Agnolo and finished in 1520, and which is one of the first examples of true Renaissance architecture (see pg. 147); and the church of Santa

Trìnita, which was built in the 11th century but whose ornate baroque facade was added by Bernardo Buontalenti in the 16th century (see pg. 136).

Porta al Prato
Viale Fratelli Rosselli

➤ Erected in 1284–1285, Porta al Prato was the city's first gate and preceded the construction of the wall itself. The poorly preserved frescoes and tabernacles were added in 1526 during modifications that lowered all three gates and supplied each with its own sculpted lion. The frescoed lunette that dons Porta al Prato, by Michele di Ridolfo del Ghirlandaio, depicts the Madonna and child with saints.

Porticina di Via delle Belle Donne (Little Wine Door of Via delle Belle Donne)
Via delle Belle Donne, near the corner of Via della Spada

➤ Walking down the streets of Florence, one can see little windows inside arches on the walls of certain ancient aristocratic palazzi. Through these windows wine was

Porta al Prato

once sold by noble families with land outside of the city. This was surplus wine from their harvests sold to their fellow citizens. This is the most interesting of these ancient wine counters.

Rotonda Barbetti
Via Il Prato

➤ In the center of the area known as the Prato, where a market used to be held, you will find the Rotonda Barbetti, built in around 1847 to offer a panoramic view of the city. It was later converted into a garage.

San Gaetano
Piazza Antinori; open: inconsistently.

➤ San Gaetano stands opposite the Palazzo Antinori. The church was mentioned in documents as early as the mid-11th century. It was completely rebuilt between 1604 and 1630 under the stewardship of Bernardo Buontalenti. The facade features two orders of fluted pilasters and is richly decorated in the

Porticina di Via delle Belle Donne

baroque style. Over the main entrance is the insignia of the Theatine order, set between two allegorical figures, Hope and Poverty. In the upper order, next to the large corniced window, note the Medici coat of arms. The interior is one of the few remaining examples of Florentine baroque. It has a single nave laid out in a Latin-cross plan with side chapels. Above, next to the chapels, are a series of important 17th-century Florentine sculptures, including marble figures of the apostles and the evangelists by Antonio Novelli and collaborators. Most of the canvases and frescoes date from the 17th century. Of particular interest is a work by Pietro da Cortona, *The Martyrdom of Saint Lawrence,* on the altar of the second chapel on the left, which was commissioned in 1637.

San Paolino
Via Palazzuolo; open: inconsistently.

➤ This humble church was built by the monks of the Dominican order in the 10th century. Its rustic ashlar facade and refined glazed terra-cotta lunette belong to the Dominican legacy, which lasted up until the early 17th century. In 1618, the church was handed over to the Carmelites who oversaw the transformation of San Paolino's interior between 1669 and 1693. Renovated in uncharacteristically sober baroque by G. B. Balatri, the late-17th-century/early-18th-

Statue on the exterior of San Gaetano

century interior consists of a single nave and an expansive transept. In the chapel of the transept is the *Wedding of Mary* by 18th-century painter Vincenzo Meucci.

SAN SALVATORE AL VESCOVO
Piazza dell'Olio; closed to the public.

➤ The facade of this Romanesque church, built in 1032 and modified in 1221 and again in the 18th century, has been incorporated into the Palazzo Arcivescovile; it is invisible from the square in the back of the palace. The facade consists of three blind arches above semi-columns.

One enters the church from the inner courtyard of the Palazzo Arcivescovile, which is decorated with Doric columns on three sides. The church was built in 1727 by Bernardino Ciurini, who also designed the courtyard, on a site once occupied by a Romanesque structure. The interior is adorned with frescoes. In the apse is a work by Giovanni Ferretti entitled *Adoration of the Shepherds* from 1735, while in the small cupola above the presbytery is the *Eternal Father and the Angels,* a piece by Pietro Anderlini, along with a chiaroscuro of the apostles, again by Ferretti.

San Salvatore al Vescovo

SPEDALE DI SAN GIOVANNI DI DIO (HOSPITAL OF SAN GIOVANNI DI DIO)
Borgo Ognissanti, 20; closed to the public.

➤ The seeds of this multifaceted complex dedicated to Saint John the Divine were sown in 1380 when the Vespucci family founded their hospital as a refuge for religious pilgrims and the poor. At the beginning of the 18th century, the Vespucci hospital was razed and rebuilt by architect Carlo Andrea Marcellini as part of an extensive project that not only included the church of San Giovanni di Dio, but also house and birthplace of the Vespucci family's most noted descendent, Amerigo. Just beyond the intricate wrought iron gate of San Giovanni di Dio's fortified entrance is a picturesque atrium, which can be seen from the street through the large glass door. It is frescoed with Vincenzo Meucci's 18th-century *Christ Healing the Sick with Angels.* Below the frescoed ceiling are handsome twin staircases, accented by the sculptural works of Girolamo Ticciati.

TERRAZZINO REALE (OR LOGGIA REALE)
Via Curtatone, at the corner of Via Il Prato

➤ Designed by Luigi Cambrai Digny to allow members of the ducal court to watch the horse races that took place here, the Terrazzino Reale was completed in 1830.

TORRE DEL SERPE (TOWER OF THE SNAKE)
Viale Fratelli Rosselli

➤ This late-13th-century structure rises on the Viale Fratelli Rosselli right off Ponte della Vittoria, and, like the Old Mint Tower (Torre della Zecca Vecchia, see pg. 116), was part of the old *arnolfiane* fortifications.

VILLA FAVARD
Via Curtatone, 1; closed to the public.

➤ Currently home to the department of economics at the University of Florence, this 19th-century villa, by Giuseppe Poggi, is located in the middle of picturesque gardens.

Museums

GALLERIA CORSINI

Via del Parione, 12, in the Palazzo Corsini; tel.: 055-218994; fax: 055-268123; open: by appointment only; admission: €8.

➣ This collection of private paintings is located in the Palazzo Corsini, a striking baroque building planned by Pier Francesco Silvani and filled with lavish aristocratic furnishings. The art collection, started in 1765 by Prince Don Lorenzo, contains some Renaissance paintings but mostly 17th- and 18th-century paintings. Particularly interesting are Filippino Lippi's *Five Allegorical Figures,* and a crucifixion attributed to Antonello da Messina. Also noteworthy is the portrait of Julius II, which is attributed to Raphael.

MUSEO DELLA CASA FIORENTINA ANTICA (MUSEUM OF THE EARLY FLORENTINE HOME)

Via Porta Rossa, 13, in the Palazzo Davanzati; tel.: 055-2388610; website: www.polomuseale .firenze.it; open: daily 8:15 A.M.–1:50 P.M.; closed: first, third, and fifth Mon. and second and fourth Sun. of each month, Jan. 1, May 1, Dec. 25; admission: free.

➣ The Museum of the Early Florentine Home is located in the austere 14th-century palazzo that used to belong to the Davanzati family. It became a museum in 1956 after undergoing heavy restoration and is furnished with 14th-century Florentine-style furniture, such as beds, kneeling stools, cabinets, and chests, which re-create the atmosphere of everyday medieval life. There are also tapestries, paintings, sculptures, pottery, and ceramic dishes. On the second floor is the Hall of Parrots with painted walls featuring geometric patterns in the lower section and a frieze of trees in the upper one. The master bedroom, also on the second floor, is called the Hall of Peacocks and is notable for its wallpaper, which is decorated with crests and geometric patterns. There is also a small exhibit featuring 16th- to 20th-century European lace and another one of antique machines, such as looms and warping mills. The Gothic courtyard, however, best captures the mood of medieval times with

its zigzagging stairway and barrel-vaulted arches, illuminated by tall shafts of sunlight. In 1904 it was bought by painter Elia Volpi, who restored it heavy-handedly.

MUSEO E CHIOSTRI MONUMENTALI DI SANTA MARIA NOVELLA (MUSEUM AND CLOISTERS OF SANTA MARIA NOVELLA)

Piazza Santa Maria Novella; tel.: 055-282187; museum and cloisters open: daily 9 A.M.– 4:30 P.M.; closed: Fri., Sun., Jan. 1, Easter, May 1, Aug. 15, Dec. 25; admission: €2.70.

➣ To the left of Santa Maria Novella's facade you will find the entrance to the museum, which is made up of a series of frescoed cloisters. Entering through the porch layered with fragments of frescoes depicting funeral scenes, one finds the Chiostro Verde, or Green Cloister, designed by Fra Jacopo Talenti in 1350. The name derives from the dominant color of the paintings here that recount scenes from Genesis. Among them are significant works of the period, such as the biblical episodes painted by the master artist Paolo Uccello between 1425 and 1430. These include *Noah and the Flood,* as well as portraits of Adam and Eve. The works were damaged during the great flood of the Arno in 1966 but underwent restoration in 1983.

Passing through an elegant entrance on the northern wall you will enter the Chapel of the Spaniards, so-named since the middle of the 16th century, when Cosimo I gave it to the Spanish retinue of Eleonora of Toledo for worship. The construction of the chapel began in 1343 by Fra' Jacopo Talenti. In the entranceway one finds a depiction of Saint Peter the Martyr attributed to Talenti. The chapel is laid out in a rectangular plan with a single vault and pointed arches. Between 1367 and 1369 Andrea di Bonaiuto and his apprentices painted the dramatic frescoes that decorate the walls. The works depict the theme of salvation and damnation and include the Journey of Saint Peter, the Resurrection, and the Ascension. Near the entrance is the Ascent from Calvary and a scene depicting the Crucifixion. On the right wall is a noteworthy fresco, *The Triumphant and Vigilant Church,* an allegorical piece depicting the work of the

Chiostri Monumentali di Santa Maria Novella

Dominican friars. Note here the portrayal of the Dominicans as whippets, the "hounds of God," who shepherd the stray sheep back into the flock. The left wall is decorated with a fresco of Saint Thomas Aquinas. Here also you will find 14 personifications of the arts and sciences, including Aristotle and Philosophy and Pythagoras and Arithmetic. The murals were repainted by Veracini from 1735–1736.

To the left, as you leave the Chapel of the Spaniards, is the entrance for the Cloister of the Dead that predates the Dominicans' presence at the church. It underwent reconstruction from 1340–1350. Onward to the left is the funeral chapel of the Strozzi family, decorated with frescoes of the Nativity and Crucifixion done by an unknown artist shortly after 1350. Note also a fresco in the portico of Saint Thomas Aquinas given to Ghiberti from Stefano Fiorentino.

In the church's refectory, which is laid out in four vaulted bays, again by Jacopo Talenti, you will see a 14th-century fresco, *Madonna and Child with the Saints.* Above this floor is the Chapel of the Popes decorated in 1515 with the *Coronation of Mary* by Ridolfo del Ghirlandaio. It also includes a Saint Veronica from the artist Pontormo. Although dating to the 14th century, the space was remodeled in 1592.

MUSEO SALVATORE FERRAGAMO

Piazza Santa Trinita, Sr, in the Palazzo Spini-Feroni; tel.: 055-3360456; website: www.salvatoreferragamo.it; open: daily 10 A.M.–6 P.M.; closed: Tues., holidays; admission: €5.

➤ This museum is housed in the 13th-century Palazzo Spini-Feroni. Its collection of 10,000 shoes documents the work of Salvatore Ferragamo and his firm from the 1920s to the present.

Via d. Porta Nuova

Via d. Pales...

26

Viale Ber...

Via G. Monaco

Via Per...

Via Ghiacciaie

Via P. da...

Via Cittadella

V.le F.lli Rosselli

Via J. da Diacceto

Via Alamanni

Staz. F.S.
Porta Al Prato

Piazzale
Porta al Prato

Via della Scala

Staz. Ce
S.ta Ma

60

...e F.lli Rosselli

il Prato

Via d. Orti Oricellari

Via della Scala

Via B. Rucellai

Via Magenta

Via Montebello

Garibaldi

29

Corso

15

Via Solferino

Italia

Via Palestro

Via
Curtatone

Via Lucia

Via

Borgo Ognissanti

16

Via dell'Albero

Via Palazzuolo

Via der

Via Melegnano

Finiguerra

Via Monte

Via Montebello

10

Lungarno A. Vespucci

'onderia

Via d. Anconella

Lungarno
di S. Rosa

Lung.

3   41

Piazza
d'Ognissanti

Vespucc

55

Ponte
A. Vespucci

P I S A N A

Zanella

Lungo
le Mura di
S.ta Rosa

Via
S. Rosa

P.za di
Verzaia

Via
Bartolini

S. Onofrio

Via
Oratoio

V. Piag-
gione

Piazza di
Cestello

Lungarno Soderini

Borgo

San

Frediano

Lu

Via F. Berni

Viale L. Ariosto

Via
S. Giovanni

Borgo

Drago d'oro

Cardatori
P.za
de' Nerli

Tessitori

V. Piag...

Piazza di
Cestello

Piazza d.
Carmine

B.go d. Stella

ALEARDI

D. Buch...

Via Pulci

Via dell'Orto

Via di
Camaldoli

Via del Leone

Piazza
Piattellina

Via S. Monaca

Via S. S

PIAZZA

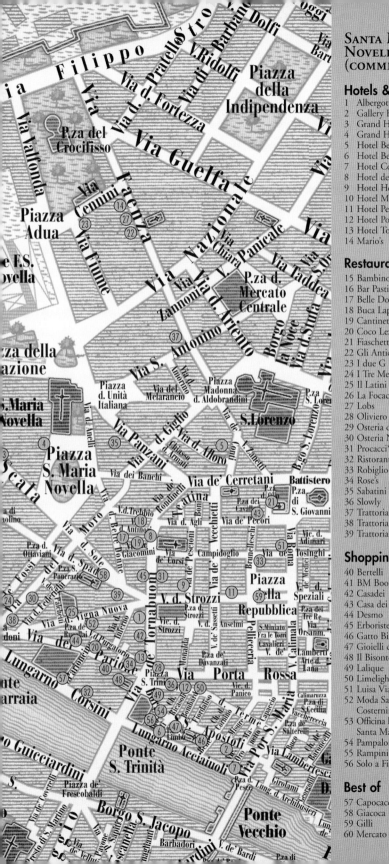

Albergotto

Via de' Tornabuoni, 13; tel.: 055-2396464; fax: 055-2398108; website: www.albergotto.com; e-mail: info@albergotto.com; category:★★★★; number of rooms: 22, including a 540-square-foot mansarda (attic) with raftered ceiling and a view of Florence's rooftops; credit cards accepted: all major; access to internet: yes; €€€.

☛Located in the center of Florence, on the city's most famous street, this is a small and very refined hotel. In the past it has hosted such illustrious characters as Verdi, Donizetti, and George Eliot.

Gallery Hotel Art

Vicolo dell'Oro, 5; tel.: 055-27263; fax 055-268557; website: www.galleryhotelart.com; e-mail: gallery@lungarnohotels.com; category:★★★★; number of rooms: 74, including a penthouse suite with two terraces and a view of downtown roofs, the Duomo, and the Palazzo Vecchio; credit cards accepted: all major; access to internet: yes; €€€€.

☛The Gallery Hotel Art is in a small piazza between Borgo Santissimi Apostoli and the Arno River, very close to the Ponte Vecchio. The hotel itself is a tower from the 1300s, but inside it has been decorated in a very modern style. A special feature at the hotel is the occasional art exhibit of well-known Italian artists on display between the bedrooms and the tearoom.

Grand Hotel

Piazza Ognissanti, 1; tel.: 055-27161; fax: 055-217400; website: www.luxurycollection.com; category:★★★★★; number of rooms: 107, including an executive suite with Renaissance-style frescoes, caisson ceiling, and tester bed; credit cards accepted: all major; access to internet: yes; €€€€.

☛The Grand Hotel is in the historic center, on the bank of the Arno River overlooking the hills surrounding Florence. The building is a 15th-century Florentine palazzo. Its rooms are decorated in Empire style.

Grand Hotel Minerva

Piazza Santa Maria Novella, 16; tel.: 055-27230; fax: 055-268281; website: www.grandhotelminerva.com; e-mail: info@grandhotelminerva.com; category:★★★★; number of rooms: 102, including a suite with a frescoed ceiling; credit cards accepted: all major; access to internet: yes; €€€.

☛One of Florence's classics, located in a palazzo dating back seven centuries. There is a roof garden and a pool with a view of the city.

Hotel Bellettini

Via dei Conti, 7; tel.: 055-213561; fax: 055-283551; website: www.hotelbellettini.com; e-mail: info@hotelbellettini.com; category: ★★; number of rooms: 27; credit cards accepted: all major; access to internet: yes; €€.

☛Try the room with a view of the Duomo, the campanile, and the Medici Chapels.

Hotel Berchielli

Lungarno Acciaioli, 14; tel.: 055-264061; fax: 055-218636; website: www.berchielli.it; e-mail: info@berchielli.it; category:★★★★; number of rooms: 76; credit cards accepted: all major; access to internet: yes; €€€€.

☛A beautiful hotel between Ponte Santa Trinita and the Ponte Vecchio. It has the air of the elegant hotels of bygone eras, yet the prices remain accessible.

Hotel Continental

Lungarno Acciaioli, 2; tel.: 055-27262; fax: 055-283139; website: www.lungarnohotels.com; e-mail: continentale@lungarnohotels.com; category:★★★★; number of rooms: 43; credit cards accepted: all major; access to internet: yes; €€€.

☛This hotel has a prime location with a splendid view of the city from its rooftop terrace. Decor is modern.

Hotel de la Ville

Piazza Antinori, 1; tel.: 055-2381805; fax: 055-2381809; website: www.hotel delaville.it; e-mail: info@hoteldelaville.it; category:★★★★; number of rooms: 75, including four junior suites with a view of Piazza Antinori and the Duomo and three suites in the rear, without a view; credit cards accepted: all major; access to internet: yes; €€€–€€€€.
☛Recently redone in classical and comfortable style, this hotel is situated in the most elegant location in the city center.

Hotel Helvetia and Bristol

Via dei Pescioni, 2; tel.: 055-26651; fax: 055-288353; e-mail: reservation.hbf @royaldemeure.com; category:★★★★★; number of rooms: 67, including two pent-house executive suites with views of the city; credit cards accepted: all major; access to internet: yes; €€€€.
☛The Hotel Helvetia and Bristol is one of the most important luxury hotels in Florence. The setting is elegant and also comfortable. All of the rooms are tastefully and uniquely decorated.

Hotel Montebello Splendid

Via Garibaldi, 14; tel.: 055-2398051; fax: 055-2747700; website: www.monte bellosplendid.com; e-mail: info@montebello splendid.com; category:★★★★★; number of rooms: 61, including a suite with a terrace facing the garden; credit cards accepted: all major; access to internet: yes; €€€.
☛An elegant hotel located in a 14th-century villa, with 1900s Parisian-style decor. Breakfast is served in a pleasant garden greenhouse.

Hotel Pensione Pendini

Via Strozzi, 2; tel.: 055-211170; fax: 055-281807; website: www.florenceitaly.net; e-mail: pendini@florenceitaly.net; category:★★★; number of rooms: 42; credit cards accepted: all major; access to internet: yes; most beautiful rooms: the seven quadruple rooms with views of Piazza della Repubblica; €€€.
☛A very central hotel that offers comfort and quiet once inside. Rooms are simple and functional.

Hotel Porta Rossa

Via Porta Rossa, 19; tel.: 055-287551; fax: 055-282179; category:★★★; number of rooms: 79; credit cards accepted: all major; €€.
☛The Hotel Porta Rossa is an old hotel on the 13th-century road to the city. It makes up part of the Palazzo Torrigiani. The rooms are spacious and decorated with antique furniture. It has been recently renovated.

Hotel Tornabuoni Beacci

Via Tornabuoni, 3; tel.: 055-212645; fax: 055-283594; website: www.tornabuoni hotels.com; e-mail: info@tornabuonihotels .com; category: ★★★; number of rooms: 28; credit cards accepted: all major; access to internet: from common area; €€–€€€.
☛One of the oldest hotels in Florence, the Hotel Tornabuoni Beacci is located amidst the most elegant designer shops. The rooms are comfortable and the suites can host several guests.

Mario's

Via Faenza, 89; tel.: 055-216801; fax: 055-212039; website: www.hotelmarios.com; e-mail: info@hotelmarios.com; category:★★★; number of rooms: 16, including one (No. 6) with a tester bed; credit cards accepted: all major; access to internet: yes; €€€€.
☛Mario's is a small, friendly hotel with rooms at reasonable prices and with a pleasant decor.

Belle Donne

Via delle Belle Donne, 16r; tel.: 055-2382609; open: daily noon–2:30 P.M., 7–10:30 P.M.; closed: Aug.; credit cards accepted: all major; €.

☛This quaint restaurant offers a limited menu of Tuscan dishes. A blackboard lists the daily specials. Cozy and pleasant, the restaurant is filled with Florentine pottery and mismatched silverware, plates, and dishes. Due to the limited seating this is not a place one can linger.

Buca Lapi

Via del Trebbio, 1r; tel.: 055-213768; fax: 055-284862; open: Mon. 7:30–10:30 P.M.; Tues.–Sat. 12:30–2:30 P.M., 7:30–10:30 P.M.; closed: Sun.; credit cards accepted: all major; €€.

☛A simple but elegant restaurant with Tuscan cuisine and a limited wine selection.

Cantinetta Antinori

Piazza Antinori, 3; tel.: 055-292234; fax: 055-2359877; open: Mon.–Fri. 12:30–2:30 P.M., 7–10:30 P.M.; closed: Sat.–Sun.; credit cards accepted: all major; €.

☛The Cantinetta Antinori has long been a mainstay of Florence's gastronomic scene because of the excellence of its cuisine and the elegance of its setting—the 15th-century Palazzo Antinori. Antinori wines need no introduction. The restaurant is run by the aristocratic, wine-producing family of the same name and offers specialties like *scamorza al forno con melanzane* (roasted scamorza cheese with eggplant) and *crema di zucchine* (zucchini cream).

Coco Lezzone

Via del Parioncino, 26r; tel.: 055-287178; open: Mon., Wed.–Sat. noon–2:30 P.M., 7:30–10 P.M., Tues. noon–2:30 P.M.; closed: Sun.; credit cards accepted: none; €.

☛This restaurant, located in a beautiful 13th-century palazzo, offers a traditional Tuscan menu. It is very popular among tourists. Specialties are *arista al forno* (roasted chine of pork), *pappa al pomodoro*, and tripe.

Fiaschetteria da Nuvoli

Piazza dell'Olio, 15r; tel.: 055-2396616; open: Mon.–Sat. 7:30 A.M.–9 P.M.; closed: Sun.; credit cards accepted: all major; €.

☛Always packed to capacity, da Nuvoli is not advisable for anyone who suffers from claustrophobia. The reason for the crowds: exceptional food and reasonable prices. One can either stand at the bar and order a glass of wine and a mixed plate of *crostini* displayed in a glass case on the counter or sit in the dining room downstairs and enjoy the wine with one of the Florentine dishes offered.

Gli Antichi Cancelli

Via Faenza, 73r; tel.: 055-218927; open: daily noon–3 P.M., 7–10:30 P.M.; credit cards accepted: all major; €.

☛This lovely trattoria is small, with about 40 seats. It serves typical Tuscan food such as *ribollita* and *pappa al pomodoro*. The menu changes daily.

I due G

Via B. Cennini, 6; tel.: 055-218623; open: Mon.–Sat. noon–2:30 P.M., 7:30–10 P.M.; closed: Sun. and public holidays; credit cards accepted: all major; €.

☛This small Tuscan trattoria serves hearty regional food such as *papardelle* in a ragu of rabbit, risotto with seasonal vegetables, ravioli with mushrooms and black truffles, tripe *alla fiorentina*, and a roast lamb with artichokes.

I Tre Merli

Via de' Fossi, 12r; tel.: 055-287062; open: daily noon–11 P.M.; credit cards accepted: all major; €€.

☛People come to I Tre Merli for its "Mediterranean cuisine"—recipes featuring in-season ingredients, fresh herbs, and the best extra-virgin olive oil. *Pasta al pomodoro* is upgraded to perfect *spaghettini al dente* (thin spaghetti), sauced with fresh plum tomatoes, basil leaves, and olive oil, and topped with melted Parmesan cheese (no garlic is used in the sauce). Tender grilled beef garnished with sage, rosemary, and olive oil is served on an oversized ceramic plate accompanied by roasted eggplant, tomatoes, fennel, and potatoes. Wines—Chianti Colli Senese or a dry Vernaccia—come by the glass. There are outdoor dining terraces on both Via de' Fossi and the quieter Via del Moro.

Il Latini

Via dei Palchetti, 6r; tel.: 055-210916; website: www.illatini.com; e-mail: info @illatini.com; open: Tues.–Sun. 12:30–2:30 P.M., 7:30–11 P.M.; closed: Mon.; credit cards accepted: all major; €.

☛If traditional Tuscan decor is an important accompaniment to classic fare, this cantina is the place to go—if you can get in. The popular spot, sporting long wooden tables, whitewashed walls, and Chianti-flask candleholders, often has a long line of hungry customers, many of them tourists, waiting to get in. Run by Torello Latini and his wife, Il Latini was founded by Torello's father, Narciso, as a *fiaschetteria,* or neighborhood drinking hole, more than half a century ago. Il Latini's house specialty is Chianina beef. Make sure not to leave without getting a bottle of wine or olive oil, proudly produced by the Latini family.

La Focaccia

Viale Corsica, 31r; tel.: 055-350663/350242; open: Mon.–Sat. 12:30–2:30 P.M., 7:30–10:30 P.M.; closed: Sun.; credit cards accepted: all major; €.

☛La Focaccia is a quiet, family-run restaurant. Its specialties include *tartara di farro con ricotta e valeriana aromatizzata al timo* (leeks tartare with ricotta), *gnocchetti in salsa di champagne e zucchine* (small gnocchi with a champagne and zucchini sauce), and fresh fish dishes.

Lobs

Via Faenza, 75–77; tel.: 055-212478; open: Tues.–Sun. 12:30–2:30 P.M., 7–11 P.M.; closed: Mon.; credit cards accepted: all major; €.

☛Lobs specializes in creative fish cuisine that even the budget diner can afford, including many seafood pastas. Among the dishes offered are seafood lasagna layered with grouper and topped with fresh shrimp, and risotto studded with fresh salmon chunks. The first courses vanish at dinner, giving way to oysters and an oven-baked sea bass fillet, head and tail intact, surrounded by grilled peppers, carrots, potatoes, zucchini, olives, and cherry tomatoes. The "grand sauté," a deep platter of mussels and clams cooked in white wine, lemon, parsley, and shallots, arrives with jumbo shrimp and crayfish. The decor is nautical, even if chicken breast and vegetable dishes are included on the menu.

Oliviero

Via delle Terme, 51r; tel.: 055-287643; open: daily 11 A.M.–3 P.M., 7 P.M.–1 A.M.; closed: Sun. and Aug.; credit cards accepted: all major; €€.

☞Near Via Tornabuoni, this elegant and friendly restaurant serves traditional Tuscan cuisine with some new twists, especially with fish. Specialties are *ravioli di anatra* (duck ravioli), *bignole di scampetti con zucchine trifoliate* (bignole with small shrimp and zucchini), *soufflé Oliviero*, and *sformatino di cavolfiore con pomodoro e olive* (cauliflower soufflé with tomatoes and olives).

Osteria dei Cento Poveri

Via Palazzuolo, 31r; tel.: 055-218846; open: daily 12:30–2:30 P.M., 7–11 P.M.; credit cards accepted: all major; €.

☞Local cuisine with an innovative touch is served at this pleasant and always-crowded restaurant. Several vegetarian dishes are offered, but their specialties are *gnocchi all'astice* (lobster gnocchi), *taglierini alle vongole* (taglierini with clams), and *tortellacci alla salsa di quaglia* (tortellini with clam sauce).

Osteria Numero 1

Via del Moro, 22; tel.: 055-284897; open: daily noon–2:30 P.M., 7–10:30 P.M.; closed: Tues. and Aug.; credit cards accepted: all major; €.

☞Inventive yet traditional cuisine is served in a historic palazzo. Specialties include *petto d'anatra all'arancia* (duck à l'orange) and *tortelli d'aragosta in salsa di gamberi* (lobster tortelli with shrimp).

*Procacci

Via Tornabuoni, 64r; tel.: 055-211656; open: Mon.–Sat. 10:30 A.M.–8 P.M.; closed: Sun.; credit cards accepted: all major.

☞A "luxury grocery store" that also serves delicious *panini tartufati* (truffle-flavored sandwiches) and wine.

Ristorante Corsini

Lungarno Corsini, 4; tel.: 055-217706; open: daily 11:30 A.M.–11:30 P.M.; credit cards accepted: all major; €.

☞The restaurant's cream-colored 14th-century vaulted ceilings and walnut paneling set the tone for a special dining experience, as do the tables outside overlooking the Arno River. The cuisine is creative: Parmesan puff pastry is filled with potato gnocchi, porcini mushrooms, and cherry tomatoes, and ravioli-like tortelloni are made with potato, melted butter, hazelnuts, and thyme. Fillet of beef is stuffed with marinated salmon and topped with a julienne of carrots and fennel.

Robiglio

Via Tosinghi, 11r; tel. and fax: 055-215013; open: daily 8 A.M.–8 P.M.; credit cards accepted: none.

☞This *pasticceria* is a breakfast institution for Florentines. Delicious cakes and pastries made on the premises are offered along with what many consider to be the best espresso in town.

Rose's

Via del Parione, 26r; tel.: 055-287090; open: Mon.–Sat. 8–1:30 A.M., Sun. 7:30 P.M.–1:30 A.M.; credit cards accepted: all major; €€.

☞A Florentine institution, Rose's is a New York–style café in decor and spirit, yet the food is prepared according to the high standards of Italian cuisine: homemade muffins at breakfast; lunch specialties such as roast turkey salad plate—shredded carrot and sliced avocado artistically layered over turkey breast that is placed on a bed of red chicory; and a vegetarian enchilada filled with grilled eggplant, zucchini, and peppers, and topped with salsa and guacamole. Rose's is also renowned for its sushi-only dinner menu. There are smoking and non-smoking sections.

RESTAURANTS & CAFÉS

Sabatini

Via dei Panzani, 9a; tel.: 055-282802; fax: 055-210293; website: www.ristorante sabatini.it; open: Tues.–Sun. 12:30–2:30 P.M., 7:30–10:30 P.M.; closed: Mon.; credit cards accepted: all major; €.

☛This longtime Florence establishment offers beautifully prepared traditional dishes and international cuisine in an elegant environment. The wine list has over 500 selections. The chef's specialties are *scampi con pomodoro* and *filetto al pepe nero* (beef fillet with black pepper).

Slowly

Via Porta Rossa, 63r; tel.: 055-2645354; open: Mon.–Sat. 10–3 A.M.; closed: Sun.; credit cards accepted: none.

☛This recently opened bar is a lively spot all day long. But it really reaches its peak in the early evening, when young Florentine professionals and tourists arrive for aperitifs and all the snacks, including pasta and sushi, that are offered with them. It is hard to find a place to sit after 7 P.M.

Trattoria Antellesi

Via Faenza, 9r; tel.: 055-216990; open: daily. noon–3 P.M., 7–10:30 P.M.; credit cards accepted: all major; €€.

☛Dine in a 15th-century cream-colored stucco setting and have the *crespelle*, ever-so-light crêpes filled with spinach-ricotta mousse and béchamel. *Spaghetti alla chiantigiana* is a popular fresh pasta dish sauced with small chunks of prime beef that have been simmered in tomato and Chianti wine. As a main course, order grilled meat or *tagliata*, strips of beef combined with arugula and balsamic vinegar. The Tuscan wine list is excellent, with offerings such as a Villa Antinori Riserva available by the half bottle. Great food and friendly service.

Trattoria Garga

Via del Moro, 48; tel.: 055-2398898; open: Tues.–Sun. 7:30–10:30 P.M.; closed: Mon.; credit cards accepted: all major; €€.

☛A colorful restaurant with good food. The menu offers a variety of dishes, nouvelle cuisine, and lots of fish. There are even cooking lessons for those curious about what goes on in the kitchen.

Trattoria Marione

Via della Spada, 27r; tel.: 055-214756; open: daily noon–3 P.M., 7–10 P.M.; credit cards accepted: all major; €.

☛Traditional Tuscan cuisine in a pleasant and comfortable setting.

SPECIALTY SHOPS

Bertelli

Via del Parione, 54r; tel.: 055-287858; open: Mon. 3:30–7:30 P.M., Tues.–Sat. 9:30 A.M.–1:30 P.M., 3:30–7:30 P.M.; closed: Sun.; credit cards accepted: all major.

☛Bertelli started this men's clothing store 40 years ago and has been running it ever since. He sells beautiful ready-to-wear men's clothes and also specializes in custom-made clothes fit to your specifications. Prices are upward of €350.

BM Bookshop

Borgo Ognissanti, 4r; tel.: 055-294575; e-mail: bmbookshop@dada.it; open: Mon.–Sat. 9:30 A.M.–7:30 P.M.; closed: Sun.; credit cards accepted: all major.

☛A reference point for the English-speaking visitor and resident, BM has the most extensive selection of books by American and British authors in town. Books on Italian art, history, cooking, design, crafts, and the most recent guidebooks are all here, and are chosen with an eye for quality. This is also the place to find literature on Florence and Italian authors translated into English, as well as paperback best-sellers.

Casadei

Via de' Tornabuoni, 33r; tel.: 055-287240; open: Mon.–Sat. 10 A.M.–1 P.M., 2–7 P.M.; closed: Sun.; credit cards accepted: all major.
☛Casadei sells beautiful, original, and comfortable shoes, as well as other leather accessories. It offers elegance at a reasonable price.

Casa dei Tessuti

Via de' Pecori, 20–24; tel.: 055-215961; open: daily 9 A.M.–1 P.M., 3:30–7:30 P.M.; closed: Mon. morning in winter, Sat. afternoon in summer; credit cards accepted: all major.
☛This shop has just about any type of fabric imaginable and will also custom tailor clothing with their material.

Erboristeria Inglese

Via Tornabuoni, 19r; tel.: 055-210628/ 2658319; open: Mon. 2–8 P.M., Tues.–Sun. 10 A.M.–8 P.M.; credit cards accepted: all major.
☛In this perfume shop you can find Harris and Penhaligon's soaps and Edwin Jagger razors.

Gatto Bianco

Borgo Santissimi Apostoli, 12r; tel.: 055-282989; open: Mon.–Sat. 10 A.M.–1 P.M., 3:30–7 P.M.; closed: Sun.; credit cards accepted: all major.
☛Gatto Bianco offers handmade jewels.

Gioielli d'Epoca

Piazza del Limbo, 8r; tel.: 055-283318; open: Mon.–Sat. 9:30 A.M.–1 P.M., 3:30–8 P.M.; closed: Sun.; credit cards accepted: all major.
☛On the corner of this ancient medieval road is the shop of Dr. Judy Gualtieri and Angelo Gandolfi, where one can buy rare period jewelry. There is also a collection of furniture.

Il Bisonte

Via del Parione, 31r; tel.: 055-215722; website: www.ilbisonte.net; e-mail: ilbisonte@ilbisonte.net; open: Mon.–Sat. 9:30 A.M.–7 P.M.; closed: Sun.; credit cards accepted: all major.
☛Although Il Bisonte now has showrooms from Paris to Tokyo, this is the original, homey, unpretentious shop featuring the creative genius of the Italian leather designer/craftsman Wanny Di Filippo. Il Bisonte carries his classic natural cowhide briefcases, backpacks, and wallets as well as bags made of striped deckchair canvas. All are instantly recognizable by their soft lines and roominess. Di Filippo's newest design—a reversible shopping bag with wool tweed on one side and black calfskin on the other—is especially popular.

Luisa Via Roma

Via Roma, 19–21r; tel.: 055-217826; website: www.luisaviaroma.com; open: Mon.–Sat. 10 A.M.–7:30 P.M., Sun. 11 A.M.– 7 P.M.; credit cards accepted: all major.

☛This upscale shop offers the most varied selection of the hottest fashions—and not just from Italian designers. In addition to clothing, the boutique also sells shoes and accessories.

Moda Sartoriale di Piero Costernino

Via del Purgatorio, 22r; tel. 055-280118; open: Mon.–Sat. 9:30 A.M.–7 P.M.; closed: Sun.; credit cards accepted: none.

☛This small tailor's shop is renowned for its sharp cut and affordable prices.

Officina Profumo- Farmaceutica di Santa Maria Novella

Via della Scala, 16; tel.: 055-216276; open: Mon.–Sun. 9:30 A.M.–7:30 P.M.; credit cards accepted: all major.

☛One of the oldest pharmacies in the world. Founded in 1612, this venerable pharmacy still uses purely natural ingredients and techniques to make the creams, soaps, and tonics that have made it famous. Don't forget the potpourri, a masterful combination of flowers and herbs from the hills around Florence (see pg. 140).

*Pampaloni

Borgo Santissimi Apostoli, 47r; tel.: 055-289094; open: Tues.–Sat. 10 A.M.–1 P.M., 3:30–7:30 P.M.; closed: Sun.–Mon.; credit cards accepted: all major.

☛Pampaloni produces beautiful silverware for Tiffany's. It also sells fine china and other wares for the home.

Rampini Ceramics

Borgo Ognissanti, 32–34r; tel.: 055-219720; website: www.rampiniceramics.com; e-mail: info@rampiniceramics.com; open: Mon.–Sat. 10 A.M.–7 P.M.; closed: Sun.; credit cards accepted: all major.

☛The extended Romano family designs, produces, and paints plates, pitchers, and canisters entirely by hand, working in an old stone house in the Chianti town of Radda. Every original ceramic table setting is a celebration of the fruit, flowers, and leaves typical of the warm Tuscan landscape. Jewel-like greens, reds, yellows, and blues are obtained with mineral oxides and glass fired at high temperatures. The shop is located on the beautiful Renaissance-era premises once belonging to Fraternità del Sacramento, a group of Florentines devoted to the worship of the Holy Eucharist and who also managed a volunteer ambulance service.

Solo a Firenze

Borgo Santissimi Apostoli, 37r; tel.: 055-216324; open: Mon.–Sat. 10:30 A.M.–1 P.M.; 2–7 P.M.; closed: Sun.; credit cards accepted: all major.

☛On a medieval road, just off Via Tornabuoni, this shop carries works by some of the best Florentine artisans: objects in silver, worked by hand; products in terra-cotta and ceramic; and reproductions of maps on cotton fabric.

Santo Spirito/ Oltrarno

By Laura Collura Kahn

anto Spirito spans the south bank of the Arno, or the Oltrarno, and is the most countryside-like area of Florence, filled with craftsmen's workshops, hilly roads, and picnic spots.

Walk west from the Ponte Vecchio to the unassuming **Piazza Santo Spirito**, a produce market during the day and a favorite hangout at night. Here stands the church of **Santo Spirito**, whose oversimplified 19th-century facade conceals a Renaissance interior. Inside, visit the lavish vestibule by Cronaca and the octagonal sacristy, designed in the 15th century in imitation of the Baptistery of San Giovanni.

Farther west is the church of **Santa Maria del Carmine**, built in 1268, destroyed by a fire in 1771, and rebuilt in 1782. The flames spared its centerpiece, the **Cappella Brancacci**, featuring landmark 15th-century frescoes by Masaccio, including his famous *Expulsion from Paradise*. Continue walking west through the working-class quarter of San Frediano, and reach **Porta San Frediano**, a city gate built in 1332–1334 by Andrea Pisano.

The stroll from the Ponte Vecchio along Via Guicciardini leads to **Piazza Pitti**, dominated by the huge facade of the **Palazzo Pitti**, a precursor of Versailles. Trying to rival the Medicis, merchant Luca Pitti commissioned it in the 15th century. Ironically, the Medicis later bought it from his impoverished heirs and finished its construction. It now houses various museums, mostly devoted to the minor arts (**Galleria Palatina**, **Galleria d'Arte Moderna**, **Museo degli Argenti**, and **Museo delle Carrozze**). The **Galleria del Costume** and the **Museo delle Porcellane** are housed in separate buildings in the **Giardino di Boboli**, behind the palazzo. An Italian-style garden, this park is a bizarre combination of mannerist sculptures and a well-groomed backdrop. As Via Guicciardini turns into Via Romana, it leads to **Porta Romana**, another remnant of the medieval walls that were torn down and turned into boulevards in the 1800s.

Yet another option at the Ponte Vecchio is to take the picturesque Costa San Giorgio up the hill to **Porta San Giorgio**, once part of an internal wall. From here, enter the **Forte Belvedere**, a 16th-century fortress with a good view of the city. The best vista, however, remains **Piazzale Michelangelo**, a spectacularly panoramic square built in the 19th century. Descending toward the city, stop at the imposing, three-story **Porta San Niccolò**.

The highest hill nearby is topped by the church of **San Miniato al Monte**.

Opposite, Fountain in the Giardino di Boboli

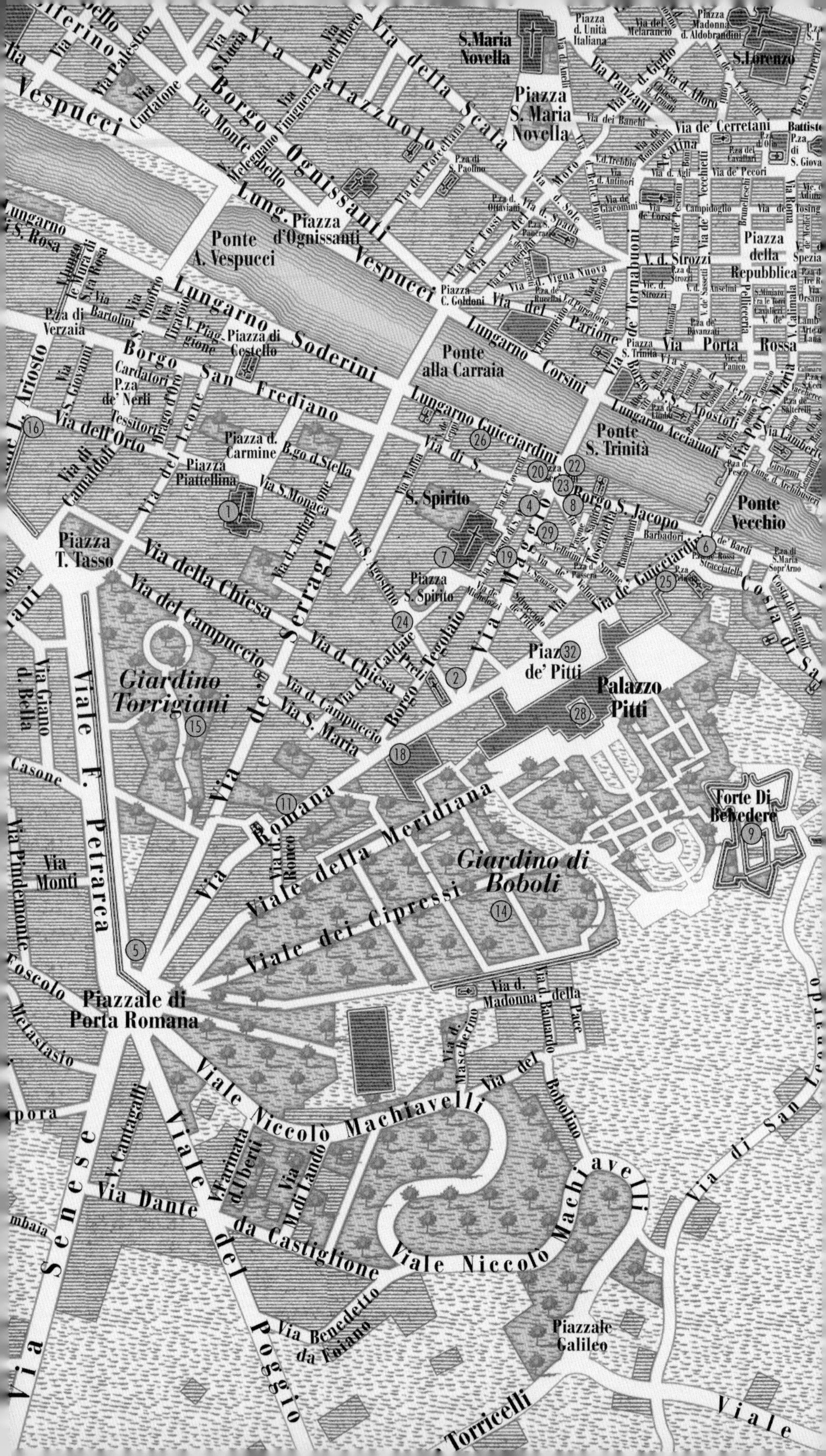

Street and place labels (map of Florence):

Via del Palazzuolo
Via della Scala
S. Maria Novella
Piazza d. Unità Italiana
Via di Giglio
Via d'Alloro
Piazza Madonna d. Aldobrandini
S. Lorenzo
Via Panzani
Piazza S. Maria Novella
Via dei Banchi
Via de' Cerretani
Battistero
P.za di S. Giova
Borgo Ognissanti
Via Monte
Via Maggio
Lung. Piazza d'Ognissanti
Piazza d. Unità
Piazza S. Paolino
Via de' Fossi
Piazza della Repubblica
V. d. Strozzi
Porta Rossa
Ponte A. Vespucci
Lungarno Vespucci
Lungarno Corsini
Piazza della
Piazza C. Goldoni
Piazza S. Trinita
Lungarno Soderini
Ponte alla Carraia
Lungarno Guicciardini
Ponte S. Trinita
Borgo San Frediano
Lungarno Acciaiuoli
Ponte Vecchio
Piazza di Verzaia
Via di Camaldoli
Via dell'Orto
Piazza d. Carmine
Piazza Piattellina
Borgo d. Stella
S. Spirito
Borgo S. Jacopo
Piazza T. Tasso
Via della Chiesa
Via de' Serragli
S. Agostino
Piazza S. Spirito
Via de' Guicciardini
Costa di S.
Piazza S. Maria Sopr'Arno
Via del Campuccio
Giardino Torrigiani
Via d. Chiesa
Borgo Tegolaio
Piaz. de' Pitti
Palazzo Pitti
Via Romana
Viale F. Petrarca
Viale della Meridiana
Giardino di Boboli
Forte Di Belvedere
Via P. Indemonte
Via Monti
Viale dei Cipressi
Piazzale di Porta Romana
Via d. Madonna della Pace
Viale Niccolò Machiavelli
Via del Poggio
Via Dante da Castiglione
Viale Niccolò Machiavelli
Via di San
Via Benedetto da Foiano
Piazzale Galileo
Viale
Torricelli

Numbered markers: 1, 2, 5, 6, 7, 8, 9, 11, 14, 15, 16, 18, 19, 22, 23, 24, 25, 26, 28, 29, 32

S.Maria Novella

Piazza d. Unità Italiana

Via di Melarancio

Piazza Madonna d. Aldobrandini

S.Lorenzo

Vespucci

Via delle Palestro

Via Curtatone

Via della Scala

Borgo Ognissanti

Via Palazzuolo

Via Monte Bello

Via del Porcellana

Piazza S. Maria Novella

Via del Giglio

Via de' Cerretani

Battiste P.za di S. Giova

Via d'Alloro

Via de' Panzani

Via de' Banchi

Via de' Cerretani

Via de' Pecori

Via Roma

Vic. d' Adimari Tosinghi

Piazza della Repubblica

Ponte A. Vespucci

Piazza d'Ognissanti

Lung. Piazza d'Ognissanti

Vespucci

P.za di S. Paolino

Via d. Porcellana

Via d'Ariento

Via d. Sole

Via d. Spada

Via d. Trebbio

Via d. Antinori

Via degli Agli

Via de' Vecchietti

Via de' Tornabuoni

Via de Corsi

Via Campidoglio

V. d. Strozzi

P.za d. Strozzi

Piazza della Repubblica

P.za di Spezia

Lungarno S. Rosa

Lungarno Soderini

Piazza C. Goldoni

Via d. Vigna Nuova

Via del Parione

Via d. Purgatorio

Piazza Rucellai

Piazza S. Trinita

Via Porta Rossa

Via de' Anselmi

P.za di pia

Borgo San Frediano

Piazza di Cestello

Lungarno Soderini

Ponte alla Carraia

Lungarno Corsini

Lungarno Acciaiuoli

Ponte S. Trinita

Via de' Pescioni

Via de' Tosinghi

Borgo San Frediano

Via de' Camaldoli

Via dell'Orto

Piazza d. Carmine

B.go d'Stella

Via S. Monaca

Via del Leone

S. Spirito

Lungarno Guicciardini

Via di S.

Piazza de' Frescobaldi

Borgo S. Jacopo

Ponte Vecchio

Piazza T. Tasso

Piazza Piattellina

Via della Chiesa

Via S. Agostino

Piazza S. Spirito

Via Maggio

Via de' Guicciardini

Costa di San

Giardino Torrigiani

Via del Campuccio

Serragli

Via d. Chiesa

Via d. Caldaie

Borgo Tegolaio

Piazza de' Pitti

Palazzo Pitti

Via Giano d. Bella

Viale F. Petrarca

Via del Campuccio

Via S. Maria

Romana

Piazza de' Pitti

Forte Di Belvedere

Casone

Via Pisana

Via Monti

Via Romana

Viale della Meridiana

Giardino di Boboli

Piazzale di Porta Romana

Viale dei Cipressi

Via d. Madonna della Pace

Via di San Leonardo

Via Senese

Viale Niccolò Machiavelli

Via del Poggio

Via Dante da Castiglione

Via Benedetto da Foiano

Viale Niccolò Machiavelli

Piazzale Galileo

Torricelli

Viale

55 36 42 51 56 62 54 53 33 41 57 47 40 63 64 35 44 62 59 58 61 60 49 43 3

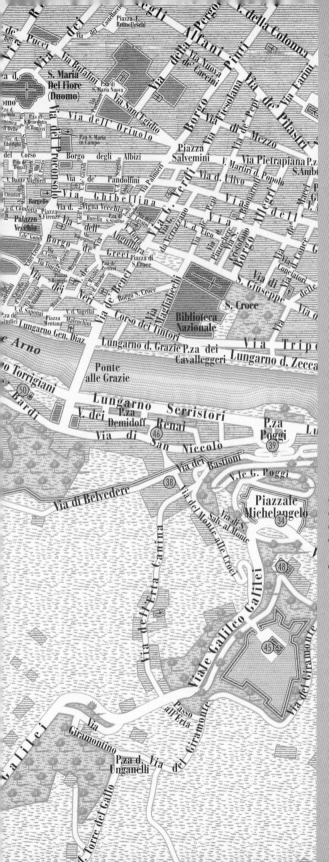

Santo Spirito/ Oltrarno (cultural)

CAPPELLA BRANCACCI (BRANCACCI CHAPEL)

Piazza del Carmine, 14; tel.: 055-2382195; website: www.comune.firenze.it; open: Mon., Wed.–Sat. 10 A.M.–5 P.M., Sun. and public holidays 1– 5 P.M.; closed: Tues.; admission: €4.

➢ The church of Santa Maria del Carmine is famous for the frescoes depicting the Life of Saint Peter in the Brancacci Chapel, located in the right transept. Begun by Masolino in 1424, they were continued by his pupil Masaccio, who died before finishing the cycle. They were completed in 1480 by Filippino Lippi. The use of perspective and simple, straightforward style in *The Tribute Money* and the realism and vivid depiction of emotions in *The Expulsion of Adam and Eve* put Masaccio at the forefront of Renaissance painting. Many great artists, including da Vinci and Michelangelo, visited the chapel to study these pioneering works. Look for the self-portrait of Masaccio in *Saint Peter Enthroned,* below the *Expulsion from Paradise.* The burly, curly-haired artist stands gazing at the viewer from a group of four men.

FORTE BELVEDERE

Via di San Leonardo; tel.: 055-2625900; open only for exhibitions and on summer evenings.

➢ Designed by Bernardo Buontalenti and don Giovanni de' Medici in 1590 during the reign of Grand Duke Ferdinando I, the structure is laid out in a polygonal plan and was built both as a defense against invading armies as well as to protect city rulers from an internal uprising. Restorative efforts since the 1950s have removed large amounts of earth around the walls to fully reveal the ramparts on the north and south ends. From its ramparts, the fort offers panoramic views of the city and surrounding hills. Inside the walls is the elegant Palazzina di Belvedere, which is open for exhibitions.

GALLERIA PALATINA (PALATINE GALLERY)

Piazza Pitti, in the Palazzo Pitti; tel.: 055-294883; website: www.polomuseale .firenze.it; open: Tues.–Sun. 8:15 A.M.–6:50 P.M.; closed Mon., holidays; admission: €8.50.

Cappella Brancacci

➢ Amassed during the Medici reign, the palazzo's collection of 16th-, 17th-, and 18th-century paintings ranks among the finest in the world. True to 18th-century custom, the paintings are scattered throughout the galleries with only decorative appeal taken into consideration, as if the chief purpose of masterpieces by Raphael, Titian, Andrea del Sarto, Caravaggio, Rubens, and Van Dyck were to complement the handsome furniture.

The parade of masterpieces begins in the first room, the Sala di Venere, with an oil painting by Titian. His portrait of Pope Julius II (1545) is copied from an early work by Raphael, located in the National Gallery in London. The virtuosity of Titian's brushstroke, however, combined with his feel for light, doubtlessly qualifies the originality of this copy. Another portrait, this time of Pietro Aretino (1545), exhibits an even finer brushstroke, rendering this writer and friend of Cosimo I in a complimentary light made of gentle browns and warm gold hues. On the opposite wall is *Concert* (1510–1512), a painting from the master's youth. The sole statue in the room is *Venere Italica,* or "Italian Venus," carved by Antonio Canova for Napoleon.

In the Sala di Apollo, two more masterpieces by Titian dominate the scene. They are *The Portrait of a Gentleman* (1540) and

Mary Magdalene (before 1548). The former painting is also known as *The Man with Grey Eyes,* even though the eyes of the subject are rendered in what seems to be an indefinable color. Together with his carefully shaded face, they emerge from a background of pitch-black darkness. The large altarpiece features the *Sacred Conversation* (1522) by mannerist master Rosso Fiorentino. It stands directly across from the *Pietà* and *Sacred Family,* late works from Andrea del Sarto, who was a contemporary of Rosso, but whose work clearly belongs to the High Renaissance.

The Sala di Marte holds two masterpieces by Rubens. *Consequences of War* (1638) is an allegorical piece that features Mars, the god of war, and Discord, also known as the Furies. *The Four Philosophers* (1611–1612), one of Rubens's final works on canvas, abounds with literary and philosophical references. The artist painted himself into the left side of the picture, seated beside his brother. The large portrait of Cardinal Bentivoglio is by Van Dyck, who lavished much attention on the opulent red robe. Even more impressive, perhaps, is Veronese's *Portrait of a Man* (1550–1560), which exhibits a remarkable sense of modernity in its use of color.

Raphael's famous *La Velata,* or "Veiled Lady," is in the Sala di Giove. The model for this masterpiece may have been the Fornarina, the artist's famous mistress.

In the next room, the Sala di Saturno, one can trace the trajectory of Raphael's artistic development. *The Madonna of the Grand Duke* (1506) is an early work, in which the artist can be seen developing da Vinci's *sfumato* technique. The Madonna emerges from darkness with features that are light, soft, and gentle, painted in the tradition of Perugino, Raphael's mentor. The portraits of Agnolo and Maddalena Doni (1506–1507) are Renaissance painting standards. The unfinished *Madonna del Baldacchino* (1507) shows signs of innovation by the artist as a young man. This early Madonna exhibits a penchant for monumentality that Raphael would crystallize in the *Madonna della Seggiola* (1513–1514), a sublime composition that practically overflows with monumental figures in vivid colors. Two more portraits, *La Gravida* (1506) and the *Madonna of the Window* (c. 1514), hang in the Sala dell'Iliade and the Sala dell' Educazione di Giove, respectively. The latter room also features the *Sleeping Cupid* (1608), completed by Caravaggio just before he died.

GIARDINO DI BOBOLI (BOBOLI GARDENS)

Piazza Pitti; tel.: 055-294883; website: www .polomuseale.firenze.it; open: Mon.–Sun. 8:15 A.M.–5:30 P.M. (Mar. and Oct.), Mon.–Sun. 8:15 A.M.–6:30 P.M. (Apr., May, Sept.), Mon.–Sun. 8:15 A.M.–7:30 P.M. (June–Aug.), Mon.–Sun. 8:15 A.M.–4:30 P.M. (Nov.–Feb.); closed: first and fourth Mon. of each month, Jan. 1, Dec. 25; admission: €6.

BOBOLI GARDENS

The Boboli Gardens are not large—you wonder how compact little Florence finds room for them within her walls. But they are scattered, to their extreme, their all-romantic advantage and felicity, over a group of steep undulations between the rugged and terraced [Pitti] palace and a still-surviving stretch of city wall, where the unevenness of the ground much adds to their apparent size. You may cultivate in them the fancy of their solemn and haunted character, of something faint and dim and even, if you like, tragic, in their prescribed, their functional smile; as if they borrowed from the huge monuments that overhang them certain of its ponderous memories and regrets.

Henry James, "Florentine Notes," *Italian Hours*

View of Florence from the Giardino di Boboli

➣ Of the many modifications the Medicis made as new owners of the Palazzo Pitti, the construction of the Boboli Gardens was the most grandiose. Designed by Niccolò Pericoli, known as Il Tribolo, refined by Ammannati, and executed in 1550 by Buontalenti, they are an eclectic blend of natural and artificial landscapes. The gardens continued acquiring new pieces until the last years of the Lorena's grand duchy.

The amphitheater that faces the palazzo inadvertently came about after a massive stone quarry left a void in the hillside. The stone went to building the palazzo; the hollow hillside was transformed into a vast stage where some of the very first operas were performed. The 2nd-century Egyptian obelisk, at the center of the amphitheater, rests upon a Roman granite basin. Climb the well-manicured hillside for an excellent view of Florence. The fountain, halfway up the hill, is Neptune's Pool (1565–1568); the statue of Neptune is by Stoldo Lorenzi. Upon climbing the hill, keep in mind that any of the paths on the right side will ultimately lead to the Viottolone, a picturesque avenue of cypresses that forms the spine of the Boboli Gardens. Planted in 1637, the cypresses form a natural corridor that frames Piazzale dell'Isolotto at its extreme

end. The L'Isolotto, or "Little Island," is considered a crowning achievement in mannerist sculpture. Surrounded by a moatlike lake, this carefully manicured island is planted with colorful orange and lemon trees and punctuated by a copy of the elegant Ocean Fountain carved by Giambologna. The original, which features Neptune at its center directing the river gods, is located in the Bargello Museum (see pg. 85). Surging from the lake's placid surface are Perseus on horseback and Andromeda. Beyond the hedges of the Isolotto complex is a semi-circular lawn marked with marble busts. Upon returning to the Palazzo Pitti, make sure to visit the Grand Grotto (1583–1588). This highly expressive structure once housed four of Michelangelo's famous *Slaves* (now in the Accademia Gallery) and still holds Giambologna's *Venus Bathing* (1565–1570).

PALAZZO PITTI

Piazza Pitti; tel.: 055-294883; website: www.polomuseale.firenze.it; open: hours vary for the different museums and apartments within the palazzo, see separate entries.

➣ Dominating the length of the piazza is the facade of the Palazzo Pitti. Upon its inception in 1458, this structure was only

PALAZZO PITTI

Of all the royal residences which I have seen, the Pitti Palace is the most desirable to live in, particularly when the attractions of the gallery are taken into account. The architecture of the facade is heavy, massive, and sombre; but that of the cortile is rich and magnificent. The rooms are spacious and imposing, and the whole air of the palace truly regal. There is nothing that speaks of decay or neglect: no faded splendor and no mouldering magnificence. It is a house to live in, as well as a palace to look at.

George Stillman Hillard, *Six Months in Italy*

a fraction of its current size. Nevertheless, it was still the largest palazzo in Florence then, far surpassing any of those owned by the Medicis. After the Pitti family fell into financial ruin the palazzo came into the possession of Cosimo I and Eleonora of Toledo, who made it home to the Medici Court in 1560. It was during this period that the palazzo underwent the majority of its enlargements. Under the direction of Bartolomeo Ammannati, the building was expanded through a scroll-like repetition of the original structure. Thus, the facade of the palazzo achieves a uniformity like no other. Entering through the center door, one passes from the piazza into a courtyard of austere porticoes supported by rustic columns. The three-storied wings, to the left and right, are by Ammannati, as well as the one-story terrace that overlooks the Boboli Gardens. Its beautiful courtyard was designed by Filippo Brunelleschi, built by architect Luca Fancelli, and later renovated by Ammannati. Under the arcade to the left is one of the very rare monuments Florentines dedicated to animals. The poor donkeys were burdened for months with the heaviest of the materials, from marble to *pietra serena*. Aside from the vital role it played for the Medici family, the palazzo also housed the Court of Savoy during Florence's brief reign as the capitol of Italy, between 1865 and 1871.

Palazzo Pitti

Palazzo Torrigiani

Piazza de' Mozzi, 5; closed to the public.

➤ This palazzo, overlooking Piazza de' Mozzi, was constructed in the first half of the 16th century by Domenico di Baccio d'Agnolo, who followed his father's project. It was renovated after the city built the Lungarno, a large road flanking the river. In 1901, a Lutheran church was also built in the palazzo's park, which in the meantime had become public property.

Piazza Pitti

➤ This gently sloping piazza rests at the foot of Boboli hill and foregrounds the expansive facade of the Palazzo Pitti. Bare of any landscaping or monuments, the piazza is filled with sunbathers during the summer months.

Piazza Santo Spirito

➤ To reach this tranquil piazza, you must leave the beaten track of tourists who flow over the Ponte Vecchio toward the Palazzo Pitti. Gently shaded by surrounding trees, the piazza hosts several quaint furniture shops and restaurants housed inside a modest set of palazzi. The most flamboyant of these is No. 10, the Palazzo Guadagni. Built by Cronaca in the early

16th century, the palazzo set a trend for the era to come with the fashionable loggia that occupies its top floor.

Piazzale Michelangelo

➤ Inaugurated in 1875, this open space offers another spot for superb views of Florence's cityscape. Here stands a monument to Michelangelo that includes bronze copies of the artist's great masterpieces, including *David*, as well as several of the marble statues for the Medici sepulcher by Giuseppe Poggi. Just up the hill from the piazzale (on the inside of the bend in the boulevard) is the Loggia-Caffè, also designed by Poggi, that was intended to house a museum of copies and original works by Michelangelo.

Porta Romana

Via Romana

➤ Built between 1328 and 1331, Porta Romana once belonged to the outermost circle of Florence's city walls. The last remaining portions of this circle are preserved in the winglike segments that flank Porta Romana. Also preserved are the original wooden doors that were once used to seal Florence off from attack. The sculptures that Paolo di Giovanni crafted

Skyline of Florence from Piazzale Michelangelo, with the cupola and campanile of the Duomo on the right and the tower of the Palazzo Vecchio to the left

... viewed from across the river, at Piazzale Michelangelo, where a copy of "David," the Giant-Killer, stands, Florence appears a level city, whose uniform low sky line is only broken by the civic tower of Palazzo Vecchio, by the Bargello, by the three great domes of Brunelleschi—the Duomo, San Lorenzo, and Santo Spirito—and by the bell towers of the Duomo, the Badia, and of the two churches of the preaching orders—Santa Maria Novella and Santa Croce.

Mary McCarthy, *The Stones of Florence*

Fundamentals

177

for Porta Romana in 1328 are now held in the Bargello Museum, but the 15th-century lunette, *Madonna and Child with Saints,* is still in situ.

PORTA SAN FREDIANO
Via Pisana

➤ Attributed to noted architect of the Gothic and early Renaissance Andrea Pisano, Porta San Frediano dominates Piazza di Verzaia with an expansive barrel-vaulted arch. This void is filled by massive wooden double doors studded with iron spikes. Among the gates of the third circle of city walls, that of San Frediano is perhaps the best-preserved.

PORTA SAN GIORGIO
Costa San Giorgio

➤ Originally belonging to the second circle of city walls and later included in the third, Porta San Giorgio (c. 1260) is among Florence's most refined gateways. The bas-relief at the face of the door depicts Saint George and the Dragon, which is a copy of the 14th-century sculptural work now kept in the Palazzo Vecchio. Between Porta San Giorgio's 13th-century capitals is Bicci di Lorenzo's *Enthroned Madonna and Child with Saints Leonardo and George* (1430).

PORTA SAN NICCOLÒ
Piazza Poggi

➤ Marooned at the center of Piazza Giuseppe Poggi (the architect whose project brought down Florence's medieval

walls in the 19th century), Porta San Niccolò (c. 1340) is the only gate in Florence to have preserved its original height over the ages. It consists of three large arches above which ramparts still run in a series of stairs and walkways.

SAN MINIATO AL MONTE
Piazzale Michelangelo, entrance from Via di San Miniato al Monte; tel.: 055-2342731; open: daily 8 A.M.– noon, 2–7 P.M. (summer), 8 A.M.–noon, 2–6 P.M. (winter); admission: free.

➤ A masterpiece of Romanesque architecture, the church of San Miniato al Monte sits on the southern foothills overlooking the Arno River, within a complex that includes the Monte alle Croci convent. The church was built in various phases between 1018 and 1207, the dates carved into the floor inside.

The site marks the shrine of the early Christian martyr, Saint Minias, an Armenian merchant who was beheaded for his beliefs by the Emperor Decius in the 3rd century.

The unique facade is a geometric patterning in green and white marble. The lower part is made up of five round blind arches set on Corinthian semi-columns. Above is the central window adorned by a mosaic depicting Christ enthroned between the Virgin Mary and Saint Minias, offering a benediction that dates from the second half of the 13th century. The top section is decorated with nine round false arches that contain inlaid allegorical figures originating from the early 13th century including an eagle, the symbol of the merchants guild, which enjoyed the

San Miniato al Monte

patronage of the church. On the left is the bell tower, based on a design by Baccio d'Agnolo and completed in 1535 to replace the tower that collapsed in 1499.

The interior spans three levels, with the presbytery sharply raised above the main floor and the crypt beneath. There is a single nave and two aisles that are marked by the alternation of two columns for each pillar, surmounted by round arches. The columns are topped by white marble capitals, in Corinthian and Composite orders that were taken from ancient buildings; those done in white terra-cotta date to the Romanesque period. The nave is decorated with fine marble intarsia, with semiprecious material inlaid on the floor. At the end of the nave, standing apart, is a formation of columns and entablatures, the Cappella del Crocifisso, designed by Michelozzo in 1448 to enshrine a crucifix (which has been moved). In its place are panels by Agnolo Gaddi dating from 1396. The barrel vault was decorated by Luca della Robbia; the two bronze eagles are by Maso di Bartolomeo.

In the presbytery, on the right, is an altar that includes a panel dedicated to the eight episodes from the life of Saint Minias, an important work by Jacopo del Casentino from around 1320. Above the main altar, the glazed terra-cotta crucifix is attributed to della Robbia. The apse is highlighted by six semi-columns in green marble with five arches that mimic those used in the facade of the building. To the right of the presbytery one finds the

entrance to the sacristy, which includes frescoes depicting the stories of Saint Benedict by Spinello Aretino and his son.

The oldest part of the church is the crypt, which includes seven small aisles with cross-vaults supported by 36 small columns consisting of an assortment of materials and capitals. In the spaces between the adjoining arches and the ceiling in the presbytery are paintings with gilt backgrounds done by Taddeo Gaddi in 1341 that depict, in remarkable colors, religious figures including the saints and prophets. On the left aisle, one finds the Cappella del Cardinale del Portogallo, a mixture of painting and sculpture considered one of the best-preserved chapels of the Florentine Renaissance. Designed by Antonio di Manetto, a pupil of Brunelleschi, it was completed in 1473 and based on the Sagrestia Vecchia of the basilica of San Lorenzo. On the vault are four medallions in glazed terra-cotta by della Robbia. On the right is a masterful piece by Antonio and Bernardo Rossellino entitled *Monument to the Cardinal.*

SANTA MARIA DEL CARMINE

Piazza del Carmine, 14; tel.: 055-212331; open: daily 7:15 A.M.–noon, 5–6:30 P.M.; closed: during mass.

➣ This massive brick and stone building houses the famed Brancacci Chapel with its exquisite frescoes. Though begun in 1268, there is evidence of a predating structure as the side walls show traces of the Romanesque-Gothic style. Completed in 1476, the church suffered a fire in 1771 and the interior was reconstructed according to a design by Giuseppe Ruggieri. The interior plan is laid out in a Latin cross that includes five chapels with altars decorated in stucco. In the third chapel on the right is a Crucifixion by Giorgio Vasari from 1560. The altar in the chapel of the left transept includes a tabernacle that holds a Madonna in the Byzantine style with 12 adoring angels that evoke the work of Botticelli. At the head of the transept is the Corsini Chapel, commissioned in 1675, where the urn containing the body of Tuscan Saint Andrea Corsini rests in a late-17th-century bronze relief.

Santo Spirito

Piazza di Santo Spirito; tel.: 055-210030; open: Sun. 8:30–11 A.M.

➢ The sun-baked facade that occupies the northern end of the piazza belongs to the church of Santo Spirito. Brunelleschi initiated its construction in 1444 and worked on it up until his death, two years later. The facade, however, is an 18th-century creation, whose unfinished surface stands in stark contrast to the refinement of Brunelleschi's design for the interior, which is the architect's true swan song. Like his design for the basilica of San Lorenzo, Brunelleschi again elegantly trims the edges of his barrel-vaulted arches in *pietra serena*, a gray stone often used in Florentine architecture. These are supported by classical columns of the same color that line both the nave and the aisles to create an overall sense of balance and unity. Underneath the organ in the north aisle is a door that leads to a vestibule. Inside the vestibule is a coffered ceiling of high opulence by Cronaca (1492–1494). The church also offers a respectable collection of artworks by Florentine masters such as Domenico Ghirlandaio, Cosimo Rosselli, and Filippino Lippi. Of these, the *Madonna and Child* (1466) by Lippi is noted for the picturesque composition of its background.

Torre dei Mannelli

On the Oltrarno side of the Ponte Vecchio, to the right

➢ The Torre dei Mannelli, renovated after World War II, was originally a medieval corner tower built to support and defend the Ponte Vecchio. During the Renaissance, Vasari designed his famous corridor so as not to disturb the tower.

Brunelleschi's nave at Santo Spirito

Walking Tour 1:

An Enchanting
Neighborhood on the Other
Side of the River

By Carla Rossi

In 1343 the official name of Santo Spirito was given to the neighborhood across the Arno River. These days it is more commonly called the Oltrarno, or "the other side of the Arno." It had its origins as the commercial area of the city. The streets were filled with wool workers and other artisan shops that thrived into the 18th century, and even to this day several persist. The neighborhood is defined by the three gates that were once part of the wall that encircled the city. To the southeast is Porta San Niccolò, where travelers to and from Arezzo arrived and departed. To the west, Porta San Frediano led the way to Pisa. And the southern border, gated by Porta Romana, obviously led to Rome. The northern edge of Santo Spirito is bordered by the Arno.

Upon crossing the Ponte Vecchio from the center of town and turning right onto Via Borgo San Jacopo, a street now open only to pedestrian traffic, one enters the actual living neighborhood of Santo Spirito. The buildings themselves are, for the most part, reconstructed imitations of the original medieval palaces that had stood here until World War II. Several towers, which were only partially destroyed during bombardments, stand tall in a sort of remembrance to a Florence that was once called the city of towers. About a block on from the Ponte Vecchio are the **Torre dei Belfredelli**, **Ramaglianti**, and **Bardadori**, all constructed in the 1200s as signs of prestige by the warring Guelph and Ghibelline factions. A bit further on at No. 17 is the **Torre dei Marsili**, an austere structure and one of the tallest towers remaining in Florence. In 1830 it was livened up with colorful della Robbian terra-cottas above the door; the current ones are copies of the originals.

The church of **San Jacopo Sopr'arno** on the opposite side of the street from the Torre dei Marsili is a 10th-century construction, with a 12th- to 13th-century three-arch loggia.

The name of the Romanesque church, which translates to Saint Jacob Above the Arno, is due to the way it was built: its apse, like the surrounding houses, is built on the so-called *sporti* (from the Italian verb *sporgersi,* to jut out). The church juts out over the Arno, and when the level of the river rises the water laps up along the bottom of its apse. Because of this, the Florentines call it the church *"con il culo in Arno"* ("with its bottom in the Arno"). The best view of the back of the church is from Ponte Santa Trìnita.

The Scopetini Canons of San Donato brought the loggia to the church in 1580. The bell tower was completed in 1660 by Gherardo Silvani. The interior is largely an 18th-century design by the Padri delle Missioni. The ancient Romanesque columns were recently restored after the damaging floods of 1966. Art historian Giorgio Vasari noted that the cupola of the Ridolfi Chapel (which was destroyed centuries ago) was a tester Brunelleschi built before his masterpiece at the cathedral of Santa Maria del Fiore. The walls are lined with 16th- and 17th-century works by Florentine artists Pier Dandini, Niccolò Lapi, and Matteo Bonechi. The fresco on the vault is by Vincenzo Meucci.

The church has now been deconsecrated and therefore is open only sporadically for cultural events. The priest at the nearby church of Santa Felicita on Via Guicciardini has the keys if the doors are closed.

In Piazza Frescobaldi note the 16th-century **Fontanella Buontalentiana**, or little fountain, at the corner of Via dello Sprone, attributed to Bernardo Buontalenti. From there make a short detour along Via dello Sprone to Piazza della Passera. You will appreciate the narrow but impressive medieval street, otherwise hidden and unknown to visitors.

Borgo San Jacopo eventually runs into what was historically one of the main thoroughfares in the neighborhood, Via Maggio. Originally named Via Maggiore because it was the road designated for major religious processions in the 1500s, it later lost this important role when the Medici family bought the Palazzo Pitti on Via Guicciardini, which then became the central passage from the center of Florence to the Oltrarno.

Via Maggio remains the best example of medieval architecture in the city. Several palaces built by the most prestigious historical figures of the 14th and 15th centuries line the road on both sides. At No. 2, family arms can be seen above the doors of the original Pitti Palace, **Casa Pitti**, adorned with a bust of Cosimo de' Medici attributed to Baccio Bandinelli. Farther along, on the right side of the road, is the **Palazzo Bianca Cappello**. Once the residence of the lover

Detail of the exterior of the Palazzo Bianca Capello

and then wife of Francesco de' Medici, it was restored by Bernardo Buontalenti between 1570 and 1574, then decorated with beautiful, ornate grotesques by Bernardino Poccetti (1579–1580).

Farther along Via Maggio, just before the church of San Felice, the **Casa Guidi** is dominated by large carriage doors. In the 1850s it was home to English poet Elizabeth Barrett Browning (where she wrote "Casa Guidi Windows," a poem imbued with Italian Risorgimento events).

The church of **San Felice** is a great example of construction throughout various architectural and artistic periods. Although the first annotations to the church date back to 1066, the actual construction is from the 1300s, with traces of the original Romanic structure and other modifications in the 14th century. The simple Renaissance-style facade is attributed to Bartolomeo Michelozzi (1452–1460). In the interior of the church, the *Pietà*, a weathered fresco attributed to Niccolò di Pietro Gerini, is dated 1405– 1410, while another fresco by Giovanni da San Giovanni is much more recent.

Take a right onto Via de' Michelozzi and you will be in Piazza Santo Spirito, one of the most beautiful in Florence. The piazza is best visited in the morning when the market takes over the square. There are several restaurants and bars inhabiting the medieval palazzi that encircle the central fountain, built by the city of Florence in 1556. Located at the corner of the piazza, bordered by Via Mazzetta, is the **Palazzo Gaudagni**, easily identified by the provocative graffiti designs etched into its exterior. When Cronaca finished the Palazzo Gaudagni in 1503, the talk of the town wasn't the graffiti, however, but the covered terrace, or loggia, that crowns the mansion's facade. Cronaca's terrace was the first in Florence to strike such an immodest pose, but it wouldn't be the last. In the years that followed, altana terraces were either added to or came standard with most fashionable Florentine mansions.

All that survives of the monastery that once stood next to the church of Santo Spirito is the refectory (*cenacolo*), one of the last works by architect Filippo Brunelleschi, who died in 1446, before it was finished. Here there is a large fresco of the Crucifixion and fragments of a Last Supper attributed to followers of Andrea Orcagna and to his brother, Nardo di Cione. It is a rare example of High Gothic religious work.

To the left of the church is the **Fondazione Romano**, a small gem of a museum. Neapolitan Antiquarian Salvatore Romano donated the collection of sculptures in the museum to the city of Florence in 1946. There are pieces from all over the country dating from the pre-Romanic period to the 15th century. The numerous

Tabernacle with the Madonna and child at the Fondazione Romano

Tabernacolo del Canto alla Cuculia

Romanesque sculptures represent some of the few works from this period that are in Florence. Among the most important pieces are the *Caryatid* and *Adoring Angel* by Tino di Camaino, the *Madonna and Child* by Jacopo della Quercia, and two bas-reliefs representing saints by Donatello, which come from the Basilica del Santo in Padua. The central work in the museum is the large fresco, *La Crocifissione,* attributed to Andrea Orcagna (1360).

Perched on the corner of Via dei Serragli and Via Santa Monaca is the **Tabernacolo del Canto alla Cuculia**, or the "Cuckoo Bird Tabernacle." Painted by Bicci di Lorenzo in 1427, the *Madonna and Child with Saints* on the tabernacle altar features a Christ child with a baby cuckoo bird in his palm. The inclusion of the bird apparently refers to the sarcasm with which this wealthy neighborhood welcomed foreign craftsmen who, like the cuckoo, laid their "eggs" in the "nests" of others. In archaic dialect, the Florentine word for "to mock" was *cuculiare,* "to cuckoo."

Passing through the piazza, taking a left back to the intersection of Via Romana, and continuing on to the right, the busy road is another typical example of medieval architecture. At No. 17 Via Romana you will find the **Museo Zoologico La Specola**, a zoological museum opened in 1775 by Grand Duke Pietro Leopoldo of Lorraine that claims to be the oldest scientific museum in Europe. It contains an impressive anatomic wax collection by such famous artists of the time as Clemente Susini and Luigi Calamai.

Farther down Via Romana is the **Giardino Corsi-Scarselli**, an English-style garden planted between 1801 and 1810 to suit the tastes of its proprietor, Tommaso Corsi, chamberlain and counselor to Leopold II of Lorena. Designed just within the city's medieval walls, the gardens actually rest upon 16th-century bastions. The loggetta, decorated in the neoclassical style, was used as box seating during ceremonial processions to and from the Palazzo Pitti.

The stores along Via Romana eventually become more interspersed with private residences, and one side of the street is dominated by the private Scarselli gardens. Lights have been hung across the narrow road, creating an enchanting tunnel of light in the evening. Just inside the ancient gate of Porta Romana is another church, the **Chiesa della Calza**, or "Church of the Stocking," mostly frequented by elderly neighborhood residents. It is an old convent founded in the 14th century by the Ingesuati monks who wore long hooded coats that resembled stockings. The facade is simple and austere, and the campanile (bell tower) was constructed after the church, around 1530.

The interior is painted in a gray-and-white-striped Gothic style, and wooden beams traverse the single nave of the church. Next door in the convent refectory, which now serves as a hotel and meeting hall, is a well-maintained fresco of the Last Supper by Franciabigio (1514), the Cappella Cardinal Mistrangelo, and a 15th-century cloister. The building was renovated most recently for the 2000 Jubilee. Via Romana ends at Piazza della Calza, enclosed by Porta Romana, which is also the defining border of the neighborhood.

FURTHER INFORMATION

Casa Guidi
Piazza San Felice, 8; tel.: 055-354457; open: Mon., Wed., Fri. 3–6 P.M. (Apr. 1–Nov. 30); closed: Tues., Thurs., Sat.–Sun.; admission: free.

Casa Pitti
Via Maggio, 2; closed to the public.

**Chiesa della Calza
(Church of the Stocking)**
Piazza della Calza, 6 (Porta Romana); tel.: 055-222287; open: daily 6–7 P.M., Sun. 8:30–11:30 A.M.

Fondazione Romano
Piazza Santo Spirito, 29; tel.: 055-287043; open: Sat. 9 A.M.– 5 P.M. (Apr.–Oct.), Sat. 10:30 A.M.– 1:30 P.M. (Nov.–Mar.); admission: €2.20.

Fontanella Buontalentiana
Piazza Frescobaldi, corner of Via dello Sprone

Giardino Corsi-Scarselli
Via Romana, 38; open: one or two weekends in May for the Giardini Aperti, or Open Gardens event (see pgs. 192, 195).

Museo Zoologico La Specola
Via Romana, 17; tel.: 055-2288251; fax: 055-225325; open: Thurs.–Tues. 9 A.M.–1 P.M., Sat. 9 A.M.–5 P.M.;

closed: Wed. and public holidays; admission: €4.

Palazzo Bianca Cappello
Via Maggio, 26; closed to the public.

Palazzo Guadagni
Piazza Santo Spirito, 10; closed to the public.

San Felice
Piazza San Felice, 7; tel.: 055-221706; open: Mon.–Sat. 8 A.M.– 7 P.M., Sun. and public holidays 8–11:30 A.M.

San Jacopo Sopr'arno
Borgo San Jacopo; open: only for concerts and exhibits.

**Tabernacolo del Canto alla Cuculia
(Cuckoo Bird Tabernacle)**
Via dei Serragli, at the corner of Via Santa Monaca

Torre dei Bardadori
Borgo San Jacopo, 54r

Torre dei Belfredelli
Borgo San Jacopo, 9

Torre dei Marsili
Borgo San Jacopo, 17

Torre dei Ramaglianti
Borgo San Jacopo, 9

FOCUS: San Frediano in Cestello

San Frediano in Cestello: Piazza di Cestello, 4; tel.: 055-215816; open: Mon.–Fri. 9 A.M.–noon, 4:30–5 P.M., Sun. 4:30–7:30 P.M.; closed: Sat.; Granaio di Cosimo III (Granary of Cosimo III): Piazza di Cestello; closed to the public.

By Stacy Meichtry

Facade of San Frediano in Cestello

At the far end of Piazza Cestello, an architectural oddity rises against the homogeneity of Florence's Renaissance landscape: the baroque church of San Frediano in Cestello. And yet the church, designed by the Roman architect Cerutti, offers more than mere stylistic contrast. Cerutti's unfinished facade and quaint bell tower also provide the sturdy shouders upon which Antonio Maria Ferri stood in 1693 to erect his resplendent cupola.

Mounted atop a drum, and frosted with windows, pediments, and pilasters, the cupola expertly blends fanciful baroque with the restraint of Florentine Renaissance, from which Ferri drew inspiration. The underbelly of this confection is frescoed with what many consider Antonio Domenico Gabbiani's definitive masterpiece, *The Glory of Mary Magdalene* (1702–1718).

Keeping the Gabbiani fresco company are works by his contemporary, Alessandro Gherardini. His *Birth of Mary* (1694) resides comfortably on the altar of the third chapel. This and each of the other five deep, lateral chapels are lit by small antique lanterns, which lend mystique to such altarpieces as the *Ecstasy of Saint Mary Magdalene de' Pazzi* (1702) by Giovanni Camillo Sagrestani.

Before leaving Piazza Cestello, note the large edifice dominating the western side of the square. The Granaio di Cosimo III was built in 1695 by Giovambattista Foggini. This early baroque granary was known better as the Granaio dell'Abbondanza, "of the abundance," for its vast storage capacity. From its sober 15th-century-inspired facade, the building stretches down Lungarno Soderini and terminates at Via Tiratoio.

Walking Tour 2:

A View of the Arno, through the Back Alleys of San Niccolò

By Olivia Ironside

The neighborhood of San Niccolò is easily overlooked in the confusion that comes with navigating the Oltrarno. After wading through the malaise of photo opportunities in progress on the Ponte Vecchio, most visitors get carried off by currents that terminate at either the Palazzo Pitti, straight ahead, or Piazza Santo Spirito, off to the right. And yet locating San Niccolò, a tightly packed cluster of medieval homes bordered by breathtaking vistas, is a fairly simple procedure. It requires neither radar nor sixth sense, but simply the will and determination to resist the currents and go left.

Doing that you will first see a decapitated column. Erected in 1381, the **Colonna di Piazza Santa Felicita** commemorates the Florentine victory over the Patarin heretics. Absent from the top of the column, however, is a statue of Saint Peter the Martyr, who made a career of persecuting the Patarins. Sainthood was achieved shortly after Peter was martyred by the vengeful heretics. The statue, sculpted by Antonio Montauti in 1700, was removed from its glorious pedestal a century later.

Just beyond the column, the low-profile facade of **Santa Felicita** crouches behind a brief stretch of the Vasari Corridor (Vasari's elevated passageway that leads from the Palazzo Vecchio, through the Uffizi, over the Ponte Vecchio, to the Palazzo Pitti). The church's current appearance reflects the work of Ferdinando Ruggieri, who completely rebuilt it from the ground up between 1736 and 1739. Its paleo-Christian foundations, however, date back to the 4th century, when San Niccolò was primarily inhabited by Syrian merchants who are now credited with spreading Christianity to Florence. Saint Felicity, aside from being a patron saint of this church, is also the patron saint of Syria.

In Santa Felicita's interior you will find the *Deposition,* mannerist painter Jacopo Pontormo's definitive masterpiece. Housed in the ornate chapel to the right of the church entrance, the painting offers a dizzying depiction of Christ carried from the cross amid a commotion of swirling bodies, limbs, and portraits, one of which (in the upper right-hand corner) belongs to the artist himself. Pontormo also frescoed the Annunciation, in the lunette, and the portraits in the tondi of the same chapel. Other notable works throughout the rest of the church include Antonio Ciseri's oil-on-panel

Martyrdom of the Brothers of Maccabeh (1863) and a Gothic polyptych (c. 1355) by Taddeo Gaddi.

Upon exiting, proceed under the Vasari Corridor, along the left side of the church, following the incline of the Costa San Giorgio. At the top of this rather steep climb, you will see the unique facade of the church of **San Giorgio e Santo Spirito alla Costa**, which houses minor works by the nearly forgotten Vincenzo Dandini, Domenico Cresti (known as Passignano), and Giovanni Battista Foggini, the baroque sculptor and architect who rebuilt the church in the 18th century. The original altarpiece, *Madonna and Child Enthroned,* attributed to the young Giotto, has been moved to the Museo Diocesano di Santo Stefano al Ponte. Still remaining, however, are the

Portal of Santa Felicita

baroque ceiling by Alessandro Gherardini that represents The Glory of Saint George, and, on the altar, the oval painting by Anton Domenico Gabbiani depicting the Descent of the Holy Ghost (1710).

Parallel with Costa San Giorgio runs Via de' Bardi. At No. 36 is the **Palazzo Capponi delle Rovinate**, which received its name after the landslides from the hill above repeatedly damaged and destroyed houses on the street. That went on until 1547, when Cosimo I prohibited the building of anything more on the site.

As a distinguished member of the Renaissance Florentine oligarchy, owner Niccolò Uzzano had his portrait frescoed above the main entrance. Niccolò himself apparently oversaw the design of the main section, but art historians quibble about who did the rest. Some say it was Brunelleschi and others, including Vasari, believe it was Lorenzo di Bicci.

Built between the 15th and 19th centuries, the mansion was extensively modified, and now parts of the original structure can be found only on the first floor. In the 17th century a chapel was added, which now houses a lunette of The Deposition, taken from the Cappella Capponi in Santa Felicita. In 1800, renovations kept the palazzo apace as frescoes were commissioned for the lofty halls of the upper floor. And to keep up with the rapidly changing face of the Lungarno Torrigiani, Count Capponi commissioned Giuseppe Poggi to modify the facade that looks out onto the Arno in the late 19th century.

The church of **Santa Lucia dei Magnoli** is a little farther down the street. Saint Lucy, a 5th-century Christian Sicilian, was famous for her chastity and her beauty. Appalled to find that a pagan admirer was obsessed with her eyes, she pulled them out. Saint Lucy is one of the most venerated Christian martyrs and is usually represented holding a plate with her eyes on it. As with the Palazzo Capponi delle Rovinate, this site also suffered landslides.

Financed by Ugaccione della Pressa and his son Magnolo, the church was built in 1078 and is one of the most ancient in Florence. In fact, according to tradition, Saint Francis and Saint Dominick met for the first time in 1211 in Santa Lucia's medieval hospital. Today, however, Santa Lucia primarily reflects reconstruction efforts in 1584 followed by restoration in 1732.

To the right of the entrance is a chapel completed

San Giorgio e Santo Spirito

in 1715, which contains a carved wooden figure of the Virgin Mary. On the *pietra serena* altar is a 14th-century panel of Saint Lucy by Pietro Lorenzetti. The *Angel of the Annunciation* by Jacopo del Sellaio covers two panels, while the panel on the high altar by Agnolo di Donino replaces the original *Sacred Conversation* by Domenico Veneziano, which now hangs in the Uffizi. Farther down Via de' Bardi is the grand **Palazzo Mozzi**, stitched together between 1260 and 1273 from a preexistent group of medieval houses and towers—one of which, though damaged, is still visible today. Between 1342 and 1343, the Mozzi mansion was home to the notoriously greedy Duke Gualtieri di Brienne, who was later captured by Florentines for his insolence. Other members of the Mozzi family were very influential in the Church and served as treasurers to the pope for generations. In fact, on July 11, 1273, with the mediation of Pope Gregory X, the peace treaty between the Guelphs and the Ghibellines was signed here, though the truce between the two factions lasted only a few days. During the 15th century, the mansion underwent heavy modifications, including the addition of a courtyard with a well in the middle.

Sharing space with the Palazzo Mozzi, in the same piazza, is the **Museo Bardini** (see pg. 191).

As Via de' Bardi runs into Via di San Niccolò, the buzz of tourists can be heard again. The workshops and studios that line Via San Niccolò are mostly behind closed doors and shutters, but if you are lucky enough to catch any open, take a peek.

Adjacent to Via di San Niccolò is Piazza Demidoff, a beautifully kept square surrounded by trees, and a good place to stop and enjoy the view of the Arno. The large monument in the center is by Lorenzo Bartolini and honors the Russian noble Nicola Demidoff.

At No. 2 Via dei Renai, where it intersects with Via del Olmo, stands the **Palazzo Serristori**, built around 1520. In the first half of the 19th century, Giuseppe Bonaparte, the elder brother of Napoleon, king of Naples and later of Spain, spent the last years of his life here. With the new lungarno, the most important facade became the one facing the river, at the rear of the palazzo, which was remodeled in 1873. Within the palace walls is a garden that, in 1721, was deemed by historian Benedetto Varchi "one of the best and most important in Florence."

The interior extolled pure decadence, and the ballroom was one of the biggest in Florence. Due to an 1877 restoration, little of the original interior remains, but you can still find some remarkable reconstructions of the original rooms together with reproductions of the furnishings.

While standing at the beginning of Via del Giardino Serristori, look up and admire the impressively tall bell tower of the church of **San Niccolò**. Built in the 12th century, the church has a single nave and three chapels in the presbytery. The renowned *Polyptic Quaratesi* by Gentile da Fabriano, now in the Galleria degli Uffizi, used to hang above the main altar of this church.

After the flood of 1966, the removal of the altarpieces from the side chapels revealed some wonderful 15th-century frescoes by the Master of Signa. The wooden Crucifixion in the second chapel to the right is attributed to Michelozzo; the stone tabernacle in the sacristy, to the school of Michelozzo.

OUR PICK

From the church, follow Via San Miniato up to Arnolfo di Cambio's famous **Porta San Miniato**, a 14th-century gate. Carried away in the flood of 1966, it was recovered, restored, and finally put back in place. This well-preserved example of Florence's medieval wall once threaded its way through the hill above Forte Belvedere. Adjacent to the gate are segments of this wall with their original ramparts, supported by a row of arches.

Finally, take the staircase up Via San Salvatore al Monte. The church of **San Salvatore al Monte**, which Michelangelo dubbed the *"bella villanella"* for its austere but elegant architectonic lines, was built between 1499 and 1504 by Cronaca. It has a humble facade of plain plaster; on the pediment is the coat of arms of the *Arte Calimala,* the merchants guild, which commissioned the church. The interior is quite simple with a single nave and a chapel on either side of the main entrance. Little remains of the Renaissance design other than the windows. Nonetheless you can still admire a glazed terra-cotta of the Deposition, attributed to Giovanni della Robbia, as well as panel paintings by Jacopo Franchi, Giovanni da Ponto, and Neri di Bicci.

Further Information

Colonna di Piazza Santa Felicita (Column of Piazza Santa Felicita)
Piazza Santa Felicita

Palazzo Capponi delle Rovinate
Via de' Bardi, 26; open: closed to the public.

Palazzo Mozzi
Piazza de' Mozzi, corner of Via San Niccolò and Via de' Bardi (in front of the Ponte alle Grazie); closed to the public.

Palazzo Serristori
Via dei Renai, 2; closed to the public.

Porta San Miniato
Via San Miniato, corner of Via di Belvedere

San Giorgio e Santo Spirito alla Costa
Via Costa San Giorgio, 32; tel.: 055-784715; open: Fri. 4–7 P.M., Sun. 9:30 A.M.–1 P.M.; closed: Mon.–Thurs., Sat.

San Niccolò
Via di San Niccolò, 48; tel.: 055-2344903; open: by appointment.

San Salvatore al Monte
Via San Salvatore al Monte, 9; open: daily 8 A.M.–noon, 1–5 P.M.

Santa Felicita
Piazza Santa Felicita, 3; tel.: 055-213018; open: daily 9 A.M.–noon, 3–6 P.M.; closed: Sun. afternoon.

Santa Lucia dei Magnoli
Via de' Bardi, 22; tel.: 055-2342436; open: Sun. 11 A.M.–noon.

Piazza de' Mozzi, 1; tel.: 055-2342427; closed for renovations.

By Stacy Meichtry

Stefano Bardini (1836–1922) was an antiquarian and a collector of architectural materials, many salvaged from churches and palazzi destroyed when Piazza della Repubblica was built in the 1860s. In 1881, Stefano Bardini transformed the 13th-century church of San Giorgio and its adjacent convent into his own private mansion. An avid collector of masonry, Bardini put his collection to work, using combinations of original stones and bricks taken from Renaissance and baroque buildings to construct a home, which he then decorated with his massive collection of sculpture, painting, furniture, ceramics, armor, and arms dating from the Etruscan period through the baroque. The fruits of Bardini's labor are now on display at the Museo Bardini, which preserves the collector's mansion and thus pays tribute to the pastiche of the 19th-century aristocracy.

Aside from the elaborate staircases and coffered ceilings that adjoin the Bardini superstructure, note the windows on the first floor, adapted for practical purposes from their original use as cornices for the demolished altars of the church of San Lorenzo in Pistoia. The elaborate windows help to shed light on some of the more important works in Bardini's art collection such as Antonio del Pollaiuolo's oil-on-panel *Archangel Michael*, a 15th-century Madonna and child, a stucco polychrome crafted in the manner of Andrea Verrocchio, the *Madonna dei Cordai* by the workshop of Donatello, and the Madonna and child attributed to the master himself.

On the ground floor, the intricate marble group *Caritas,* by 13th-century Sienese architect Tino Camaino, holds court over pieces by the workshops of his contemporaries.

Relief panel with the Madonna and child at the Museo Bardini

Walking Tour 3:

Florence's Secret Gardens

By Carla Rossi

Florence in May is a spectacle of gardens in bloom, but the average visitor would never know walking through a city center in which the color green is almost completely absent.

The Giardino di Boboli (see pgs. 173–174) is the most renowned of the Medici gardens in Florence, expanding behind the Santo Spirito neighborhood and bridging the city landscape with the semi-rural hills behind. Although it is the largest garden in the area, it is not the only one. In the Santo Spirito neighborhood, the somber facades of the Florentine villas and palazzi hide a treasure of courtyards and even full-fledged gardens behind their gates. Once a year, these gates, among many others throughout the city, are opened to the public, who are allowed a weekend to peruse the cool, tranquil, green corners tucked inside. The Giardini Aperti (Open Gardens) event allows visitors into the gardens two Sundays a year. With such a limited amount of time to see so many incredible gardens it is advised that visitors follow an itinerary covering just one of the neighborhoods of Florence.

Starting on Via Maggio, there are several courtyards worth peeking into, great examples of open spaces created in the smallest and busiest of quarters. The **Palazzo Ricasoli-Firidolfi**, a two-story structure with large, ashlar-framed windows and decorated with a facade of ornate family arms, boasts the largest internal courtyard in the neighborhood.

The palazzo was built by Senator Giovanni Francesco Ricasoli in the early 1500s, under the direction of architect Baccio d'Agnolo. The courtyard was designed in the style of Cronaca. It has three porticoed sides, and a fourth side with a series of semi-arches and a full arch. The columns in *pietra serena* are topped by capitals with an acanthus-leaf design, typical of private homes of this period. The wall decorations are alternating coats of arms of the Ricasoli and Firidolfi families along with a sculpture of what is presumed to be Saint Giovanni Battista, the protector of Francesco Giovanni Ridolfi. This courtyard is one of great architectural harmony and exemplifies the open space created for the urban dwellers of Florence.

Continuing down toward the river and then left onto Via Santo Spirito, you will find the **Palazzo Frescobaldi**, which was originally built in the 13th century but succumbed to many restorations. It has a very long facade with several interior courtyards. One must pass through an entrance hall, a gate, and a courtyard of ornate columns to reach the garden behind, which is bordered on one side by the apse of the basilica of Santo Spirito. In the 1800s the garden was divided into four parts. The fountain in the center is covered

Garden at Palazzo Frescobaldi

in baroque sculptures and displays a statue of Pan. It is surrounded by potted azaleas that border the surrounding flower beds. From the garden's little terrace you can see the dome of Santo Spirito. In 1301 the palace was host to Prince Charles of Valois, who came to Florence with a mission sponsored by the pope that eventually caused the exile of Dante.

Moving on along Via Santo Spirito and then left onto Via dei Serragli, the **Giardino Torrigiani** is by far the largest private garden inside the city's walls. Covering more than 15 acres of land, it is an exquisite example of Florence's interpretation of the Romantic English garden.

In the mid-1700s, before the land was turned into a garden, botanist Pier Antonio Micheli worked here. He was determined to create a botanical garden and, in fact, founded the first Italian botanical society here. In 1813, it was turned into the magnificent garden it is today. Luigi Torrigiani, whose family had owned the property since the 1500s, wanted to create a garden with a landscape symbolic of the voyage through life, death, and resurrection. Although the esoteric plans of the garden remain elusive to the average visitor, its beauty is readily apparent.

Upon entering the garden, designed by Luigi de Cambray-Digny and finished by Gaetano Baccani between 1813 and 1819, a grandiose row of plane trees shades the driveway leading to the neoclassical Villa Torrigiani. These trees were planted before the garden was designed and even before the villa was constructed in the mid-1700s. The path to the rest of the gardens veers immediately to the right of the entrance at the statue of the Osiris (the Egyptian god of the underworld and of vegetation), following under white roses that cling to a Chinese fence. In fact, at the time the garden was designed there was great interest in planting exotic plants, mainly from the Far East and India. Ahead, to the right, there is the Tempietto dell'Arcadio. Inside this temple is the sculpture of a lion assaulting a bull, one of many stone pieces that decorate the garden.

Farther along, the English garden theme becomes more evident with the sinuous paths that open onto large grassy fields surrounded by small, artificial, rolling hills bordered by a dense plantation of trees, giving a depth and

Giardino Torrigiani

variety to the landscape. These forests in miniature include various exotic, secular trees, the best example being the huge gingko biloba that looms over the stable behind the villa. There are also several foreign oaks and sequoias among the more classical Italian garden evergreens, like holm oaks, cedars, and laurels.

At the highest point in the garden a neoclassical tower was built, alluding to the family name and coat of arms. It stands over 98-feet tall but at present is in perilous ruin, and entrance is no longer possible.

At the opposite end of the garden is a circular field, designed to create a sort of small hippodrome. At one time horse races did take place here. It is now decorated with benches, vases, and statues, and constitutes the oldest part of the garden.

Across from the villa there are also several greenhouses that serve as the base for the large nursery un by the current owner.

Proceeding along Via dei Serragli then left onto Via Romana, a bit of garden peeps over large stone walls on the opposite side of the street from the Giardino di Boboli. This is the Giardino Corsi-Scarselli (see also pg. 183), owned at one point, like most other things in Florence, by the Medici family. On the corner of Via Romana and Via de' Mori a temple was constructed above the wall of the garden. It is in full view of passersby on Via Romana, who are greeted by a statue of Mercury, the protector of travelers, erected inside the temple. The entrance to the garden is farther along at No. 38. Two statues of muses, their feet interestingly finished in terra-cotta and one holding a harp, introduce the theme of the garden, which is dedicated to music. Designed and built between 1801 and 1810 by architect Giuseppe Manetti, it became the first Florentine Romantic English-style garden, in strong contrast with the more common Italian geometric garden of the late 1700s.

The winding and crisscrossed paths, typical of the Romantic garden, lead the visitor along the wall, which was originally constructed to protect the city against the Sienese army that threatened it in the 1500s. In fact, the wall and the mountains of rubble left behind after its partial demolition created the foundation around which Manetti built the garden.

In this garden, which measures about 2 1/2 acres, the vegetation is in large part made up of box, laurel, and holm oaks. There are also varieties of more exotic trees such as magnolias, cedars, and palms. A pond is situated in front of the neoclassical greenhouses graced with stone fruit garlands on the walls. Above a nearby fountain, a lapis with a Latin inscription by Ferdinando III consents to the use of the water supply for the Giardino di Boboli via a now-defunct underground aqueduct. Various other inscriptions throughout the garden add to the feeling of philosophical meditation it was created to inspire.

Further Information

The Associazione Dimore Storiche Italiane (Sezione Firenze) and Città

Nascosta collaborated with the owners to create the Giardini Aperti, or Open Gardens intitiative. They can be contacted for more information about gardens that will be open in May throughout the city (tel.: 39-055-6801680; e-mail: info@ cittanascosta.it or info@ adsi-toscana.itx).
For future Giardini Aperti schedules call 055-6802590.

Palazzo Frescobaldi
Via Santo Spirito, 13; closed to the public.

Palazzo Ricasoli-Firidolfi
Via Maggio, 13; tel.: 055-282951; fax: 055-217963; closed to the public.

Giardino Torrigiani
Via dei Serragli, 146; tel.: 055-224527; closed to the public (call to obtain special authorization to visit).

If you are interested in this wonderful garden we suggest you call and ask for a special "personalized" visit. You will be asked for a contribution to help maintain the garden, but it will be worth it.

FOCUS: Irises and Roses

Giardino dell'Iris (Iris Garden): Piazzale Michelangelo; open: daily in the month of May 10 A.M.–12:30 P.M., 3–7 P.M.; closed: June–Apr.; Giardino delle Rose (Rose Garden): Viale Giuseppe Poggi, 2; open: when the roses are in bloom (approx. May–June) 8 A.M.–1 P.M.; closed: July–Apr.

By Carla Rossi

There are two public gardens worth noting in the Oltrarno: the Giardino dell'Iris (Iris Garden) and the Giardino delle Rose (Rose Garden). Located just below Piazzale Michelangelo, they deserve a visit just for their views. Benches and walls overlook the Florentine skyline at such close range that they give the feeling that with one false move you might fall into Piazza San Giovanni, right in front of the Duomo.

Being the official flower of Florence, the iris has most appropriately been given a garden of its own. Open only during the month of May, when the flowers are in full bloom, the rows of irises are a spectacle of colors. All sorts of hybrids and heirloom varieties are to be found and after the winner of the annual international competition is chosen for the best hybrid, the flower is added to the collection that includes all winners since the competition began in the 1800s.

The garden, which is actually a terraced olive orchard, is dotted with benches that usually remain empty, although the entrance to the garden is a gate in the middle of the overcrowded Piazzale Michelangelo, which offers an almost identical panorama of the city.

At the bottom of the garden a pond contains water irises and lilies that bloom in such abundance they almost drown the goldfish swimming below.

The Giardino delle Rose has successfully managed to remain hidden just below the piazzale for more than 100 years. In 1865 the city of Florence named architect Giuseppe Poggi director of a beautification project for the then-future capital city of Italy, and the garden was designed to improve the riverbank opposite to the center. Inside there is an array of different types of roses and various other flowering plants, and a small Japanese garden.

Istituto e Convento di San Francesco di Sales

Other Points of Interest

FORTIFICAZIONI DI MICHELANGELO
Viale dei Colli

➤ Heading toward San Miniato al Monte, up the Viale dei Colli, you will come across a series of fortifications that were designed by Michelangelo in 1529. Made from beaten earth and crude brick, the outpost offered a commanding view to monitor approaching enemy troops. It was converted into a permanent fortress using sturdier bricks in 1552.

ISTITUTO E CONVENTO DI SAN FRANCESCO DI SALES
Viale Ariosto, 13; open: to arrange a visit to the convent, contact the Istituto at tel. 055-224190.

➤ This 18th-century convent by Antonio Ferri holds a number of contemporaneous works of art in its small church. Most notable among these are the frescoes by Giovanni Antonio Pucci. Look for *The Glorification of the Virgin with Saints Francesco di Sales and Giovanna Francesca di Chantal*. The *Visitation* and the *Crucifixion between Two Saints* decorate the lateral altars.

PALAZZO CAPPONI
Lungarno Guicciardini, 1; closed to the public.

➤ This 14th-century structure is noted for its magnificent salon. Located on the first floor, it features wall-to-ceiling frescoes (1585) courtesy of Bernardino Poccetti and lit by a handsome stone fireplace. The frescoes depict a variety of grotesques, allegorical figures, and stories of the Capponi family.

PALAZZO DELLE MISSIONI
Piazza Frescobaldi, 1; closed to the public.

➤ Part of the convent of the Scopetini, also known as the Padri delle Missioni or Barbetti, this palazzo features a baroque facade built in 1640 by Bernardino Radi. On the exterior, four oval niches house the busts of the grand dukes of Florence. The building was used as the seat of the Navy Ministry during the short time Florence was capital of Italy.

PALAZZO GUICCIARDINI
Lungarno Guicciardini, 7; closed to the public.

➤ Once celebrated for its garden, rich with exotic essences, the Palazzo Guicciardini underwent remodeling in the 17th century, followed by further renovations in the 19th

Palazzo Capponi

century that ultimately uprooted its claim to fame. It was later updated in the 18th century by Giuseppe Poggi.

PALAZZO GUICCIARDINI
Via Guicciardini, 15; closed to the public.

➤ This building is the home where Florentine writer Francesco Guicciardini, famous for his *History of Italy* and his political theories, was born in 1483. Originally, the site housed the residence of Luigi di Piero Guicciardini, the standard-bearer of justice, which was burnt down in 1378 during a revolt by the so-called Ciompi, or textile workers. Renovated in the first part of the 17th century, the palazzo houses, in the courtyard, a large stucco bas-relief representing Hercules and Cacus, attributed to Antonio del Pollaiuolo.

SAN BARTOLOMEO A MONTEOLIVETO
Via di Monteoliveto, Monticelli; open: to arrange a visit, contact the former home of the Monache Oblate Benedettine at Via di Monteoliveto, 72.

➤ Now operating as a military hospital, the church of San Bartolomeo was commissioned by Bartolomeo Capponi in 1377 for the monks of Monteoliveto. Prior to the church's construction, this Sienese monastery had been practicing out of an oratory perched in the hills nearby. In 1472, the monks were treated to renovations by Michelozzo, who sought to update the building in the Rennaissance style. Michelozzo's graceful design was later embellished upon during two different interventions that took place in the baroque era. Dominating the facade is an exceptional stone-carved portal, flanked by vestal virgins. The virgin on the right is attributed to 16th-century artist Giovanni Caccini; her partner was finished much later in the 17th century. The entire arrangement is decorously surmounted by a mullioned window. The interior of the church contains frescoes by Bernardino Poccetti on the west wall, a *Last Supper* by the painter known as Sodoma, and the *Entry of Christ into Jerusalem* by Santi di Tito on the high altar.

SAN PIETRO IN GATTOLINO (OR SAN PIETRO DI SERUMIDO)
Via Romana; open: inconsistently (contact the parish priest at 055-222233 for further information).

➤ Past Scarselli Garden on Via Romana, on the left, you will find the church of San Pietro in Gattolino. It was built on the site of an earlier 5th- or 6th-century structure.

In the Cappella del Sacramento, frescoed in 1776, is a Madonna with Child by Alessandro Fei del Barbiere, dated 1568, while the choir chapel displays an Enthroned Madonna with Child and Saints by the Maestro di Serumido. On the left wall is a 16th-century wooden crucifix.

SANTA MONACA
Via Santa Monaca, 6; open: inconsistently.

➤ The modest facade of the church of Santa Monaca is decorated with the Capponi coat of arms, which hang above its entrance. Inside are an elegant wood-carved choir, a 17th-century organ, and the *Deposition*, painted by Giovanni Maria Butteri in 1583. The fresco depicting the Glory of Saint Martin is by Cosimo Ulivelli.

Tabernacolo di Via de' Serragli

Tabernacolo del Ghirlandaio nel Torrino di Santa Rosa (Ghirlandaio's Tabernacle on Torrino di Santa Rosa)

Lungarno Soderini

➤ This 19th-century tabernacle has a fresco from the beginning of the 16th century representing the Pietà. It is attributed to Ridolfo del Ghirlandaio.

Tabernacolo di Piazza del Carmine (Tabernacle of Piazza del Carmine)

Piazza Piattellina, at the corner of Via del Leone

➤ This tabernacle is adorned with the fresco *Madonna, the Child and the Archangels Michael and Raphael*, believed to be the work of the Maestro di San Miniato or Francesco Botticini.

Tabernacolo di Via de' Serragli (Tabernacle of Via de' Serragli)

Via de' Serragli, corner of Via della Chiesa

➤ On the left side of Via de' Serragli is a large tabernacle decorated with a fresco by Cosimo Ulivelli. It depicts the Florentine Saint Philip Neri at the feet of the Madonna.

Torre di Bellosguardo (Torre di Bellosguardo Hotel)

Via Roti Michelozzi, 2; tel.: 055-2298145

➤ Ideally positioned for panoramic views of Florence, this 13th-century castle is now a hotel. Built at the behest of the Cavalcanti family, the castle was restored to medieval glory at the turn of the 20th century, setting the stage for its current vocation. Prior to this renovation, the castle had been temporarily transformed into a villa in the years following 1583. Much of Bellosguardo's artwork dates from this period. The marble group above the main entrance of the hotel depicts the Charities, executed in 1603 by Francavilla. The lobby, meanwhile, boasts a frescoed version of the Charities by noted mannerist painter Bernardino Poccetti.

Villa dell'Ombrellino

Piazza di Bellosguardo, 12; closed to the public.

➤ Adjacent to the Torre di Bellosguardo is the Villa dell'Ombrellino, which has served as a sumptuous convention center ever since the restoration of its grounds in 1988. Prior to this update, the villa hosted Galileo Galilei between the years 1617 and 1631. In the garden lies a monument to the many illustrious poets who lived in the villa's vicinity, including Ugo Foscolo, who passed several months of 1813 in a nearby building called "La Torricella." This structure no longer stands, but the numerous fragments Foscolo composed there live on in his famous poem "Le Grazie."

Museums

Palazzo Pitti, Appartamenti della Duchessa d'Aosta (Apartments of the Duchess of Aosta)

Palazzo Pitti; tel.: 055-294883; closed for renovations.

➤ These apartments, located inside the Palazzo Pitti, were used as a winter residence by the Savoy family during their visits to Florence from 1865 to the early 20th century. The paintings from the Lorena period, illustrating traditional Florentine celebrations and exhibited in the Chinese room, are of particular interest.

Palazzo Pitti, Appartamenti Reali (Royal Apartments)

Palazzo Pitti; tel.: 055-294883; website: www.polomuseale.firenze.it; open: Tues.–Sun. 8:15 A.M.–6:50 P.M.; closed: Mon., Jan. 1, May 1, Dec. 25; admission: €8.50 (includes entry to the Palatine Galleries).

➤ The royal apartments, on the first floor of the south wing of the palazzo, were built in the 17th century and were inhabited by the Medici, Lorraine, and Savoy families. As you walk through the richly decorated and furnished rooms, it is particularly interesting to note the changes in taste and style that characterize the different time periods during which the apartments were occupied. The rooms are decorated with frescoes by various Florentine artists and portraits of the Medici family by Justus Sustermans, a Flemish painter who worked in the court from 1619 to 1681. The dukes of Lorraine redecorated the apartments when they succeeded the Medici dynasty, adding the neoclassical details on the ceilings, frescoes, and the rococo-style stucco. Victor Emmanuel II's family lived here from 1865 to 1871, when Florence was the capital of a newly united Italy. Umberto and Margherita of Savoy made further changes to the apartments, adding the overworked decorations characteristic of the late 1800s as well as furniture, paintings, and tapestries, many of which were taken from the palaces of Parma and Lucca.

The Sala Bianca (White Room) is actually an enormous hall named for the bright light and white stuccoed decorations. The Sala dei Pappagalli (Parrot Room), covered in a crimson fabric full of birds, leads to the apartment of Queen Margherita, which is decorated with rich wall hangings, carpets, and furniture, most of which were installed by the House of Lorraine. The chapel, which until the turn of the 18th century was a bedroom in the apartment of Ferdinando de' Medici, is one of the few examples of late-baroque decoration in the Palazzo Pitti.

CASA-MUSEO DI RODOLFO SIVIERO

Lungarno Serristori, 3; tel.: 055-2345219; open: Sat. 10 A.M.–1:30 P.M., 4:30–7 P.M., Sun.–Mon. 10 A.M.–1 P.M.; admission: free.

➤ This museum was once the residence of Rodolfo Siviero (1911–1983), who was responsible for recovering many works of art stolen from Italy by the Nazis during World War II. After his death, the Casa Rodolfo Siviero was bequeathed to the Regione Toscana and then opened to the public in 1992. The house/museum contains his private collection of artwork dating from the Etruscan era to the 20th century, and features drawings and paintings by Giorgio de Chirico, and a restored fragment of a Roman mosaic from the 4th century.

GALLERIA D'ARTE MODERNA (MODERN ART GALLERY)

Piazza Pitti, 1, in the Pitti Palace; website: www.polomuseale.firenze.it; tel.: 055-294883; open: Tues.–Sun. 8:15 A.M.–6:50 P.M. (last admission 30 minutes before closing); closed: Mon. and Jan. 1, May 1, Dec. 25; admission: €8.50.

➤ The gallery, located on the second floor of the Palazzo Pitti, primarily has paintings from the 18th and 19th centuries that were collected by the Lorraine dukes to decorate the Palazzo Pitti. The museum combines this collection with pictures donated by the state and various private collections. Of particular interest are the works of the *macchiaioli* (spotmakers), a group of late-19th-century artists who painted the Tuscan landscape with bright splashes of color. They are said to be the Italian counterparts of the French Impressionists, if not their predecessors. Two paintings by Camille Pissarro are in the same room as these paintings, and there are also works by Giovanni Fattori, Silvestro Lega, Telemaco Signorini, Adriano Cecioni, and Federico Zandomeneghi.

GALLERIA DEL COSTUME (COSTUME GALLERY)

Piazza Pitti, 1; tel.: 055-294883; website: www.polomuseale.firenze.it; open: daily 8:15 A.M.–4:30 P.M. (Nov.–Feb.), 8:15 A.M.–5:30 P.M. (Mar.), 8:15 A.M.–6:30 P.M. (Apr., May, Sept., Oct.), 8:15 A.M.–7:30 P.M. (June–Aug.), last admission one hour before closing; closed: first and last Mon., Jan. 1, May 1, Dec. 25; admission: €6.

➤ Founded in 1983, the Costume Gallery is located on the ground floor of the Palazzina della Meridiana—the wing of the Palazzo Pitti that faces the Boboli Gardens. The museum recounts the history of clothing in Italy during the past two centuries. It is situated in rooms with frescoed ceilings and furniture dating from the 18th and 19th centuries. The collection, made up of private donations, includes men's and women's garments and accessories and a collection of theatrical and cinematographic costumes. There are also 16th-century garments, some worn by Eleonora of Toledo, and some of the rooms have been restored to correspond to a 1911 inventory, with original furniture and wall hangings.

Galleria del Costume

MUSEO DEGLI ARGENTI

Piazza Pitti, 1; tel.: 055-294883; website: www.polomuseale.firenze.it; open: daily 8:15 A.M.–4:30 P.M. (Nov.–Feb.), 8:15 A.M.–5:30 P.M. (Mar.), 8:15 A.M.–6:30 P.M. (Apr., May, Sept., Oct.), 8:15 A.M.–7:30 P.M. (June–Aug.); closed: first and last Mon. of each month, Jan. 1, May 1, Christmas; admission: €6.

➤ The Museum of Silver is located in the Palazzo Pitti and features an astounding display of the riches of the Medici dynasty. The rooms, once used by the Medici family as their summer apartments, are furnished with ebony furniture inlaid with *pietre dure* (semi-precious stones). Rare Roman ivory, carpets, glassware, and crystal are exhibited along with works by Florentine and German goldsmiths and other precious objects. Anna Maria Luisa de' Medici's cameo and jewel collection, and the refined cutlery and dinner services used by the family, are also on display. Of particular interest is the collection in the Sala Buia (Dark Room) of 16 vases from the ancient Roman and Byzantine periods that are laden with semi-precious stones and once belonged to Lorenzo the Magnificent. Also noteworthy is the beautiful Room IV, frescoed by Giovanni da San Giovanni between 1634 and 1642.

MUSEO DELLE CARROZZE (CARRIAGE MUSEUM)

Piazza Pitti, 1; tel.: 055-294883; website: www. polomuseale.firenze.it; closed for renovations.

➤ Located on the ground floor of the Palazzo Pitti, the Carriage Museum features several sedan chairs and carriages from the 18th and 19th centuries that belonged to the Lorraine grand dukes and the royal house of Savoy. Of particular interest is an elaborately decorated 18th-century carriage that belonged to Ferdinando II, king of Naples, and was brought to Florence by the Savoys, as well as three magnificent Berlin carriages in sculpted, painted, and gold-plated wood, built in Florence in 1818.

MUSEO DELLE PORCELLANE (MUSEUM OF PORCELAIN)

Piazza Pitti, 1, in the Boboli Gardens; tel.: 055-294883; website: www.polomuseale .firenze.it; same as "Silver Museum"; admission: €6.

➤ The Museum of Porcelain, located in the Casino del Cavaliere rooms in the upper section of the Boboli Gardens, features a beautiful collection of porcelain objects that belonged to the houses of Medici and Lorraine. Most of the pieces were manufactured in 18th-century Viennese factories and in the French factories of Tournais, Vincennes, and Paris. The museum has interesting Egyptian- and Greek-style dinner sets (1790–1800) and porcelains from the Real Fabbrica di Napoli (Royal Factory of Naples) such as the *School for Bears* and 18 statuettes of Neapolitan Common Women. Two 18th-century statuettes of Turkish Women are from the famous manufacturer Ginori di Doccia.

Lungarno di S. Rosa

Lung. Piazza d'Ognissanti

Ponte A. Vespucci

Pza. d'Oltarno

Via de' Rossi

Pza. S. Pancrazio

Via d. Sole

Via de' Giacomini

Via d. Antinori

Via d. Corsi

Via de' Cerchi

Via de' Federighi

Via d. Vigna Nuova

La Purgatoria

Via de' Tornabuoni

V. d. Strozzi

Via d. Strozzi

Vic. de' Strozzi

Piazza C. Goldoni

Piazza Rucellai

Via de' Palchetti

Via del Parione

Pza. S. Trinita

Via Porta Rossa

Piazza Davan...

Via

Lungarno Soderini

Lungarno Vespucci

Ponte alla Carraia

Lungarno Corsini

Ponte S. Trinita

Ponte Acciai...

Pza. di Verzaia

Via Bartolini

Pza. di Cestello

Piazza di Cestello

Piaggione

Lungarno Guicciardini

Lungarno di S...

Piazza de' Frescobaldi

Borgo S. Jacopo

Barbad...

Borgo San Frediano

Cardatori P.za de' Nerli

Tessitori

Via del Leone

Piazza d. Carmine

B.go d'Stella

Via S. Monaca

Via S. Agostino

S. Spirito

Via Maffia

Via del Presto di S. Martino

Via de' Coverelli

Piazza de' Frescobaldi

Piazza Santo Spirito

Via de' Camaldoli

Via dell'Orto

Piazza Piattellina

Via della Chiesa

Via delle Caldaie

Via de' Preti

Borgo Tegolaio

Via Mazzetta

Sdrucciolo de' Pitti

Via de' Vellutini

Piazza de' Pitti

Viale L. Ariosto

Via di S. Giovanni

Borgo d'Greci

Piazza T. Tasso

Via della Chiesa

Via del Campuccio

Via de' Serragli

Via S. Agostino

Via Sant'Agostino

Via del Campuccio

Via S. Maria

Palazzo Pitti

Via S. Paolo

Via Giano d. Bella

Giardino Torrigiani

Viale F. Petrarca

Via Romana

Via d. Ronco

Viale della Meridiana

Giardino di Boboli

Via del Casone

Via Pisana

Via Monti

Via Pindemonte

Viale dei Cipressi

Via d. Madonna della

Via d. Baluardo

Piazzale di Porta Romana

Via del Bobolino

Foscolo

Metastasio

Via Mascherino

Via del Boboli...

Via Senese

Viale Niccolò Machiavelli

Via Cantagalli

Via Marsilio d'Alberti

Via del Tasso

Viale Niccolò Machiavelli

Via Dante da Castiglione

Viale Niccolò Machiavelli

Viale del Poggio

Via Benedetto da Foiano

Piazzale Galileo

Via Senese

lombaia

Tricelli

SANTO SPIRITO/ OLTRARNO (COMMERCIAL)

Hotels & Inns

1 Grand Hotel Villa Cora
2 Hotel Annalena
3 Hotel David
4 Hotel Lungarno
5 Palazzo Magnani Feroni
6 Pensione Sorelle Bandini
7 Torre di Bellosguardo
8 Villa Carlotta

Restaurants & Cafés

9 All'Antico Ristoro dei Cambi
10 Alla Vecchia Bettola
11 Angiolino
12 Antico Borgo
13 Bar Rifrullo
14 Beccofino
15 Ben Vobis
16 Brindellone
17 Cabiria
18 Caffè Ricchi
19 Camillo
20 Capannina di Sante
21 Carlino Diladdarno
22 Celestino
23 Ciao Bella
24 Da Ginone
25 Enoteca Fuori Porta
26 Enoteca Le Barrique
27 Il Cantinone
28 Il Guscio
29 La Casalinga
30 Latteria Frilli*
31 Le Volpi e L'Uva
32 Momoyama
33 Osteria Antica Mescita
34 Osteria Santo Spirito
35 Pane e Vino
36 Ruggero
37 Taverna Machiavelli
38 Trattoria Beppin
39 Trattoria del Carmine
40 Trattoria 4 Leoni
41 Trattoria Pandemonio
42 Vanesio

Shopping

43 Alessandro Dari
44 Antico Setificio Fiorentino
45 Cassetti
46 Flair
47 Giovanni Manetti
48 Giulio Giannini e Figlio
49 Il Torchio*
50 L'Auriga
51 L'Ippogrifo
52 Lisa Corti Home Textile Emporium*
53 Lorenzo Villoresi*
54 Mannina*
55 Massimo Poggiali
56 Paolo Pagliai
57 Roberto Ugolini
58 Rosadi
59 Traslucido Art Deco
60 Vetrerie Locchi

Best of

61 Certini

Grand Hotel Villa Cora

Viale Machiavelli, 18; tel.: 055-271840; fax: 055-27184199; website: www.villacora.it; e-mail: reservations@villacora.it; category: ★★★★★; number of rooms: 48, including the Imperial suite, about 328 square feet, with a tester bed and view of downtown; credit cards accepted: all major; access to internet: yes; €€€–€€€€; currently being refurbished.

☛What was originally a mansion immersed in the lush vegetation around Florence is now a luxury hotel that is still surrounded by foliage, although it is just a five-minute taxi ride from the city center.

Hotel Annalena

Via Romana, 34; tel.: 055-222402; fax: 055-222403; website: www.hotelannalena.it; category: ★★★; number of rooms: 20, including 6 rooms with a balcony; credit cards accepted: all major; access to internet: yes; €€.

☛A small pensione with traditional decor and small but comfortable rooms just across the street from the Boboli Gardens. Most rooms look out onto the courtyard where a plant nursery is located.

Hotel David

Viale Michelangelo, 1; tel.: 055-6811695; fax: 055-680602; website: www.davidhotel.com; category: ★★★; number of rooms: 25, including 1 with an antique tester bed; credit cards accepted: all major; access to internet: yes; €€€.

☛A small hotel with charming decor. Each room, filled with interesting antique pieces, is unique.

Hotel Lungarno

Borgo San Jacopo, 14; tel.: 055-27261; fax: 055-268437; website: www.lungarno hotels.com; e-mail: lungarnohotels@lungarno hotels.com; category: ★★★★; number of rooms: 69, including the Palazzo Capponi suite, 650 square feet with a view of the Arno; credit cards accepted: all major; access to internet: yes; €€€€.

☛This hotel is in the historical center of the Oltrarno, with a view of the Ponte Vecchio and Ponte Santa Trìnita. Recently renovated, it is very luxurious.

Palazzo Magnani Feroni

Borgo San Frediano, 5; tel.: 055-2399544; fax: 055-2608908; website: www.florence palace.com; category: ★★★★★; number of rooms: 12 suites, including deluxe suites measuring 328 square feet; credit cards accepted: all major; access to internet: yes; €€€–€€€€.

☛According to E. Grifi, author of the authoritative 19th-century guidebook *Saunterings in Florence*, "Palazzo Magnani-Ferroni is a good building in the Renaissance style, built after a design by Zanobi del Rosso." The ambience of an aristocratic home of the 1800s is evident in the decor: overstuffed armchairs and couches are upholstered in gray-green silk, the bathrooms are decorated in warm reddish porphyry-colored tiles and period-inspired fixtures. Several suites have a private courtyard or terrace, and the walls of the smallest—Smeralda—are entirely covered by an authentic period fresco. A contemporary counterpoint to a delightful marble fireplace is provided by satellite TV in every suite.

Torre di Bellosguardo

Via Roti Michelozzi, 2; tel.: 055-2298145; fax: 055-229008; website: www.torrebellos guardo.com; e-mail: info@torrebellosguardo .com; category: ★★★★; number of rooms: 16, including the Tower suite on top of the tower with 360-degree view; credit cards accepted: all major; access to internet: no; €€€€.

☛Situated on the green hills just outside Porta Romana, it's still just a short walk to the center of Florence. There is a large garden and a swimming pool, and all rooms have their own unique decor.

HOTELS & INNS

Villa Carlotta

Via Michele di Lando, 3; tel.: 055-2336134; fax: 055-2336147; website: www.hotelvil-lacarlotta.it; email: info@hotelvillacarlotta.it; category: ★★★★; number of rooms: 32; credit cards accepted: all major; access to internet: yes; €€€–€€€€.

☛This old patrician villa in a quiet part of Florence behind the Boboli gardens offers modern and comfortable rooms and service.

RESTAURANTS & CAFÉS

All'Antico Ristoro dei Cambi

Via Sant'Onofrio, 1r; tel.: 055-217134; open: Mon.–Sat. 12:15–2:30 P.M., 7:30–10:30 P.M.; closed: Sun.; credit cards accepted: all major; €.

☛This is a very popular and noisy restaurant in the Oltrarno. It offers, in various forms, the tripe and offal characteristic of the real Florentine kitchen. A surprisingly extensive wine list is available, including some of the better-known Brunellos, at very reasonable prices.

Alla Vecchia Bettola

Viale Vasco Pratolini, 3-5-7r; tel.: 055-224158; open: Tues.–Sat. noon–2:30 P.M., 7:30–10:30 P.M.; closed: Sun.–Mon.; credit cards accepted: none; €.

☛In the Oltrarno, it's one of the less touristy joints in town. Specialties are *taglierini con funghi* (taglierini with mushrooms), *porcini gnocchi al pomodoro* (gnocchi with porcini mushrooms and tomatoes), and carpaccio.

Angiolino

Via Santo Spirito, 36r; tel.: 055-2398976; open: daily noon–2:30 P.M., 7–10:30 P.M.; credit cards accepted: all major; €.

☛A typical Tuscan trattoria with the usual decor. It's a nice place to get a hearty plate of *pappa al pomodoro* or *ribollita,* or to try a cold plate like *panzanella* or carpaccio with bresaola (a type of prosciutto), arugula, and Parmesan. There are tasty homemade desserts.

Antico Borgo

Piazza Santo Spirito, 6r; tel.: 055-210437 (reservations required); open: daily noon–midnight; credit cards accepted: all major; €.

☛One of the busiest restaurants in the Oltrarno, Antico Borgo serves homemade gnocchi in large portions. Seating is available within the café-style dining room or outside in the picturesque piazza.

Bar Rifrullo

Via San Niccolò, 55r; tel.: 055-2342621; open: daily 7–1 A.M.; credit cards accepted: all major.

☛Near Porta San Miniato is Bar Rifrullo, not particularly noted for its wine list, but where a glass of Antinori spumante can be enjoyed in the charming raised garden bordering the road or in the English-style pub inside.

Beccofino

Piazza Scarlatti, 1r (Lungarno Guicciardini); tel.: 055-290076; open: Mon.–Sat. 12:30–2:30 P.M., 7–10:30 P.M., wine bar open until midnight; closed: Sun.; credit cards accepted: all major; €.

☛Tuscan ingredients combined with inventiveness in its own small piazza on the Arno River. In summer, tables are placed on the piazza looking across the Arno to Palazzo Corsini, with its baroque statuary on perpetual sentry duty. Beccofino combines the best of the London/New York bustling bistro style with imaginative and generously portioned meals of Tuscan inspiration.

Take the simple but satisfying *pasticcio di fave*, a concoction of slightly mushy broad beans perfumed with rosemary and oil, lying on a bed of spinach leaves and scattered with shavings of Parmesan. If it's truffles you are after, try them with poached eggs atop braised onions courted by a Tuscan chardonnay from the Fattoria della Rendola in the Valdarno. Roast suckling pig with overtones of sesame and buttressed by potato deserves the full whack of a Super Chianti: the Castello di Fonterutoli Riserva 1997 allows the Sangiovese grape to display its power without losing the elegance, a hallmark of the house of Mazzei, winemakers since 1435.

Bene Vobis

Via dei Serragli, 78r; tel.: 055-218952; open: Mon. 6:30 P.M.–3 A.M., Tues.–Sun. 11:30 P.M.–3 A.M.; credit cards accepted: all major.
☛An amazing selection of wines—over 80 Tuscan reds alone—is available to taste by the glass or bottle at little more than the standard retail price, and there are plenty of local cheeses, hams, and salamis to be consumed under the magnificent brick-vaulted ceilings. The sommelier has a well-founded weakness for the big red wines of Rocca di Castagnoli in deepest Chianti. Open until late and with occasional musical interludes.

Brindellone

Piazza Piattellina, 10; tel.: 055-217879; open: Tues.–Sun. noon–2 P.M., 7:30–10 P.M.; closed: Mon.; credit cards accepted: all major; €.
☛Named after the exploding cart rigged with fireworks each Easter Sunday morning, Il Brindellone is a good lunch spot. The decor is "rustic country" and the food is "poor country," according to the owner, despite a convenient inner-city location. Pasta is cooked to order, and the salads come with imaginative toppings.

Cabiria

Piazza Santo Spirito, 4r; tel.: 055-215732; open: Wed.–Mon. 8–1:30 A.M.; closed: Tues.; credit cards accepted: none.

☛A very relaxed place that serves everything from brunch and light lunch to drinks in the evening. The outdoor seating is located right under the church of Santo Spirito.

Caffè Ricchi

Piazza Santo Spirito, 8r; tel. 055-215864; open: Mon.–Sat. noon–3 P.M., 7:30–11 P.M.; closed: Sun.; credit cards accepted: all major; €.
☛An outdoor terrace in the middle of Piazza Santo Spirito is what makes this restaurant so appealing. The crowded tables in the shade of the piazza's trees and church are the perfect spot to enjoy lunch on a warm spring day. The restaurant and bar are elegant and the outside dining area is literally hedged off from the piazza, turning it into a garden oasis. The menu varies according to what the daily catch brings—expect carpaccio of sea bass, oysters, and gratinéed scallops among the starters. *Primi* include *riso nero,* where the ink of the cuttlefish is added to the rice to give it a deceptively sinister look, and classics such as *pasta con le vongole* (pasta with clams). As in all good seafood restaurants in Italy, the best ingredients are simply allowed to speak for themselves with no more than a squeeze of lemon and a drizzle of olive oil to enhance the freshness of the fish. The restaurant is also open for breakfast and between lunch and dinner, serving drinks and appetizers at the bar.

Camillo

Borgo San Jacopo, 57r; tel.: 055-212427; fax: 055-212963; open: Thurs.–Tues. noon–2:30 P.M., 7:30–10:30 P.M.; closed: Wed; credit cards accepted: all major; €.
☛One of Florence's best traditional restaurants with good Tuscan cuisine. Highlights are the house's *Peposo, taglierini con asparagi* (taglierini with asparagus, made when the vegetable is in season), *tagliatelle al tartufo* (tagliatelle with truffles), and grilled meats. Patronized by Florentines and tourists alike.

Capannina di Sante

Piazza Ravenna, 1r; open: Mon.–Sat. 7:30–10:30 P.M.; closed: Sun.; credit cards accepted: all major, except Diners Club; €€.

☛Capannina di Sante is considered one of the best places in Florence for fish. Although it is not centrally located, it is worth a trip: dishes are based on traditional recipes. Originally a hut beside the river ferry in the days before the construction of the Ponte da Verrazzano, it is now a somewhat chichi restaurant with most un-hutlike prices, but many will enjoy the setting.

Carlino Diladdarno

Via dei Serragli, 108r; tel.: 055-225001; open: 12:30–3:30 P.M., 7:30 P.M.–midnight; closed: Mon. and Tues. at lunch; credit cards accepted: all major; €.

☛Chiefly frequented by locals, old-fashioned in conception, and more or less free from the ravages of mass tourism, Carlino Diladdarno, on the busy Via dei Serragli leading up to Porta Romana, has a quiet, white-walled patio at the back, covered by a luxuriant spreading vine. The roasted and grilled meats are exceptional. There is pleasant shady outdoor seating in the summer. Carlino buys its cakes and tarts from Dolce e Dolcezze, the city's finest patisserie (see pg. 122).

Celestino

Piazza Santa Felicita, 4r; tel.: 055-2396574; fax: 055-292185; open: daily noon–2:30 P.M., 7–10:30 P.M.; closed: Sun. from Nov. to Mar.; credit cards accepted: all major; €.

☛One of the oldest restaurants between the Ponte Vecchio and the Palazzo Pitti, it serves homemade pastas and soups, risotto, fresh fish, and grilled meats. Garden seating.

Ciao Bella

Piazza Tiratoio, 1r; tel.: 055-218477; fax: 055-283519; open: Wed.–Mon. noon–3 P.M., 8 p.m.–1 A.M.; closed: Tues.; credit cards accepted: all major; €.

☛A blue-eyed, mustachioed Sicilian and his German wife prepare light, flavorful, generous portions of Southern specialties such as *penne alle sarde* (short pasta with sardine fillets, wild fennel, pine nuts, raisins, bread crumbs, and saffron), *maccheroni* topped with fried eggplant and salted ricotta, grilled swordfish accompanied by tomato and capers, and even the occasional Tuscan recipe. The desserts are homemade and usually come with a glass of homemade *limoncello* liqueur. Ciao Bella is located in a former 12th-century convent.

Da Ginone

Via de' Serragli, 35r; tel. and fax: 055-218758; open: Mon.–Sat. noon–2:30 P.M., 7–10 P.M.; closed: Sun.; credit cards accepted: all major; €.

☛This friendly trattoria serves traditional country fare such as fettuccine topped with ragu of wild hare. Follow this with the house specialty, *Toscano Fritto*, a fried assortment of chicken, hare, and lamb.

Enoteca Fuori Porta

Via Monte alle Croci, 10r; tel.: 055-2342483; website: www.fuoriporta.it; e-mail: info @fuoriporta.it; open: daily noon–12:30 A.M.; credit cards accepted: all major.

☛Fuori Porta is located outside the old gate of Porta San Miniato. Here, a few strategically placed benches offer imbibers an eerily evocative view of one of the few remaining stretches of the old walls of the city, for the most part destroyed when Florence became capital of Italy in 1867. The wine list is extensive and notably strong on Tuscan reds.

Enoteca Le Barrique

Via del Leone, 40r; tel.: 055-224192; open: Tues.–Sun. 7 P.M.–midnight; closed: Mon.; credit cards accepted: all major.

☛In the same area, and with the advantage of its own tranquil garden at the back, is Le Barrique, another of the new generation of wine bar/restaurants. The owners have almost completely turned their backs on Tuscan cuisine and have struck out on their own imaginative path, accompanying the food with a list offering wines not only from Italy but also France and South Africa. A Hoffstater Muller Thurgau from the Alto Adige region would go well with the crusty sea bass fillet in a mussel sauce.

Il Cantinone

Via Santo Spirito, 6r; tel.: 055-218898; open: Tues.–Sun. 12:30–2 P.M., 7:30–10:30 P.M.; closed: Mon.; credit cards accepted: all major; €€.

☛This is a classic Chianti restaurant. Here, wine is not savored to accompany food, but vice versa. The menu offers typical Tuscan cuisine served in a dining room with stone vaulted ceilings. House prices range from house wine at about €6, to special wines (up to €250).

Il Guscio

Via dell'Orto, 49a; tel.: 055-224421; open: Tues.–Sat. 8–11 P.M.; closed: Sun.–Mon. and all of Aug.; credit cards accepted: all major; €.

☛Located in the heart of San Frediano, Il Guscio attracts a mainly Florentine crowd who come time and time again. Kitchen staff cook all day, preparing the homemade fish broth added to the plum tomatoes, chopped mullet, and squid of the slightly spicy *spaghetti al trabaccolare*. Crêpes are homemade, rolled around delicate eggplant mousse with a touch of béchamel. Owner Francesco is on hand to suggest wines by the glass from the 13-page Italian, French, and "foreign" wine list. For dessert, try the baked, almost caramelized slices of apple, peach, and grape served with cream.

La Casalinga

Via del Michelozzo, 9r; tel.: 055-218624; open: Mon.–Sat. noon–2:30 P.M., 7–9:45 P.M.; closed: Sun. and Aug.; credit cards accepted: all major; €.

☛Family-run restaurant patronized by locals. A good place to eat local fare at reasonable prices. Specialties include *ribollita* and *pappa al pomodoro*.

Latteria Frilli

Via San Miniato, 5r; open: Thurs.–Tues. 11 A.M.–midnight (summer), Thurs.–Tues. 11 A.M.–8 P.M. (winter); closed: Wed.

☛The tiniest and probably the best gelaterie in town. The shop offers just a few select flavors of freshly made ice cream.

Le Volpi e L'Uva

Piazza dei Rossi, 1r; tel.: 055-2398132; open: Mon.–Sat. 10 A.M.–9 P.M.; closed: Sun.; credit cards accepted: all major.

☛Just steps from the Ponte Vecchio on the Oltrarno, Le Volpi e L'Uva is an enticing summer retreat from the crowds and the city streets. It has tables that spill onto the tiny Piazza dei Rossi and an impressive wine selection. Owners Riccardo and Emilio cater to a laid-back clientele and take great pride in their tiny enoteca. At the marble-topped bar (mounted on giant wine barrels), up to 20 different wines are available by the glass. There is also a selection of high-quality snacks (porcini sandwiches, fine Tuscan hams and salamis, Tuscan and French cheeses, local breads from the Pugi bakery).

Momoyama

Borgo San Frediano, 10r; tel.: 055-291840; open: Tues.–Sun. 7:30–11:30 P.M.; closed: Mon.; credit cards accepted: all major; €.

☛Sushi heaven. Before the diner's eyes, sushi chefs Eric Stedman from San Diego and Miwa Inumana prepare the dragon roll—smoked salmon, cream cheese, avocado, and cucumber shaped into a dragon, decorated with carrot curls—as well as platters of paper-thin raw tuna and salmon fillets, shrimp, and octopus—atop a counter in the non-smoking section. From the Japanese menu, try the excellent miso soup and torikara (crunchy fried chicken nuggets complemented by a soy sauce batter, sesame seeds, and bean sprouts). Fusion cuisine such as mussels cooked with lemongrass and basil is featured on the "inventive" menu. The atmosphere is serene and comfortable.

Osteria Antica Mescita

Via San Niccolò, 60r; tel.: 055-2342836; open: Mon.–Sat. noon–2 P.M., 7 P.M.–1 A.M.; closed: Sun.; credit cards accepted: all major; €.

☛A traditional cantina, with a simple but good menu, in a beautiful environment in the crypt of San Niccolò.

Osteria Santo Spirito

Piazza Santo Spirito, 16r; tel.: 055-2382383; open: daily 12:30–2:30 P.M., 7:30–11:30 P.M.; credit cards accepted: all major; €.

☛A popular tavern with a fixed menu, as well as tables in the piazza when the weather permits it. Their specialty is gnocchi in truffle-flavored cheese.

Pane e Vino

Via San Niccolò, 60; tel.: 055-2476956; open: Mon.–Sat. 7–10:30 P.M.; closed: Sun. and all of Aug.; credit cards accepted: all major; €.

☛In the quiet area of San Niccolò, open until late at night. Elegant but relaxed, with traditional Tuscan cuisine. Menu changes regularly, always using fruits and vegetables in season. Specialties include *ravioli neri ripieni di pesce con porri* (ravioli filled with fish and leeks) and *bocconcini di capretto in salsa di melanzane* (cheese with eggplant).

Ruggero

Via Senese, 89r; tel.: 055-220542; open: Thurs.–Mon. noon–2 P.M., 7–10 P.M.; closed: Tues.–Wed.; credit cards accepted: all major; €.

☛Home-style, local cuisine at a very reasonable price. Reservations are essential. *Ribollita* and *pappardelle alla lepre* (pappardelle with hare sauce) are the specialties.

Taverna Machiavelli

Viale Machiavelli, 18; tel.: 055-2298451; open: daily noon–2 P.M., 7–10:30 P.M.; credit cards accepted: all major; €€.

☛Elegant and charming. Try the *terrina di pescatrice e astice* (lobster terrine), *crema di piselli con gnocchetti di ricotta e magro* (cream of peas with small ricotta gnocchi), or *tortelli all'ortica con burro e tartufo* (tortellini with butter and truffles).

Trattoria Beppin

Via di Ripoli, 13r; tel.: 055-6810505; open: noon–3 P.M., 7–10:30 P.M.; closed: Tues. evening and Wed.; credit cards accepted: all major; €.

☛Typical trattoria, specializing in fish dishes.

Trattoria del Carmine

Piazza del Carmine, 18r; tel.: 055-218601; open: Mon.–Sat. 12:15–2:30 P.M., 7:15–10:30 P.M.; closed: Sun.; credit cards accepted: all major; €.

☛Informal, with formica furnishings and home-style cooking. Especially good are the *coniglio* (rabbit) *alla maremmana* and the desserts.

Trattoria 4 Leoni

Via dei Vellutini, 1r, in Piazza della Passera; tel.: 055-218562; website: www.4leoni.com; e-mail: info@4leoni.com; open: daily noon–2:30 P.M., 7–11 P.M.; closed: Wed. for lunch; credit cards accepted: all major; €.

☛The outdoor seating located in the quiet piazza is a respite from the throngs of visitors around the Palazzo Pitti and Santo Spirito. The style of the trattoria and its food could be described as "rustic panache" and none the worse for the slight air of invented tradition that hangs over it. The cleaned-up piazza is a rare haven in this part of the city, and the food is good enough for actor Anthony Hopkins, who is frequently spotted here, though hardly up to the fastidious standards of his alter ego, Dr. Hannibal Lecter. The menu offers typical Tuscan dishes as well as a variety of salads. There is also an extensive dessert list.

Trattoria Pandemonio

Via del Leone, 50r; tel.: 055-224002; open: Mon.–Sat. 12:30–2:30 P.M., 7:30–10:30 P.M.; closed: Sun.; credit cards accepted: all major; €.

☛This long, narrow restaurant has lots of seating that extends back to an outdoor garden. The service is efficient, and the menu offers several typical Tuscan dishes, as well as homemade *limoncello* for after dinner.

*Alessandro Dari

Via San Niccolò, 115r; tel.: 055-244747; website: www.alessandrodari.com; e-mail: alessandrodari@libero.it; open: Mon.–Sat. 9 A.M.–1 P.M., 3:30–7:30 P.M.; closed: Sun.; credit cards accepted: all major.

☛An elegant and very original collection of jewels fills the shop of this master jeweler and artist.

Antico Setificio Fiorentino

Via Bartolini, 4; tel.: 055-213861; website: www.anticosetificiofiorentino.com; open: Mon.–Fri. 9 A.M.–1 p.m., 2–5 P.M.; closed: Sat.–Sun.; credit cards accepted: all major.

☛Antico Setificio Fiorentino (old Florence silk products) has been in business since 1700, as has the Florentine factory where the famous 100-percent tessuti silks are made. The factory provides the store with silk that can be bought as is or transformed into other items, such as dresses. The larger and made-to-order clothes are quite pricey, but it is possible to get smaller items for as little as €50.

Cassetti

Ponte Vecchio, 52–54r; tel.: 055-287361/2396028; open: Tues.–Sat. 10 A.M.– 7 P.M. (Jan.–Feb.), Mon.–Sat. 10 A.M.–7 P.M. (Mar.–Dec.); closed: Sun.–Mon. (Jan.–Feb.), Sun. (Mar.–Dec.); credit cards accepted: all major.

☛Well known for the quality of their products, this shop sells jewels of their own production as well as antique pieces.

Flair

Piazza Scarlatti, 2r; tel.: 055-2670154; fax: 055-2676316; website: www.flair.it; e-mail: info@flair.it; open: Mon. 3–7:30 P.M., Tue.–Sat. 10 A.M.–1 P.M., 3–7:30 P.M.; closed: Sun.; credit cards accepted: all major.

☛Former Gucci and Ralph Lauren merchandiser Franco Mariotti and his wife, Alessandra Tabacchi, mix furniture and design accessories from different periods and places (Italy, France, Austria, England), personalizing interior design to mirror a contemporary lifestyle. Mariotti is found at Piazza Scarlatti, while Tabacchi oversees the furnishings department at Piazza Frescobaldi: Plexiglas lamps, wooden tables topped with a parchment surface, and armchairs reupholstered with 19th-century African fabric or zebra hide.

Giovanni Manetti

Borgo San Jacopo, 55r; tel. and fax: 055-214702; open: Mon.–Fri. 9 A.M.–1 P.M., 3:30–8 P.M., Sat. 9 A.M.–1 P.M.; closed: Sun.; credit cards accepted: Visa and American Express.

☛This small artisan jeweler is famed for his creative collections, such as his line of animals made of precious stones and metals.

Giulio Giannini e Figlio

Piazza Pitti, 37r; tel.: 055-212621; e-mail: giannini@giuliogiannini.it; open: daily 10 A.M.–7:30 P.M.; credit cards accepted: all major.

☛Directly across from the Costume Gallery is one of Florence's finest bookbinding workshops, specializing in skillfully made, elaborate marbled paper. Five generations of the Giannini family have worked at this location since 1856, re-adapting the centuries-old Oriental technique of marbled paper to create the classic peacock design as well as the more recent stone motif. This colorful hand-designed paper, along with paper stenciled with original Italian folk patterns, is used to cover notebooks, planners, frames, photo albums, and other gift items.

*Il Torchio

Via de' Bardi, 17; tel.: 055-2342862; open: Mon.–Fri. 9:30 A.M.–1:30 P.M., 2:30–7 P.M., Sat. 9:30 A.M.–1 P.M.; closed: Sun.; credit cards accepted: all major.

☛This paper shop is crammed with paper goods and a bookbinding workshop that spills into the display area. A unique assortment of hand-decorated paper, photo albums, address books, and diaries are piled high around a central table where the products are made.

L'Auriga

Sdrucciolo dei Pitti, 20r; tel. and fax: 055-294928; open: Mon. 3:30–7:30 P.M., Tues.–Sat. 10 A.M.–1 P.M., 3:30–7:30 P.M.; closed: Sun.; credit cards accepted: all major.

☛This antique shop sells beautiful and precious furniture imported from China.

L'Ippogrifo

Via Santo Spirito, 5r; tel.: 055-213255; open: Mon.–Fri. 10 A.M.–1 P.M., 3–7 P.M., Sat. 3–7 P.M.; closed: Sun.; credit cards accepted: all major.

☞Artist Gianni Raffaelli has opened up this shop to sell his watercolor engravings. Works can also be commissioned.

*Lisa Corti Home Textiles Emporium

Via de' Bardi, 58; tel.: 055-2645600; website: www.lisacorti.com; e-mail: firenze @lisacorti.com; Mon. 3:30–7:30 P.M., Tues.–Sat. 10 A.M.–1 P.M., 3:30–7:30 P.M.; closed: Sun.; credit cards accepted: all major. Piazza Ghiberti, 33; tel.: 055-2001200; open: Mon. 3:30–7:30 P.M., Tues.–Sat. 10 A.M.– 2 P.M., 3:30–7:30 P.M.

☞The creatively designed curtains, bed-covers, and pillows in organza, silk, and velvet make for a lively and colorful shop.

*Lorenzo Villoresi

Via de' Bardi, 14; tel.: 055-2341187; fax: 055-2345893; open: (see p. 19) by appointment only; credit cards accepted: all major.

☞Although he has perfumes already prepared, you need an appointment with Lorenzo Villoresi to have a personalized perfume created. He has lots of famous clients and a great location, with a huge window overlooking the city. There aren't too many like him in Italy.

*Mannina

Via Guicciardini, 16r; tel.: 055-282895; open: daily 9:30 A.M.–7:30 P.M.; credit cards accepted: all major.

☞Beautiful custom-made handmade shoes.

Massimo Poggiali

Borgo Tegolaio, 32r; tel.: 055-2398945; open: 8:30 A.M.–12:30 P.M., 2:30–6:30 P.M.; closed: Sat.–Sun.; credit cards accepted: none.

☞Poggiali does artistic work in bronze and he is almost one of a kind, working on his own in a small shop. He does a lot of work for antiques dealers but also has a small showroom with lights and other items.

Paolo Pagliai

Borgo San Jacopo, 41r; tel.: 055-282840; fax: 055-2398167; open: Mon.–Fri. 9 A.M.– 7:30 P.M., Sat. 9 A.M.– 1 P.M.; closed: Sun.; credit cards accepted: all major.

☞Mr. Pagliai comes from a tradition of silversmithing, starting in 1930 as an apprentice in his father's shop. He is especially adept at re-creating pieces that are missing from objects. His shop displays his own works as well as period pieces.

Roberto Ugolini

Via Michelozzi, 17r; tel. and fax: 055-216246; website: www.roberto-ugolini.com; open: Mon. 9 A.M.–1 P.M., Tues.–Sat. 9:30 A.M.–1:30 P.M., 3:30–7:30 P.M.; closed: Sun.; credit cards accepted: all major.

☞Handmade shoes of the highest quality are created here by craftsman Roberto Ugolini.

Rosadi

Borgo San Jacopo, 7r; tel.: 055-282301; open: Mon–Sat. 9 A.M.–8 P.M. (closes Dec.–Jan. between 1 P.M. and 2:30 P.M.); closed: Sun.; credit cards accepted: all major.

☞Right off the Ponte Vecchio, this small shop has a marvelous collection of Mazzini bags and accessories.

Traslucido Art Deco

Via Maggio, 9r; tel.: 055-212750; open: Mon.–Fri. 10 A.M.–1 P.M., 4–7:30 P.M., Sat. 10 A.M.–1 P.M. (summer), Mon. 4–7:30 P.M., Tues.–Sat. 10 A.M.–1 P.M., 4–7:30 P.M. (winter); closed: Sun.; credit cards accepted: all major.

☞They have beautiful furniture, lamps, and artwork from the art deco period.

Vetrerie Locchi

Via Burchiello, 10; tel.: 055-2298371; fax: 055-229416; open: daily 8:30 A.M.–1 P.M., 3–6:30 P.M.; credit cards accepted: all major.

☞Famous throughout Italy, these artisan and export glassblowers can create almost any object a client conjures up and are also capable of repairing broken crystal and glassware.

Outside Florence

By Laura Collura Kahn

E ven in the early Renaissance, Florence was a burgeoning city that could not remain cooped up within its walls. Consequently, its harmonious architecture spilled out into the countryside. As always, the Medici dynasty played a major role—most notably renovating villas while respecting the geometric rules of the Renaissance.

The **Villa Medicea della Petraia** was bought by the Medicis in 1530 and, even after renovation, kept its original shape as a medieval fortification. In the 1800s it was used by Italy's first king as a hunting lodge. Its park includes a hanging garden, the Piano della Figurina.

Not far from this rises the **Villa Medicea di Castello**, also originally a medieval fortification that was bought by the Medicis in 1477 and entirely renovated. Later destroyed by the Medicis' opponents, it was again restored in 1527 by Niccolò Tribolo, a pupil of Michelangelo. Today, the garden is open to the public but the villa, which houses the Accademia della Crusca, an institution protecting the purity of the Italian language, is closed.

Some 11 miles (18 kilometers) northwest of Florence stands the **Villa Medicea di Poggio a Caiano**, a true Renaissance "country residence" in the style outlined by Leon Battista Alberti. Lorenzo the Magnificent bought it from the Strozzi family in 1480 and had it redone, and the king of Italy used it in the 19th century.

A different route south of the city will lead to the **Certosa del Galluzzo**, a charterhouse founded in the 14th century by Niccolò Acciaiuoli, a member of Florence's high bourgeoisie. The Certosa includes a **Pinacoteca**, or painting gallery, featuring five frescoed lunettes by Jacopo Pontormo.

The hill town of Fiesole, north of Florence, was considered a strategic spot by both the Etruscans and the ancient Romans, and later became a favorite haunt of the Medicis. **San Romolo**, the city's cathedral, is a Romanesque church built on the site of the ancient forum, today Piazza Mino da Fiesole.

From here, Via Giovanni Dupré leads to the archaeological area. The **Teatro Romano**, built under Augustus and unearthed in the 1800s, held as many as 3,000 people. On its right stand the ruins of the **Terme Romane**, ancient baths complete with a swimming pool and the remains of the heating system. A small path west leads past the Etruscan walls and to the **Tempio Romano**, built over the ruins of an Etruscan temple, whose pediment is still visible.

Leaving the archaeological area behind, the Via Portigiani leads up to the **Antiquarium Costantini**, showcasing a collection of 170 ceramic objects.

Once back at San Romolo, climb up a steep alley to the 14th-century convent of **San Francesco**, built on the site of the ancient acropolis.

Opposite, Florence as seen from the hill town of Fiesole

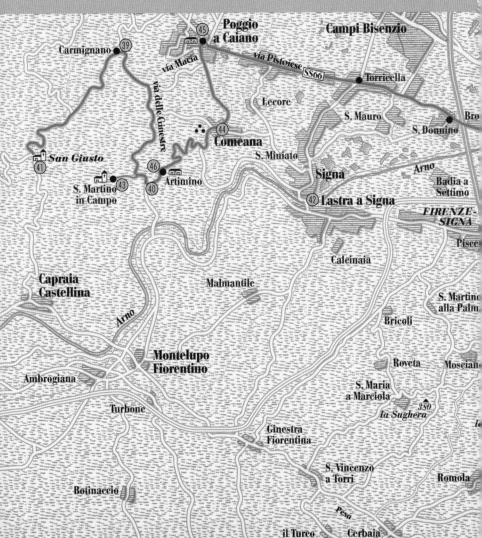

ITINERARIES

In this chapter, you will find excursions to towns just outside of
Florence with exceptional sites:

Northeast
• Fiesole

East of Florence
• Maiano
• Martino a Mensola
• Settignano

South of Florence
• Arcetri
• Galluzzo
• Giogoli
• Impruneta
• Mezzomonte
• Poggio Imperiale
• Rosano
• San Felice a Ema
• Scandicci
• Settimo

West of Florence
• Artimino
• Capraia e Limite
• Carmignano
• Comeana
• Lastra a Signa
• Poggia a Caiano

Northwest of Florence
• Careggi
• Castello
• Cercina
• Sesto Fiorentino

North of Florence
• Pratolino
• Vaglia

OUTSIDE FLORENCE

Beyond the walls, the whole sweet Valley of the Arno,
the convent at Fiesole, the Tower of Galileo, Boccaccio's house,
old villas and retreats; innumerable spots of interest,
all glowing in a landscape of surpassing beauty steeped in
the richest light; are spread before us.

Dickens, *Pictures from Italy*

Northeast of Florence

Fiesole

Situated in the hills above Florence is the village of Fiesole. Founded as an Etruscan colony, the town rose to prominence in Roman times when it was considered the region's most important settlement. Most of the development that Fiesole experienced during this period, however, would be destroyed a thousand years later. Florence, threatened by the small town's strategic position, overwhelmed Fiesole, attacking and burning the majority of its architectural heritage to the ground. Today, Fiesole is best known for the unparalleled panoramas it offers of its once-hostile neighbor.

Directions: From Piazza della Libertà (Porta San Gallo) in Florence take Viale Don Minzoni, then turn right on the overbridge, Cavalcavia delle Cure. Once you cross the overbridge, take Via Borghini and continue on Via Faentina. Take Via Togliatti and turn onto Via della Badia dei Roccettini. After about 600 yards turn left on Via Vecchia Fiesolana. At the end of the road you will reach Piazza Mino da Fiesole, the center of Fiesole. You can also take ATAF bus No. 7 from Piazza della Stazione in Florence.

FURTHER INFORMATION

Tourist Office
Via Portigiani, 3/5; tel.: 055-598720;
open: Mon.–Sat. 9 A.M.–6 P.M.,
Sun. 10 A.M.–6 P.M.

Anfiteatro Romano in Fiesole

ARCHAEOLOGICAL AREA

Tel.: 055-59477; admission: €13 (includes entry to the entire archaeological area of Fiesole and the Museo Bandini).

➢ From Piazza Mino da Fiesole, the street behind the cathedral of San Romolo leads to Fiesole's archaeological area, with a Roman theater, temple, and baths, as well as a museum displaying ancient objects.

• ANTIQUARIUM COSTANTINI (COSTANTINI ANTIQUITY MUSEUM)

Via Portigiani, 1; open: daily 9:30 A.M.–7 P.M. (summer), daily 9:30 A.M.–5 P.M. (winter); closed: Tues.

➢ This building was donated to the town of Fiesole by Alfiero Costantini in 1985 and is positioned next to the archaeological area. It holds an impressive collection of ancient ceramic objects from the Attic, Etruscan, and Magna Grecia eras (about 170 altogether). On the ground floor are a series of documents relating to the excavations conducted in the surrounding area in recent years, which brought to light objects dating from the 2nd century B.C. to the Roman era.

• TEATRO ROMANO (ROMAN THEATER)

Via Portigiani, 1; open: daily 9:30 A.M.–7 P.M. (summer), daily 9:30 A.M.–5 P.M. (winter);

closed: Tues.

➢ Work on the Roman Theater was first initiated under Augustus and was completed under Emperor Claudius. At that time, it could hold up to 3,000 spectators. Its horseshoe-shaped auditorium is built into the hill but partly supported by a man-made wall. Three small flights of steps divide it into four parts. The seats on the right are still intact and original, while the others have been replaced with smaller blocks of stone. The authorities used to be seated in the orchestra, in front of the stage. On the right side of the stage lie the interesting remains of a horseshoe-shaped iron room, which once housed a device used to raise the curtain. The theater is still used for performances and concerts during the Estate Fiesolana, a summer festival in Fiesole.

• TEMPIO ROMANO (ROMAN TEMPLE)

Via Portigiani, 1; open: daily 9:30 A.M.–7 P.M. (summer), daily 9:30 A.M.–5 P.M. (winter); closed: Tues.

➢ Located northwest of the Roman Theater, this temple was built in the first century B.C. on the ruins of an earlier Etruscan temple that had burned down in a fire. It was rebuilt larger and taller than the original one, but it kept the Etruscan tradition of terra-cotta decorations (they are now kept in the Antiquarium Costantini. A seven-step stairway, with a 70-foot-wide base, is located on the east side of the ruin. Although the temple's arcade has long disappeared, the ruins of five of the columns that used to hold it up are still visible on the site.

• TERME ROMANE (ROMAN BATHS)

Via Portigiani, 1; open: daily 9:30 A.M.–7 P.M. (summer), daily 9:30 A.M.–5 P.M. (winter); closed: Tues.

➤ These Roman baths were originally built under the reign of Augustus and extended in the 3rd and 4th centuries. They house three pools. The first, in a large courtyard, was used for swimming. The other two, higher up on the terrace, could also have been used to filter water. The chambers, down some steps, are located to the right of these latter pools. They include the hypocausis, where burners heat the water; the adjoining caldarium, where the air was distributed through pipes, transforming it into some sort of sauna; the frigidarium, a cooling-down area for those exiting the caldarium; and the tepidarium, which contained the warm water people dipped into in preparation for the caldarium.

SAN FRANCESCO

Via San Francesco, 13; tel.: 055-59175; open: Mon.–Sat. 10 A.M.–noon, 3–6 P.M., Sun. and public holidays 3–6 P.M.; admission: free.
✐ DIRECTIONS: Follow directions to Piazza Mino da Fiesole (see pg. 217). Via San Francesco starts at Piazza Mino da Fiesole.

➤ Crowning the highest hill in the town is the convent of San Francesco. Founded in the 14th century, the convent was taken over by the Franciscan order in the 15th century and used to house its friars, one of whom was Saint Bernardine of Siena. The cloisters at the center of the convent date back to the 14th century. Climb an adjacent flight of stairs to the first floor, where the monks' cells are located. Several of these are still furnished with the meager accoutrements that the friars once enjoyed.

The convent's church was also constructed in the 14th century and still possesses its original Gothic facade. The interior holds two noteworthy paintings: the *Immaculate Conception* by Piero di Cosimo and the *Annunciation* by Raffaellino del Garbo.

Cloister of San Francesco

SAN ROMOLO
(OR CATHEDRAL OF FIESOLE)

Piazza della Cattedrale, 1; tel.: 055-599566;
open: daily 7:30 A.M.–noon, 3–6 P.M.
(summer), daily 7:30 A.M.–noon, 3–5 P.M.
(winter); admission: free.

⌁ DIRECTIONS: Follow directions to Piazza
Mino da Fiesole (see pg. 217). Piazza della
Cattedrale is next to it.

➤ This Romanesque cathedral, dedicated to Saint Romulus, was begun in 1028, enlarged in the 13th and 14th centuries, and restored between 1878 and 1883 by Michelangelo Maiorfi, who designed the current facade. The tall, distinctively shaped bell tower was built in 1213.

The Romanesque interior of the church is divided into a high nave and two aisles with truss roofs. The arcades' columns have very well-preserved capitals, two of which (the fourth on each side) were originally part of a Roman building. A 1521 terracotta statue by Giovanni della Robbia of Saint Romulus, bishop of Fiesole and the church's patron saint, stands in a garlanded niche just above the central portal.

The left side of the presbytery leads to the Canonical Chapel, while the right side leads to the Salutati Chapel, frescoed by Cosimo Rosselli. The bust in this chapel is by Mino da Fiesole, as is the altar front depicting the Madonna adoring the child, Saint John the Lesser, Saint Leonard, and Saint Remigius.

The crypt under the presbytery, added in the 13th century, is divided into a nave and two aisles separated by thin marble columns with capitals of different shapes.

Bell tower of San Romolo, the cathedral of Fiesole

A number of works are kept here, including frescoed medallions from the 15th and 19th centuries and a baptismal font by Francesco del Tadda (1569). In the left aisle is a monument with a self-portrait by del Tadda (1576).

The sacristy has a red-velvet miter embellished with gold and silver leaf that belonged to bishop Leonardo Salutati, and a reliquary bust of Saint Romulus. Both, however, are rarely displayed. On the high altar is a multipaneled painting, *Madonna on the Throne with the Child and Saints*, by Bicci di Lorenzo.

FIESOLE

Placed on the summit of a lofty and broken eminence it
looks down on the vale of the Arno, and commands Florence with
all its domes, towers, and palaces, the villas that encircle it,
and the roads that lead to it. The recesses, swells, and breaks of the
hill on which it stands, are covered with groves of pines, ilex,
and cypress. Above these groves rises the dome of the cathedral;
and in the midst of them reposes a rich and venerable
abbey founded by the Medicean family. Behind the hill at a
distance swell the Apennines.

John Chetwode Eustace, *A Classical Tour through Italy; An. 1802*

Itinerary:

Fiesole Under the Fold

By Stacy Meichtry

I n *Invisible Cities,* Italo Calvino writes: "I could tell you how many steps there are in the streets made of stairs, of the curve in the arches that form the arcades, of which roofs are recovered in layers of zinc, but then I might as well tell you nothing at all. Not of this is the city made, but of relations between the measurements of its space and the events of its past."

Taken at face value, Fiesole plays a charming second fiddle to Florence's blend of artistic, cultural, political, and economic virtues. The Roman amphitheater and Etruscan ramparts of the archaeological zone are the town's principal tourist haunts and promise a pleasant contrast for those looking to bookend their trip to Florence, cradle of the Renaissance, with an excursion to "ancient" Fiesole. Beyond the archaeological zone, however, lies a city whose actual dimensions cannot be articulated in descriptions of the apparent. Like one of Calvino's invisible cities, Fiesole is not made of masonry, but of the ephemeral relationships between its past and present.

Take the basilica of **Sant'Alessandro** for example. Wedged between escalatorlike sidewalks that communicate between Fiesole's cathedral and the monastery of San Francesco, this basilica easily escapes notice. Its neoclassical facade, while elegant in composition, belies its ancient history.

Built on the foundations of a Roman temple dedicated to Bacchus, the building's Christian history began in the 6th century, when Theodore I, king of the Goths, transformed the temple into a church. It would later be dedicated to Saint Alexander, bishop of Fiesole, after his martyrdom in 820. Visible proof of this history is found within the church, in the form of ancient pillars, which still support the church's trussed roof, and Etruscan tombs, recently discovered underneath the sanctuary.

The only other church in Fiesole that spans time as gracefully as Sant'Alessandro is the **Badia Fiesolana,**

Badia Fiesolana

San Domenico

located about a kilometer southwest of the town center, perched above the Mugone River valley. Identified by the patch of 15th-century marquetry that precociously covers the center section of its sun-burnt facade corresponding to the nave, the Badia Fiesolana served as Fiesole's main cathedral from the years in which the town rivaled medieval Florence up until 1028, when Fiesole completed a brand-new, centrally located cathedral to mark its own resurrection.

Although the Badia could no longer boast pride of place among Fiesoleans, it nevertheless received attention worthy of a cathedral. The order of Carmelite monks who took over the church after its demotion partially rebuilt it, adding a monastery to its complex. In 1456 Cosimo the Elder took a special interest in the Badia, expanding the church to its current proportions. The Romanesque green and white marquetry that distinguishes the facade, in fact, remains unfinished due to Cosimo's early death in 1464. Vasari attributes the designs for this unrealized exterior, as well as those of the lofty, barrel-vaulted interior of the church, to none other than Filippo Brunelleschi. Vasari's attribution, however, is open to discussion, considering the fact that the great architect had been dead for nearly ten years by the time work started on the Badia.

Among the works of art dotting the Badia's vast interior space is the *Crucifixion,* a 16th-century oil painting executed by Lombard master Bernardo Campi during a rare visit to Florence. The rococo frescoes in the neighboring chapel depict the Annunciation, adapted to 17th-century aristocratic mores by Raffaellino del Garbo. The marble relief of the Madonna and child, in the first chapel on the right, is attributed to the school of Jacopo della Quercia.

Recognizable by the elegant loggia that gallops along its facade in graceful arches of *pietra serena,* **San Domenico** should not be omitted from any tour of Fiesole. As the headquarters of the Domenican order up until the construction of the complex of San Marco in Florence, the church and its adjacent convent

OUR PICK

housed some of the order's most illustrious members including Saint Anthony, the archbishop of Florence, and Domenico Buonvincini, who was burned at the stake in 1491 with Girolamo Savonarola for his support of the infamous preacher and reformist.

The most enduring presence in the religious order, however, is that of Fra Giovanni da Fiesole, the convent's resident artist, better known as Fra Angelico. Born and raised in Fiesole, this Dominican friar would go on to fresco Florence's convent of San Marco, eventually becoming one of the city's most prominent early Renaissance artists. His monumental *Annunciation* in San Marco is widely regarded as one of the age's inaugural images.

Before beginning his tenure at San Marco, however, Fra Angelico spent a considerable amount of time at San Domenico honing his skills. Among the works that the artist left behind there are the monumental fresco of the Crucifixion, housed in the convent's capitular hall, and an oil-on-panel triptych, *Madonna and Child with Saints Thomas Aquinas, Barnabus, Dominic and Peter the Martyr*. Painted in 1425, the triptych later had its borders removed by Lorenzo di Credi, who transformed Fra Angelico's composition into a rectangular panel, fusing the separate saints into a harmonious ensemble united by a single architectonic background. Lorenzo di Credi is also the author of the *Baptism of Jesus*, in the second chapel, which pays tribute to works of the same subject by Andrea del Verrocchio and Leonardo da Vinci, now housed in the Uffizi.

While Fra Angelico's early works at San Domenico lack the sense of proportion and perspective that he commanded in his maturity, they nevertheless witness a departure from the primitivism that pervaded Florentine art at the time. The "primitive" style, as it was labeled by 19th-century art critics, was mastered by artists like Taddeo Gaddi, who promoted mystical representations of religious subjects through stiff, woodlike figures, painted on gold-leaf backgrounds.

Taddeo Gaddi's Annunciation *at the Museo Bandini*

A fine example of Gaddi's artistic range is seen in the *Annunciation*, painted between 1330 and 1366, currently housed in the **Museo Bandini**. It depicts the swooning Virgin about to be injected with the Holy Spirit by an arrow-shaped dove. Located in the heart of Fiesole, between the Roman Amphitheater and the cathedral of San Romolo, this museum exhibits the collection of Angelo Maria Bandini. Librarian to the Biblioteca Laurenziana and the Biblioteca Marucelliana, Bandini was a collector of medieval and Renaissance art dating from 1200 to 1400.

The museum collection also includes works by Gaddi's contemporaries such as Nardo di Cione's radiant *Madonna of Birth and Donor* (c. 1365), Bernardo Daddi's *Saint John the Evangelist* (c. 1348), and Lorenzo Monaco's *Christ on the Cross between the Virgin, Saint John the Evangelist, and Saint Francis.*

Occasionally, the museum strays from its devotion to primitive painters and instead indulges in the sins of early Renaissance works like the *Triumphs of Love and Chastity,* an enigmatic work by Jacopo del Sellaio, which depicts members of a love triangle bound to a flaming cauldron. Its flames jump into the air and lick the heels of Cupid, who pirouettes above the trio, already poised to fire his arrow at another target. Behind the ensemble, a landscape stretches in blue and gold hues. To their right and left, crowds gather to speculate over their entanglement.

Further Information

Badia Fiesolana
Via della Badia dei Roccettini; tel.: 055-59155; open: Mon.–Fri. 9 A.M.–5 P.M.; Sat. 9 A.M.–noon; closed: Sun.
⌀ DIRECTIONS: From Piazza della Libertà (Porta San Gallo) in Florence take Viale Don Minzoni, then turn right on the overbridge, Cavalcavia delle Cure. Once you cross the overbridge, take Via Borghini and continue on Via Faentina. Take Via Togliatti and turn onto Via della Badia dei Roccettini. You can also take ATAF bus No. 7 from Piazza della Stazione in Florence. Get off a few stops before the center of town at the church of San Domenico. The narrow street that runs tangentially to this bus stop leads to the Badia.

Museo Bandini
Via Giovanni Duprè, 1; tel.: 055-59477; open: daily 9:30 A.M.–7 P.M. (summer), daily 9:30 A.M.–5 P.M. (winter); admission: €13 (includes entry to the entire archaeological area of Fiesole).
⌀ DIRECTIONS: Follow directions to Piazza Mino da Fiesole (see pg. 217). From Piazza Mino da Fiesole take Via Giovanni Duprè.

San Domenico
Piazza di San Domenico; tel.: 055-59230; open: daily 8 A.M.– noon, 4–6 P.M.
⌀ DIRECTIONS: From Piazza della Libertà (Porta San Gallo) in Florence take Viale Don Minzoni, then turn right on the overbridge, Cavalcavia delle Cure. Once you cross the overbridge, take Via Borghini and continue on Via Faentina. Take Via Togliatti and turn onto Via della Badia dei Roccettini. At the end of Via della Badia dei Roccettini turn right onto Piazza San Domenico. You can also take ATAF bus No. 7 from Piazza della Stazione in Florence.

Sant'Alessandro
Via San Francesco; open: daily 9:30 A.M.–7:30 P.M.
⌀ DIRECTIONS: Follow directions to Piazza Mino da Fiesole (see pg. 217). Via San Francesco starts at Piazza Mino da Fiesole.

FOCUS: Villa Medici di Belcanto

Via Beato Angelico, 2; tel.: 055-59417; open: Mon.–Fri. 9 A.M.–1 P.M.; admission: €6.
⮑Directions: From Piazza Mino da Fiesole take Fra Giovanni da Fiesole detto l'Angelico.

By Stacy Meichtry

While the Villa Medici di Belcanto was built between 1451 and 1457 for Giovanni de' Medici, it was Lorenzo the Magnificent, his nephew, who called it home. In fact, 12 years after its completion, Lorenzo would inherit the estate, where he and his court of humanist poets and artists habitually gathered. These guests included Pico della Mirandola, Marsilio Ficino, Politian, and the villa's architect, Michelozzo.

Among the finest builders of secular architecture in the Florentine Renaissance, Michelozzo employed all of his ingenuity and technical know-how to complete this villa. Perched on a hillside just beneath Fiesole, its layout consists of several ledges that descend from the main house toward panoramic views of Florence in a succession of gardens, peristyles, and staircases.

The lowest of these ledges hosts the villa's highly symmetrical Italian garden. Redesigned in 1915 by architects Geoffrey Scott and Cecil Pinsent, it is dominated at its center by a circular basin flanked by concentric parterres and box bushes. One ledge above the garden and spanning its entire length is a flower-laden peristyle that leads to the Belvedere Terrace. The diametrical opposition of the terrace at the back of the house and the driveway in the front enhances the stature of the villa itself. From the terrace, the villa looks down upon all of Florence, while the richly landscaped driveway with its closely shaven path provides a graceful introduction to Belcanto's bristling white facade.

Viewed from the Italian garden below, the driveway forms the highest ledge on the stairway, surmounting the peristyle with its procession of potted citrus trees. Though the driveway was designed in the late 18th century, the citrus trees harken back to the Medici era. Giovanni, a botanical collector, made the trees a mainstay at the Medici villas, importing them for their dietary and pharmaceutical value from as far south as Sicily.

Villa Medici di Belcanto

225

Other Points of Interest

FONDAZIONE PRIMO CONTI

Via Giovanni Duprè, 18, in the Villa le Coste; tel.: 055-597095; website: www.fondazione primoconti.org; Mon.–Fri. 10 A.M.–2 P.M.; admission: €3.

⊘ DIRECTIONS: From Piazza Mino da Fiesole (directions pg. 217) take Via Giovanni Duprè.

➤ This foundation, housed in the 16th-century Villa le Coste, contains a large collection of works by artist Primo Conti (1900–1988). Conti was buried in a chapel embellished with 17th-century decorations located in the villa's garden.

PALAZZO PRETORIO (NOW FIESOLE CITY HALL)

Piazza Mino da Fiesole, 24–26; closed to the public.

⊘ DIRECTIONS: Follow directions to Piazza Mino da Fiesole (see pg. 217).

➤ This municipal building was first built in the 14th century, but it was repeatedly renovated from the 15th century onward. The portico has an architrave with an upper story displaying a series of coats of arms. Outside the palazzo is the 1906 monument by Oreste Calzolari that depicts the 1860 encounter between King Victor Emmanuel II and Giuseppe Garibaldi that occurred in the southern Italian city of Teano and completed Italy's unification campaign.

PALAZZO VESCOVILE

Piazza Mino da Fiesole; closed to the public.

⊘ DIRECTIONS: Follow directions to Piazza Mino da Fiesole (see pg. 217).

➤ This building was originally built in the 11th century, but the facade dates back to 1675. Rarely accessible, the bishop's private chapel inside the building has frescoes depicting Saint Romulus, Saint Jacob, and God in Benediction. Annexed to the palazzo is the San Jacopo Maggiore oratory, with its *Crowning of Mary with Saints*, a fresco by Bicci di Lorenzo and another Gothic painter. In 1853, the fresco was retouched by Antonio Marini, who also added the figure of Saint Jacob (in the center of the picture). At the far end of the gardens are the remains of the Etruscan walls that were part of the acropolis.

SANTA MARIA PRIMERANA

Piazza Mino da Fiesole; tel.: 055-599566; open: closed for restoration.

⊘ DIRECTIONS: Follow directions to Piazza Mino da Fiesole (see pg. 217).

➤ First mentioned in 966, this church was rebuilt at the end of the 16th century, when it gained its present mannerist-style facade. The unusual porch was added in 1801. The interior has faded frescoes by Niccolò di Pietro Gerini with stories of the Virgin Mary. In the right transept are two marble bas-reliefs by Francesco da Sangallo (one is a self-portrait, the other depicts Francesco del Fede). The *Crucifix with the Madonna and the Saints*, executed by Andrea della Robbia, is situated in the left transept, while the 16th-century crucifix on a wooden panel ascribed to Bonaccorso di Cino is positioned on the right wall. In the presbytery, placed on the high altar designed by Bernardino Ciurini and built between 1745 and 1767, is a 15th-century Gothic tabernacle depicting the Madonna on the throne with the Christ child, by the 13th-century Maestro da Rovezzano.

VILLA IL RIPOSO DEI VESCOVI

Via Vecchia Fiesolana, 62; closed to the public.

➤ This privately owned villa was established in the 16th century as a "resting stop" for the bishops of Fiesole, who routinely commuted up the hill from their homes in Florence. In the 19th century, the villa came under Dutch and Swiss ownership, which resulted in the transformation of the building in the Jugendstil style. These alterations were completed after Dutch painter W. O. J. Nieuwenkamp (a pupil of Paul Gauguin) purchased the villa in 1926.

VILLA SAN MICHELE (OR VILLA DOCCIA)

Via Doccia, 4; tel.: 055-5678200.

➤ This villa, facing the valley, was once owned by the Davanzati family. In 1486 it became a convent (until 1808), and now is a hotel. Santi di Tito rebuilt it between 1599 and 1600. On its grounds is a former two-story church with a portico.

Hotel Villa Fiesole

Via Beato Angelico, 35; tel.: 055-597252; fax: 055-599133; website: www.villafiesole.it; e-mail: info@villafiesole.it; number of rooms: 28; credit cards accepted: all major; access to internet: available in some rooms; €€–€€€.
DIRECTIONS: From Piazza della Libertà (Porta San Gallo) in Florence take Viale Don Minzoni to Piazza delle Cure. Take Viale Alessandro Volta, which turns first into Via San Domenico, then into Via Giuseppe Mantellini. Once you reach Largo Leonardo da Vinci, take Via Fra Giovanni da Fiesole (also called Via Fra Giovanni da Fiesole, detto l'Angelico).

☛Originally a private mansion, this villa, which was turned into a peaceful little hotel in 1995, has an excellent view of Florence and a pretty swimming pool huddled beneath a medieval tower. The rooms, almost identical in dimensions and decor, are spacious and tastefully decorated with rich blue and white tones. Although it does not have a formal restaurant, the hotel nevertheless offers breakfast, a light lunch, dinner, and a simple buffet supper.

Villa San Michele

Via Doccia, 4; tel.: 055-5678200; fax: 055-5678250; e-mail: reservations@villasan michele.net; category:★★★★★; number of rooms: 21 doubles, 20 junior suites, and 5 suites; credit cards accepted: all major; access to internet: yes; closed: Nov.–Mar.; €€€€.
DIRECTIONS: From Piazza della Libertà (Porta San Gallo) in Florence take Viale Don Minzoni to Piazza delle Cure. Take Viale Alessandro Volta, which turns first into Via San Domenico then into Via Giuseppe Mantellini. Once you reach Largo Leonardo da Vinci, take Via Fra Giovanni da Fiesole (also called Via Fra Giovanni da Fiesole, detto l'Angelico). Turn left on Via Doccia.

☛This very elegant and luxurious hotel, with its view of Florence, the antique decor, the impeccable management, and the excellent dinners, is unforgettable. A converted 15th-century monastery, the building is said to have been designed by Michelangelo himself. All the bedrooms, lounges, and dining rooms have been exquisitely decorated, and the gardens and terraces are also beautiful. Dinner can be enjoyed either in the refined dining room or on the attractive outside veranda. To add to the beauty, a gorgeous swimming pool is available on one of the secluded terraces.

RESTAURANTS & CAFÉS

Perseus

Piazza Mino da Fiesole, 9r; tel.: 055-59143; open: daily noon–2:30 P.M., 7:30–11:30 P.M.; €.
DIRECTIONS: Follow directions to Piazza Mino da Fiesole (see pg. 217).

☛This Tuscan restaurant is beautifully situated in Fiesole. It is large, with many rooms, and both a terrace and a garden. The classic Tuscan pastas are well done, but the emphasis of the restaurant is on meat. Some typical *primi* are pasta with ragu and a ravioli with sausage and blue cheese.

Trattoria Le Cave di Maiano

Via Cave di Maiano, 16; tel.: 055-599504; open: Mon.–Sat. 12:30–2:30 P.M., 7:30–10:30 P.M.; closed: Sun.; €.
DIRECTIONS: From Piazza della Libertà (Porta San Gallo) in Florence take Viale Don Minzoni to Piazza delle Cure. Take Viale Alessandro Volta, which turns first into Via San Domenico then into Via Giuseppe Mantellini. Once you reach Largo Leonardo da Vinci, take Via Benedetto da Maiano, then turn left on Via Cave di Maiano.

☛Going to this trattoria is a bit like going to a Tuscan household for a meal—the atmosphere is casual and the food is good and authentic. An added bonus is that it is in the country and has outdoor seating.

East of Florence

Itinerary:

Around the Villa Gamberaia

By Stacy Meichtry

I n his 1948 *Diaries,* Bernard Berenson—the art critic and unofficial "dean" of artistic Florence—described the garden of the **Villa Gamberaia** as a "great boat, sailing through space." He was referring to its expansive terrace, which, like the deck of a ship, floats above the Arno River plain, rippling its terra-cotta surface into miniature domes and toylike towers.

Edith Wharton was no less prosaic in 1904, when she praised the "breadth and simplicity of composition" that the garden achieves "without the least sense of overcrowding." The cypress corridor, the water parterre, the bowling green, the *boschetto,* the grotto garden, represent only a few of the many components

Villa Gamberaia

Villa I Tatti

that Gamberaia so seamlessly compacts into its garden. Exploring this assorted landscape of emerald pools and budding topiary art is like wandering into a dream in which discordant images suddenly crystallize in music to the eyes.

Before the noble Caponi family purchased the estate and transformed its grounds into one of Europe's finest gardens, Villa Gamberaia, like most other Florentine villas, was a farmhouse. Founded in the 14th century by the neighboring convent of San Martino a Mensola, its name derives from the *gamberi,* or shrimp, that once inhabited freshwater ponds near here. But with the exception of these ponds, the landscape that encircled the farmhouse probably resembled that which is still seen beyond the garden: olive groves and cypress trees rolling in foothills that conform to the contours of the Arno River valley.

The convent survives in the form of the church of **San Martino a Mensola**. Prefaced by a handsome, barrel-arched portico, the church's current facade dates back to its Renaissance reconstruction in 1460. Founded in the 9th century, the church reached its zenith in the years during which it owned the farmhouse that turned into Villa Gamberaia.

San Martino's altarpieces testify to this success. The polyptych at the end of the right aisle, *Enthroned Madonna with Saints Lucy and Margaret,* was painted by Taddeo Gaddi, one of the 14th century's leading painters. One of Gaddi's prominent contemporaries, Neri di Bicci, painted the *Enthroned Madonna* in the left aisle.

Connecting the villa to the church of San Martino is the historic town of Settignano. This tiny burg is the place where many of Florence's greatest sculptors passed their formative years. The early Renaissance sculptor Desiderio da Settignano was born here in 1428 and is memorialized by the bronze statue in the piazza named after him, which opens up to a panorama of Florence. Desiderio was followed by mannerist sculptor and architect Bartolomeo Ammannati, born in 1511, whose master, Michelangelo, was raised in Settignano. Architect Bernardo Rosellino and his brother Antonio were actually onetime residents of the Villa Gamberaia. Their father, Matteo di Domenico, was the villa's first secular owner, purchasing it in the early 15th century.

Despite their childhood roots, none of these artists contributed to their hometown church, **Santa Maria Assunta**, located in Piazza Tommaseo. Recorded as early as the 12th century, the church's features are now predominately 16th century, owing to renovations carried out in 1518 and 1595. The second altar preserves an early-15th-century polychrome terra-cotta of Saint

OUR PICK

Villa di Maiano

Lucy by Michelozzo. This sober work is surrounded by an elaborate framework of frescoes, painted in 1593 and attributed to Santo di Tito. Among the church's other significant works are the *pietra serena* pulpit, carved by Gherardo Silvani in 1602, and a glazed terra-cotta of the Madonna and child, by the della Robbia workshop.

In 1905 Bernard Berenson settled near Settignano in yet another former farmhouse now known as **Villa I Tatti**, located along Via San Martino a Mensola, a couple of miles past the church. In the following years, Berenson transformed the property into an oasis of artistic and cultural refinement. British architect Cecil Pinsent was brought in between 1908 and 1915 to design a vast *giardino all'italiana,* or Italian-style garden, with a distinctly English border garden at its core.

While at the villa, also visit the **Collezione Berenson**. Berenson curated the interior decoration himself, meticulously arranging his oriental tapestries and furniture so as not to clash with the Italian oils from the 14th to 16th centuries, which include *Saint Francis in Glory* by Sassetta, two small oil-on-panels attributed to Giotto, and a Madonna by Domenico Veneziano. This tasteful living space, complete with a world-renowned library and photo archive, was bequeathed to Harvard University after the historian's death in 1959.

As a British land owner and collector in Florence, Berenson had few peers in the 20th century, but in the 19th century there had been a similar figure, another Briton, John Temple Leader. Monte Ceneri, or "Ash Mountain," is the pine-covered mound that rises behind Settignano, to the northwest. Around 1840, Leader purchased the entire mountain as a sort of backdrop to his home, the **Villa di Maiano**.

Located at the foot of Maiano, a historic mining community down the road from Berenson's villa, the Villa di Maiano was the 15th-century residence of the Pazzi family. Among the Pazzis' more illustrious members was Saint

Mary Magdalene de' Pazzi, who resided at the villa before becoming a nun. When Leader took the reigns of the Villa di Maiano in the 19th century, he looked to revive the spirit of the Pazzi legacy through architectural enhancements, hiring Felice Francolini to restore the villa in the style of early Renaissance architect Michelozzo. It was Francolini who added the distinctive crenellated tower that sprouts from the villa's terra-cotta roof, as well as the sets of twin Ionic columns that line its ocher facade.

Like Berenson, Leader also took a special interest in the interior of his home that, at times, bordered on obsession. The mammoth gray fireplace that dominates the tapestry room, for example, was carved in England, from sandstone that was imported from Florence, and then shipped back to Maiano in massive segments for assembly. The red room, with its walls and furniture upholstered in monochromatic silk and accented with gold leaf, has been featured in movies like Franco Zeffirelli's *Tea with Mussolini* and James Ivory's *Room with a View*.

For a view of the Leader legacy, descend the garden's stairlike layout to its lowest shelf, the Italian garden. This level, planted with geometrically hedged box bushes, offers an imposing perspective of the villa with its powerful tower in the foreground. In the distant background, nestled amidst the pines of Monte Ceneri, is the **Castello di Vincigliata**.

Covered in florescent layers of ivy, the castle's robust, fortressed structure strikes a medieval pose that belies the fact that it was completely rebuilt in the 19th century. Its intricate network of interior courtyards and exterior ramparts had been reduced to mere ruins by the time Leader discovered it in 1840. All that remained standing was its mighty military tower, which supposedly seduced Leader with its panoramic views of Florence, backed by the blue hills of Chianti.

Castello di Vincigliata

In search of Vincigliata's "medieval intrigues," Leader traced the castle's history all the way back to the 11th century. Mixing this tradition with that of the castle's Renaissance owners, the dei Alessandri, Leader rebuilt the castle from the ground up, commissioning an army of artisans, sculptors, glassblowers, painters, and antiquarians to restore Vincigliata to its former glory.

FURTHER INFORMATION

Castello di Vincigliata

Via di Vincigliata, 21, Fiesole; tel.: 055-599556; fax: 055-599166; open: by appointment only.
⚘ DIRECTIONS: From Piazza Cesare Beccaria (Porta alla Croce) in Florence take Via Vincenzo Gioberti. At Piazza L. B. Alberti, turn left onto Via Lungo l'Affricco and then right onto Via Gabriele d'Annunzio. Turn left onto Via di Corbignano, and continue on Via di Vincigliata.

San Martino a Mensola

Via San Martino a Mensola, 4, Martino a Mensola; tel.: 055-602115; open: daily 9 A.M.– 6 P.M. (summer), 9 A.M.– 5 P.M. (winter); admission: free.
⚘ DIRECTIONS: See above. Instead of turning left onto Via di Corbignano, cross Viale Eleonora Duse, passing the crossroad near Ponte a Mensola. The road eventually runs along the small Mensola River. On the right is Via San Martino a Mensola.

Santa Maria Assunta

Piazza Tommaseo, Settignano; tel.: 0571-673025; open: inconsistently.
⚘ DIRECTIONS: See Castello di Vincigliata. Instead of turning left onto Via di Corbignano, continue on Strada Provinciale 55 (SP 55) for about one mile and then turn right onto Piazza Niccolò Tommaseo.

Villa di Maiano

Via Benedetto da Maiano, 11, Maiano; tel.: 055-598631; open: by appointment only, with a minimum of 10 people; admission: €10.
⚘ DIRECTIONS: See San Martino a Mensola. Continue past the church of San Martino until the road runs into Via Poggio Gherardo, which goes slightly uphill, running through a series of private properties until it reaches Via Benedetto da Maiano.

Villa Gamberaia

Via del Rossellino, 72, Settignano; tel.: 055-697205; fax: 055-697090; website: www.villagamberaia.com; open: daily 9 A.M.– 6 P.M. (groups are advised to make an appointment); admission: €10 (€8 for groups of 10 or more).
⚘ DIRECTIONS: See Santa Maria Assunta. From Piazza Niccolò Tommaseo turn left onto Via del Pianerottolo. After 130 yards turn right on Strada Provinciale 55 (SP 55) and then right again onto Via del Rossellino.

Villa I Tatti and Collezione Berenson

Via di Vincigliata, 26, Maiano; tel.: 055-603251; fax: 055-603383; website: www.itatti.it; open: guided tours only on Tues. and Wed. afternoon with faxed request; admission: free.
⚘ DIRECTIONS: See Castello di Vincigliata.

FOCUS: San Salvi

Via di San Salvi, 16, Florence; tel.: 055-2388603; open: Tues.–Sun. 8:30 A.M.–2 P.M.; closed: Mon.; admission: free. ⌁DIRECTIONS: Follow directions for Santa Maria Assunta (see pg. 232).

By Stacy Meichtry

The gray sandstone loggia that underlines the facade of San Salvi gives a sunny disposition to a building with a tempestuous past. This turbulence is encapsulated by the church's patchwork interior: the inaccessible fragment of stairway in the right transept that begins in midair and leads to nowhere; the fractured masonry of the left transept, blown to pieces by a bolt of lightning just as mass was beginning on April 12, 1994; the Romanesque pillars to the right of the sanctuary that date back to the church's founding in 1048 by Saint John Gualberto.

Gualberto also founded the Vallombrosan order of monks, which ran the church from the time of his assassination until 1784. The order was expelled from Florence in 1808, under a Napoleonic decree that suppressed monastic life throughout the city. During this period, San Salvi faced the constant threat of demolition but was saved by the grace of its artwork. Allegedly, French troops, under orders to raze the complex, were dissuaded by the beauty of the frescoed *Last Supper*.

This work, executed by Andrea del Sarto in 1528, is considered a masterpiece of Italian mannerism. Framed by the barrel-vaulted ceiling of the refectory, the fresco forms a giant lunette, wherein Christ foretells the treachery that will lead to his tragic death. The drama unfolds under the observation of two unrelated figures, who occupy a balcony above the dinner table. Arcing around the entire ensemble at a right angle to the fresco are medallions with portraits of Saint John Gualberto, Saint Salvi, Saint Bernard degli Ulberti, and Saint Benedict. The refectory and its adjacent cells currently form the church's museum, which displays many mannerist works of art brought here for protection during the Napoleonic decree and the Nazi occupation.

Among these are several Madonnas by Pontormo as well as a Benedetto da Rovezzano marble relief depicting the Vallombrosan monks of San Salvi. Carved between 1505 and 1513 for the tomb of Saint John Gualberto (which was never completed), the relief was vandalized in 1530, when each of its figures was decapitated.

Refectory at San Salvi with Andrea del Sarto's Last Supper

Other Points of Interest

MUSEO DEL CENACOLO DI ANDREA DEL SARTO
(MUSEUM OF ANDREA DEL SARTO'S *LAST SUPPER*)

Via di San Salvi, 16; tel.: 055-2388603; open: daily 8:15 A.M.–4:50 P.M.; admission: free.

➤ This small museum, set in some of the rooms in the former Vallombrosan monastery of San Salvi, is a long gallery containing paintings from 16th-century Florence. The back of the room has fragments of the funerary monument of Saint Giovanni Gualberto by Benedetto da Rovezzano (1507–1513). In the convent's refectory there is an enormous fresco of the *Last Supper* by Andrea del Sarto that covers an entire wall. The fresco, painted between 1526 and 1527, is a masterpiece of late Renaissance painting.

HOTELS & INNS

Pensione Bencistà

Via Benedetto da Maiano, 4, Fiesole; tel./fax: 055-59163; website: www.bencista.com; e-mail: info@bencista.com; category:★★★; number of rooms: 40; credit cards accepted: all major; access to internet: none; most beautiful rooms: 18 and 21; €€.

⌂ DIRECTIONS: From Piazza Cesare Beccaria (Porta alla Croce) in Florence take Via Vincenzo Gioberti. At Piazza L. B. Alberti, turn left onto Via Lungo l'Affrico and then right onto Via Gabriele d'Annunzio. In the town of Coverciano, turn left onto Via Benedetto da Maiano.

➥This family-owned pensione, with a panoramic view of Florence, offers unpretentious yet very charming accommodations for those wanting to visit the city while lodging in the countryside. The owners are very friendly and helpful and have tastefully decorated the pensione with antique furniture and travel souvenirs. Many guests return to the Bencistà year after year, choosing to stay in their own favorite rooms.

Villa La Massa

Via della Massa, 24, Candeli; tel.: 055-62611; fax: 055-633102; website: www.villalamassa.com; e-mail: info@villalamassa.com; category: ★★★★★ luxury; number of rooms: 35; credit cards accepted: all major; access to internet: yes; facilities: swimming pool; €€€€.

⌂ DIRECTIONS: From Della Libertà (Porta San Gallo) in Florence, take Viale Matteotti and follow the ring road through Viale Gramsci until you reach the Arno River. Turn left onto Lungarno Colombo and cross the river on the bridge, called Ponte Varlungo. Follow signs for Bagno a Ripoli and Pontassieve (do not enter the highway). The villa is located on Via La Massa, in Candeli.

➥A five-star hotel located only five miles outside of Florence, this villa used to belong to the Medici family and was chosen by David Bowie for his wedding celebration. The interiors are beautiful, with arcades and vaults decorating the great hall and the dining room. The rooms showcase old furniture and flower prints, which give them a discreetly luxurious style. Access to Florence is easy: a shuttle bus leaves every hour to and from the Ponte Vecchio between 9 A.M. and 7 P.M.

CERTOSA DEL GALLUZZO (OR CERTOSA DI FIRENZE, OR DI VAL D'EMA)

Via della Buca di Certosa, 2, Galluzzo; tel.: 055-2049226; open: Tues.–Sun. (guided tours only) 9:15, 10:15, 11:15 A.M., 3:15 and 4:15 P.M., and 5:15 P.M. (from April–Sept.); closed: Mon.; admission: donation suggested.

⌂ DIRECTIONS: From Piazzale di Porta Romana in Florence take Via Senese. After about two miles turn right onto Via di Colle Ramole. After 200 yards turn right again on Via della Buca di Certosa.

➤ The Certosa del Galluzzo was founded in 1342 by Niccolò Acciaioli, seneschal to King Robert of Naples. Many Florentines donated to the collection and it was, over time, enlarged and enriched. Since 1958 it has been inhabited by Benedictine monks.

After the entrance ramp there is a large piazza and then the church of San Lorenzo, which was built around the 13th century and renovated in the 16th century. Inside the church, the monks' choir has fine vaulting (covered in the 17th century with frescoes by Orazio Fidani) and beautiful 16th-century stalls. On the east wall is a fresco by Bernardino Poccetti (1591–1592). Beyond a corridor with side chapels (brightly decorated in 1794–1801), is the church of Santa Maria, built in 1404–1407 (with a stained-glass window by Niccolò di Pietro Gerini) and restored in 1841. Beneath the lay brethren's choir is a chapel with the magnificent tomb-slab of Cardinal Agnolo II Acciaioli, thought to be the work of Francesco da Sangallo. Also here are three other beautiful pavement tombs of the Acciaioli family, and the Gothic monument to the founder, Niccolò Acciaioli (1365).

The secluded great cloister is decorated with 66 majolica tondi of saints and prophets, by Andrea and Giovanni della Robbia. In the center is a well from 1521 and the cemetery that the monks use. One of the monks' quarters may be visited.

The *foresteria*, where popes Pius VI and Pius VII both stayed, has 18th-century frescoes and a Murano glass chandelier. The Palazzo degli Studi was begun by Niccolò Acciaioli as a meeting place for young Florentines to study the liberal arts. The splendid Gothic hall was designed by Fra Jacopo Passavanti. The upper floor houses a picture gallery (see pg. 244).

Certosa del Galluzzo

Itinerary:

A Picturesque Periphery over the River and into the Hills

By Stacy Meichtry

I n 1865, architect Giuseppe Poggi tore down sections of Florence's medieval walls to pave a long and winding road through the hillsides south of the Arno. In doing so, he authored the only fundamental change to Florence's urban plan in modern times and gave his town what many Italian cities unfortunately lack: a picturesque periphery.

While big-city life in Italy is often divided into well-groomed historic centers and dull industrial outskirts, the suburbs just south of the historic Santo Spirito quarter are an aesthetically pleasing composition of public gardens, rough-hewn churches, and palatial villas, all of which are fed by Poggi's tree-lined artery, known as the Viale dei Colli.

Bisecting this conduit is the twiglike Via di San Leonardo. A quick jog down this open-air corridor of sun-dried brick bears fruit in the form of the church of **San Leonardo**: an 11th-century church, restored to idyllic form in the years 1899 and 1929. Preceded by a meticulous patchwork of hedges and flower beds, the church's rustic facade can be distinguished from that of the average countryside house by the glittering mosaic lunette (1928) above its doorway. Fashioned from *pietre forti,* or semiprecious stones, by the historic Opificio delle Pietre Dure workshop (see pg. 57), the lunette depicts Saint Leonard between two angels, based on iconic drawings by Giuseppe Castellucci.

OUR PICK

Actual distemper-on-panel icons are on display inside the church, underneath the broad apex of its wood-trussed ceiling. These include works by late Gothic and early Renaissance master Neri di Bicci (1419–1491) whose *Annunciation with Eternal Father and Angels* and *Madonna della Cintola and Saints* flank the main alter at the right and left respectively. The first of these works deserves a closer look as it circumscribes a miniature tabernacle. Attributed to the shop of Giuliano da Maiano, the tabernacle is virtually incorporated into Bicci's "framework." Standing between Bicci's panels, on the main altar, is a late-13th-century triptych, the *Madonna and Child with Four Saints,* attributed to Lorenzo di Niccolò.

The unofficial centerpiece of the church, meanwhile, is the wide pulpit, which protrudes out into the nave. This two-legged, block-shaped balcony balances a portion of its girth on a pair of slim columns and leans the rest of its weight against the left wall of the nave. Carved from marble between 1193 and 1250, the pulpit has hosted such luminary speakers as Saint Anthony and Dante Alighieri. The cycle of bas-reliefs that form the pulpit's decorous perimeter depict the Adoration of the Magi, the Nativity, the Tree of Jesse, the Baptism, and the Presentation of Christ at the Temple.

San Leonardo's mix of architectural rusticity and artistic refinement is somewhat rare for a church of its location and size. **San Felice a Ema** has seen less success in preserving its heritage: all that remains of the original church is the lunette above its central door.

Carved from green and white marble in intricate geometric patterns, this Romanesque creation dates back to the church's founding, recorded as early as the 12th century. In the 13th century, the church's parish, dedicated to the priest from Nola who was martyred in the year 266, gained considerable influence in spheres beyond religion due to the patronage of powerful families like the Canigiani. Among the family's more historically notable members is Eletta Canigiani, mother of humanist poet Francesco Petrarch.

In the centuries that followed, however, San Felice underwent a number of restorations that inevitably tarnished its image. Most damaging among these was the restoration conducted by Giovanni Rivani between 1790 and 1796, which submerged the primitive charm of the church's Romanesque beginnings in the opulent dressings of the rococo. While sections of Rivani's labors were successfully eradicated by yet another restoration in 1966, these efforts more closely resembled damage control, toning down the flamboyance of the interior and reinventing an archaic facade for its exterior. Although the nave and lateral aisles still remain in Rivani's rococo style, portions of the columns that line the nave reveal remnants of the Romanesque skeleton.

Villa del Poggio Imperiale

Rising from behind the symmetrically cut grass of the semicircular lawn at the corner of Via San Felice a Ema and Via San Leonardo is the mammoth neoclassical facade of the **Villa del Poggio Imperiale**. Begun by Pasquale Poccianti and finished by Giuseppe Cacialli in 1823, the facade of this 15th-century villa consists of two registers, or levels, that are identical in form, but different in style. The lower register, composed of long horizontal ashlars broken up by the arches of its portico, exudes the harmony and simplicity of the Renaissance. The upper register mimics these forms with a loggetta, an enclosed loggia, visible through arched windows. The clock, however, flanked by angels carved in relief, and the triangular pediment supported by Ionian columns are more typical of neoclassical ornamentation.

With its drapes drawn, the interior of Cacialli's loggetta sets the tone for the rest of the villa. Its floors rigorously patterned in polished stone, its vaulted ceiling frosted over with grotesques, the loggetta's well-mannered mix of sobriety and ostentation achieves a harmony that is at once disorienting and refined.

Cacialli put together similar combinations throughout the upper floor. The villa's ballroom assembles all the trimmings of classical architecture in an inverted wedding cake of monochromatic pilasters, pediments, cornices, grotesques, and bas-reliefs. The neoclassical bathroom down the hall to the left is fully functional despite its illusory character. The miniature bathtub is carved from marble to complement the checkered pavement of this closet-sized room. The fountain that ostensibly feeds the tub, however, is a trompe l'oeil, as is the cylindrical niche in which it rests. The fountain is nevertheless capable of filling the tub through the copper faucets protruding from its base.

The best features of the bathroom, ballroom, and loggetta are brought together in Cacialli's design for the villa's chapel, which occupies the east wing. A collision of various shapes and patterns, the chapel successfully manages its contrasting floral, diamond, and checker schemes with an unbroken cornice that wraps around the nave and even circles behind the main altar to underline the chapel's semispherical posterior. Supporting the cornice are polished Corinthian columns that divide the nave from the lateral aisles, which are trimmed with bas-relief panels dating from the 19th century but inspired by 15th-century della Robbian panels. The finest bas-relief in the chapel, *Christ Giving the Keys of the Church to Saint Peter* by Bertel Thorwaldsen, decorates the main altar. Cacialli extends his neoclassical touch to the ground floor with a pair of lateral courtyards, but there his influence ends. The rest of the lower floor reflects the legacy of Grand Duchess Maria Maddalena, widow of Cosimo II, who oversaw the reconstruction and amplification of the villa until her death in 1631. The sister of Emperor Ferdinand II of Austria, Maddalena not only gave the Villa del Poggio Imperiale its "imperial" status, but also made it worthy of the promotion. In 1622 she asked architect Giuseppe Parigi, who designed the central courtyard, to transform the villa from the modest country home it had been since its founding in 1427 into the palatial mansion it is now. She also assembled a team of painters that included Matteo Rosselli, Ottavio Vannini, Giovambattista Vanni, Domenico Pugliani, and Anastasio Fontebuoni to fresco the ground-floor apartments. Led by Rosselli, the group executed the cycle now known as the *History of Illustrious Reigns,* which captures some of the more ceremonious moments in the totalitarian reigns of Maddalena's father, her brother, and Cosimo II, and frames them with colorful grotesques.

Since 1865, the villa has operated as a campus to the Educandato Statale della Santissima Annunziata. This state-run boarding school has turned many of Poggio Imperiale's decorous apartments into fully functional classrooms. Before leaving the villa make sure to visit its cafeteria; its richly frescoed hall includes the *Vittoria della Rovere* by Ferdinando Tacca and Giacinto Marmi (1681–1682).

FURTHER INFORMATION

San Felice a Ema
Via San Felice a Ema, 47, San Felice a Ema; tel.: 055-2049248; open: Sun. 7 A.M.–noon, 5–6:30 P.M.; closed: Mon.–Sat.

⤷ DIRECTIONS: From Piazzale di Porta Romana in Florence take Viale Niccolò Machiavelli to Piazzale Galileo, then take Viale Galileo. Continue for 100 yards, then turn right onto Via San Leonardo, which turns into Via San Felice a Ema. The church is about half a mile from the viale.

San Leonardo
Via San Leonardo, 25, Florence; tel.: 055-223084; open: Sun. mass from 11 A.M., other days you must ring doorbell.

Villa del Poggio Imperiale
Piazzale del Poggio Imperiale, 1, Poggia Imperiale; tel.: 055-226171; fax: 055-2298085; website: www .poggio-imperiale.it; open: Mon.–Fri. 10 A.M.–noon (by appointment only); closed: Sat.–Sun., all of Aug.; admission: free.

⤷ DIRECTIONS: From Piazzale di Porta Romana in Florence follow Viale del Poggio Imperiale until you reach the villa.

FOCUS: Santa Maria all'Impruneta

Piazza Buondelmonti, Impruneta; tel.: 055-2313729; open: daily 8 A.M., 6 P.M. (for mass), Sun: 10:30 A.M. (mass)
↗DIRECTIONS: From Piazzale di Porta Romana take Via Senese, then turn left onto Via Accursio. After one mile turn right onto Via di San Felice a Ema and then left onto Via Gherardo Silvani. Take Via Imprunetana toward Pozzolatico, and after 4¾ miles you will reach Impruneta. Turn left onto Piazza Buondelmonti.

Cloister of Santa Maria all'Impruneta

By Stacy Meichtry

Ever since the Middle Ages, religious pilgrims have flocked to Impruneta hoping to get close to the image of the Madonna dell'Impruneta, which, legend has it, was painted by Saint Luke the Evangelist. Under the protection of Saint Romulus and his followers, the painting was carried to Tuscany, in flight from religious persecution. There, Romulus buried the image *in prunetis*, "between the plum trees," from which the name Impruneta derives.

A sapling church grew into a full-scale basilica in the 15th century as the Medicis became invested in the welfare of the image. In fact, by 1348, members of Florence's most powerful families had already formed the cult of Santa Maria all'Impruneta, combining spiritual devotion to the image with financial devotion to the town.

The facade of the basilica is preceded by a portico, flanked by an 18th-century clock tower and a 13th-century bell tower. The interior, in Renaissance style, has a single nave with four lateral altars decorated with 17th-century paintings. In the chapel on the right, you will find the interesting 15th-century tombstone of Antonio degli Agli and, over the altar, a crucifix by Felice Palma.

To the sides of the presbytery, there are two small chapels attributed by some to Michelozzo and decorated with terra-cottas by Luca della Robbia. The chapel on the right is called the Cappella della Croce because it is said to hold a piece of the Holy Cross donated to the church in the 15th century by a Florentine knight. The chapel on the left is the Cappella della Madonna and holds the venerated image of the Madonna all'Impruneta, a medieval work completely repainted in 1758. To its sides are Luca della Robbia's terra-cottas of Saints Peter and Paul.

Above the Romanesque main altar, in white and green marble, there is a 14th-century polyptych by Pietro Nelli, the *Madonna with Child and the Apostles*.

From the portico you can access the two cloisters. The first, in the style of Michelozzo, was built in the middle of the 15th century. The second, which leads to the crypt underneath the presbytery of the basilica, was built in the 14th century. From the right-hand side of this cloister you can also enter another 13th-century underground room, called the Cantinone, or large cellar.

Other Points of Interest

BADIA DI SAN SALVATORE A SETTIMO

Via San Lorenzo a Settimo, Settimo (a *frazione*, or part, of the Commune of Scandicci); tel.: 055-790015 (parish); website: www.badiadisettimo.it.; open: call for guided tours; admission: free.
⊘ DIRECTIONS: From Piazzale di Porta Romana in Florence take Via Senese toward the A1 highway (Autostrada del Sole). Take the A1 highway at the entrance of Firenze Certosa and exit at Firenze Signa. Then turn left onto Via delle Nazioni Unite. Turn left onto Via del Botteghino and left again on Via del Borgo. Continue on Via dei Pratoni and then Via della Pieve. Turn left onto Viale la Comune di Parigi and continue on Via San Colombiano. Turn right on Via San Lorenzo a Settimo.

➤ Documented as early as 988, this Romanesque church first prospered under the patronage of the powerful Cadolingi family, who later donated the building to the Benedictine Order of Cluny in 1004. The church still retains most of its early structure. The interior, with a trussed ceiling and rustic pillars, and parts of the exterior, most notably the left apse, all date back to the Cadolingi legacy. The facade, however, was extensively made over by the Cistercians of San Galgano, who came into possession of the church in 1236 and later added the dominant rose window.

Among the most important works of art contained in the church are Domenico Ghirlandaio's medallions depicting an angel and the Annunciation (1487), kept in the choir along with Giuliano da Maiano's magnificent tabernacle in *pietra serena* and polychrome majolica. Other works include an ornate sarcophagus of the countesses Cilla and Gasdia, members of the Cadolingi line who died in 1096.

The cluster of private buildings next to the church is what remains of San Salvatore's former monastery. Its 13th-and 15th-century cloisters are lined with Ionic columns and artwork that includes a cycle of frescoes attributed to Giovanni da San Giovanni and a glazed terra-cotta from the della Robbia workshop. Among the monastery's most notable residents was a humble monk known as Peter. According to legend, Peter miraculously disproved accusations of simony, brought against him by Bishop Pietro Mezzabarba, by walking into two piles of burning wood and emerging unscathed.

MONASTERO DI SANTA MARIA (MONASTERY OF SANTA MARIA)

Borgo del Monastero, 13, Rosano; tel.: 055-8303006; open: by appointment only. Only church can be visited.
⊘ DIRECTIONS: From Piazzale di Porta Romana in Florence take Viale del Poggio Imperiale. After 1/2 mile turn left onto Viale Torricelli. Continue to Piazzale Galileo, then take Viale Galileo. At Piazzale Michelangelo take Viale Michelangelo. In Piazza Ferrucci turn right onto Ponte San Niccolò and then right onto Lungarno del Tempio. Continue through Lungarno Cristoforo Colombo, then Lungarno Aldo Moro. Take Via Enrico de Nicola and then Via Carlo Alberto dalla Chiesa. Take Strada Statale 67 (SS67), or Tosco-Emiliana, for about eight miles. Once you arrive in Pontassieve, cross the Arno River. The monastery is a little more than one mile outside the center of Rosano.

➤ Located in the very peaceful area of Rosano, the Monastery of Santa Maria was founded in 780 and is still home to about 70 Benedictine nuns. It underwent several restorations in the 12th, 13th, 16th, and 18th centuries, and after World War II, when the medieval structures were brought back to light (at the expense of the 18th-century stuccoes).

The interior of the Romanesque church is divided into a nave and two aisles with trussed roofs standing on quadrangular pillars. In the right aisle is a baptismal font in *pietra serena*, made in 1423. In the presbytery, raised above a crypt, is a 15th-century fresco of Saint Apollonia. In the crypt itself, which still preserves parts of the original Romanesque apse, is an altar with a green and white marble frontal. Similar patterns also decorate the medallion portrait placed on the 12th-century floor. In the 16th-century apse is *The Annunciation* by Giovanni Del Ponte, a triptych that depicts Saint Lawrence, Saint Benedict, Saint John the Baptist, and Saint Nicholas. Above the high altar is a crucifix by an unknown artist, the Master of

Rosano, who worked in the monastery between the 12th and 13th centuries. The 12th-century bell tower houses *The Annunciation* by Jacopo di Cione, painted in 1365. *Mary with Child and Saints* by Master Vico l'Abate is kept in the cloister section of the monastery.

The monastery has very strict rules and limits concerning tours, as the nuns follow the Benedictine rules of seclusion. Mass is celebrated with Gregorian chants at 7 A.M. on weekdays and 10 A.M. during the holidays.

ORATORIO DI SANTA CATERINA ALL'ANTELLA (ORATORY OF SANTA CATERINA ALL'ANTELLA)

Via del Carosa, at the corner of Via di Montisoni

⟶ DIRECTIONS: From Piazzale di Porta Romana in Florence take Via Senese toward the A1 highway (Autostrada del Sole). Enter the A1 highway (Autostrada del Sole) at Firenze Certosa toward Rome and exit at Firenze Sud. Continue on Strada Provinciale 127 (SP 127) and then Strada Statale 222 (SS 222). Take Via dell'Antella and turn right onto Via Brigate Partigiane. Continue on Via Simone degli Antelli and turn left onto Via Ubaldino Peruzzi, then left again onto Via dell'Antella. The oratory is in the main piazza of Antella.

➤ Located in the fields near Ponte a Ema, this 14th-century church is simple in design. The interior is highlighted with pointed arches and decorated with 14th-century frescoes that include works depicting the stories of Saint Catherine of Alexandria and the evangelists by Spinello Aretino, and other frescoes by Maestro di Barberino.

PIEVE DI SANT'ALESSANDRO A GIOGOLI

Via di Giogoli, 1, Giogoli (a *frazione,* or part, of the Commune of Scandicci); tel.: 055-741453 (parish); open: call for hours.

⟶ DIRECTIONS: From Piazzale di Porta Romana in Florence take Via Senese. After about two miles, turn right onto Via Volterrana. After about 1 1/2 miles turn right again onto Via di Giogoli.

➤ Recorded as early as 1035, the church of Sant'Alessandro lost its Romanesque appearance due to an 18th-century makeover that fashioned its facade and matching three-tiered bell tower. The interior of the church is laid out in a basilican plan with a nave, flanked by two aisles, that terminates in a single apse. At the foot of this apse is the tomb of parishioner Baldo Naselli, who died in 1397. He is depicted in the relief that dominates the sarcophagus. Under the canonic loggia, decorated with Ridolfo del Ghirlandaio's fresco of the Madonna and child, lies a plaque, carved in 1513, with a transcription of Pope Gregory VIII's papal bull (1187). The frescoes at the back of the church and in the transept are 18th-century works by Pietro Pertichi and Francesco Manetti, respectively.

SAN BARTOLOMEO A BADIA A RIPOLI

Via di Ripoli, 219; tel.: 055-6820507; open: daily 7 A.M.–noon, (summer), daily 7 A.M.–noon, 4–5:30 P.M., (winter); to visit the cloister and refectory, contact the Istituto di Badia a Ripoli at tel. 055-6530395.

➤ The 16th-century church that dominates the Piazza Ripoli with its porticoed facade and massive bell tower actually dates back to 790, making it the oldest monastery in the territory of Florence. Founded as a Benedictine convent, the church was taken over by an order of Vallombrosan monks in the 13th century. Despite significant enlargements that took place in 1598, which gave the exterior its current look, the interior has managed to maintain a modest appearance over the centuries. It consists of a single nave and crypt arranged along a Latin-cross plan. The frescoes in the sacristy (1585) are attributed to mannerist painter Bernardino Poccetti, as is the *Marriage of Cain* (1601–1604), located in the convent refectory adjacent to the church.

SAN GIULIANO A SETTIMO

Via della Pieve, 44, Scandicci; tel.: 055-7310077; open: call for hours.

⟶ DIRECTIONS: From Piazzale di Porta Romana in Florence take Via Senese toward the A1 highway (Autostrada del Sole). Take

the A1 highway (Autostrada del Sole). Take the A1 at the entrance of Firenze Certosa and exit at Firenze Signa. Turn left onto Via delle Nazioni Unite, then right onto Strada Statale 67 (SS 67), Tosco-Romagnola. After about 1/2 mile turn right onto Via della Pieve.

➢ Built toward the end of the Middle Ages, the church of San Giuliano, with its three-aspe posterior and mighty bell tower, provides a rare example of a fully intact Romanesque structure. The interior consists of a nave lined by stone pillars and narrow aisles, typical of the 12th-century style. The elegant sandstone trimming, however, dates from 17th-century interventions, which also resulted in the addition of the harmonious exterior portico. On the first altar to the right, note the vibrant terra-cotta bas-relief, the *Madonna of the Flowers*, attributed to the school of Antonio Rossellino. A 1st-century sarcophagus, decorated with masks, cupids, and garlands, is housed in the adjacent cloister.

SANTA MARGHERITA A MONTICI

Via Santa Margherita a Montici, 62, Arcetri; tel.: 055-689698; open: call for hours.
⤤ DIRECTIONS: From Piazzale di Porta Romana in Florence take Viale del Poggio Imperiale. After 1/2 mile, turn left onto Viale Torricelli. Continue to Piazzale Galileo, then take Viale Galileo. At Piazzale Michelangelo take Viale Michelangelo for about 1 1/2 miles and turn right onto Via Santa Margherita a Montici.

➢ Santa Margherita a Montici is a characteristic 14th-century church, with its bell tower shaped like a battlement. Inside are early-14th-century panels by the Master of Saint Cecilia depicting Saint Margaret and a Madonna with child. In the apse is a work by Tuscan sculptor Andrea Sansovino, *Tabernacle with Adoring Angels.*

TORRE DEL GALLO

Via del Giromontino, Arcetri
⤤ DIRECTIONS: From Piazzale di Porta Romana in Florence take Viale Niccolò Machiavelli to Piazzale Galileo. Then take Viale Galileo. Continue for 100 yards, then turn right onto Via San Leonardo. Next, turn left onto Via Viviani and left again onto Via

del Pian dei Giullari. Turn left one more time onto Via della Torre del Gallo. Immediately after, turn right onto Via del Giromontino.

➢ Rebuilt between 1904 and 1906 by renowned art collector and historian Stefano Bardini, the Torre del Gallo nevertheless retains its medieval appearance. Surrounding this structure is a patchwork of gardens recently made public that are easily spotted, stretching out against the hillside, when looking south of the Arno.

VILLA CORSINI DI MEZZOMONTE

Via Imprunetaria per Pozzolatico, 116, Mezzomonte; closed to the public.
⤤ DIRECTIONS: From Piazzale di Porta Romana in Florence take Viale del Poggio Imperiale and then Via San Felice a Ema. Follow directions to Pozzolatico. Once you pass the village of Pozzolatico, continue along the main road to Mezzomonte. The villa is just outside the center of Mezzomonte.

➢ Positioned in a beautiful landscape of vineyard and olive groves on the outskirts of Florence, the Villa Corsini di Mezzomonte was built in the 16th century and belonged to prominent families, including the Buondelmontes, the Panciatichis, Lorenzo de' Medici, and Cardinal Giovan Carlo de' Medici. Between 1630 and 1644, under the ownership of the Corsini family, the villa was redecorated with frescoes by Giovanni di San Giovanni, Francesco Alani, Pandolfo Sacchi, and Passignano. The villa is now privately owned and usually used for private receptions; it is therefore difficult to visit.

VILLA I COLLAZZI

Via Volterrana, 7, Cerbaia; tel.: 055-7309002; open: call for hours.
⤤ DIRECTIONS: From Piazzale di Porta Romana in Florence take Via Senese. After about two miles, turn right onto Via Volterrana.

➢ This beautiful mannerist villa was built by Agostino Dino in 1560. Santi di Tito painted the altarpiece representing the Wedding at Cana (1593). The garden has fine trees, including cypresses, oaks, and ilexes. There is a parterre on a terrace below the villa.

Museums

Museo di Santa Maria all'Impruneta (Museum of Santa Maria all'Impruneta)

Piazza Buondelmonti, Impruneta; tel.: 055-2036408 (Commune of Impruneta); open: Sat.–Sun. 9 A.M.–12:30 P.M., 3:30–6:30 P.M.; admission: €2.50.

⌁ DIRECTIONS: From Piazzale di Porta Romana take Via Senese, then turn left onto Via Accursio. After one mile turn right onto Via di San Felice a Ema and then left onto Via Gherardo Silvani. Take Via Imprunetana toward Pozzolatico, and after 4³/4 miles you will reach Impruneta. Turn left onto Piazza Buondelmonti.

➤ The collection of the Museum of Santa Maria all'Impruneta includes illuminated manuscripts, silver objects, gold jewelry, and donations to the basilica collected over the course of the centuries. In the first room to the left of the ticket office, there is a Florentine 14th-century fresco from the tabernacle of the Ricci family with an enthroned Madonna with angels and saints. In the third room, there are a dozen 14th- and 16th-century illuminated manuscripts. To the right of the ticket office, in the Silvani Room, which overlooks the portico of the facade of the basilica, is the *Finding of the Image of the Madonna,* a bas-relief attributed either to Michelozzo, Filarete, or Luca della Robbia.

Pinacoteca della Certosa del Galluzzo (Picture Gallery of the Certosa del Galluzzo)

Via della Buca di Certosa, 2, Galluzzo; tel. 055-2049226/2048617; open: Tues.–Sun. (guided tours only) 9:15, 10:15, 11:15 A.M., 3:15 and 4:15 P.M., and 5:15 P.M. (from April–Sept.); closed: Mon.; admission: donation suggested.

⌁ DIRECTIONS: From Piazzale di Porta Romana in Florence take Via Senese. After about two miles turn right onto Via di Colle Ramole. After 200 yards turn right again on Via della Buca di Certosa.

➤ This art gallery was inaugurated after World War II and it exhibits paintings from the 14th to 17th centuries. Particularly interesting are the frescoes from the cloister, including *The Passion of Christ,* by Pontormo. They were painted when he took refuge in the cloister to escape the plague in Florence (1523–1525).

Castello di Cafaggio

Via del Ferrone, 58, Impruneta; tel.: 055-2012085; fax: 055-2314633; website: www.castellodicafaggio.com; e-mail: info@cafaggio.com; number of rooms: 4 apartments; credit cards accepted: all major; access to internet: yes; €€.

⊘ DIRECTIONS: From Piazzale di Porta Romana in Florence take Via Senese, which will turn into Via Cassia (SS 2). Once you reach the town of Tavernuzze, take the road for Impruneta. Once in Impruneta, follow the main street into Piazza Buondelmonte. At Piazza Buondelmonte take Via Giuseppe Mazzini, then turn right into Piazza A. Da Bagnolo and take Via del Ferrone.

☛This 14th-century castle rises on the top of a hill among a grove of olive trees in Impruneta, a wine-growing town. The apartments, decorated country-style, are located in the main part of the castle. The smaller apartments have kitchenettes, while the larger ones have proper kitchens. The only apartment with two bedrooms is the Ulivo; all the others have only one bedroom, as well as a living room with a folding bed.

La Querce II

Via Treggiaia, 128, La Romola (San Casciano); tel.: 055-827014; fax: 055-827169; number of rooms: 3 apartments; credit cards accepted: none; access to internet: none; €€.

⊘ DIRECTIONS: From Piazzale di Porta Romana in Florence take Via Senese. After about two miles turn right onto Via Volterrana. Follow the directions for Volterra/Cerbaia. As you follow Via Volterrana, you will pass the Certosa del Galluzzo on the left. At the Chiesa Nuova junction, take the road leading toward the Romola 3, on the right. Continue along this road until you reach the top of the hill. Do not take the road on the right leading to Poggio Vallicaia, but the road on the left, with no indications. Follow this past a villa and a yellow house. The red house following these is La Querce II.

☛La Querce II is located in the countryside just outside Florence and on the opposite side of the valley from Fiesole.

Apartments of varying sizes and at very reasonable prices can be rented daily or weekly. There is a pool.

Tenuta Le Viste

Via del Leone, 11, Mosciano (Scandicci); tel.: 055-768543; fax: 055-768531; website: www.tenuta-leviste.it; e-mail: info@tenuta-leviste.it; number of rooms: 5; credit cards accepted: all major; access to internet: yes; facilities: swimming pool; €€–€€€.

⊘ DIRECTIONS: From Piazzale Porta al Prato take Viale Fratelli Rosselli and go over Ponte della Vittoria. From Piazza Taddeo Gaddi take Via Bronzino, turn right onto Via Fra Diamante Masolino, right again onto Via dell'Olivuzzo, and left onto Via di Scandicci. Once you arrive in Scandicci, follow the directions toward Mosciano. The Tenuta Le Viste is at the end of the first small road found on the left past the church.

☛The lawn of the Tenuta, only five miles outside Florence, offers a beautiful view of the city and the surrounding countryside. There are only four rooms, decorated with a mix of ancient and modern furnishings. The largest and most luxurious room is a duplex with Jacuzzi.

Villa Belvedere

Via B. Castelli, 3, Florence; tel.: 055-222501; fax: 055-223163; website: www.villabelvederefirenze.it; e-mail: reception@villabelvederefirenze.it; category: ★★★★; number of rooms: 26, including 7 with large balconies and views of downtown; credit cards accepted: all major; access to internet: yes; €€–€€€.

⊘ DIRECTIONS: From Piazzale di Porta Romana in Florence take Via Senese, and turn left on Via B. Castelli.

☛Views of the city and a quiet garden surround the Villa Belvedere. The large rooms were recently redecorated.

HOTELS & INNS

Villa Montartino

Via Gherardo Silvani, 151, Florence; tel.: 055-223520; fax: 055-223495; website: www.montartino.com; e-mail: info @ montartino.com; category:★★★★; number of rooms: 4, plus 10 apartments; credit cards accepted: all major; facilities: air-conditioning, satellite TV, safe, heated swimming pool, Jacuzzi, and sauna; access to internet: yes; €€€.

⊘ DIRECTIONS: From Piazzale di Porta Romana in Florence take Viale Poggio Imperiale and follow it until you reach Via San Felice a Ema. Turn left onto Via Gherardo Silvani.

☛This small deluxe hotel is only two miles from Florence, but its beautiful surroundings will give you a sense of countryside seclusion.

RESTAURANTS & CAFÉS

Bibe

Via delle Bagnese, 1, Florence; tel.: 055-2049085; open: Mon., Tues., Thurs., Fri. 7:30–11 P.M., Sat.–Sun. 12:30–2:30 P.M., 7:30–11 P.M.; closed: Wed. and second half of Nov.; credit cards accepted: all major; €€.

⊘ DIRECTIONS: From Piazzale di Porta Romana in Florence take Via Senese. The restaurant is before the town of Galluzzo, right at the corner of Via delle Bagnese.

☛Bibe is a very intimate restaurant on the outskirts of Florence. They serve dishes such as macaroni with rabbit ragu, duck in herb and orange sauce, and a cheese torte with lemon sauce. They also have an excellent wine and grappa list.

Marchino

Piazza Buondelmonti, Impruneta; open: Sat. 8 A.M.–2 P.M.; closed: Mon.–Fri., Sun.; credit cards accepted: none.

⊘ DIRECTIONS: From Piazzale di Porta Romana (Oltrarno) take Via Senese, which will turn into Via Cassia (SS 2). Once you reach the town of Tavernuzze, take the road for Impruneta. Once in Impruneta follow the main street into Piazza Buondelmonti, the main piazza in town. Marchino is on the right.

☛For 19 years, Marco Bucciarelli has parked his sandwich stand in front of Santa Maria all'Impruneta during the Saturday marketplace. A self-proclaimed "genius of the *panino*," Marco grants wishes in the form of hearty porchetta sandwiches.

Omero

Via Pian dei Giullari, 11r, Arcetri; tel.: 055-220053; website: www.ristoranteomero.it; open: Wed.–Mon. 12:30–2 P.M., 7:30–10 P.M.; closed: Tues. and month of Aug.; credit cards accepted: all major; €.

⊘ DIRECTIONS: From Piazzale di Porta Romana in Florence take Viale Niccolò Machiavelli to Piazzale Galileo, then take Viale Galileo. Continue for 100 yards, then turn right onto Via San Leonardo. Turn left on Via Viviani and left on Via Pian dei Giullari.

☛Omero is an elegant tavern with a garden that serves up home-style cooking. Their menu is strong on grilled meat.

Osteria del Vicario (Inn and Restaurant)

Via Rivellino, 3, Certaldo Alto; tel./fax: 0571-668228/668676; website: www.osteriadelvicario.it; e-mail: info @osteriadelvicario.it; number of rooms: 4; credit cards accepted: all major; access to internet: no; €.

⊘ DIRECTIONS: From Piazzale di Porta Romana in Florence take Via Senese until you arrive at Firenze Certosa. Take the Superstrada Firenze Siena, toward Siena. Take the first exit to Poggibonsi and follow the road until you reach Certaldo (after about seven miles). Follow the directions to Certaldo Alto.

☛This village inn has preserved the original features of an old townhouse. The rooms are attractive although not very spacious. The restaurant offers carefully prepared Tuscan food and a good selection of regional wines.

Villa Medicea di Poggio a Caiano

Piazza dei Medici, 14, Poggio a Caiano; tel.: 055-877012; website: www.polomuseale. firenze.it; open: daily 8:15 A.M.–4:30 P.M. (Jan.–Feb., Nov.–Dec.), 8:15 A.M.–5:30 P.M. (Mar.), 8:15 A.M.–6:30 P.M. (Apr.–May, Sept., Oct.), 8:15 A.M.–7:30 P.M. (Jun.–Aug.); closed: second and third Mon. of each month and holidays; admission: free.

⏐ DIRECTIONS: From Piazzale Porta al Prato in Florence, turn onto Viale Belfiore and then right onto Via Guido Monaco. From here turn left onto Viale Belfiore again and right onto Via Benedetto Marcello. Follow the road, which will first become Viale Francesco Redi and then Via di Novoli. After about one mile turn right onto Via Enrico Forlanini. Turn right again onto Viale Alessandro Guidoni and again on Viale XI Agosto, then left on Via Zoroastro da Peretola. Continue along the Viadotto dell'Indiano and then turn left on Via Pistoiese, which will take you directly to Poggio a Caiano. From there, follow the signs to the villa.

➤ The Villa Medicea di Poggio a Caiano was acquired by Lorenzo the Magnificent in 1480. He then commissioned Giuliano da Sangallotto to rebuild it, transforming it into his favorite country villa. It was used by other members of the Medici dynasty, and subsequently by the Austrians, French grand dukes, and the kings of Italy. Victor Emmanuel II gave it to the state in 1919.

The villa is a rectangular building on a broad terrace surrounded by a colonnade. A classic portico with Ionic columns on the first floor shows the Medici arms and bears a beautiful frieze, which is a copy of the original, now displayed inside the villa. A representation of a Platonic myth, the frieze was designed to celebrate the Medici dynasty. It is attributed by some scholars to Andrea del Sansovino and dated to about 1490–1494, but others consider it a later work.

On the ground floor, there is a vestibule covered in monochromatic frescoes by Luigi Catani (after 1811), detailing the history of the villa.

The salon was designed by Lorenzo's son, Pope Leo X, to celebrate the return of the Medici family to Florence. It has a carved and gilded barrel vault with the Medici arms, by Andrea Feltrini and Franciabigio. The frescoes were begun by Franciabigio, Andrea del Sarto, and Pontormo (1519–1521) and completed by Alessandro Allori (1579–1582). The subjects were designed by Paolo Giovio and illustrate incidents in Roman history that are paralleled in the lives of Cosimo the Elder and Lorenzo the Magnificent, as well as mythological scenes celebrating the return of the Medici dynasty. *The Return of Cicero from Exile*, by Franciabigio, alludes to the return of Cosimo the Elder to Florence, while *The Consul Flaminius at the Council of the Achaean League*, by Allori, alludes to Lorenzo the Magnificent's intervention at the Diet at Cremona. The decorative scheme culminates in the remarkable lunette by Pontormo (c. 1520) illustrating the story of Vertumnus and Pomonas, told by Ovid. On the right are three female figures with white stoles; on the left, on either side of a dog, are Vertumnus (as an old man and as a young man), with Bacchus seated above.

Beneath the loggia, on the facade, are remains of a fresco by Filippino Lippi, part of Lorenzo's original decoration.

Itinerary:

At the Crossroads of Montalbano

By Stacy Meichtry

Like many wine-producing areas in Tuscany, the hills of Montalbano have ripened in recent years, bringing prestige to their labels and prosperity to their communities. It therefore takes a considerable stretch of the imagination to visualize its tawny landscape soaked with blood. But as the annals of local history report, Montalbano was among Tuscany's most popular battlegrounds during the Middle Ages. Situated between the bellicose Communes of Prato, Pistoia, and Florence, the territory couldn't help but find itself well within harm's way whenever war came to pass. Even in times of peace, rogue armies and soldiers of fortune frequently roamed the hillsides in search of diversions more intense than the average wine-tasting itinerary.

For those with earnest travel plans in mind, such as religious pilgrims or members of the clergy, trekking through Montalbano required guile, good fortune, and, most importantly, a place to rest. Providing the last of these requirements were a number of Romanesque churches and the religious orders that ran them.

Built by Lombard settlers after the fall of the Roman Empire, these churches became points of reference for travelers moving along the network of country trails. While the majority of these buildings have either been demolished

San Giusto

Interior of San Martino in Campo

or converted into more modern structures, others were so deeply immersed in Montalbano's rich vegetation that they went unaltered through the course of history to the present day.

Buried deep within the pine forests of eastern Montalbano is the church of **San Giusto**, considered one of the most important stations along the secret pilgrimage routes. According to legend, the church was erected over the course of a single night by the French monk and local hermit known as Giustone. To compound his adversity, Giustone had to share his only shovel with another monk, named Baronto, who had a similar project in mind but at a separate location. The pair pushed ahead with their separate plans on the same night. By dawn, each monk had managed to finish his own church, aided by the "providential elongation" of their arms, which allowed them to pass the shovel back and forth across miles of territory.

Having been repeatedly sacked in medieval times, the monastery that originally accompanied the church to form the abbey has all but vanished. What remains is the church itself in a vacant shell of stone blocks, still solidly stacked in the Romanesque style of 13th-century Italy. Situated at the dead end of a tree-lined gravel road, the church maintains its Latin-cross layout, its fortified bell tower, and even its shingled roof, but its insides are fully gutted and charred, as the church was deconsecrated in the 18th century and relentlessly vandalized thereafter. The stone altar, lit by a solitary beam of sunlight that enters the church through a twin mullion window in the facade, supports a makeshift cross, propped up by loose rocks and cobwebs.

For a better indication of what the abbey of San Giusto might have looked like at its genesis, visit the newly restored abbey of **San Martino in Campo**, perched above olive groves on the edge of the thick woods that border Montalbano to the south.

OUR PICK

Dating back to as early as the 10th century, San Martino in Campo was once the area's most prominent abbey with a nave three aisles wide and five pillars deep.

These proportions were permanently altered in the 12th century, when the nave was subjected to "mutilations" that reduced its length from five to three arches. One of these arches was later destroyed in 1464, when troops from Lucca raided the building and set it ablaze. The two surviving pillars, distinct for the vegetal and zoomorphic motifs that decorate their capitals, form what is considered the ancient core of the church.

Also surviving the blaze was the late-14th-century fresco in the sacristy, the *Enthroned Madonna and Saints.* The work, attributed to Pietro and Francesco Miniati di Prato, was discovered in 1950 during a restoration effort that removed all of the extraneous decorations accumulated over the baroque and rococo periods. This restoration also led to the rediscovery of the sandstone architrave over the main door, which also dates back to the 14th century and features a relief sculpture of Christ the Redeemer, flanked by a lion and a wolf.

The oldest of Montalbano's Romanesque churches also happens to be its best preserved. Mentioned in imperial documents as early as 998, the **Pieve di San Leonardo** bares deep military roots. Planted at the foot of the hilltop town of Artimino, the church's bell tower originally served as a lookout tower to the medieval walls of the town's castle, which now lies in ruins nearby. Even after the Countess Matilda of Canossa commissioned the construction of the church, its tower continued to function in a military capacity up until the early Renaissance. Looming over dry grass and pine trees, against the three sandstone apses that form the church's elegant rear end, the brick monolith offers San Leonardo its unflinching protection to this very day.

The timeworn relief works embedded in the church's exterior were molded in plaster by San Leonardo's Lombard builders from original Etruscan cinerary urns. These urns are now kept in the Museo Archeologico Nazionale di Firenze. The molds, meanwhile, confirm the belief that, by the Middle Ages, builders were using artifacts to enhance the beauty of their architecture.

Apse and bell tower of the Pieve di San Leonardo

Cloister of the Parrocchiale di San Michele

The beauty of San Leonardo's interior, on the other hand, is enhanced by less ancient artwork. The statuettes of Saint Leonard and Saint Anthony, each of which inhabits its own niche, were carved in the late 14th century. The pillars that divide the nave into three aisles date back to the church's foundations, while the wood-trussed ceiling that they support was added in the 1300s. The organ in the right aisle is particularly noteworthy for the oil-on-canvas of David strumming his harp mounted above its ivory keys. This painting retracts like a blind to reveal the organ's polished pipes underneath.

Among the other fascinating revelations in the church are two polychrome terra-cotta statuettes, located at the end of the left aisle. Depicting the Visitation, the terra-cotta group by the della Robbia workshop is a modest work that wouldn't merit mention if not for the removable pieces of pavement at its feet. After obtaining permission from the church management, remove the pavement to reveal a tiny grave. With dimensions measured at roughly four feet in length and a foot and a half in width, the grave is believed to have been that of an Etruscan infant.

A far more stirring depiction of the Visitation is located in the **Parrocchiale di San Michele** in the town of Carmignano. It was founded in 1100, was originally built in the Romanesque style of San Leonardo, underneath the *mura della rocca,* a medieval military wall that now rests in ruins. In 1349, a Gothic building replaced the ancient structure, while the graceful portico was added during the Renaissance, completing the church's current appearance.

These alterations to the church's ancient roots can be forgiven, since its interior contains what many contemporary art critics regard as the definitive masterpiece of early Florentine mannerism. The *Visitation,* executed by mannerist painter Pontormo in 1528, communicates a simple image—four women meeting in the street—through one of the painter's most psychologically complex compositions. Two of the women, Mary and Saint Elizabeth, embrace one another in acknowledgment of their mutual impregnation.

Their handmaidens stand behind them, casting hypnotic stares outside the painting, as if to distract the viewer from the encounter. Notice the striking resemblance that Mary bears to Saint Elizabeth, as well as to the other two women: Pontormo cloned each member of the quartet from the exact same model. Thus, the youthful Virgin embraces an elderly version of herself in her kinswoman Elizabeth, eyes softened by sagging lids and crow's feet, the ravages of time carried out by strokes of the painter's brush.

FURTHER INFORMATION

You can take the CAP, COPIT, and LAZZI buses from Piazza Della Stazione.

Parrocchiale di San Michele
Piazza Santissima Francesco e Michele, 1, Carmignano; tel.: 055-8712046; open: daily 7:30 A.M.–6 P.M.
⊘ DIRECTIONS: Follow directions for the Villa Medicea di Poggio a Caiano to Poggio a Caiano (see pg. 247). From here, turn left onto Strada Provinciale 45 (SP 45) and at Piazza della Stazione turn right onto Via delle Ginestre. Follow it around, past Artimino, and then toward the left, when it becomes Via la Serra. Take Strada Provinciale 44 (SP 44), turn right onto Strada Provinciale 43 (SP 43), and you will arrive in the center of Carmignano.

Pieve di San Leonardo
Via della Chiesa, 19a, Artimino; open: Mon.–Fri. by appointment only, Sat.–Sun. 10:30 A.M.–noon, 4–6 P.M. (summer), Sat.–Sun. 10:30 A.M.–noon, 2–4 P.M. (winter).
⊘ DIRECTIONS: Follow directions for the Villa Medicea di Poggio a Caiano to Poggio a Caiano (see pg. 247). From here, turn left onto Strada Provinciale 45 (SP 45) and at Piazza della Stazione turn right onto Via delle Ginestre, which will take you to Artimino. The pieve is outside the village.

San Giusto
Via Montalbano, 7, Carmignano; open: contact the Antica Trattoria di San Giusto at tel. 055-8712022.
⊘ DIRECTIONS: Follow directions for the Parrocchiale di San Michele to Carmignano. Then take Via Vergheretana up the hill past Santa Cristina to the Montalbano provincial road. Stay on this road until you reach Pinone, where you should follow the directions for Vitolini-Vinci. About a third of a mile after the turn, you will come across a shaded road to the left called Via del le Ginestre that descends toward the restaurant Antica Trattoria di San Giusto. The road ends at the church. The restaurant keeps the key of the church if you want to visit the interior.

San Martino in Campo
San Martino in Campo, 2, Capraia e Limite; tel.: 0571-910118; open: Mon.–Fri. by appointment only, Sun. 8:45 A.M.–1 P.M., 3–7 P.M.; closed: Sat.
⊘ DIRECTIONS: Follow directions for the Parrocchiale di San Michele to Carmignano. From there, follow the signs to the abbey. It is just outside the village.

Viale Papa Giovanni XXIII, Artimino; tel.: 055-8751426; open: by appointment only; admission: free self-guided visits, or up to €140 with an expert guide.

⏿DIRECTIONS: Follow directions for the Villa Medicea di Poggio a Caiano to Poggio a Caiano (see pg. 247). From here, turn left onto Strada Provinciale 45 (SP 45) and at Piazza della Stazione turn right onto Via delle Ginestre, which will take you to Artimino. From there, follow the signs to the villa.

By Stacy Meichtry

Seen from the terrace of the Villa Medicea la Ferdinanda, on the adjacent hill, Artimino is the crown that rests atop the highest peak in eastern Montalbano. And its dominating jewel is the embattled clock tower that rises up on the edge of town.

During the Middle Ages, this tower was the lynchpin of Artimino's defense against Florentine invaders as it was part of the town's military fortifications, commissioned in 998. Over the next 200 years, Artimino was repeatedly passed back and forth between Pistoia and Florence, until the latter definitively conquered the area in 1228.

During Medici rule, Artimino was a favorite haunt of Ferdinando I, who built the villa across the way and named it **Villa Medicea la Ferdinanda**. Currently connected to Artimino by a street that swoops between the clock tower and the villa facade in an unbroken, tree-lined parabola, la Ferdinanda is also known as the "villa of the hundred chimneys" for the multitude of ornamental smokestacks that rise from the roof like pieces on a chessboard.

Built between 1596 and 1600, the villa marks Artimino's passage into an era of relative peace, in which wealthy Florentine families began venturing out into the countryside for recreation and relaxation. This tradition lives on today in the form of the servants' quarters, which have been converted into a four-star hotel (see Hotel Paggeria Medicea, pg. 255), and in the ancient town itself.

Villa Medicea la Ferdinanda

Other Points of Interest

San Martino a Gangalandi

Via Leon Battista Alberti, 37, Lastra a Signa; tel.: 055-8720008; open: daily 8 A.M.–12 P.M.

⤢ DIRECTIONS: From Piazzale Porta al Prato in Florence take Viale Fratelli Rosselli toward the south, away from the center. Follow it over the bridge, Ponte della Vittoria, then turn right onto Lugarno del Pignone. Once you reach Piazza Paolo Uccello, turn onto Via del Sansovino. Then from Piazza Pompeo Batoni take Viale Francesco Talenti and after about a quarter of a mile you will reach Viale Etruria. Follow this until you get to the entrance to the superstrada for Livorno. Take the Superstrada Pisa-Livorno and exit at Lastra a Signa. Then take Via Livornese. Turn left onto Via XXV Aprile and left again onto Via San Martino. Via Leon Battista Alberti is the first road on the left.

➤ Located in Lastra a Signa, on the way to Empoli, this Romanesque church dates from 1108 but was later remodeled in several phases. The portico is from the 15th century. Of note inside is the Cappella del Battistero, whose octagonal sides are adorned with frescoes by Bicci di Lorenzo (c. 1433). The octagonal-shaped baptismal font in marble dates from 1423 and is attributed to a disciple of Lorenzo Ghiberti. The apse is believed to be the work of Leon Battista Alberti, who was a benefactor of the church between 1432 and 1472. Adjoining the church is a small museum that includes a painting by Lorenzo Monaco titled *Madonna of Humility*.

Tombe Etrusche di Comeana (Etruscan Tombs of Comeana)

Via Monterfortini, 43, Comeana (a *frazione*, or part, of the Commune of Carmignano); tel: 055-8719741; open: Mon.–Sat. 9 A.M.–2 P.M.; closed: Sun.; admission: free.

⤢ DIRECTIONS: Follow directions for the Villa Medicea di Poggio a Caiano to Poggio a Caiano (see pg. 247). At the crossroad of Via Pistoiese with the Strada Statale 66 (SS 66) Firenze-Pistoia, turn left toward Florence. Then at the first light turn right. After a few hundred yards, at the next light, turn left and follow directions for Comeana. From there, follow the signs to the Etruscan Tombs.

➤ Discovered in the 1950s and 1960s during a series of excavations performed in the area of Comeana, these Etruscan tombs are among the best preserved in the territory of Florence. The first of these, the Tomba dei Boschetti, or Tomb of the Little Woods (along the uphill road to town, near the cemetery), is believed to have been built in the 7th century and consists of two funerary chambers. The Tomba di Montefortini (Montefortini Tomb) offers a more complex layout, featuring a false vault, preceded by a monolith that once sealed the entrance to the real one. The monolith now frames a long corridor that leads into an inner vault, distinguished by a domelike ceiling. This feat of ancient architectural ingenuity uses giant, ring-shaped stones, stacked one on top of the other, to achieve a concave ceiling, supported by a solitary six-meter-high column at its center.

HOTELS & INNS

Hotel Paggeria Medicea

Viale Papa Giovanni XXIII, 3, Artimino; tel.: 055-875141; fax: 055-8751470; website: www.artimino.com; e-mail: hotel@artimino.com; category:★★★★; number of rooms: 37; credit cards accepted: all major; facilities: tennis courts, swimming pool, gymnasium; access to internet: yes; most beautiful rooms: those on the first floor facing south; €€.

⌂ DIRECTIONS: From Piazzale Porta al Prato in Florence take Viale Fratelli Rosselli toward the south, away from the center. Follow it over the bridge, Ponte della Vittoria, then turn right onto Lugarno del Pignone. Once you reach Piazza Paolo Uccello, turn onto Via del Sansovino. Then from Piazza Pompeo Batoni take Viale Francesco Talenti and after about a quarter of a mile you will reach Viale Etruria. Follow this until you get to the entrance to the *superstrada* for Livorno. Take the Superstrada Pisa-Livorno and exit at Montelupo Fiorentino. Follow the highway toward Florence, and after three miles you will find a junction, which, on the left, heads toward Artimino. Follow it and when you have passed over a bridge, you will find a little road on the right that leads to the Villa Medicea (signposted). The hotel is next door.

☛ Located next to Grand Duke Ferdinando I's hunting lodge, the Villa Medicea la Ferdinanda, this luxurious hotel used to be the servants' lodgings. But do not be fooled—the rooms and suites are more than luxurious. The restaurant offers products grown on the grounds of the hotel, as well as great service.

RESTAURANTS & CAFÉS

Da Delfina

Via della Chiesa, 1, Artimino; tel.: 055-8718119; website: www.dadelfina.it; e-mail: posta@dadelfina.it; open: Wed.–Sat. 12:30–2 P.M., 7:30–10 P.M., Sun. 12:30–2 P.M., Tues. 7:30–10 P.M.; closed: Mon.; credit cards accepted: none; €.

⌂ DIRECTIONS: Follow directions for the Villa Medicea di Poggio a Caiano to Poggio a Caiano (see pg. 247). From here, turn left onto Strada Provinciale 45 (SP 45) and at Piazza della Stazione turn right onto Via delle Ginestre, which will take you to Artimino. From there, follow the signs to the restaurant.

☛ Da Delfina is about a 30-minute drive from Florence and has outdoor seating in the summertime. The food is classic Tuscan such as *ribollita, pappardelle con ragù,* and rabbit made in the oven with pine nuts.

Northwest of Florence

VILLA MEDICEA DELLA PETRAIA

Via della Petraia, 40, Castello; tel. 055-452691; website: www.polomuseale.firenze.it; open: daily 8:15 A.M.–4:30 P.M. (Jan.–Feb., Nov.–Dec.), 8:15 A.M.–5:30 P.M. (Mar.), 8:15 A.M.–6:30 P.M. (Apr.–May, Sept.–Oct.), 8:15 A.M.–7:30 P.M. (Jun.–Aug.); closed: second and third Mon. of each month and holidays; admission: free.

⌂ DIRECTIONS: From the Fortezza da Basso in Florence take Via dello Statuto. It will turn into Via Guasti after Piazza Muratori, Via Gianni after Piazza G. Viesseux, and Via Tavanti after Piazza Leopoldo. Toward the end it bends toward the left: turn with it and you will find yourself on Via Vittorio Emanuele II. Follow it for about 50 yards and then turn right onto Via Celso and right again onto Via Taddeo Alderotti. Keep on this road until you reach Via del Garbo, which turns into Via Santo Stefano in Pane. Turn left and follow it until you find Via Reginaldo Giuliani on the right. After about a mile or so, turn right onto Via della Petraia. You can also take ATAF bus No. 28 from Piazza della Stazione in Florence, toward Sesto Calenzano or No. 2 from Piazza Dalmazia.

➤ This complex was built by Brunelleschi and acquired in 1530 by the Medici family, who hired Bernardo Buontalenti to undertake renovations. It has frescoes by Volterrano depicting feats of the Medici family and Saint Stephen's Knights. Particularly interesting is the interior decoration, much of it from the 19th century. King Victor Emmanuel II of Savoy and his wife lived here from 1865 to 1870, and some of their possessions still remain. In the garden there is a hanging fountain of the Venere-Fiorenza (Venus-Florencia) by Tribolo and a statue by Giambologna.

VILLA MEDICEA DI CAREGGI

It was an especial favourite among the dwellings of Lorenzo the Magnificent, who made it the scene of some of the most distinguished literary meetings of his most distinguished literary age. A statue of Plato was solemnly placed in the gardens of this villa by Lorenzo, who caused them to be laid out according to his notions of the groves of Academus; and on every 7th of November, the anniversary of the philosopher's birth was celebrated there by a splendid festival.

Frances Trollope, *Italy and the Italians*

Villa Medicea di Careggi

VILLA MEDICEA DI CAREGGI

Viale Pieraccini, 17, Careggi; tel. 055-4279981; open: by appointment only (contact the local hospital at tel. 055-4279755).

⏃ DIRECTIONS: From the Fortezza da Basso in Florence take Via dello Statuto. It will turn into Via Guasti after Piazza Muratori, Via Gianni after Piazza Viesseux, and Via Tavanti after Piazza Leopoldo. Toward the end it bends toward the left: turn with it and you will find yourself on Via Vittorio Emanuele II. At Piazza Dalmazia, turn right onto Viale G. B. Morgagni. After about 150 yards, turn left onto Viale Pieraccini.

➢ Used as offices by the nearby Careggi hospital, the Villa Medicea di Careggi stands amidst a wooded park at the top of a hill.

The villa was built as a farmhouse in the 14th century. The Medicis bought it in 1417. After being exiled to Venice, Cosimo the Elder, the family patriarch, returned to Florence and hired the architect Michelozzo to enlarge the villa. This expansion took place in 1434.

The site soon became one of the Medicis' favorite residences, and the garden was opened to a group of Renaissance artists and intellectuals, such as Marsilio Ficino and Pico della Mirandola, who called themselves the Platonic Academy and met there regularly. Both Cosimo the Elder and his most famous descendant, Lorenzo the Magnificent, died here. Sacked and burned down in the 16th century, when the Medicis were expelled from Florence, the villa was renovated once again by Cosimo I and underwent final alterations in the 19th century. Overall, the building preserves its original medieval shape, including a crenellated wall, but achieves the symmetry that is typical of Renaissance architecture.

VILLA MEDICEA DI CASTELLO

Via di Castello, 46–47, Castello; tel.: 055-452691; website: www.polomuseale .firenze.it; open: daily 8:15 A.M.–4:30 P.M. (Jan.–Feb., Nov.–Dec.), 8:15 A.M.–5:30 P.M. (Mar.), 8:15 A.M.–6:30 P.M. (Apr.–May, Sept.–Oct.), 8:15 A.M.–7:30 P.M. (Jun.–Aug.) (villa and park); closed: second and third Mon. of each month and holidays; admission: free.

⏃ DIRECTIONS: Follow directions for the Villa Medicea della Petraia (see pg. 256). Continue on Via della Petraia, then turn left onto Via di Castello.

➢ This villa, one of the most beloved residences of the Medici family, lies on the top of a hill where an old cistern— *castellum*, in Latin—once stood and which gave name to the surrounding area. The commissioned artist Niccolò Tribolo to change its height and decorate its facade with a sequence of new windows. The central rusticated portal and the balcony above it were added later, probably during the renovation by Bernardo Buontalenti. On the first floor of the villa, in what used to be the guard's room, is a fresco by Baldassare Franceschini Volterrano, called *The Allegory of Sleep and Vigilance.* However, the interior of the building, which, since 1974, has been occupied by the literary institution the Accademia della Crusca, cannot be visited, except for its small museum (see pg. 264).

Behind the villa lies a beautiful garden, also commissioned by Cosimo as a symbol of the duchy and a commemoration to his family. Unfortunately, not much remains of the original path designed by Niccolò Tribolo and Benedetto Varchi, which initially started at the highest point of the garden (in order to reach it, follow the drive that begins at the entrance gate on the right side of the building). In a pond surrounded by cypress trees and helm oaks is a statue by Bartolomeo Ammanati (c. 1563) that represents either the Apennine mountains or the month of January (when Cosimo became a duke). In the villa's Italian-style garden is a very

peculiar man-made cave—the Grotta degli Animali—started by Tribolo and completed by different artists under the supervision of Giorgio Vasari. The structure and embellishments, consisting of shells, stalactites, and calcareous decorations, together with the two basins containing marine animals, are all Tribolo's work. The vast range of stone animals, are by various artists, including Bartolomeo Ammannati, Antonio and Stoldo Lorenzi, and Giambologna. Water from the main basin once flowed into the grotto, giving life to the spurts in the two artificial basins, and then carried on irrigating the gardens.

In the central axis of the garden there is also another work by Tribolo, the Fountain of Hercules and Antaeus, with an octagonal basin and two circular shallow dishes placed on a marble stem and adorned with putti. The top part of the fountain was once adorned with sculptures of Hercules crushing Antaeus by Bartolomeo Ammannati, made between 1558 and 1559, as an allusion to Cosimo's victory against the enemies of the Medicis.

Villa Medicea di Castello

Itinerary:

Russian Grandeur Meets Florentine Taste

By Stacy Meichtry

S esto Fiorentino has long been considered more of a reference point for some other destination than an important town in itself. Along the Roman road to Pistoia, it marked a sixth (*sesto,* in Italian) of the distance traveled from Florence.

Amid the sea of signs along the Viale Milton, a curious quintet of muscovite cupolas rise up, marking the way to Sesto Fiorentino. The bulbous domes, in swirling patterns of green, purple, and yellow ceramic shingles, are set on candlestick-like bases and belong to Italy's first **Russian Orthodox Church**. Designed by Michail Preobrasheniskij in 1883, the church marks a coming of age for the Russian community in Florence. After nearly a century of worship in family chapels and embassy churches, Russian aristocrats and artists built a monument to their faith. It was completed in 1902.

A glittering mosaic depicting Znamenie, or the Mother of God, just beyond the church's intricately designed wrought iron gates, leads to the upper floor of the two-story church. While adhering to the Byzantine vision of a church as an "incarnation of heaven on earth," the inside of which should encapsulate the entire span of history, Preobrasheniskij's design for the interior also needed to instruct Roman Catholic Florentines on the peculiarities of orthodoxy. Hence, the iconic frescoes covering the walls and ceilings depict scenes from the Life of Christ, as well as an iconic rendering of Photius, defender of orthodox purity. The iconostasis, depicting Saint Lawrence, Saint Stephen, and Saint Nicholas, dominates the quadrangular plan of the church.

The lower level is luxuriously furnished with wood-carved iconastases donated by the Demidoff family upon their relocation to the Medici Villa of Pratolino in 1879. The pieces had originally occupied the chapel of the family's former residence in San Donato. In acquiring the former Medici property, the Russian prince Pavel Demidoff secured his place near the top of Florence's expatriate aristocracy. His investment in the Orthodox church, meanwhile, affirmed him a place within the greater Russian community.

Expatriate communities, like that lead by the Demidoffs, found their footing just as Florence's native aristocracy was on its last leg. Evidence of this fall can be seen in the **Villa La Quiete**, where Anna Maria Luisa, the last leaf on the Medici family tree, sought succor after the death of her beloved father, Grand Duke Cosimo III, in 1723.

OUR PICK

Nestled in the hills of Castello, a small village that borders Sesto Fiorentino on one side and Florence on the other, the villa provided Anna Maria with a creative outlet of sorts. Over a string of "spiritual retreats," which she spent at La Quiete, she took to carving an immense Renaissance-style garden out of Castello's grassy slopes. Stretching her sadness over an expanse of geometrical hedges, box bushes, and cypress trees, Anna Maria pushed her garden all the way to the edge of the property line, where its stone walls currently crumble.

But long before she decided to make the villa her home away from home, La Quiete had been an emblem of Medici glory. Pier Francesco de' Medici purchased the estate roughly a decade after its construction in 1438, turning it into yet another reservoir for the dynasty's burgeoning art collection.

Among the works currently held inside are a glazed terra-cotta lunette by Giovanni della Robbia depicting the Doubting Thomas, a panel illustrating the wedding of Saint Catherine of Alexandria by Rodolfo Ghirlandaio, and the *Coronation of the Virgin* by the workshop of Sandro Botticelli. La Quiete derives its name from a fresco Giovanni da San Giovanni executed for the villa's upper floor, *The Quiet that Calms the Wind*.

The **Villa Ginori** was built in the span of history between the decline of the Medici family and the beginning of French occupation. Located in the hills of Doccia, just north of Sesto Fiorentino, the villa was transformed from a country home into a full-scale porcelain factory in 1737 by its owner, the Marquis Carlo Andrea Ginori. From its very beginning, Ginori envisioned his villa as a place of enterprise rather than retreat. Using examples from the Medici art collection, Ginori stamped scaled-down reproductions of the Renaissance's greatest hits onto the precious pottery and then sold them as rare art objects. In the years that followed, his successors would one-up him, borrowing archetypal images from the Orient, as well as from the Renaissance and baroque eras, and stamping them on teacups and tray tables to be delivered to the dinner tables of high society.

When train tracks reached Sesto Fiorentino in the 19th century, the Ginori enterprise relocated from the hilltop to the train depot. New methods of distribution created new demand among different classes. The best-selling tulip pattern underwent constant redesign to keep up with the changing tastes of the continent, while requests for virtuoso creations like Gaspero Bruschi's three-foot porcelain fireplace (1754) petered out. Both the fireplace and some 20 versions of tulip-patterned wares are on display at the **Museo delle Porcellane di Doccia**, on the hilltop just above the train tracks, off Viale Pratese.

The museum can be visited by appointment for anyone interested in the evolution of the Ginori brand. In the museum's second-floor gallery are porcelain specimens drawn from the baroque, rococo, neoclassical, art nouveau, and art deco periods. Works of modernist Giò Ponti, a Ginori designer, are also represented.

Among the few centrally located, historically pertinent properties to survive the Ginori expansion is the **Villa Guicciardini Corsi Salviati**, now owned by the University of Michigan. It was built in 1502, although the baroque facade that stretches along Via Antonio Gramsci is the fruit of renovations that took place between 1632 and 1736. These renovations radically altered the villa's relationship with the outside world, creating a giant barrier to conceal its luxurious gardens from traffic along the viale.

Villa Guicciardini Corsi Salviati

For an idea of how the villa must have looked at its conception, visit its ground-floor studio, where Alessandro Fei del Barbiere frescoed his *Views of the Villa* in 1570. These ceiling frescoes depict the Villa Guicciardini Corsi Salviati free of its current confines: a domestic landscape that harmoniously blends with its natural surroundings.

Missing from these depictions is the Teatro della Limonaia, a 17th-century open-air theater that stretches between the villa and the Italian gardens in an expanse of low-cut grass, lined by potted lemon trees. The Limonaia's basic design takes its inspiration from 16th-century amphitheaters like the one in the Giardino di Boboli, where Giacomo Corsi, Villa Guicciardini's first owner, supposedly conducted some of the very first operas in conjunction with the illustrious Camerata dei Bardi.

The rest of the garden, planted in 1740, is threaded with gravel paths and spiraling hedges. Within this network, plots of daisies bloom in orange, allegorical statues of vegetation rise in various stages of decay, and a central fountain nonchalantly trickles away as ducklings wander in and out of a lily-covered pond.

FURTHER INFORMATION

Sesto Fiorentino is the final stop on ATAF bus #27, which originates in Florence at Piazza della Stazione. By car, from the Fortezza da Basso in Florence, take Via dello Statuto and continue north through Via Guasti, Via Gianni, Via Tavanti, Via Vittorio, Via Reginaldo Giuliani, and Via Antonio Gramsci.

Museo delle Porcellane di Doccia (Porcelain Museum of Doccia)

Viale Pratese, 31, Sesto Fiorentino; tel.: 055-4207767; open: Wed.–Sat. 10 A.M.–1 P.M., 2–6 P.M.; admission: €6.

⬈ DIRECTIONS: From Piazzale Porta al Prato in Florence take Viale Belfiore, then turn left onto Viale Francesco Redi. After the bridge, Ponte di San Donato, turn right onto Via Enrico Forlanini and then left onto Viale Alessandro Guidoni. After 200 yards, turn right onto Via Umberto Maddalena and continue on Via di Caciolle. Pass Piazza Enrico Mattei and continue on the left onto Via Panciatichi (later Via de Perfetti Ricasoli). After some 350 yards, turn right on Via Pietro Fanfani, continue on Via del Sodo, then turn left on Via Sestese. Continue until you reach Via Antonio Gramsci, and then continue straight to Viale Pratese.

Russian Orthodox Church

Via Leone X, 8, Florence; tel.: 055-490148; open: Mon.–Fri. 4–7 P.M., Sat. 6–8 P.M., Sun. 10 A.M.–1 P.M. (subject to change).

Villa Ginori

Via Doccia, 3, Sesto Fiorentino; open: contact the Museo delle Porcellane di Doccia at tel. 055-4207767; admission: free.

⬈ DIRECTIONS: Follow directions for the Museo delle Porcellane di Doccia. From Via Antonio Gramsci turn right onto Via Santa Caterina, then right again onto Via Carlo Pisacane, and left onto Piazza San Francesco. Continue for about 150 yards, then take the first left onto Via Nazario Sauro, then right onto Via Cesare Battisti, and right again on Via di Colonnata. Take Via Carlo Cafiero, turn left onto Via Camillo

Benso Conte di Cavour, and then take Via Vittorino da Feltre, through Piazza Mario Rapisardi and Piazza San Romolo. Take Via Ginori, turn right on Via Giotto, and right again on Via Nino Bixio. Take Via delle Porcellane, then Via della Fabbrica. Turn right on Via del Tiglio and then left on Via Doccia.

Villa Guicciardini Corsi Salviati

Via Antonio Gramsci, 426, Sesto Fiorentino; tel.: 055-443778; fax: 055-2346863; open: villa closed to the public, garden can be visited with faxed request.

⬈ DIRECTIONS: Follow directions for the Museo delle Porcellane di Doccia.

Villa La Quiete

Via di Boldrone, 2, Florence; tel.: 055-450634; open: by appointment only via faxed request (contact the University of Florence at fax: 055-2757429, attention Prof. Augusto Marinelli).

⬈ DIRECTIONS: From the Fortezza da Basso in Florence take Via dello Statuto. It will turn into Via Guasti after Piazza Muratori, Via Gianni after Piazza G. Viesseux, and Via Tavanti after Piazza Leopoldo. Toward the end it bends to the left: turn with it and you will find yourself on Via Vittorio Emanuele II. Continue to Piazza Dalmazia, then turn right onto Viale G. B. Morgagni. Once at Largo G. A. Brambilla, turn right and you will reach Largo Palagi. Turn left onto Viale Pieraccini, and then left onto Via delle Oblate. Continue until you cross a small bridge, and turn right onto Via della Quiete. Take the first street on your right, Via Pietro Dazzi, and continue to the first street on your right, Via di Boldrone.

FOCUS: Museo Stibbert

Via Federico Stibbert, 26, Florence; tel. 055-475520; website: www.museostibbert.it; open: Mon.–Wed. 10 A.M.–2 P.M., Fri.–Sun. 10 A.M.–6 P.M. (last admission one hour before closing); closed: Thurs., Jan. 1, Easter, May 1, Aug. 15, Dec. 25; admission: €6.

⌖DIRECTIONS: From Piazza della Libertà (Porta San Gallo) in Florence take Via del Ponte Rosso, turn left onto Via XX Settembre, and right again on Via Vittorio Emanuele II. After about 1/2 mile, turn right onto Via Federico Stibbert. The museum is on your right.

By Stacy Meichtry

Despite its warlike ramparts and insuperable retaining walls, the complex at the top of Via Federico Stibbert is neither a fortress nor a castle. It belongs, rather, to the legacy of Frederick Stibbert, a collector of armor and weaponry, who, in 1891, transformed his country home into the Museo Stibbert, with roughly 50,000 objects in 60 rooms.

Dubbed a "man of exceptional talent" on road signs directing traffic to the museum, Stibbert went to extraordinary lengths to put his collection on display, fashioning thematic settings specific to each of his armories. Thus, antique mannequins with distinctly Asiatic features brandish samurai swords and spears in a salon dedicated to Japanese armory, while their Arab counterparts march through mosquelike interiors dedicated to Middle Eastern armory.

The latter collection apparently takes its inspiration from Stibbert's grandfather, the governor of Bengal, who commanded the armed forces of the East India Company in the 18th century. These military campaigns produced spoils large enough to create an expansive fortune for the Stibbert family.

After inheriting this fortune at 22, Stibbert discovered his talents as a collector. He began by amassing pieces from 16th- and 17th-century Italian and German armor, which the museum currently displays in fully assembled suits, mounted on model horses that line the vaulted corridors. The surrounding walls are studded with a relentless barrage of helmets, stirrups, and breast plates of every possible size and shape. A black suit of armor, behind a wall of glass near the front of the procession, belonged to Giovanni delle Bande Nere, a 15th-century mercenary. The Cavalcade Room includes a procession of Italian and German knights and a procession of Ottoman knights from the 16th to 18th centuries. There are also examples of Indian arms and armor (hall 8) and a painting of a group of Japanese samurais (hall 50).

The last part of the museum features the family furniture, an interesting collection of 16th- and 17th-century costumes, and a collection of 14th- to 17th-century paintings by Luca Giordano, Carlo Crivelli, Neri di Bicci, and Pietro Lorenzetti. The highlights among these include a Virgin and child, attributed to Sandro Botticelli, and a portrait of Francesco de' Medici, attributed to Bronzino.

Other Points of Interest

Tomba Etrusca della Montagnola (Etruscan Tombs of Motagnola)

Via Fratelli Rosselli, 95, Sesto Fiorentino; tel.: 055-448451; open: call ahead.

⤴ DIRECTIONS: From the Fortezza da Basso in Florence take Via dello Statuto. It will turn into Via Guasti after Piazza Muratori, Via Gianni after Piazza Viesseux, and Via Tavanti after Piazza Leopoldo. Toward the end it bends toward the left: turn with it and you will find yourself on Via Vittorio Emanuele II. Follow it for about 50 yards and then turn right onto Via Celso and right again onto Via Taddeo Alderotti. When you reach Via del Garbo, turn left; this road will turn into Via Santo Stefano in Pane. Continue until you find Via Reginaldo Giuliani on the right. Turn right on Via XX Settembre and right again on Via Fratelli Rosselli.

➤ Dating all the way back to the 6th or 7th century B.C., this Etruscan tomb has earned the love and affection of Florentines for its unique underground roofing system. It was discovered in 1959 by local researchers and was named *"la montagnola"* ("the little mountain") because it was found under a tumulus shaped as a natural hill. The corridor that leads down into the crypt is flanked by

mammoth monolithic stones, which meet at the top to form a pointed roof. The crypt itself is a work of collective genius. It features a small dome of stacked concentric circles, supported by a solitary pillar.

Villa Corsini a Castello

Via della Petraia, 38; tel.: 055-450752; open: temporarily closed.

⤴ DIRECTIONS: Follow directions for the Villa Medicea della Petraia (see pg. 256).

➤ Originally built between the 15th and 16th centuries, this baroque villa was renovated by Antonio Maria Ferri between 1698 and 1699. The facade is decorated with pillars that slightly project from the wall and a clock with garlands and stuccoes. Frescoes depicting subjects of life in the countryside and white stucco ornaments adorn the ceiling of the reception hall, an area that can only be visited with authorization from the local Archaeological Superintendent. Through the loggia you can access an impressive Four Seasons Garden at the back of the house, with statues in *pietra serena* representing the different seasons.

Museums

Museo dell'Accademia della Crusca (Museum of the Crusca Academy)

Via di Castello, 46, Castello; tel.: 055-454277; open: guided tours by appointment only; admission: free.

⤴ DIRECTIONS: Follow directions for the Villa Medicea della Petraia (see pg. 256). Continue on Via della Petraia, then turn left onto Via di Castello.

➤ The offices of the Accademia della Crusca, founded in 1583, have been housed in the Villa di Medicea Castello (a home of the Medici family) since 1974. The Accademia was founded to publish the *Vocabolario*, Italy's version of the *Oxford English Dictionary*, meant to standardize proper Italian language. The small museum exhibits objects, manuscripts, and portraits of illustrious academics. Particularly interesting is the collection of side tables painted with various quotes from the scholars of the Crusca academy.

Villa Corsini a Castello

Residence Leopoldo

Via Fabroni, 68; tel.: 055-4630811; category: ★★; number of rooms: 25 studios; credit cards accepted: all major; facilities: air-conditioning, TV, direct-dial telephone, covered garage; access to internet: no; €.

⌖ DIRECTIONS: From the Fortezza da Basso in Florence take Via dello Statuto. It will turn into Via Guasti after Piazza Muratori and Via Gianni after Piazza G. Viesseux. Turn right onto Piazza Leopoldo. Take your first right onto Via Fabroni. The Residence Leopoldo is on the right.

☛While situated in a quiet, residential neighborhood, the Residence Leopoldo does not sacrifice location for tranquility. It is a stone's throw from the Fortezza da Basso, and a hop, skip, and a jump away from Via Bolognese. The complex is composed of various one-bedroom apartments, each with a kitchen and terrace.

Villa Villoresi

Via Ciampi, 2, Colonnata (Sesto Fiorentino); tel.: 055-443212; fax: 055-442063; website: www.ila-chateau.com/villores; e-mail: civillor@tin.it; category: ★★★; number of rooms: 28, plus 5 suites; credit cards accepted: all major; access to internet: yes; €€–€€€.

⌖ DIRECTIONS: From the Fortezza da Basso in Florence take Via dello Statuto. It will turn into Via Guasti after Piazza Muratori, Via Gianni after Piazza G. Viesseux, and Via Tavanti after Piazza Leopoldo. Toward the end it bends toward the left: turn with it and you will find yourself on Via Vittorio Emanuele II. Follow it for about 50 yards and then turn right into Via Celso and right again onto Via Taddeo Alderotti. Keep on this road until you reach Via del Garbo, which turns into Via Santo Stefano in Pane. Turn left and follow it until you find Via Reginaldo Giuliani on the right. After less than a mile, turn onto Via Antonio Gramsci. This will lead to a roundabout, from which you turn right onto Via I Maggio. Follow this street until you reach Via Carlo Cafiero, on the left. At the junction at the end of it, turn right onto Via del Cuoco. Via Carlo Ciampi is on the right along this road.

☛A 12th-century fortress transformed into a country home during the Renaissance, these days the Villa Villoresi offers an ideal spot for tourists to relax just outside of bustling Florence. The interior has a beautiful range of frescoed ceilings, allegoric or panoramic murals, and portraits of ancestors hanging on the walls, as well as the longest loggia in Tuscany, which runs through the whole length of the second floor. A few bedrooms are of enormous dimensions, and the gallery in the house offers an impressive sight. If in need, Signora Villoresi can provide you with helpful advice on cultural sightseeing. Italian cooking lessons are also available.

Restaurants & Cafés

Dulcamara

Via Dante da Castiglione, 2, Sesto Fiorentino; tel.: 055-4255021; website: www.ristorantedulcamara.it; e-mail: info@usodicucina.it; open: Tues.–Sun. 7:30–11:30 P.M.; closed: Mon.; credit cards accepted: all major; €.

⌖DIRECTIONS: From the Fortezza da Basso in Florence take Via dello Statuto. It will turn into Via Guasti after Piazza Muratori, Via Gianni after Piazza G. Viesseux, and Via Tavanti after Piazza Leopoldo. Toward the end it bends toward the left: turn with it and you will be on Via Vittorio Emanuele II. At Piazza Dalmazia take Via Reginaldo Giuliani. Take the first right onto Via delle Panche and then turn right onto Via delle Gore. Stay on this for about two miles (direction Serpiolle-Cercina). The restaurant is in the first house you will find in Cercina, in a red villa behind a gate.

☛Set in the countryside but only about 15 minutes by taxi from Florence, it has a beautiful garden and is worth the trip on a summer evening. The food is Tuscan but with inventive twists, such as tortelli with fava beans and pecorino cheese and tagliette with tuna.

North of Florence

Itinerary:

Up Via Bolognese: Expatriate
Acquisitions of Medici Glory

By Stacy Meichtry

Arco Trionfale dei Lorena

The triumphal arch that dominates Piazza della Libertà in Florence seems appropriate enough. It stands in a square designed in 1865 upon the unification of Italy under the House of Savoy, which ostensibly "liberated" its people from foreign rule. In accordance with the parameters of nationalistic ornamentation, a melee of marble statuary gallops over the ocher horizon of the arch to announce the birth of Italy's nationhood and the selection of Florence as its provisional capital.

And yet the arch is not dedicated to the Savoy, nor does it have anything to do with liberty. Its dedication belongs to François Stephan of the House of Lorraine, the first foreign duke to rule Florence. When French architect Jean-Nicholas Jadot unveiled his creation to the public on January 20, 1739, it was noted that the

Garden at Villa La Pietra

arch rested outside the city walls, just 100 feet beyond Porta San Gallo, so as not to provoke the resentment of an already restless native population.

While the eventual incorporation of the **Arco Trionfale dei Lorena** into the nationalistic framework of Piazza della Libertà satisfied certain aesthetic needs, it did not overwrite the historical shift to which the arch originally bore witness. The arrival of the Lorraine dynasty definitively marked the decline of the Florentine aristocracy, a recession that even nationalistic pride failed to arrest. The Medici line had worn itself out by the time Anna Maria Ludovica, its last descendant, died in 1743, and the network of wealthy families that initially prospered during the rise of the Medici clan now crumbled along with it. Palatial villas fell into decay, and illustrious art collections were sold off en masse.

On the receiving end of this liquidation were many foreign aristocrats, Anglophones, in particular, who found themselves in a position to acquire Florentine culture piecemeal, through the individual purchases of valuable artworks, and fill the aristocratic vacuum that the fallen Medici family had created. They colonized the Florentine hillsides, moving their fortunes into the dilapidated estates and restoring these properties to "authentic" Renaissance form. With this backdrop in place, they could immerse themselves in the respective roles of Renaissance dukes or duchesses.

Few families put this lifestyle into practice quite as literally as the Actons, who transformed their villa into a hub for high-society eccentrics: a place where expatriates convened for garden parties in full Renaissance costume one night, Persian the next. In 1903, Arthur Acton, a British-born artist and collector, relocated to the **Villa La Pietra** with his wife, Hortense, the daughter of a wealthy Chicago banker, and his two sons, Harold and William. In purchasing the estate, the Actons inherited the legacy of its 15th-century owners, the Sassetti family. But while Francesco Sassetti, the lynchpin of the Medici bank, directed the initial construction of the villa, it was Arthur Acton who returned the villa to its original luster.

OUR PICK

The gates to Villa La Pietra lie precisely one mile beyond Porta San Gallo in Piazza della Libertà on Via Bolognese. In fact, the name of the estate, "The Stone Villa," derives from the conception of the villa as Florence's glorious "mile-stone." From these gates, a corridor of cypresses descends from Via Bolognese and rises to frame a baroque facade at its opposite end. This viale, a tree-lined avenue typi-cal of the Renaissance, was added by Acton himself and offers a first glimpse into the principles that governed him in his unique treat-ment of space outside the home.

Inside the home, Acton the collector was meticulous in his pre-sentation of valuable objects. The furniture that fills the dining room,

The Appennino *in Villa Demidoff*

for instance, is coordinated with the works that hang on the walls, guiding the eye toward *The Adoration* by Vasari and Donatello's marble relief of the Madonna and child in a most aesthetically pleasing manner.

Outside the home, Acton the gardener applied the same principles to exert a similar level of control over perspective. The garden flows from behind the villa in a succession of "rooms," which Acton carved out of cypress, umbrella pine, and laurel trees, furnishing them with topiary sofas fashioned from geometrically carved boxwood and punctuating the entire ensemble with the occasional fountain. In the *teatrino,* a two-tiered lawn where the Actons once held amateur theatricals, the rounded box bushes at the edge of the upper tier, or "stage," evoke the presence of footlights, while lateral rows of cypresses double for "wings."

With these horticultural "rooms" in place, the panoramic views of Florence that border the estate to the southwest are not allowed to dominate the scenery but are, instead, harnessed and presented like any other object in Acton's art collection. As Vasari's oil-on-panel hangs in the dining room, Brunelleschi's cupola sprouts up beyond the garden, framed by cypress rows and rotting statues.

The **Villa Demidoff** is buried too deeply down Via Bolognese to incor-porate the Florentine skyline into its mise-en-scène. Fortunately for the Russian prince Pavel Demidoff, who purchased this former Medici villa in 1872, the estate came complete with its own Renaissance monuments. Unfortunately for Demidoff, these works represented only a fraction of the park that was once considered a true masterpiece of Tuscan mannerism.

Built by Bernardo Buontalenti in the 16th century, the estate's palatial villa, then known as the Villa di Pratolino, for the name of this suburban area, quickly fell into ruin when the Lorraine family abandoned the property following their succession of the Medici. In the 19th century, Ferdinando III of Lorraine turned the attention back to the dilapidated villa only to demolish it in preparation for his own artistic project: a hackneyed version of an English romantic park.

Upon taking over the grounds, Demidoff converted the servant's quarters, which had somehow survived Ferdinando's ruthless artistry, into a villa fit for a prince. He also devoted his labors to restoring those mannerist works spared by Ferdinando's campaign. These include Buontalenti's chapel, whose innovative design features a missile-shaped dome skirted by a hexagonal portico, under which servants could attend mass.

Among the series of grottoes executed by Giambologna, as the Flemish artist Jean de Boulogne was known in Italy, to complement the exterior of the original Medici villa, only the Laghetto della maschera (Fish Pond of the Mask) remains intact. The pond, which currently holds waters worthy of a swamp, was originally designed as a type of swimming pool where hot baths could be taken. The pond earns its name from the gentleman wearing a ghastly facial expression at its far end.

Giambologna saved his finest efforts for the *Appennino,* the colossal stone statue that forms the centerpiece of the Villa Demidoff. Carved between 1579 and 1580, the crestfallen giant crouches amid a shallow skyline of oak trees. A shock of white granite against a background of black foliage, the *Appennino* is pitted against the flow of nature itself, his efforts to rise to his feet thwarted by the weight of his overgrown beard.

Further Information

Arco Trionfale dei Lorena
Piazza della Libertà, Florence.

Villa Demidoff
Via Fiorentina, 282, Pratolino; tel.: 055-409427/409155; open: Sun. 10 a.m.–8 p.m. (Mar. and Oct.); Thurs.–Sun. 10 a.m.–8 p.m. (Apr.–Sept.); closed: Nov.–Feb.; admission: €3.
⬈DIRECTIONS: From Piazza della Libertà (Porta San Gallo) in Florence take Via del Ponte Rosso, which turns into Via Bolognese. Before Pratolino you will see Via Fiorentina and the Villa Demidoff on the right side. You can also take ATAF bus No. 25/A from Piazza della Stazione in Florence.

Villa La Pietra
Via Bolognese, 120, Florence; tel.: 055-50071; open: guided tours by appointment only; admission: free.
⬈DIRECTIONS: From Piazza della Libertà (Porta San Gallo) in Florence take Via del Ponte Rosso, which will turn into Via Bolognese. You can also take ATAF bus No. 25/A from Piazza della Stazione in Florence.

FOCUS: Convento di Monte Senario

Via Monte Senario, 3474, Vaglia; tel.: 055-406441; open: daily 7 A.M.–12:30 P.M., 3–8 P.M.; admission: free.

⤢ DIRECTIONS: From Piazza della Libertà (Porta San Gallo) in Florence take Via del Ponte Rosso, which will turn into Via Bolognese (Strada Statale 65, or SS 65). This leads toward San Piero a Sieve. Continue on SS 65 until you reach the area of Pratolino. At the top of the hill turn right, following Via da Bivigliano in the direction of Monte Senario. Continue on this road (do not turn left toward Bivigliano) until you reach a triple crossroad. Continue straight, uphill, until you reach the convent.

By Stacy Meichtry

Via da Bivigliano is a backwoods road that branches off of Via Bolognese a couple of miles north of Florence, just after the town of Pratolino. Its sun-dappled pavement threads through dense patches of woods, dashes through intermittent fields of wheat, and scales a decisive hillside before coming to a most natural and logical conclusion: the Convento di Monte Senario.

Framed by Pompilio Ticciati's twin statues of Saint Filippo Benizi and Saint Bonfiglio Monaldi, the convent's rustic skyline looms over the Sieve Valley like a hilltop fort. Beyond the Ticciati sentinels stretches a broad piazza that surrounds the complex and offers 360-degree panoramas of Sieve's arcadian expanse. The brief flight of stairs at the center of the square leads up to yet another piazza, above which the facade to the Church of the Adoration rises.

Founded as early as 1412, the church was completely rebuilt in 1717 according to the baroque sensibilities of prolific Florentine architect G. B. Foggini. The portico, which dominates the facade, and the posterior 17th-century bell tower are the only structures to survive these renovations. The interior presents a sumptuous nave soberly trimmed in baroque trademarks. Among these are the frosted cherubs that hover about Antonio Domenico Gabbiani's monumental fresco, *The Assumption of Mary*.

The Oratory of San Filippo Benizzi, the oldest section of the convent, is located behind the altar, to the right to the sacristy. It is here that the Virgin Mary supposedly appeared to the founders of the order in 1240, thus planting the spiritual seed of Monte Senario and inspiring a second name for the oratory: the Chapel of the Apparition. In the sacristy, note yet another *Assumption of the Virgin*, an oil-on-panel by Giuseppe Bezzuoli (1849).

The cloisters, accessed through the elegant clock tower to the right of the church facade, also belonged to the convent's medieval nucleus, but the majority of its decorations are as recent as the 17th century. Among these is a sober lunette by Jacopo Vignali depicting the Pilgrims of Emmaus.

Convento di Monte Senario

Other Points of Interest

PIEVE DI SANT'ANDREA A CERCÌNA

Via Dante da Castiglione 32, Cercìna (commune of Sesto Fiorentino); tel.: 055-402006; open: call ahead for hours.
⊘ DIRECTIONS: From Piazza della Libertà (Porta San Gallo) in Florence take Via del Ponte Rosso, which will turn into Via Bolognese. Turn left onto Pian di San Bartolo and continue for 2 1/2 miles until you see the sign for the Pieve.

➤ Documented as early as 880, this Romanesque church is presently defined by its 15th-century portico and imposing bell tower. Baroque renovations have covered up much of the interior's original medieval decoration with richly coffered ceilings. The right aisle, however, terminates in a typical Romanesque apse that harmoniously frames a fresco of Saints Jerome, Barbara, and Antonio Abate, executed in 1562 by Renaissance master Domenico Ghirlandaio and his brother David. At the end of the left aisle is the parish's venerated polychrome statue of the Madonna. It was carved in wood sometime between the 12th and 13th centuries.

VILLA SALVIATI

Via Salviati, Florence; open: closed to the public.
⊘ DIRECTIONS: From Piazza della Libertà (Porta San Gallo) in Florence take Via del Ponte Rosso, which will turn into Via

Villa Salviati

Bolognese. Turn right on Via Salviati. You will find the villa on your right.

➤ A 14th-century castle converted into a 15th-century villa by Giuliano da Sangallo, the Villa Salviati boasts one of the most palatial interiors on the hillsides north of Florence. The ornate sgraffiti designs that decorate the villa's internal courtyard were executed by Giovan Francesco Rustici around the time of the Sangallo renovation. Rustici also had a hand in the decoration of the villa chapel, authoring the grotesques and medallions along the nave, as well as the marble bas-reliefs depicting the Annunciation and the Madonna and child.

HOTELS & INNS

Hotel Villa Demidoff

Via San Jacopo, 51A, Pratolino; tel.: 055-409772; website: www.hotel-demidoff.it; category: ★★★★; number of rooms: 98; credit cards accepted: all major; access to internet: yes; facilities: free parking, swimming pool; €€.
⊘ DIRECTIONS: From Piazza della Libertà (Porta San Gallo) in Florence take Via del Ponte Rosso, which will turn into Via Bolognese (Strada Statale 65, or SS 65). Take

SS 65 for about eight miles until you reach Pratolino. Take the right turn toward Bivigliano. The Hotel Villa Demidoff is situated about a mile down this road.

➤ Located inside the Demidoff historic park, the Hotel Villa Demidoff comes equipped with 98 rooms, elevators for the disabled, and an indoor swimming pool. Concerts, performances for children, and other events are held here throughout the summer.

Hotel Villa Le Rondini

Via Bolognese Vecchia, 224, Trespiano; tel.: 055-400081; fax: 055-268212; website: www.villalerondini.it; e-mail: mailbox@villalerondini.it; category:★★★★; number of rooms: 30; credit cards accepted: all major; access to internet: no; facilities: swimming pool, tennis court; €€–€€€.

⚗ DIRECTIONS: From Piazza della Libertà (Porta San Gallo) in Florence take Via del Ponte Rosso, which will turn into Via Bolognese (SS 65). You will pass Via Salviati on the right and in the area of La Lastra, take a left onto Via Bolognese Vecchia. You can also take bus No. 25/A from Piazza della Stazione as above. Get off at the LA RAI stop.

☛A vast olive grove leads the way to this magnificent villa, with very easy access to the city of Florence (the bus stop is just in front of the villa's gate, and buses run every 20 minutes). The view of the city is beautiful, especially during the spring and early summer, when the countryside is in bloom. The guest rooms are distributed in three equally comfortable buildings, although the rooms in the two annexes are not as pretty as the ones located in the original villa.

Villa Campestri (Inn and Restaurant)

Via di Campestri, 19/22, Vicchio di Mugello; tel.: 055-8490107; fax: 055-8490108; website: www.villacampestri.com; category: ★★★★; number of rooms: 25; most beautiful rooms: 49, 59, and 60; credit cards accepted: all major; access to internet: yes; facilities: swimming pool; €€.

⚗ DIRECTIONS: From Piazza della Libertà (Porta San Gallo) in Florence take Viale Don Minzoni. From here follow directions toward Via Faentina. At Piazza delle Cure take Via Borghini and then turn right onto Via Faentina (toward the north). Continue along this road and pass the towns of Caldine, Olmo, Polcanto, and Faltona. Exit onto the road heading for Sagginale. Once you have passed the town of Sagginale, you will find, on the right, directions toward Campestri, Cistio, and Arliano. Take this road and stay on the right. Once past Cistio and Lastricata, you will arrive at Villa Campestri.

☛Once belonging to the famous Medici family, this villa is now a very pretty hotel overlooking the Mugello Valley. The interior is exquisitely decorated with antique furniture, and the bathrooms have all that one could wish for. Tuscan food is served, with the products coming directly from the villa's farm. The suites are suitable for families.

RESTAURANTS & CAFÉS

Ricchi

Via della Docciola, 14, Cercina; tel.: 055-402045; open: Tues. 7–10:30 P.M., Wed.–Sun. noon–2:30 P.M., 7–10:30 P.M.; closed: Mon.; credit cards accepted: major; €.

⚗ DIRECTIONS: From the Fortezza da Basso in Florence take Via dello Statuto. It will turn into Via Guasti after Piazza Muratori, Via Gianni after Piazza G. Viesseux, and Via Tavanti after Piazza Leopoldo. Toward the end it bends toward the left: turn with it and you will find yourself on Via Vittorio Emanuele II. At Piazza Dalmazia take Via Reginaldo Giuliani. Take the first right onto Via delle Panche and then turn right onto Via delle Gore. Stay on this road for about four miles (direction Serpiolle-Cercina) and you will reach Cercina. From there, follow the signs to the restaurant.

☛Located in the hills just outside Florence and with plenty of outdoor seating, this is the ideal place to go to get away from the hot city. Their specialty is the *ragnatela*, a technique for making battered, fried food look like it is covered in spiderwebs.

AIR TRAVEL

Aeroporto Amerigo Vespucci (also known as Peretola)

The airport is about 3 miles (5 kilometers) north of Florence. Tel.: 055-3061300, for general information; for arrival and departure information: 055-30615.

☛The biggest airlines that fly into Florence are Alitalia (tel.: 055-27881) and Meridiana (tel.: 055-2302314/199-111339). However, Peretola is a small airport and there are no intercontinental flights so if you are coming from outside Europe you must fly into Milan or Rome and then take a train or a connecting flight to Florence.

From Peretola to the center of Florence, a taxi ride takes about 30 minutes and costs about €20–€25. There is also a charge for luggage and an extra charge on Sundays and holidays.

A SITA bus leaves from the front of the airport and goes to the center of Florence. There is a bus every half hour between 5:30 A.M. and 11:30 P.M. The bus ride takes about 20 minutes, and you can buy the tickets, which cost €4, from the bar at the airport.

Lost Luggage

If you lose your baggage at the airport, call 055-3061302.

BICYCLE AND SCOOTER RENTALS

You need a credit card, passport, and cash deposit to rent a bicycle or scooter.

Alinari, Via San Zanobi, 38r; tel.: 055-280500. Bikes are €12–€18 a day depending on the type. Scooters are €30 a day for one person and €65 for two people.

Florence by Bike, Via San Zanobi, 120r; tel.: 055-488992. Bikes are €12–€23 a day depending on the type. Scooters start at €40 per day.

CARS

☛Car rentals are great for exploring the countryside, but not necessary for city driving. Rentals cost between €300 and €400 for a medium-sized car for a week.

Some major agencies are:
Avis, tel.: 06-65011531/199-100133
Hertz, tel.: 06-542941
Maggiore National, tel.: 06-65011508
Travel Car, tel.: 190-180180

You need a credit card, passport, and license to rent a car, and you must be at least 25 years old.

Driving in Italy is on the right and regulations are similar to those in the United States. There are certain towns where the horn is forbidden (this is indicated by a sign saying ZONA DI SILENZIO). Speed limits are 130 kph (80 mph) on the autostrade, or toll-highways, and between 70 and 90 kph (43 and 56 mph on toll-highways) on smaller roads unless otherwise marked. There are large fines for drinking and driving which may include the suspension of a license and the possibility of six months imprisonment. There is a network of autostrade (toll-highways) as well as superstrade (free expressways). When you enter an autostrade you are issued a ticket and you must return that ticket when you exit and pay a toll. On some shorter highways, a toll is paid on entry.

Gas stations on the autostrade are open 24 hours a day. Gas (benzina) generally costs over €1 per liter.

Autostrade Information: 06-43632121 (24 hours a day); website: www.autostrade.it.

CONSULATES

U.K. Consulate: Lungarno Corsini, 2; tel.: 055-284133; open: Mon.–Fri. 9:30 A.M.– 12:30 P.M., 2:30–4:30 P.M.
U.S. Consulate: Lungarno Amerigo Vespucci, 38; tel.: 055-266951; open: Mon.–Fri. 9 A.M.–12:30 P.M.

CREDIT CARDS

To report lost or stolen credit cards, call the appropriate number for your card carrier: American Express (800-874333); Master Card (800-870866); Visa (800-877232).

CURRENCY EXCHANGE

You can change currency at any bank or you can withdraw money from ATMs (there is usually a fee of $1–$5 for a withdrawal and a withdrawal limit of $500 per day). Most U.S., Canadian, or U.K. bank cards, MasterCards, and Visas can be used at ATMs in Florence.

CUSTOMS AND DUTIES

When shopping in Florence, keep receipts for all of your purchases. To get a V.A.T. (Value-Added Tax) refund (about 12% of the cost of your purchase), you must spend more than €150 at a store and request a V.A.T. form at the store where you purchase the goods. At the airport, get your form stamped by Italian customs, which will give you specific information about receiving your refund. If you paid by credit card, you will get the reimbursement credited to your account; if you paid by cash, you will get a check sent to your home address.

Residents of the U.K. do not have to pass through customs to reenter their home country.

Residents of the U.S. over the age of 21 can bring in 200 cigarettes, or 50 cigars, or 2 kilograms of tobacco; 1 liter of alcohol; and gifts worth $100. Prohibited items include meat products, seeds, and plants.

Residents of Canada can bring in C$500 worth of duty-free goods if they have been away for more than seven days, C$200 if they've been away between 48 hours and seven days, and C$50 for less than 48 hours.

GUIDED TOURS IN ENGLISH

Guided tours in English can be arranged Associazione Guide Turistiche di Firenze (contact) Nobel Viaggi, Borgo Ognissanti, 3r; tel.: 055-288633).

HOURS

Business hours vary depending on the stores and the season, but most stores are open Mon.– Sat. 9 or 9:30 A.M.–1 P.M. and then from 3:30 or 4 P.M. –7 or 7:30 P.M.

In more touristy areas of Florence, some stores stay open throughout lunch time and may be open for limited hours on Sunday. In general, stores in Florence are closed on Saturday afternoons in the summer and on Monday mornings in the winter.

Museum hours vary greatly, but most are open from 8:30 or 9 A.M.–5 or 6 P.M. without a break. It is best to call the museum to check the specific hours. Many museums are also closed one day a week, usually on Monday.

Banks are open weekdays 8:30 A.M.–1:30 P.M. and 2:45–3:45 P.M.

Churches are usually open from early morning until noon or 12:30 P.M. They open again in the afternoon until about 7 P.M. However, many churches in Florence do not have resident priests, so they are open inconsistently (as is noted in the guide). Major cathedrals are open all day.

INFORMATION BOOTHS

There are information stands (Informazione Turistiche) at Piazza Stazione, 4 (tel.: 055-212245), at Via Cavour, 1r (between Via Gori and Via Guelfa; tel.: 055-290832/ 290833), and at Borgo Santa Croce, 29r (tel.: 055-23404444). They have maps, bus and museum schedules, and information on guided tours. The people running the booths speak English.

INTERNET CAFÉS

Internet Train is one of the biggest Internet cafés in Florence and has locations near the Santa Maria Novella Station, the Dumo, and the Ponte Vecchio (tel.: 055-2654212). Cost is €3–€5 an hour (there are discounts for students).

Late-Night Pharmacies

Farmacia Comunale 13, in Santa Maria Novella Station; tel.: 055-216761; open: 24 hours.

Farmacia Molteni, Via dei Calzaiouli 7r; tel.: 055-215472; open: 24 hours

☛Other pharmacies rotate night and Sunday openings—look for the schedules posted on their doors.

Mail

☛Postcards and letters to the U.S. and Canada cost €0.77. Postcards and letters to the U.K. cost €0.44. You can buy stamps (francobolli) at tobacco stores (tabacchi), recognizable by the black "T" sign.

Post offices are open Mon.–Fri. 8:15 A.M.–1:30 P.M. and Sat. 8:30 A.M.–12:30 P.M.

Medical Care in English

☛The Associazione Volontari Ospedalieri (tel.: 055-2344567) is an organization with volunteer interpreters who speak French, German, or English and can clarify medical questions. The Tourist Medical Center has English- and French-speaking doctors (Via Lorenzo Il Magnifico, 59; tel: 055-475411).

Newspapers

☛Tuscany's main newspaper is *La Nazione*, but you can find the *International Herald Tribune* at most newsstands in town.

Passports and Visas

☛U.S. citizens do not need a visa to visit Italy unless they plan to stay longer than three months, in which case they must apply for a permesso di soggiorno. Contact the closest Italian consulate for further information. U.K. citizens only need a passport.

Pets

☛Most animals can enter Italy if they are accompanied by their owner and a certificate of good health issued by a certified veterinarian in the country of origin no more than 30 days before the departure date. These certificates are available on the internet (www.italemb.org) or can be requested from the closest Italian consulate. The certificate does not need to be authenticated by the embassy.

Religious Services

American Episcopal: Via Bernardo Rucellai, 9; tel.: 055-294417.

Church of England: Via Maggio, 16; tel.: 055-294764.

Synagogue: Via Luigi Farini, 4; tel.: 055-245252.

Methodist Church: Via de' Benci, 9; tel.: 055-288143.

Taxis

☛Only take official taxis, which are white and have a "Taxi" sign on the roof. There are added charges for baggage, for riding between 10 P.M. and 7 A.M., and for riding on Sundays and public holidays. When you call for a taxi they begin the meter from the moment you call so it may already be up to a few euro by the time it reaches you. Alternatively, you can get one at a taxi stand (you will find them at Santa Maria Novella Station and Piazza San Marco) or you can hail one (they will usually stop if empty). You do not need to tip unless you have baggage.

Radiotaxi, tel.: 055-4798/4242/4390.

Telephones

☛Telephone cards (carta telefonica) can be purchased at newsstands or tabacchi. To call the U.S. or Canada, dial 001 then the number. To call the U.K., dial 0044 then the number. To use a calling card, dial the international number for your calling card and you will be connected with an operator. (AT&T, tel.: 172-1011; MCI, tel.: 172-1022; and Sprint, tel.: 172-1877.)

Tipping

☛There is a service charge included in most restaurants, but it is customary to leave an additional 5–10% tip, depending on the quality of the service. We suggest a tip of 10% for a bill up to €50, and 5% over €50. Tip a chambermaid a minimum of €1 per day and the bellhop or porter €1 per bag. Tip €0.10 for drinks at the counter of a bar and €0.50 for a round of drinks.

Train Travel

For information on schedules and ticket costs, you can refer to www.ferroviedellostatio.it or call Information at 147888088 from 7 A.M. to 9 P.M.

☛There are a few types of trains on the Italian railway, Ferrovie dello Stato (FS). The fastest is the Eurostar, which operates on many main lines including Rome-Florence-Milan. Reservations are always advisable.

You can buy tickets in the ticket office, or biglietteria, or at one of the self-ticketing machines at the station. You can buy them at a travel agent with an FS sticker. Tickets can be purchased up to two months before travel but must be stamped immediately before boarding at the orange machines located at the beginning of the tracks. There is a fine for unstamped tickets.

There are two stations in Florence: Santa Maria Novella Station is the main one. It is located in the center of Florence, and trains from Paris and Frankfurt also stop there. Rifredi Station is at No. 1 Via dello Steccuto (about 2 miles/3 kilometers from Santa Maria Novella Station) and local trains and some Eurostars stop there.

Transportation around Florence

☛There is no metro in Florence, but the bus system is good and runs until 9:30 P.M., with some buses continuing until midnight. Bus tickets can be purchased at newsstands, bars, or tabacchi displaying the ATAF sign and cost €1 for one trip. You must validate the tickets by stamping them in the orange machine when you enter the bus; they expire one hour after they have been stamped. You can get routes and bus schedules from the ATAF office, or from the tourist office.

ATAF Ufficio Informazioni & Abbonamenti, Piazza della Stazione; tel.: 055-5650222/800-424500.

Acknowledgments

This has been the collective effort of the staff of the Italian supplement of the *International Herald Tribune,* many of its regular contributors, and a number of other people and entities.

I would like to thank all of the authors whose bylines appear in this guide-book; Alessandro Tortorici, Stacy Meichtry, and Alessandro Nanì for their photographs; Luisa Milanese for her research work, and, more importantly, for coordinating the work of our contributors; Sarah Leiwant, Ivan Carvalho, Sara Carobbi, Carla Rossi, and Rosanna Cirigliano for their contributions as researchers and writers; *la signora* Maddalena Gentile for pointing us to some of the most wonderful but lesser known architectural and artistic jewels of her beloved city; Linda Rauch, Riccardo Catola, and Lorenzo Villoresi for their excellent suggestions for our commercial listings; and Luigi Sinigaglia of LS Cartography for the beautiful maps.

I would also like to thank Ermanno Bonomi and the Azienda di Promozione Turistica of Florence (Via Manzoni 16; tel. 055-23320; fax 055-2346286; web site: www.pisoft.it/apt/apt.html). Mr. Bonomi and his team in the Image Division, led by Maurizio Paradisi, spent months working with and for us, providing an extraordinary amount of help in a short amount of time.

I also would like to thank Maurizio Bossi, head of the Centro Romantico, or Center for Studies on Romanticism and XIXth Century Civilization, of the Gabinetto Vieusseux, who selected the descriptions by famous authors on some of the most interesting sites in Florence.

Finally, I would like to thank art historian Lucia Bassignana who helped us devise our special itineraries and reviewed the entire manuscript for artistic and historical accuracy; graphic artist Lisa Vaughn; editorial assistant Tiffany Sprague; editor Tricia Levi; and the series editor Isabel Venero.

Claudio Gatti
Editorial Director

CONTRIBUTORS

Rosanna Cirigliano is an American journalist, writer, and publisher who lives in Florence. A graduate of Boston University, she wrote a daily column in English for the Tuscan pages of *La Repubblica* for several years and her articles have appeared in the Italian supplement of the *International Herald Tribune* and the *European,* as well as nationally circulated periodicals in Italy and Israel. Author of five travel books on American cities and one on California, in collaboration with the photographer Andrea Pistolesi, she also wrote *Studying in Florence: A Guide.* Her company, Magenta Editrice, publishes *Vista, Florence & Tuscany,* a quarterly English-language magazine that provides a panorama of the region's culture and cultural events in addition to *Month by Month,* an electronic newsletter reporting on local current events. *A Guide to the Pistoia Province* is slated for publication in 2003.

Olivia Ironside graduated from St. Martins School of Art and Design in 1998. After completing her degree, she decided to stay in London and began working as a photographer/writer. Interested in London life, she set about recording contemporary streetlife and began freelancing as a writer for various publications while exhibiting her photographic work in and around London. Here she met Alessandro Nanì, an Italian photographer who she began to work with regularly. They moved to Florence in 2000 and set up Oxygen, a photographic studio that was to become their base for the following three years. Olivia recently returned to the UK where she continues to freelance as a writer and photographer.

Sarah Rose Leiwant, a graduate of Wesleyan University, has been living in Italy for the past two years. She first fell in love with Florence when she studied there for her junior year semester abroad. She has written a number of travel articles for the Italian supplement of the *International Herald Tribune.*

Stacy Meichtry is the assistant editor of *Bell'Italia magazine,* an art and travel publication devoted to Italy. In 2001 he received his B.A. from New York University, where he studied both at the university's Casa Italiana in New York and the Villa La Pietra in Florence. Throughout 2002 Stacy wrote and reported for the Italian supplement of the *International Herald Tribune.* A native of Van Nuys, California, Stacy has resided in Florence, Catania, Milan, and Siena.

Alessandro Nanì was born and grew up in Florence, Italy. He had a passion for two things in life, photography and horses. Over the years, Alex has, and is, continuing to work to fulfill both of them. Having moved from Florence to London in order to study photography at the London College of Printing, he then remained in London for another 3 years before returning to Florence with a fellow photographer, Olivia Ironside. There they set up a photographic studio and for the next 3 years worked in and around Florence. He moved back to the UK in 2002 in order to train at the Talland School of Equitation, as one day he intends to bring his passions together with a photojournalistic expedition on horseback.

Carla Rossi, a San Francisco native of Florentine origin, has collaborated with various media in Florence. Her first experience was writing for an Internet site for the European Internet festival, held every year in the historical center of Florence. She then helped create and write for the online English version of *La Nazione,* the city's largest and oldest newspaper, covering news ranging from travel to fashion and local and national events. She is a contributor to the Italian supplement of the *International Herald Tribune,* writing travel itineraries for Florence. Her latest exploration into life in the Renaissance city is the initiation of a weekly radio show on Controradio, part of the national Radio Popolare network that covers local news and events of interest to both visitors and residents.

The following photographs are © Azienda di Promozione Turistica di Firenze: pages 22 (The Cupola del Duomo); 33 (Mercato Centrale, interior); 64 (Biblioteca Laurenziana); 91 (Replica of Michelangelo's *David* in Piazza della Signoria); 96 (The Synagogue of Florence); 130 (Palazzo Rucellai); 131 (Courtyard of Palazzo Strozzi); 178 (San Miniato al Monte); 235 (Certosa del Galluzzo)

The following photograph is © Azienda di Promozione Turistica di Firenze and Biblioteca Marucelliana: page 65 (interior)

The following photograph is © Azienda di Promozione Turistica di Firenze and Cappelle Medicee of San Lorenzo: page 30 (Michelangelo's Tomb of Lorenzo the Magnificent)

The following photograph is © Azienda di Promozione Turistica di Firenze and Cenacolo del Fuligno: page 44 (Detail of the Cenacolo del Fuligno)

The following photograph is © Azienda di Promozione Turistica di Firenze and Galleria dell'Accademia: page 31 (Michelangelo's *Dying Slave*)

The following photograph is © Azienda di Promozione Turistica di Firenze and Galleria del Costume: page 201 (interior)

The following photograph is © Azienda di Promozione Turistica di Firenze and Fondazione Romano: page 182 (Tabernacle with the Madonna and child)

The following photograph is © Azienda di Promozione Turistica di Firenze and Museo Bardini: page 191 (Relief panel with Madonna and child)

The following photograph is © Azienda di Promozione Turistica di Firenze and Museo della Casa Fiorentina: page 148 (interior)

The following photograph is © Azienda di Promozione Turistica di Firenze and Museo di "Firenze Com'Era": pages 66–67 (Pianta delle Catena of Florence in 1470)

The following photograph is © Azienda di Promozione Turistica di Firenze and Museo di Storia della Scienza: page 100 (*Sfera armillare*, armillary sphere, interior)

The following photograph is © Azienda di Promozione Turistica di Firenze and Museo Nazionale del Bargello: page 85 (Donatello's *David*)

The following photograph is © Azienda di Promozione Turistica di Firenze and San Lorenzo: page 42 (Brunelleschi's Sagrestia Vecchia, interior)

The following photographs are by Stacy Meichtry: pages 48 (Orto Botanico); 50 (Chiostro delle Donne at the Ospedale degli Innocenti); 52, 53 (Courtyard and door of Santa Maria Maddalena de' Pazzi); 54 (Torre della Pagliazza); 55 (Loggia del Bigallo); 59 (Trompe l'oeil by Giuseppe del Moro at the Palazzina di Livia, interior); 106 (Palazzo Gondi); 107 (Chiostro degli Aranci); 142 (Tondi at the Palazzo Corsini); 145 (Exterior of the Casa-Galleria di Giovanni Michelazzi); 172 (Brancacci Chapel, interior); 176 (View from Piazzale Michelangelo); 179 (Santo Spirito, Brunelleschi's Nave); 221 (Badia Fiesolana); 222 (San Domenico); 225 (Villa Medicea di Belcanto); 229 (Villa I Tatti); 230 (Villa di Maiano); 231 (Castello di Vincigliata); 233 (Refectory at San Salvi with Andrea del Sarto's *Last Supper*); 240 (Cloister of Santa

Maria all'Impruneta); 248 San Giusto; 249 (Interior of San Martino in Campo); 250 (Apse and bell tower of the Pieve di San Leonardo); 251 (Cloister of the Parrocchiale di San Michele); 253 (Villa Medicea la Ferdinanda); 267 (Garden at Villa La Pietra); 271 (Convento di Monte Senario); 272 (Villa Salviati)

The following photograph is by Stacy Meichtry, courtesy of Museo Bandini: page 223 (Taddeo Gaddi's *Annunciation* at the Museo Bandini)

The following photographs are by Alessandro Nanì: pages 28 (Doors of the Baptistery of San Giovanni); 46 (San Barnaba); 62 (San Giovanni degli Scolopi); 82 (Detail of the Fontana del Puttino); 95 (Loggia del Pesce); 98 (Cimitero degli Inglesi); 113 (Porta alla Croce); 138 (Santa Maria Maggiore); 151 (Porta al Prato); 152 (Porticina di Via delle Belle Donne); 153 (San Salvatore al Vescovo); 183 (Tabernacolo del Canto alla Cucilia); 185 (San Frediano in Cestello); 188 (San Giorgio e Stanto Spirito); 193 (Garden at Palazzo Frescobaldi); 194 (Giardino Torrigiani); 197 (Istituto e Convento di San Francesco di Sales); 198 (Tabernacolo di Via de' Serragli); 218 (Teatro Romano in Fiesole); 228 (Villa Gamberaia); 237 (Villa del Poggio Imperiale); 257 (Villa Medicea di Careggi); 258 (Villa Medicea di Castello); 261 (Villa Guicciardini Corsi Salviati); 264 (Villa Corsini a Castello); 268 (Giambologna's *Appennino* in Villa Demidoff)

The following photographs are by Alessandro Tortorici: pages 29 (Giotto's Campanile); 34 (Palazzo Medici-Riccardi); 35 (Piazza Santissima Annunziata); 92 (Ponte Vecchio and the Arno); 37 (Detail of a statue on the facade of San Marco); 40 (Cloister of Santissima Annunziata); 53 (Door of Santa Maria Maddalena de' Pazzi); 63 (Detail of San Giovannino dei Cavalieri); 74 (Detail of the facade of Santa Croce); 80 (Cappella de' Pazzi); 81 (Corridoio Vasariani); 86 (Orsanmichele); 89 (Palazzo Vecchio); 92 (Ponte Vecchio); 93 (Santa Croce); 101 (Fondazione Horne); 110 (Tribunal of the Complesso di San Firenze); 112 (Palazzo Cocchi Serristori); 133 (Santa Maria Novella); 133 (Garden in the Old Cemetery at Santa Maria Novella); 136 (Central portal of Santa Trìnita); 137 (Facade of Santa Trìnita); 141 (Colonna della Croce al Trebbio); 144 (Giovanni della Robbia's Coronation of the Virgin lunette, above the portal of the church of Ognissanti); 149 (Palazzo Spini-Feroni); 150 (Piazza Santa Trìnita and the Colonna della Giustizia); 152 (Statue on the exterior of San Gaetano); 155 (Chiostri Monumentali di Santa Maria Novella); 166 (Fountain in the Giardino di Boboli); 174 (Giardino di Boboli); 175 (Palazzo Pitti); 181 (Palazzo Bianca Capello); 187 (Portal of Santa Felicita); 197 (Palazzo Capponi); 212 (Florence seen from the hill town of Fiesole); 219 (Cloister of San Francesco); 220 (Bell tower of San Romolo, the cathedral of Fiesole); 267 (Arco Trionfale per Lorena)

The following photograph is © Associazione Museo dei Ragazzi: page 104 (Activities in Palazzo Vecchio)

The following photograph is © Galleria degli Uffizi: page 83 (Botticelli's *Allegory of Spring*)

The following photograph is courtesy of the Opificio delle Pietre Dure and Basilica di Santa Maria Novella: page 134 (Giotto's crucifix)

The following photograph is by Tiffany Sprague: page 39 (Duomo and Campanile as seen from the Palazzo Vecchio)

Undiscovered Italy ®
from cottages to castles ®

Once you've met Davide, visited the Medici and made your way from

the Pitti Palace to the Gucci outlets on the outskirts of Florence, wouldn't it be

grand to be within a short drive of your villa overlooking it all? Throw off your

shoes, open a bottle of fabulous wine and watch the sun set over the

vineyards as you plan the next few days?

The Parker Company invites you to experience Italy, not just tour it.

We have dozens of villas and apartments for rent in and around Firenze

and hundreds more throughout Italy. Call us for a free catalog or visit our

villas online. Either way, we'll find the right one for you.

Now imagine spending an afternoon with an Italian artist, a craftsman,

a chef or a vintner, or going on a truffle hunt or a day-long Tuscan safari. Such

personal invitations into the hearts, homes and workplaces of Italy's finest artisans

can be booked online and experienced in person.

800.280.2811

www.theparkercompany.com

Casini
Ombrone
Quarrata
Catena
Fontanelle
Colonic
Poggetto
Poggio
a Caiano
Carmignano
via Macia
via Pistoiese
SS66
via delle Ginestre
Lecore
Comeana
San Giusto
S. Miniato
San
Martino
in Campo
S. Martino
in Campo
Artimino
Capraia
Castellina
Malmantile
Arno
Montelupo
Fiorentino
Ambrogiana
Turbone
Ginestra
Fiorentina